Key Reviews in Managerial Psychology

Concepts and Research for Practice

Edited by

Cary L. Cooper
and
Ivan T. Robertson

*University of Manchester
Institute of Science & Technology, UK*

JOHN WILEY & SONS

Chichester · New York · Brisbane · Toronto · Singapore

The chapters in this volume were originally published by John Wiley & Sons
in the *International Review of Industrial and Organizational Psychology*
and are copyright for the dates shown:
Chapter 1 (Kanfer) Volume 7, 1992, pp 1–53; Chapter 2 (Smith & George)
Volume 7, 1992, pp. 55–97; Chapter 3 (Fiedler & House) Volume 3, 1988,
pp. 73–92; Chapter 4 (Smith & Misumi) Volume 4, 1989, pp. 329–369;
Chapter 5 (Wall & Martin) Volume 2, 1987, pp. 61–91; Chapter 6
(Koopman & Pool) Volume 5, 1990, pp. 101–148; Chapter 7 (Driver)
Volume 3, 1988, pp. 245–277; Chapter 8 (Baldwin & Padgett) Volume 8,
1993, pp. 35–85; and Chapter 9 (Bedeian) Volume 2, 1987, pp. 1–33.

Library of Congress Cataloging-in-Publication Data

Cooper, Cary L.
    Key reviews in managerial psychology : concepts and research for
practice / edited by Cary L. Cooper and Ivan T. Robertson.
        p.   cm.
    Includes bibliographical references and index.
    ISBN 0-471-95010-6 (paper)
    1. Psychology, Industrial.   2. Management—Psychological aspects.
I. Robertson, Ivan.   II. Title.
HF5548.8.C597   1994
158.7—dc20   93-47088
                                                            CIP

British Library Cataloguing in Publication Data

A catalogue record for this book is available from the British Library

ISBN 0-471-95010-6 (paper)

Printed and bound in Great Britain by
Biddles Ltd, Guildford and King's Lynn

Key Reviews in
Managerial Psychology

CONTENTS

CONTRIBUTORS

Cary L. Cooper
Editor

Manchester School of Management, University of Manchester Institute of Science & Technology, PO Box 88, Manchester M60 1QD, UK.

Ivan T. Robertson
Editor

Manchester School of Management, University of Manchester Institute of Science & Technology, PO Box 88, Manchester M60 1QD, UK.

Timothy T. Baldwin

School of Business, Indiana University, 10th and Fee Lane, Bloomington, Indiana 47405, USA.

Arthur G. Bedeian

Department of Management, Louisiana State University, Baton Rouge, Louisiana 70803, USA.

Michael J. Driver

Department of Organizational Behavior, Graduate School of Business Administration, University of Southern California, Los Angeles, California 90007, USA.

Fred E. Fiedler

Department of Psychology, University of Washington, Seattle, Washington 98195, USA.

Dave George

KPMG Peat Marwick, Peat Marwick House, 135 Victoria Street, Wellington 1, New Zealand.

Robert J. House

Department of Management, Wharton School, University of Pennsylvania, Philadelphia, Pennsylvania 19104, USA.

Ruth Kanfer

Department of Psychology, University of Minnesota, Elliott Hall, 75 East River Road, Minneapolis, Minnesota 55455, USA.

Paul L. Koopman
Faculty of Psychology, Department of Work and Organisational Psychology, Vrije Universiteit, De Boelelaan 1081, 1081 HV Amsterdam, The Netherlands.

Robin Martin
MRC/ESRC Social and Applied Psychology, University of Sheffield, Sheffield S10 2TN, UK.

Jyuji Misumi
Department of Social Psychology, Tchikushi Women's University, Japan.

Margaret Y. Padgett
College of Business Administration, Butler University, 4600 Sunset Avenue, Indianapolis, Indiana 46208, USA.

Jeroen Pool
Dutch National Hospital Institute, The Netherlands.

Mike Smith
Department of Psychology, Victoria University of Wellington, Private Bag, Wellington, New Zealand.

Peter B. Smith
School of Social Sciences, University of Sussex, Falmer, Brighton BN1 9QN, UK.

Toby D. Wall
MRC/ESRC Social and Applied Psychology, University of Sheffield, Sheffield S10 2TN, UK.

EDITORIAL FOREWORD

Organizational psychology developed basically from attempts to apply theories and research of psychology to practical problems in the workplace. Historically, the beginning of managerial psychology took root in the field of personnel selection during World War I. In the US, a massive programme of psychological testing was instituted by the US Army, the results being used to help allocate military personnel to jobs and training courses in line with their abilities and aptitudes. During World War II, psychological and psychometric techniques were used widely in the US and throughout Europe. Subsequently, their use spread in industry, commerce and the public sector until today personnel selection, recruitment and appraisal are major areas of activity carried out by occupational psychologists in the work environment.

In addition to the practical problems of fitting the 'right person to the right job', psychologists also became interested in other person-centred or 'personnel/industrial psychology' topics like motivation, leadership, work attitudes, and decision making. From the 1950s a variety of scholars from other psychological disciplines, particularly social psychology, began to take an interest in developing a broader scientific understanding of organizational behavior and psychology within work environments, focussing on topics such as career development, job design, management development, organizational theory and development. Indeed, during the 1960s and 1970s more organization-orientated research, in contrast to personnel-orientated, was undertaken (Cooper, 1991). Organizational psychology had by the 1980s, therefore, caught up with its older cousin 'personnel/industrial psychology', to form a strong and cohesive field exploring a range of issues in the workplace.

In 1986, we edited the first in an annual series of scholarly reviews, which were designed to provide state of the art information on research and theory in industrial and organizational psychology: *The International Review of Industrial and Organizational Psychology* (Cooper & Robertson, 1986–1994). Chapters included in the series have spanned the full range of industrial and organizational psychology, including careers, stress at work, organizational development and analysis, personnel selection, training and corporate culture. As Professors of psychology working within the framework of a management school, we recognise that management scientists have found, subsumed within this broad spectrum of industrial and organizational psychology, a number of topics that directly affect the behaviour of managers in organizations, which have become the focal point of 'managerial psychology'. These topics range from the individually-orientated ones of selecting individuals for jobs, to motivating them, through to developing them for their managerial potential; to job- and organizationally-orientated issues such as job design, decision making, career development and organizational behavior and theory.

It is the purpose of this volume to put together some of the most relevant reviews of research and theory in the more global field of industrial and organizational psychology that relate specifically to managerial behavior and psychology. These are drawn from recent volumes of *The International Review of Industrial and Organizational Psychology*, the most comprehensive and up-to-date compendium of reviews available in the field. It is hoped that exposure of these key reviews on significant topics of managerial interest will inform the *practice* of management within organizations, both in North America and Europe, where many of these reviews originated. We cover those topics we feel have direct relevance to the problems faced by managers within organizations; motivation, selection, leadership, Japanese management practice, job design, decision making, career development, management development, counselling at work and organization theory. Many other topics could also have been included but given the limited space available, the more relevant managerial and organizational issues are included. We hope that this collection of reviews will not only help future research in managerial psychology but also contribute to the practice of management and creating healthier and more productive work environments.

REFERENCES

Cooper, C. L. (1991) *Industrial and Organizational Psychology*, Volo 1 and 2, Aldershot. Edward Elgar Publishing; New York: New York University Press.
Cooper, C. L., & Robertson, I. T. (1986–1994) *International Review of I/O Psychology*, Chichester: John Wiley.

CLC
ITR
December, 1993

Chapter 1

WORK MOTIVATION: NEW DIRECTIONS IN THEORY AND RESEARCH

Ruth Kanfer
University of Minnesota, USA

INTRODUCTION

The topic of motivation continues to command substantial attention in the field of industrial/organizational psychology. Motivational concepts, such as goal choice, valence, self-efficacy, and expectancy, are often used to understand and predict a wide array of organizationally-relevant perceptions, attitudes, and behaviors such as job satisfaction, leadership, employee withdrawal, performance, and persistence. Over the past four decades, progress in work motivation theory and research has yielded a wealth of information about both the factors and the processes that affect the direction, intensity and persistence of behavior in the workplace. Comprehensive reviews by Campbell and Pritchard (1976), Landy and Becker (1987), Locke and Henne (1986), and Miner (1980), along with selective reviews by Mitchell (1982b) and Zedeck (1977) document advances in work motivation through the early 1980s. Ilgen and Klein (1988) and Katzell and Thompson (1990) provide recent integrative overviews of different work motivation perspectives. Detailed reviews of specific theoretical perspectives in the industrial/organizational domain are also provided by Mitchell (1982a; expectancy theory), Greenberg (1982; equity theory), Deci and Ryan (1980; intrinsic motivation), Luthans and Kreitner (1985; behavior modification), Hackman and Oldham (1980; job characteristics theory), and Locke, Shaw, Saari, and Latham (1981; goal-setting). An edited volume by Kleinbeck, Quast, Thierry, and Hacker (1990) provides summaries of recent progress from a variety of work motivation perspectives. In a major review of the recent literature, R. Kanfer (1990) noted two major trends; (a) continuing emphasis on cognitive theories and research in work motivation, and (b) the maturation, consolidation, and integration of extant theories of work motivation (cf. O'Reilly, 1991).

At the same time, however, new developments have taken place in several of the allied fields, including cognitive/information-processing, personality, and instructional psychology. As advances in these areas have spread across the discipline, they have served to challenge extant work motivation perspectives and to profoundly influence how industrial/organizational psychologists think about, study, and attempt to influence motivation in the workplace. For example, motivation has long been regarded as a complex, dynamic, and multiply-determined system. Through the early 1980s, however, most theory and research focused on a specific facet of the system at one point in time. In contrast, contemporary approaches have begun to refocus on the dynamic aspects of motivation and the interactive effects of different inputs to the system. The major thrust of such research has been to raise questions that cannot be readily addressed by current perspectives; questions such as "how do individual differences in dispositions interact with motivational interventions (such as goal-setting) to affect long-term job performance?"

Prior to the late 1970s, work motivation could be best described as a problem of understanding the determinants of choice. The accelerating pace of research, in both the United States and Europe, directed at understanding the determinants and consequences of an individual's goals has clearly broadened the scope of the problem, and has encouraged investigation of problems in volition. In addition, research on the beneficial effects of self-regulatory activities on performance has fostered interest in the study of psychological processes that affect the implementation or execution of goals.

Finally, advances in the mapping of the criterion domain have had a noteworthy impact on conceptualizations of how motivation processes affect job performance. In contrast to early work that focused on broad measures of performance, such as supervisory ratings, contemporary work aims to predict motivational effects on specific components of performance, such as effort, persistence, pacing, and dependability. A potential advantage of the contemporary approach lies in the extent to which specific motivational interventions may ultimately be mapped to remediate specific deficits in job performance.

The infusion of new ideas from allied fields of psychology has been accompanied by growing concern that prevailing theories of motivation are insufficient for addressing contemporary problems in the workplace. To date, for example, theories of work motivation have not clearly distinguished the effects of motivation processes in simple and complex jobs, the effects of motivation during different phases of training, how motivation processes operate in team contexts, or how and why some individuals sustain effort in the face of failure where others give up. Forecasted changes in both the demographic composition of the workforce and the technological characteristics of the workplace during the next two decades suggest that motivation researchers will need to pay increasing attention to these and related problems.

The purpose of this chapter is not to summarize past research on work motivation but rather to examine new trends and to identify recent developments that show promise for advancing the field. This chapter is organized into three sections. The first section provides a heuristic for organizing motivation theories and constructs. This framework is then used to identify emerging trends in the fields of motivational psychology and work motivation research. The second section focuses on advances in select research paradigms and their implications for applied settings. Consistent with the organizational framework presented earlier, material in this section is classified into three broad areas on the basis of the portion of the motivation system the theory and research targets. Review of recent developments pertaining to distal constructs highlights progress in dispositional approaches, motive-based (e.g. motivational orientation, justice/fairness, and intrinsic motivation) analyses, and cognitive choice/decision theories (e.g. expectancy-value theories). In the proximal constructs portion of this section, emphasis is placed on theories and research that focus on goals and psychological processes underlying goal-directed action. The third segment of this section addresses progress aimed at clarifying the interface between choice and volition. The final section of this chapter summarizes trends in each area and suggests future research directions in work motivation psychology.

OVERVIEW

An Heuristic Organization

At the broadest level, an individual's motivation for a specific task or job is determined by environment, heredity, and their interactions (such as learning). These factors influence individual characteristics such as personality, motives, affect, attitudes, beliefs, knowledge, skills, and abilities. In turn, these characteristics affect one's choice of goals and actions, the intensity and character of effort, and the endurance of goal-directed behaviour over time.

Specific theories of work motivation can be organized within the broader context of environment, heredity, and their interactions by considering which determinants and processes the various theories target. Figure 1.1 provides a general heuristic framework upon which diverse motivation approaches may be mapped. As implied in the figure, theories and their associated constructs can be organized in terms of their conceptual proximity to action. Theories of distal constructs, such as achievement motivation and expectancy-value, stress the impact of non-cognitive individual differences on choice. Other distal perspectives, such as cognitive evaluation theory and organization justice theories, emphasize the influence of activation of particular motives, such as challenge or injustice. These constructs are termed distal because the impact of such constructs on behavior and performance is often indirect. Personality determinants of action, for example, may exert a regular influence on goal choice, and thereby indirectly affect long-term patterns of behavior across

Constructs   *Theories*

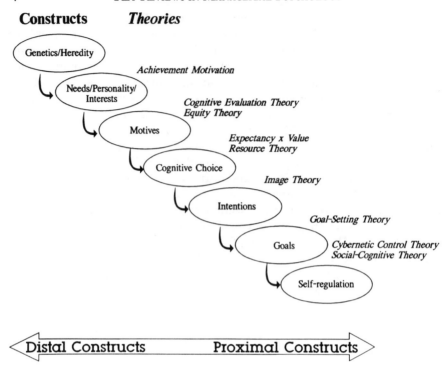

Figure 1.1   A heuristic framework of motivation constructs and examplar motivation theories

situations. To obtain unequivocal support for these theoretical models, however, it is necessary to map and test the full pathway by which these factors affect performance. To date, most distal theories of motivation have enjoyed their greatest success in predicting other diotal oonotructo, ouch as predecision and decision processes and intentions, rather than behavior or performance.

Proximal construct theories focus on motivational constructs at the level of purposive action. Analyses of motivational processes in these theories tend to begin with the individual's goals rather than with the factors that have shaped the individual's objective. Such theories concentrate on the processes and variables that affect the goal–behaviour/performance relation. Social-learning/ social-cognitive theories, self-regulation models and goal-setting approaches represent several of the more well-known proximal theories.

The heuristic framework presented in Figure 1.1 implies that most extant distal theories of motivation most strongly influence intermediate cognitive choice processes. These processes determine an individual's intentions, rather than behavior or performance *per se*. Choice processes yield intentions that set the stage for action. When intentions can be accomplished with relative ease, distal models often yield accurate predictions of an individual's behavior.

However, when accomplishment of an intention is difficult, or requires a complex sequence of behaviors, additional motivational constructs are needed to explain how persons sustain goal-directed action. Self-regulation and volitional activities pertain to the portion of the motivational system through which persons translate goals into action. These constructs and processes, such as goals and self-reactions, are termed proximal since the product of these processes typically exerts a direct influence on behavior.

Choice and volition

In Figure 1.1, the distinction between distal and proximal constructs and theories is based upon the call for differentiation of the motivational processes underlying choice and volition (e.g. see Ajzen, 1985; Heckhausen & Kuhl, 1984; Kuhl, 1982, 1984; Kuhl & Beckmann, 1985; Gollwitzer, 1990). At the turn of the twentieth century, motivation was broadly viewed as conation, or the processes involved in both choice and implementation of action (e.g. James, 1890; Woodworth, 1929). Woodworth (1929), for example, noted that, "the motive plays a part in determining what response shall be made to the stimulus . . . [and] motivation is the producing of such a state or activity" (p. 228)

In American psychology, the advent of cognitive theories of motivation during the early and mid-twentieth century, for example by Lewin (1938), Tolman (1932), and Rotter (1954) led many researchers to focus almost exclusively on the cognitive processes underlying choice, rather than volition. The impact of this perspective on industrial/organizational psychology was tremendous; during the 1960s and 1970s distal choice theories dominated the published literature.

The recent revival of volitional constructs has its origins in both American and European theories. In American psychology, advances in self-regulation theory and research by clinical, experimental, and instructional psychologists have demonstrated the importance of motivational processes that take place in the context of action. In European psychology, the increasing emphasis on volition and the interface between distal and proximal constructs may be traced to the expansion of achievement motivation models (Heckhausen, 1977) and to cognitively-focused theories of action (e.g. Nuttin, 1984; Von Cranach, Kalbermatten, Indermühle, & Gugler, 1982). Heckhausen (see Gollwitzer, 1990), for example, offered the analogy of "crossing the Rubicon" to refer to the distinct differences between motivational processes underlying the formation of intentions and those processes affecting volition. A similar distinction is made by Klinger (1975, 1987) in his conceptualization of the fundamental changes in information-processing associated with the emergence of a "current concern".

In industrial/organizational psychology, issues related to volition first appeared in the context of goal-setting research. In 1968, Locke proposed that an individual's goals served as the immediate regulator of action. Scores of studies investigating the basic tenets of Locke's goal-setting model showed that explicit goal assignments exert a substantial impact on task performance. Attempts to understand the psychological processes underlying these phenomena, in turn, led to increasing interest in self-regulation, social-cognitive, and volitional concepts.

The heuristic framework presented in Figure 1.1 organizes theoretical developments in terms of their primary, but not exclusive focus. During the past ten years, several new models of motivation have been proposed that represent a mix of both distal and proximal constructs. Goal-setting researchers, for example, have included distal constructs, such as need for achievement (Hollenbeck & Klein, 1987). Social-personality theorists have also expanded their models to consider how dispositional tendencies may directly affect behavior and performance through their impact on proximal activites, such as self-regulation (e.g. Carver & Scheier, 1981; Kuhl, 1984, 1985). Theories and research directed specifically at the intention-goal interface will be discussed in detail later.

Behavior and performance

It is common to evaluate and compare theories of work motivation by the extent to which they successfully predict job performance. Nonetheless, most motivation theories are not intended to predict performance but rather to predict decision processes and volitional behavior. Although the distinction between behavior and task/job performance is typically not made in broader theories of human motivation, it is essential to recognize this in industrial/organizational research. In organizational settings, persons engage in a wide variety of motivated behaviors. Not all behaviors, however, relate to an individual's job performance. An individual's performance is typically determined on the basis of evaluation of some *subset* of workplace behaviors. Moreover, job performance ratings typically refer to an *evaluation* of the product of the individual's behavior. Motivation theories aim at the prediction of behaviors—either in isolation or over time. Although motivational effects on patterns of work behaviors can certainly affect job performance, the prediction of performance *per se* requires consideration of several additional factors, including for example, individual differences variables (e.g. abilities, task comprehension) and environmental factors (e.g. situational constraints, task demands) (R. Kanfer, 1990).

The distinction between behavior and performance has become more important over the past decade. In complex jobs and tasks involving a great deal of behavioral latitude, similar levels of performance may be accomplished via different constellations of behavior. For example, a high level of sales performance may be accomplished through changing what one does (making phone calls instead of visiting potential clients), doing more of a behavior (increasing the number of phone calls made), or changing one's environment (getting a cellular phone to reduce the likelihood of missing important calls from potential clients). Analysis of the effects of motivational interventions on job performance requires more fine-grained assessment of the behaviors that contribute to performance than is typical using an aggregate, or composite performance rating. Recent self-regulation research, for example, indicates that particular goal assignments may be mapped to particular forms of cognitive and behavior change (e.g. Nolen, 1988).

Recognition of the distinction between behavior and performance has also led to greater care in the selection of criterion variables used in laboratory and field research. In the laboratory, many researchers have moved toward use of longitudinal and repeated-measure designs in attempts to capture the dynamic and cumulative effects of motivational processes on behaviors that contribute to task performance. The results of this shift are most notable with respect to the increasing use of computer technologies to create complex and multimodal tasks that simulate real-world conditions. These developments in laboratory methodology, along with the increased emphasis on behavioral measures in field settings, have substantially lessened concerns about the distinction between laboratory and field research (see, e.g. Campbell, 1986).

Trends in Work Motivation Theorizing

As a prelude to discussion of recent advances, it is important to consider how previous concerns about motivation in industrial/organization psychology have shaped the current state of affairs. In the 1940s, work motivation often referred to the influence of incentives. The limits of this approach were recognized by Blum (1949) when he noted that "the major error in industry has been the oversimplification of the concept of motivation" (pp. 132–133). In 1964, Vroom acknowledged increasing sophistication in dealing with motivation concepts, but also noted that "research in industrial psychology is still largely atheoretical with little use being made of the concepts and models which are an integral part of current theories of motivation" (1964, p. 4).

By the mid-1980s, concerns about the oversimplification of the motivation domain and the paucity of theoretical approaches had virtually disappeared. In their place, new concerns were raised about the *multitude* of theories and the lack of a unified framework. Locke and Henne (1986), for example, note that "theories abound, yet somehow they do not seem to fit in with either the research findings or with each other" (p. 1). Further, several researchers began to question the appropriateness of studying work motivation in isolation from other determinants of job performance, such as cognitive abilities and situational constraints (e.g. R. Kanfer & Ackerman, 1989; Peters & O'Conner, 1980). As Mitchell (1986) noted, by mid-1980s scientific activity in the field had progressed from the simple question of "Can motivation make a difference [in performance]?" to two related, but more difficult questions: (1)

"How does motivation make a difference?", and (2) "When does motivation make a difference?"

The shift toward "how" and "when" questions in work motivation has generated a host of new challenges, as well as resurrecting several enduring problems in motivational psychology. Abiding problems include difficulties in the measurement of cognitive effort, difficulties in the assessment of dispositional tendencies, and practical problems associated with the measurement of environmental influences on intermediate cognitive processes. New problems tend to be associated with research that investigates motivation in the context of complex skill learning and in long-term performance of complex tasks, such as computer programming (rather than in repetitive, well-learned behaviors, such as assembly-line work). In these new arenas, critical issues include: (1) developing an adequate conceptualization of how individual differences in cognitive abilities, affect, and task demands may influence, mediate, or otherwise transform select portions of the motivational system; and (2) how to employ procedures that permit full analysis of interactive and dynamic motivational processes. Findings obtained from studies using multiple criterion measures, complex task paradigms, and longitudinal research designs, for example, suggest that motivational processes influence skill learning and complex job performance through their effects on: (1) how information is organized and processed; (2) long-term patterns of work behavior; and (3) persistence in the face of difficulties.

The explosion of different theoretical perspectives during the the 1960s and 1970s, along with greater emphasis on "how" and "when" questions, has also prompted a basic shift in the aim of theory development. Most contemporary work motivation theorizing has been directed toward the coordination and integration of existing work motivation models (e.g. Ilgen & Klein, 1988; Katzell & Thompson, 1990). Several researchers have made conceptual arguments for the integration of expectancy and goal-setting approaches (see e.g. Hollenbeck & Klein, 1987; R. Kanfer, 1986, 1987; Locke, Motowidlo, & Bobko, 1986; and Naylor & Ilgen, 1984). Other scientists have suggested frameworks that integrate well-known work motivation approaches, such as goal-setting, with newer developments in the broader field of motivational psychology, such as cybernetic control theory (e.g. Lord & Hanges, 1987) and social-cognitive theory (e.g. Bandura & Cervone, 1983, 1986). And still other researchers have begun investigation of motivational influences in the workplace from a dispositional, individual differences perspective (e.g. Helmreich, Sawin & Carsrud, 1986; McHenry, Hough, Toquam, Hanson, & Ashworth, 1990).

The direction and focus of recent work motivation theory and research correspond closely to new developments in the broader field of motivational psychology. During the past ten years, major integrative theories of human motivation have been proposed by clinical, instructional, social, and personality researchers, including theories by Bandura (1986, 1988), Carver and

Scheier (1981), Heckhausen and Kuhl (1985), F. Kanfer and Hagerman (1981), Klinger (1975, 1987), Kuhl (1985; Kuhl & Kraska, 1989), Nicholls (1978, 1984; Nicholls & Miller, 1984), and Weiner (1985, 1986). Broad theoretical statements and overviews of research on human motivation from particular perspectives can be found in books by Ford (1987), Heckhausen, Schmalt, and Schneider (1985), and McClelland (1985), and in edited volumes by Frese and Sabini (1985), Halisch and Kuhl (1987), Kuhl and Beckmann (1985), and Pervin (1989). Many new research directions in work motivation complement and extend one or another of these more general theories of motivation. For example, several recent formulations in goal-setting incorporate concepts from both social-cognitive and cybernetic control theories. Research derived from these integrative approaches, in turn, provides critical empirical evidence for the potential viability of a unified theoretical paradigm.

The heuristic framework shown in Figure 1.1 is used to organize diverse new developments discussed in this chapter. The next section provides a review of these advances. The first portion of this section focuses on distal constructs, such as individual differences in personality, motives (intrinsic motivation and organizational justice), and cognitive choice processes. Next, advances in proximal theories and research, including goal-setting, social-learning/social-cognitive, cybernetic control theory, and self-regulation approaches, are presented. The final portion of this section covers integrative approaches that emphasize the relationship between distal and proximal constructs.

DISTAL CONSTRUCTS: DISPOSITIONS, MOTIVES, CHOICE

Personality-based theories, such as need-achievement models, focus on the joint effects of dispositional tendencies and environmental conditions; motive-based approaches, such as justice and intrinsic motivation theories, stress the role of the environment in activating higher-order psychological states, which in turn affect choice and behavior. During the 1970s and early 1980s, motive formulations received far more attention than personality approaches. Recently, however, researchers have used modern formulations of personality to study workplace behavior and performance. Because dispositional and motive approaches differ substantially, advances in each area will be discussed separately.

Dispositional Approaches

Theoretical developments and research in this section emphasize the role of non-cognitive individual differences (such as dispositional tendencies) on choice and work behavior. During the 1970s, these perspectives were relatively unpopular in the organizational psychology literature. Criticisms of dispositional approaches during the situation-versus-trait debates of the 1970s (e.g. Mischel, 1973; see Weiss & Adler, 1984) and the poor showing of many personality measures in predicting performance (e.g. Guion & Gottier, 1965) contributed strongly to this trend. In the area of work motivation, the study of dispositions was associated most closely with early models of motivation that were losing favor, such as Maslow's Need Hierarchy theory (Maslow, 1943, 1954) and Alderfer's Existence-Growth-Relatedness (ERG; Alderfer, 1969).

During the past few years, however, conceptual and empirical advances in personality psychology, advances in theories of performance, and new lines of inquiry in motivational psychology have prompted renewed interest in dispositional determinants of work behavior. Implications of recent research for theories of work motivation derive from programmatic research in three broad areas: (1) the factor structure of personality and patterns of work behavior and performance; (2) personality determinants of information-processing; and (3) dispositional influences on self-regulation processes. The next section summarizes theoretical and research developments in each of these areas.

The factor structure of personality and patterns of work behavior and performance

During the past decade, personality researchers have made significant progress in the identification and measurement of basic personality dimensions (see McCrae & Costa, 1990; Pervin, 1990; Tellegen, 1985; Watson & Tellegen, 1985). The results of this work have led to general agreement regarding the existence of five basic personality dimensions, or traits. McCrae and Costa (1990) refer to these factors as: (a) Neuroticism, (b) Extraversion, (c) Openness to Experience, (d) Agreeableness, and (e) Conscientiousness. Of the five factors, Conscientiousness, also called Will to Achieve (Digman & Takemoto-Chook, 1981), represents the trait dimension most closely associated with motivation or volitional processes. McCrae and Costa, for example, describe persons high on this dimesion as hardworking, achievement-oriented, and persevering. Other researchers, such as Hough, Eaton, Dunnette, Kamp, and McCloy (1990), summarize this factor as Dependability, with the associated characteristics of planfulness, responsibility, and carefulness.

Initial investigations of personality in the organizational context focused on the study of dispositional determinants of job satisfaction (e.g. Levin & Stokes, 1989; Staw, Bell, & Clausen, 1986; see Arvey, Carter, & Buerkley, 1991 for a review). Recently, however, researchers have begun to explore the association between personality dimensions and different dimensions of job performance. Barrick and Mount (1991), for example, conducted a meta-analysis exploring the relation between each of the five major personality dimensions and three job performance criteria (job proficiency, training proficiency, and personnel data). Results obtained indicated that only one personality dimension, Conscientiousness, showed consistent relations (estimated true correlation, $\rho = 0.26$) with all job performance criteria across the five occupational groups studies. As Barrick and Mount (1991) note, "those individuals who exhibit traits associated with a strong sense of purpose, obligation, and persistence generally perform better than those who do not" (p. 18). Barrick and Mount (1991) also found that Openness to Experience was related to training proficiency criteria (estimated true correlation, $\rho = 0.25$), but not to job proficiency criteria. Persons high on this dimension are typically characterized as inquisitive and open-minded. Barrick and Mount (1991) suggest that persons high on this trait may be more likely to possess positive attitudes toward learning experiences in general. As a consequence, such persons may be more "training ready" and more likely to benefit from training programs than persons low in this dimension.

As Weiss and Adler (1984) have stated, the impact of individual differences in dispositional tendencies on work performance is likely to be most apparent in weak situations characterized by repeated free choice in the direction, intensity, and persistency of action over time. Several recent field studies provide additional empirical evidence for this notion and the relation of these tendencies to motivational processes in the job context. The assumption underlying this line of research is that individual differences in dispositional tendencies with motivational properties may influence variability in job performances where persistence is an important component of successful job performance.

Helmreich, Sawin, and Carsrud (1986), for example, examined the influence of individual differences in three forms of achievement motivation on training and job performance of airline reservation agents. In this study, two dependent measures of performance (percentage of time spent on the telephone with customers and percentage of time agents were available to receive calls) were obtained at three time periods; 1–3 months, 4–6 months, and 7–8 months following hire. Results of this study showed that motive orientations were unrelated to job performance measures at the early stage of tenure, but were significantly related to performance at the two later stages of tenure. Similar results were obtained by Day and Silverman (1989) in a field investigation of trait determinants of job performance among accountants. In their study, trait measures derived from the Jackson Personality Research Form were used to assess the extent to which dispositional tendencies predicted dimensions of job performance (beyond that predicted by cognitive ability measures alone). They found that work orientation, ascendancy, and interpersonal orientation scales added significantly to the prediction of component job performance ratings.

Further evidence for the influence of motivationally-related dispositions on job performance was recently provided by Campbell and his colleagues in their report of the results of the US Army Selection and Classification Project (Project A; see Campbell, 1990). In this large-scale research program, predictor and criterion constructs were independently identified for a broad sample of jobs. Six broad personality constructs were identified. Next, a noncognitive inventory, called the Assessment of Background and Life

Experiences (ABLE), was developed to provide measures of these constructs (Peterson, Hough, Dunnette, Rosse, Houston, Toquam, & Wing, 1990). Empirical evidence for the predictive validity of the ABLE was obtained in concurrent and longitudinal field studies involving several thousand military personnel. In the longitudinal study, four composite scores, assessing achievement orientation, dependability, adjustment, and physical condition, were computed from the ABLE for use in predicting five job performance factors. Analyses of the incremental validity of ABLE composites, above that obtained when using general cognitive ability composites alone, revealed significant and substantial improvement in the predictive validities for three job performance factors; effort and leadership, personal discipline, and physical fitness and military bearing (McHenry et al., 1990). The incremental validity of the effort and leadership and personal discipline factor suggests that individual differences in dispositions may play a role in naturally occurring instances of goal choice and self-regulatory activity in the workplace.

Personality determinants of information-processing

Humphreys and Revelle (1984) have organized the personality, motivation and performance literature from a cognitive, information-processing framework. In contrast to the field studies described in the previous section, these researchers have focused on delineating the precise effects of personality dimensions on cognitive task performance. They proposed a theory linking individual differences in Extroversion, Achievement Motivation, and Anxiety to information processing components of complex task performance. According to their theory, individual differences in personality interact with situational factors to affect two separate motivational constructs: on-task effort and arousal. The influence of these motivational constructs is then mapped to three components of task performance: sustained information transfer, long-term memory, and short-term memory. A graphic illustration of the model and operationalization of constructs is provided in Figure 1.2.

Building on taxonomic work by Eysenck and Gray, Revelle and his colleagues have focused largely on two personality dimensions; Impulsivity and Anxiety (see Revelle, 1989). As shown in Figure 1.2, individual differences in impulsivity are posited to affect performance via their efforts on arousal. In contrast, individual differences in state anxiety are predicted to affect performance through their influence on on-task effort. Zinbarg and Revelle (1989), for example, investigated the interactive effects of impulsivity, anxiety, and stimulus valence (reward or punishment) in four studies involving performance on a discrimination task. Results provided support for the model, and showed that anxiety and impulsivity interacted in their effects on performance. In conditions where the response led to a reward, high anxiety coupled with low impulsivity facilitated performance, but high anxiety and high impulsivity hindered performance.

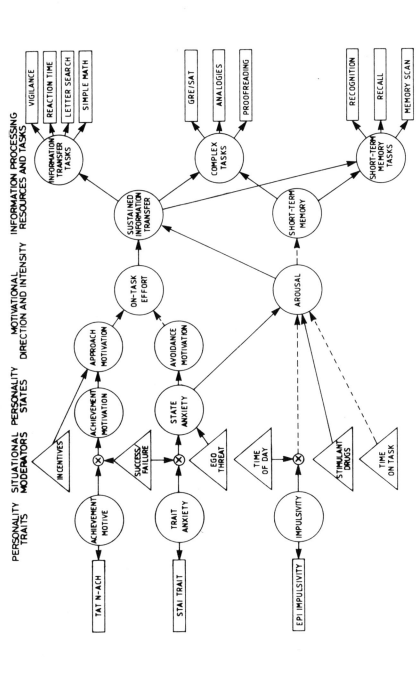

Figure 1.2 Humphreys and Revelle conceptual model of the effects of personality, situational moderators and motivational states on information processing and cognitive performance. Solid lines indicate positive influences, dashed lines indicate negative influences. From Humphreys & Revelle (1984). Copyright © American Psychological Association. Reprinted by permission

The Humphreys and Revelle (1984) formulation indicates the complexity of the pathway through which individual differences in personality affect learning and performance. Although most research using this conceptualization involves analyses of cognitive task performance in laboratory settings, several organizationally-relevant predictions may be derived from the theory. For example, Humphreys and Revelle (1984) predicted that persons high in impulsivity will benefit more from interventions that increase on-task effort than persons low in impulsivity (Humphreys & Revelle, 1984).

Dispositional influences on self-regulation processes

A third stream of personality-linked theory and research seeks to demonstrate the influence of non-cognitive individual differences on self-regulation. Two major individual differences constructs have been proposed: (a) self-focus, and (b) action/state orientation. Theoretical formulations associated with both constructs share the view that dispositional tendencies affect the direction and form of attention during action.

According to Carver and Scheier (1981), self-focus refers to the pattern of preference exhibited with respect to the source and subject of one's attention. Persons high in self-focus are characterized as attending to self-generated sources of information about the self. In contrast, persons low in self-focus are characterized as attending to environmental sources of information and subjects other than the self. Individual differences in self-focus are often assessed using a self-report measure, such as the Self-Consciousness Scale (Fenigstein, Scheier, & Buss, 1975).

Carver and Scheier propose that high self-focus, or high self-awareness, promotes the activation of self-regulatory processes. In particular, high self-focus is proposed to increase the frequency of comparison processes between the current state of affairs and some standard or goal. In the event of a discrepancy between the current state and the standard, high self-focus is proposed to promote behavioral attempts to reduce this discrepancy.

In Europe, Kuhl and his colleagues have proposed a related individual differences construct, namely action control (see Kuhl, 1984, 1985; Kuhl & Beckmann, 1985). Individual differences in action control refer to dispositional tendencies in the content of an individual's cognitions and affect associated with anticipated or ongoing activity. Individual differences in action control are typically assessed by the Action Control Scale (see Kuhl, 1985; Kuhl & Beckmann, in press). This self-report measure assesses action orientation in three dimensions: cognition, performance, and decision-making.

According to Kuhl, persons who are high in action control orientation are posited to direct attention toward task resolution rather than on internal emotional states associated with task performance. In contrast, persons who are low in action control, or state-oriented, are proposed to focus attention on internal emotional states and external conditions unrelated to task accomplishment. Similar to Carver and Scheier (1981), Kuhl (1985) also proposes that individual differences in action control influence the activation and efficiency of self-regulation during task performance.

Empirical evidence for the influence of individual differences in self-focus on self-regulation mechanisms has been provided by Carver and Scheier (see Carver & Scheier, 1981, for a review). Additional evidence for the basic tenets of the Carver and Scheier formulation has also been provided in the industrial/organizational domain by Campion and Lord (1982) and Hollenbeck and his colleagues (Hollenbeck, 1989; Hollenbeck & Williams, 1987). Hollenbeck and Williams (1987), for example, investigated the impact of self-set goals, goal importance, and self-focus on sales volume performance. They found that self-persons high in self-focus who viewed the goal as important set the highest goals for themselves. Hollenbeck (1989) found that among salespersons, outcome expectations and organizational commitment were more closely related among persons high in self-focus compared to persons low in self-focus.

Research by Kuhl and his colleagues (e.g. Beckmann & Kuhl, 1984; Kuhl & Koch, 1984) also provides empirical evidence supporting various aspects of action control theory. Several studies (e.g. Kuhl & Geiger, 1986; Kuhl & Wassiljew, 1985) have demonstrated differences in performance associated with stable individual differences in action/state orientation. Specifically, state orientation was associated with lower levels of performance; action orientation was associated with higher levels of performance. Inductions of state and action orientations via instructions also demonstrate the mediating effects of this variable on goal enactment (e.g. Kuhl & Weiss, 1985).

The conceptual origins of Carver and Scheier's self-regulatory constructs and Kuhl's action control construct lie in cybernetic and information-processing approaches to motivation, respectively. Relatively little is currently known about the relations between these constructs and basic personality dimensions, making it difficult to map these individual differences constructs to the five-factor framework of personality used in field research on performance and by Humphreys and Revelle.

Recent studies investigating the relations between Kuhl's action control scales and higher-order personality dimensions provide one potentially fruitful avenue for future integrative research. Based on empirical research conducted over the past decade, Tellegen and his colleagues have proposed that personality dimensions may be further organized in terms of two distinguishable mood-dispositional dimensions: Positive Affectivity and Negative Affectivity. Positive Affectivity refers to dispositional tendencies toward the experience of pleasurable engagement, and most closely corresponds to trait measures of extraversion. In contrast, Negative Affectivity refers to tendencies toward unpleasurable engagement and corresponds to trait measures of anxiety and neuroticism. Recent research by Klinger and Murphy (in press) correlating measures of Negative and Positive Affectivity with the Action Control subscales suggests substantial similarity between portions of the action control construct and Negative Affectivity.

Summary and implications for work motivation

Interest in delineating the influence of dispositions on job performance is clearly on the rise. Building on advances in personality psychology, researchers have shown that non-cognitive individual differences influence long-term patterns of work behavior, information-processing, and patterns of self-regulation. Yet very little is known about how specific dispositions, such as Conscientiousness, affect the motivational pathways underlying these effects. Although Humphreys and Revelle (1984) spelled out the independent and joint influence of dispositional and environmental influences on motivational processes and task performance, aptitude-treatment frameworks of this type have not been widely adopted among researchers investigating personality-job performance relations. Such frameworks are sorely needed to delineate the precise mechanisms by which individual differences factors, such as Conscientiousness, have their impact on motivational processes such as self-regulation.

Theory and research in social-personality psychology also suggest that more circumscribed non-cognitive individual differences, such as action control, also play a role in task performance through their influence on proximal self-regulation processes, such as self-monitoring and self-evaluation. Future research is needed to ascertain whether dispositions that affect the proximal portion of the motivational system are related to dispositions shown to affect long-term patterns of performance.

Recent theory and research in mood and emotion pose another important challenge to existing models of work motivation. Investigations of individual differences in affectivity represent a portion of the burgeoning body of research directed toward understanding the influence of affective tendencies on cognitive choice processes. Research on the effects of mood on decision-making indicates that positive and negative mood states influence the perception, organization and recall of information (e.g. Broadbent & Broadbent, 1988; Isen, Means, Patrick & Nowicky, 1982). Since these perceptual and cognitive processes serve as the foundation for choice behavior in the motivational system, it is quite possible that individual differences in mood tendencies account for substantial variance in choice behavior. In the domain of self-regulation, several studies indicate the influence of mood inductions on self-efficacy expectations and behavioral persistence (Kavanaugh & Bower, 1985; Wright & Mischel, 1978). Although affective self-reactions are generated in self-regulatory activity, dispositional mood tendencies may mediate the influence of these reactions and thus the effectiveness of the self-regulatory system. Future research investigating the influence of affective tendencies on specific motivational components is likely to shed light on the intermediate processes by which emotions influence important components of job performance, such as interpersonal relations.

One major drawback of personality-based theories of motivation in the past has been a lack of precision in predicting job-related behavior. Recent research has minimized this problem by use of multiple criterion measures of performance *based on theoretically-derived expectations* of the components of performance most likely to be affected. For example, in the Helmreich, Sawim, and Carsrud (1986) study, persistence measures of job performance, rather than ratings of performance adequacy, were used to test the influence of individual differences in particular forms of achievement motivation.

Motive Approaches

Motive-based work motivation theories, such as equity and intrinsic motivation theories, focus on the influence of a single or small set of universal and psychologically-based motives, such as mastery, control, competence, and the desire to reduce psychological tension created by perceptions of imbalance in social exchange. In contrast to personality formulations, motive theories place less emphasis on individual differences in motive strength and more emphasis on the conditions that activate the motive. In general, motive-based theories also tend to more fully specify the cognitive processes by which the motive affects behavior.

Among all the motive-based approaches, noteworthy progress has been made in organizational justice and intrinsic motivation paradigms. The following sections describe recent advances in each of these paradigms, respectively.

Organizational justice/fairness theories

The basic premise of organizational justice theories is that individuals seek fairness and justice in the employee–employer social exchange relationship. Perceptions of imbalance in this relation (perceived unfairness or injustice) are posited to create psychological tension that initiates cognitive and behavioral changes directed toward the reduction of the tension. Review of this area indicates two distinct forms of fairness in organizational settings: (a) distributive fairness, and (b) procedural fairness. As distinguished by Thibaut and Walker (1975, 1978), distributive fairness pertains to perceptions with respect to the distribution or allocation of outcomes; procedural fairness refers to perceptions about the organizational procedures used to make outcome decisions. Early research focused almost entirely on delineating the determinants and consequences of perceptions of distributive justice. In organizational psychology, equity theory (Adams, 1963, 1965) provided the dominant framework for studying motivational implications of perceptions of distributive unfairness. Studies of the impact of perceived unfairness in the allocation of outcomes conducted during the 1960s through early 1980s focused primarily on the cognitive and behavioral effects of perceived unfairness in outcomes created through underpayment or overpayment (see Campbell & Pritchard, 1976; Greenberg, 1982). During the 1980s, several studies examined equity predictions in the context of other organizational outcomes, such as job titles (e.g. Greenberg & Ornstein, 1983). Other researchers have focused on extending equity formulations to account for behavior over time (see, e.g. Coser & Calton, 1983).

During the past decade, however, interest in equity theory has been eclipsed by theoretical, empirical, and applied progress in procedural theories of justice and fairness (see Lind & Tyler, 1988, for a review). Research in procedural justice first emerged in the legal domain of dispute resolution as Thibaut and Walker (1975) showed that providing persons with the opportunity to provide input into the decision-making process enhanced perceptions of procedural fairness *independently* of the outcome obtained. As applied to the work setting, findings in the legal domain suggested that the opportunity to provide input to a decision-maker should enhance perceptions of fairness in the context of performance appraisal and performance evaluation. During the 1980s, support for this notion was provided by several studies of procedural fairness in formal work settings (e.g. Greenberg, 1987; R. Kanfer, Sawyer, Earley, & Lind, 1987; Landy, Barnes, & Murphy, 1978; Landy, Barnes-Farrell, & Cleveland, 1980). These studies indicated that perceptions of fairness in performance evaluation were enhanced by procedures that afforded process control, or the opportunity to provide input to the evaluator.

In 1987, Greenberg proposed a theoretical framework that related the effects of variations in organizational procedures to cognitive and motivational processes. By integrating expectancy and procedural/distributive models, Greenberg suggested that perceptions of procedural injustice instigate cognitive or behavioral change when procedures, such as performance evaluations, are interpreted by the employee as a terminal outcome, or "end in themselves". In contrast, when procedures are interpreted by the employee as first-level outcomes, or as "means to an end", perceptions of procedural fairness *per se* are less influential than perceptions of distributive fairness (fairness in the second-level outcome). In essence, the framework suggests that the motivational power of injustice perceptions may be closely linked to the individual's goals.

More recently, a number of researchers have suggested that interpersonal aspects of the implementation of a procedure also play an important role in individuals' judgments of procedural fairness (e.g. Tyler & Bies, 1990; Tyler, 1988). Building upon Leventhal's (1980) analysis of the features of procedures that contribute to perceived fairness, Folger and Bies (1989) and Tyler and Bies (1990) suggest five norms that contribute to perceptions of fairness: (a) adequate consideration of an employee's viewpoint, (b) suppression of personal bias, (c) consistent application of criteria across employees,

(d) provision of timely feedback after a decision, and (e) providing employees with an adequate explanation for the decision.

A related approach to conceptualizing the influence of perceived fairness on motivation, behavior, and performance stems from theory and research on participative decision-making. Participative decision-making (PDM) procedures refer to organizational procedures that provide the employee with some form of input to a decision-maker. Participative procedures range from those that permit token input opportunities to interactions that permit the employee full control over the decision.

PDM has long been advocated as a means of enhancing work motivation and job performance. Nonetheless, reviews of PDM studies suggest that such procedures enhance job satisfaction but exert little or no influence on performance (see Locke & Schweiger, 1979; Schweiger & Leana, 1986). In the goal-setting research arena, Locke and his colleagues argue that participatively set goals enhance performance expressly through their effects on goal commitment as well as the difficulty of the goal that the individual chooses to adopt. In a series of studies designed to test this hypothesis, Latham, Erez, and Locke (1988) found that performance differences in participative and assigned goal conditions could be attributed to differences in the extent to which persons are given a rationale, prior to performing the task, for the goal assignment. Use of a "tell and sell" procedure in the assigned goal condition resulted in similar levels of goal commitment and performance compared with subjects in the participatively-set goal condition. Conceptually, the "tell and sell" procedure represents and explicit operationalization of the explanation norm described by Folger and Bies (1989). Integration of the Latham, Erez, and Locke findings with contemporary work in the procedural justice domain suggests that adherence to norms for procedural fairness may exert indirect, but non-trivial motivational effects through commitment and choice in direction and intensity of effort allocations (e.g. Greenberg, 1990).

Intrinsic motivation

Similar to developments in the organizational justice paradigm, there has been a substantial shift in the direction and content of intrinsic motivation theorizing during the past decade. Deci's Cognitive Evaluation Theory (Deci, 1975; Deci & Ryan, 1980) represents the most well-known and extensively studied theory of intrinsic motivation in industrial-organizational psychology. Scientific interest in Deci's formulation began with investigation of the potential undermining effects of extrinsic rewards on intrinsic task interest and task persistence (for reviews, see Condry, 1977; Deci & Ryan, 1980; Lepper & Greene, 1978; Notz, 1975). As research accumulated, it became clear that extrinsic rewards, such as pay, did not always reduce intrinsic motivation (e.g. Fisher, 1978; Guzzo, 1979). These findings led Deci to elaborate his theoretical formulation into what is currently known as Cognitive Evaluation Theory

(CET; Deci, 1975). According to this theory, the detrimental effects of extrinsic events on intrinsic motivation depend on the perceived salience of "controlling" versus "informational" properties of the extrinsic event.

During the past decade, investigations in the CET paradigm have broadened to include examination of other extrinsic events, such as rewards, feedback, and goal assignments. More importantly, however, results of these studies have led to new theorizing that proposes different forms of intrinsic motivation with associated differences in their consequences for task interest, learning, and behavior. Since reviews of classic CET research are provided elsewhere (e.g. Deci & Ryan, 1980; R. Kanfer, 1990), the following discussion will focus on recent theoretical developments pertaining to distinctions among forms of intrinsic motivation.

Two broad conceptualizations that emphasize the distinction between different types of intrinsic motivation have been put forth recently by Malone and Lepper (1987) and Bandura (1986). Malone and Lepper (1987) organized intrinsic motives into three clusters on the basis of theories about various forms of intrinsic motivation. One cluster contains theories that emphasize curiosity, incongruity, and discrepancy motives (e.g. Berlyne, 1966; Hunt, 1965). In these theories, intrinsic motives refer to needs for stimulation and arousal. A second cluster of theories stresses competence, mastery, effectance, and challenge motives (e.g. White, 1959). These theories view intrinsic motivation as stemming from the individual's needs to demonstrate and exercise personal competencies. The third cluster of theories emphasizes personal control over the environment and self-determination (e.g. deCharms, 1968; Deci, 1975). In organizational psychology, intrinsic motivation has been studied most from the perspective of the latter two clusters of theories, rather than from theoretical perspectives that emphasize stimulation and arousal (although see Gardner & Cummings, 1988 for recent theorizing from the activation/arousal perspective).

Bandura's (1986) framework distinguishes between different forms of intrinsic motivation and extrinsic motivation based upon locus of the outcome and type of behavior-outcome contingency. Outcomes that occur within the person, such as self-satisfaction, are termed internal. External outcomes refer to incentives that originate in the environment (e.g. job termination). Natural contingencies refer to behavior-outcome relations that occur reliably across situations, such as fatigue (internal outcome) following strenuous physical activity (behavior). Arbitrary contingencies refer to the establishment of behavior-outcome relations via cognitive mechanisms. For example, level of pay is an arbitrary outcome that gains meaning and influence over behavior through intermediate cognitive processes.

The Bandura (1986) and Malone and Lepper (1987) frameworks complement one another. Both frameworks emphasize the point that similar intrinsically motivated behaviors can have different origins. More important, however, is the point that many organizational events, such as a pay rise, may involve both intrinsic and extrinsic outcomes (cf. Campbell & Pritchard, 1976). The problem of delineating the person and situation features that influence interpretation of an organizational event has begun to occupy the attention of many intrinsic motivation researchers. Attempts to address this problem have led to research in two directions: (1) determining how characteristics of an event facilitate intrinsic forms of motivation; and (2) investigating the specific combinations of task-person factors that affect an individual's motivational orientation toward task engagement. By adopting a motivational orientation perspective, the question of the relationship between intrinsic and extrinsic motivation is recast into the question of identifying the unique conditions that induce shifts from one orientation to the other.

According to Deci's theory, events that are interpreted by the individual as informational should facilitate intrinsic task interest, particularly when the information provided conveys a sense of personal competency. Harackiewicz (1979), for example, found that the detrimental effects of extrinsic rewards could be offset if the informational aspects of the reward were stronger than the controlling aspects. Several studies testing this aspect of Deci's theory provide further empirical evidence indicating that a variety of extrinsic organizational events, such as rewards, goal-setting, feedback, and modelling may also affect task interest, enjoyment, and behavior (Cellar & Barrett, 1987; Cellar & Wade, 1988; Harackiewicz & Larson, 1986; Harackiewicz, Sansome, & Manderlink, 1985; Manderlink & Harackiewicz, 1984).

Investigation on the effects of performance feedback further indicate the critical importance of the competency information in cultivating intrinsic task interest. In an attempt to interpret inconsistent findings with respect to the influence of performance feedback on intrinsic task interest, Sansone (1986) suggested that performance feedback would enhance intrinsic task interest only if such feedback provided the individual with a means of assessing personal competency. Sansone (1986) examined the effects of three feedback procedures on intrinsic task interest among college students performing a word puzzle task. Students who obtained performance feedback that permitted assessment of competency relative to others reported higher perceptions of competence and greater task enjoyment relative to persons in the no-competence information feedback and no-feedback conditions.

Research on determinants of intrinsic task interest indicates that features of the task environment play a critical role in the development and maintenance of intrinsic task interest. From an organizational perspective, these findings have potential implications for both training and management of work performance. Findings by Harackewicz and Sansone suggest that cultivation of an intrinsic motivation orientation may be achieved through the use of instructional embellishments, goal-setting procedures, and provision of positive competency feedback about performance. However, findings by Manderlink and Harackiewicz (1984) also suggest that some procedures may be more or less useful at different stages of skill acquisition/performance. For example, new employees may perceive performance feedback as informational, while longer-tenured employees may interpret such feedback as controlling. Similarly, the use of proximal goal assignments may be more beneficial among employees engaged in difficult or novel task assignments, whereas distal goal assignments may be more effective among persons engaged in repetitive or skilled task performances.

Flow states

A radically different approach to intrinsic motivation stems from Csikszentmihayli's (1975, 1978) research on identifying the job–person features that characterize intrinsically motivated behaviors over time. In a series of semi-structured interviews with skilled performers, such as surgeons, rock climbers, and dancers, Csikszentmihayli asked persons to describe the situations and conditions of work that were most enjoyable. Through rational analysis and factor analysis of the responses, Csikszentmihayli proposed the construct of "flow state" to denote periods of high intrinsic motivation. Features that characterize flow include undivided task attention, an organized set of action opportunities, a limited stimulus field, clear goals and feedback, and perceptions of personal control over the activity.

The concept of flow differs in several ways from previous conceptualizations of intrinsic motivation. In contrast to CET, the state of flow pertains to a psychological state that results from the *integration* of cognitive processes, task characteristics, and multiple intrinsic motives. In CET, perceptions of control and competence are represented as sufficient conditions for intrinsic motivation. However, these perceptions appear to represent necessary but not sufficient conditions for flow. In addition to these perceptions, it is also necessary that one's attention be directed toward regulation of action for the sole purpose of task accomplishment. Other essential features of flow, such as opportunities to limit the stimulus field, depend on the nature of the task. Once the indiviudal is engaged in a flow experience, however, superordinate cognitive processes appear to provide at least temporary protection against competing demands for attention. For example, Csikszentmihayli (1975) reports that persons engaged in flow frequently report perceptual distortions of time while engaged in the activity.

A recent study by Csikszentmihayli and LeFevre (1989) provided initial evidence on the incidence of flow in the workplace. In this study, 78 employed adults provided self-reports of their activities, motivation, and their subjective perceptions of the quality of their experience seven times per day (at random intervals within 2-hour periods) in response to a pager signal. The authors found that more flowlike experiences were reported in work contexts than leisure contexts. Of greater importance, however, they found that the individual's motivation for the activity (assessed through the item, "Did you wish you had been doing something else?") was more strongly influenced by the formal category (work or leisure) than by the experience of flow or non-flow. That is, the individual's classification of the activity as work or leisure had a stronger effect on activity preference than did the existence of the intrinsic motivational state.

Csikzentmihalyi and LeFevre's findings indicate that flow states wax and wane across a range of jobs, although it was also the case that flow states *per se* may be insufficient for sustaining task activity. Similar findings by Cellar and Barrett (1987) suggest that the benefits of flow conditions depend in part on the individual's cognitive schemas and work goals. In the context of work, the individual's goal for task engagement, or individual differences in motivational orientation, appear likely to moderate the beneficial effects of conditions conducive to flow.

The use of a time-sampling procedure for assessing flow and motivational processes represents a substantial departure from traditional methods of assessing intrinsic motivational states. Although this method is more costly and raises some concerns about the validity of self-report measures, an approach of this type does appear to be potentially advantageous in terms of providing on-line assessment of motivational processes in the workplace.

Summary and implications for work motivation

Two broad themes characterize recent motive-based research: (1) identification of the organizational conditions that activate particular motives; and (2) investigation of the influence of motives on specific components of the motivational system, such as job commitment, task interest, and motivational orientation. In the area of organizational justice, widespread interest in equity theory evident during the 1970s has given way to investigations of the determinants and consequences of procedural justice. Among intrinsic motivation researchers, there is growing recognition that different forms of intrinsic motivation have different implications for action. Research derived from CET has led to a steady stream of studies demonstrating the importance of the individual's goals in task engagement when attempting to decompose the effects of extrinsic events on intrinsic task interest. The move away from prediction of task behavior, and the corresponding emphasis on predictions of task interest and enjoyment, reflect the growing recognition that such theories have their greatest value in predicting the activation of a pattern of motivational processing rather than behavior *per se*. Individual differences in knowledge, skills, and abilities, as well as dynamic changes in situational demands further influence the extent to which an intrinsic motivational orientation will influence behavior.

Theory and research during the past decade suggest that broad, higher-order motives are activated in myriad and often unintentional ways in the organizational context. Recent theorizing in procedural justice, for example, outlines the elements of interpersonal dynamics in performance appraisals and decision-making procedures that may directly affect perceptions of fairness and an individual's commitment to job and organizational goals. The analysis of procedural fairness concerns from this perspective might be also usefully applied to leadership. Future research is needed to assess which components of these procedures carry the most impact, and to determine the ubiquity of such effects in cultures that emphasize different work values.

Recent advances in intrinsic motivation also suggest several new directions for research in organizational psychology. The coordination of various forms of intrinsic motivation into broader frameworks of motivational orientation has direct implications for the design and structure of training and management programs to facilitate and sustain learning and performance. In the instructional realm, for example, premature loss of interest in enhancing task performance can often result in failure to achieve asymptotic level of skill acquisition. The advent of computerized or simulated task-training environments should enable the inclusion of particular instructional embellishments to sustain intrinsic motivation throughout all phases of training. Further research investigating the effects of various instructional embellishments and procedures that activate different forms of motivation is needed to take full advantage of these technological advances. For example, curiosity and challenge motives for persistence may wane as persons become more experienced at the task. Procedures that sustain in intrinsic motivation orientation through different motives, for example recognition, cooperation, or increased arousal (by increasing task complexity), may be particularly useful during later phases of training.

Finally, the multidimensional and dynamic nature of intrinsic motivation suggests that it may be unrealistic to search for a single set of management procedures that will consistently sustain intrinsic task interest and persistence. As Csikszentmihayli's work with skilled performers suggests, intrinsic motivation may be more aptly conceptualized as episodic and temporally bounded rather than continuous.

Cognitive-Choice/Decision Approaches

Cognitive choice theories emphasize two determinants of choice and action: (a) the individual's expectations, and (b) the individual's subjective valuation of expected consequences associated with various alternative actions. The popularity of these theories in psychology reached a peak in the early 1980s, with extensive research programs associated with Expectancy X Value (E X V) type theories in social psychology (e.g. Fishbein & Ajzen, 1975; Triandis, 1979), personality psychology (Atkinson & Birch, 1974; Atkinson & Feather, 1966; Heckhausen, 1977; Raynor, 1969), and industrial/organizational psychology (e.g. Campbell & Pritchard, 1976; Graen, 1969; Naylor, Pritchard, & Ilgen, 1980; Porter & Lawler, 1968; Vroom, 1964). Through the early 1980s, organizational research focused on tests of basic tenets of the theory and investigations into the predictive validity of various models. Results of this period indicated conceptual difficulties with some of the basic assumptions of E X V models and lower than expected levels of predictive validity for task and job performance. [Excellent reviews of progress made during this period can be found in Feather (1982), Heckhausen, Schmalt, and Schneider (1985), and Mitchell, (1982a)]. Since the early 1980s, researchers in this area have directed their attention toward the resolution of difficulties identified in the 1970s. These efforts have resulted in the elaboration and revision of the original models, the refinement of methodological procedures for testing model components, and identification of the boundary conditions associated with choice conceptualizations.

Most E X V models of motivation share two basic assumptions. First, persons are assumed to behave hedonistically when choosing between tasks or levels of effort. This assumption implies that persons strive to maximize positive affect and minimize negative affect by engaging in behaviors to attain outcomes associated with the greatest perceived positive overall value. The hedonistic assumption is found in most E X V models, although there has been considerable disagreement regarding the calculative process by which persons select the alternative associated with the greatest perceived gain (see Mitchell & Beach, 1977).

Second, most E X V models are considered episodic. That is, these models account for behavior change in terms of changes in the individual's expectancies and anticipated valences. Change in motivation is depicted in terms of changes in either of these components. However, as Atkinson and Birch (1974) and Kuhl and Atkinson (1984) have noted, episodic models cannot readily account for behavior change when expectancies and incentives do not change. The episodic nature of E X V models has proven to be a major limitation in both the theoretical and practical usefulness of these models.

E X V formulations are intended to predict an individual's choices or decisions, not necessarily subsequent performance. This distinction is of critical importance when considering the effectiveness of these models in prediction of task and job performance. The focus on prediction of purposive choice means that the effect of an individual's choice on behavior is indirect, and will depend upon other factors such as situational constraints and ease of implementing the choice. In addition, these models contain no special provisions for conceptualizing motivational processes that may be enlisted for the purpose of overcoming difficulties in the accomplishment of one's intentions during task engagement. That is, most E X V models cannot readily explain the motivational processes underlying the translation of choice into long-term behavioral accomplishments.

Growing recognition of the boundary conditions associated with effective use of E X V models for predicting work behavior has led to a general decline in research from classic E X V perspectives. As more sophisticated frameworks have emerged, two decision theories of motivation and organizational behavior have captured research attention: Naylor, Pritchard, and Ilgen's

(1980) theory of organizational behavior, and Beach and Mitchell's (1987, 1990) Image Theory. Both theories incorporate the classic assumptions of expectancy-value approaches within a broader, more inclusive framework of decision-making.

Resource theory

Naylor, Pritchard, and Ilgen (1980) proposed a comprehensive resource theory of organizational behavior. According to this theory, motivation is defined as "the process of allocating personal resources in the form of time and energy to various acts in such a way that the anticipated affect resulting from these acts is maximized" (p. 159). Similar to traditional E X V approaches, Naylor, Pritchard, and Ilgen (1980) cast the problem in motivation as determining the factors and processes that influence choice in the direction of behavior.

Several features of the theory distinguish it from previous E X V organizational theories. By conceptualizing choice in terms of a resource allocation process, the theory permits analysis of decisions involving a range of events and outcomes. Second, Naylor, Pritchard, and Ilgen (1980) propose that persons make choice decisions based upon the form of perceived contingencies. For example, a computer programmer may perceive a positive monotonic relation between the amount of time he/she allocates to a particular assignment and the quality of the resulting product. According to Naylor, Pritchard, and Ilgen (1980), allocation decisions are made on the basis of the perceived forms of the contingency. Finally, Naylor, Pritchard, and Ilgen (1980) refine the instrumentality contingency by separating it into two distinct contingencies: (a) an outcome-evaluation contingency, and (b) an evaluation-reward contingency. Outcome-evaluation contingencies pertain to the perceived relation between amount of an outcome and likely evaluation of that outcome by other organizational personnel. In contrast, evaluation-reward functions pertain to the perceived relation between an evaluation of a product and the level of organizational reward provided for that product. As applied to organizational contexts, the distinction emphasizes two potential sources of difficulty in organizational procedures that affect motivation.

Naylor, Pritchard, and Ilgen (1980) also identify a wide variety of individual difference and situational determinants of decision-making. Pritchard, Jones, Roth, Stuebing, and Ekeberg (1988) developed a productivity measurement system based upon the Naylor, Pritchard, and Ilgen (1980) model and the form/function view of contingency relations. Pritchard et al. (1988) then conducted a large-scale investigation to assess the effects of group-level feedback, goal-setting, and incentives on productivity using the new measurement system. Results obtained with five organizational US Air Force units demonstrated the feasibility of this measurement approach to organizational productivity and the positive effects of group-based feedback and goal-setting.

Several researchers have focused on factors affecting the development of perceived contingencies and the effects of those contingencies on resource allocation decisions (e.g. Sawyer, 1990; Sniezek, May, & Sawyer, 1990; Switzer & Sniezek, 1991). Using a multiple cue probability learning task, Sawyer (1990) found that uncertainty affected resource allocation decisions. Subjects allocated fewer resorces to contingencies that were uncertain than to those what were certain. Sniezek, May, and Sawyer extended this analysis to investigate the role of uncertainty on resource allocation decisions in group contexts. They found that reducing social uncertainty through provision of feedback about other group member's allocations increased subject commitment of resources to the group.

To date, the bulk of empirical research using Naylor, Pritchard, and Ilgen's (1980) theory has focused on determinants of judgment and decision processes. Further applications of the theory to prediction of performance based on decision processes appear feasible. Naylor and Ilgen (1984), for example, used the Naylor, Pritchard, and Ilgen theory to propose an alternative framework for predicting the effects of difficult and specific goal assignments on task performance. Future research directed at assessing other applications and innovative features of the Naylor, Pritchard, and Ilgen approach is likely to yield information that integrates and extends existing motivation theories.

Image theory

Beach and Mitchell (Beach, 1990; Beach & Mitchell, 1987, 1990) have proposed a descriptive theory of decision-making that unifies cognitive and motivational structures within a decision paradigm. According to the theory, individuals maintain three distinct, but related structures: (a) value image, (b) trajectory image, and (c) strategic image. These images, whether they be developed through visual, mental, or cognitive formats, represent the basic information structures used in decision-making. The value image contains knowledge related to principles used in judging the "rightness/wrongness" of decisions. The trajectory image accommodates the individual's goals and timelines for accomplishing various outcomes. The strategic image structure is posited to maintain plans and strategies for implementing goals.

Beach and Mitchell distinguish two basic forms of decision-making in their formulation. Adoption decisions refer to the selection among a choice of possible courses of action. Progress decisions occur in the context of a previously selected plan or goal. These decisions refer to evaluation of whether a particular plan is producing satisfactory progress toward goal attainment. Both adoption and progress decisions are proposed to begin with a cognitive process by which persons assess the range of potential decisions in terms of their compatibility with relevant images. In the progress decision, the Compatibility test results in either continuation or change in one's goals. In adoption decisions involving only one candidate course of action, the individual is proposed to either adopt or reject the course of action. When the compatibility test results in the survival of more than one possible decision, a further cognitive process is conducted. The objective of this secondary process, called the Profitability Test, is to identify the best decision among those candidates still under consideration.

The Beach and Mitchell formulation suggests that images provide the representational structure by which an individual's knowledge influences the decision-making process. The model also emphasizes a simplified decision-making process by which persons either accept or reject a particular course of action, rather than considering all alternatives. Mitchell and Beach (1990) describe five studies that provide preliminary support for basic elements of Image Theory in individual decision-making.

Summary and implications for work motivation

The long accumulating evidence challenging the validity of classic expectancy-value models has led organizational researchers into several new directions. One area of investigation closely related to basic research in decision-making pertains to identifying conditions that bias underlying basic judgment processes in learning context (e.g. Sniezek, May, & Sawyer, 1990). Another approach, exemplified by Pritchard *et al.* (1988), builds directly on Naylor, Pritchard, and Ilgen's theory and focuses on the organizational implications of form conceptualizations of contingencies. A third approach, followed by Mitchell and Beach (1990), applies advances in cognitive, information-processing psychology to formulate a descriptive model of decision-making processes in organizational contexts.

Communalities between Resource theory and Image theory make salient some of the more important issues facing researchers in this area. For example, both formulations explicitly acknowledge that personal and situational factors affect the decision-making process. In addition, both theories emphasize the view that decision-making encompasses consideration of a wide range of anticipated outcomes and events. Naylor, Pritchard, and Ilgen (1980) proposed that these factors affect the form of perceived contingencies used in decision-making: Mitchell and Beach proposed a more radical approach in which these factors are incorporated within the image structures upon which decisions are evaluated. These approaches suggest that traditional conceptualizations of choice processes used by work motivation theorists during the 1960s and 1970s will undergo substantial revision during the next decade.

PROXIMAL CONSTRUCTS: GOALS AND SELF-REGULATION

Theoretical and empirical interest in proximal motivation constructs have increased steadily over the past two decades. Two forces have contributed to growth in this area: practical concerns about how to enhance work motivation, and renewed interest in the theoretical integration of cognition, motivation, and emotion. As Nuttin (1987) noted: "the major challenge at the moment is to explain how behavior dynamics are affected by their interaction with higher cognitive functions in man [sic] and how the behavioristic gap between cognitively processed needs and action is effectively bridged" (p. 320). Three issues dominate current theory and research in this broad area: (1) How do cognitive representations of outcomes gain salience and control over behavior? (2) How are choices translated into action? and (3) What characterizes the process of commitment to action?

In industrial and organizational psychology, the dominant research paradigm for studying work motivation has been the goal-setting paradigm established by Locke and his colleagues. Research in this framework has focused primarily on the attributes of assigned goals that facilitate task and job performance. As empirical demonstrations of the beneficial effects of difficult and specific goal assignments on performance accumulated during the 1970s, investigators began to concentrate on understanding the processes and mechanisms by which this effect occurred. Recent studies examining these process issues often conceptualize the goal–performance relations from social learning/social-cognitive, control, and resource allocation perspectives. This section provides a brief overview of prevailing conceptualizations and research on goals and self-regulation processes.

Locke's Goal-Setting Model

Locke (1968) proposed that persons assigned (and who adopt) difficult and specific goals outperform persons provided "do your best" (vague and nonspecific) goal assignments. Numerous studies and the results of recent meta-analyses of goal-setting research show support for Locke's notion (Latham & Lee, 1986; Locke et al., 1981; Mento, Steel, & Karren, 1987; Tubbs, 1986; Wood, Mento, & Locke, 1987). Evidence demonstrating the beneficial effects of difficult and specific goal assignments on work performance has prompted widespread use of goal-setting techniques in industry (see Locke & Lathum, 1984). Reviews of the goal-setting literature may be found in Austin and Bobko (1985), Locke and Latham (1991), Locke et al. (1981), and R. Kanfer (1990).

Locke et al. (1981) proposed that goals influence task behavior through four mechanisms: (1) directing attention; (2) mobilizing on-task effort; (3) encouraging task persistence; and (4) facilitating strategy development. Locke et al. (1981) also specified two relevant goal attributes: intensity and content. Goal content refers to features such as difficulty, specificity, complexity, and multiplicity of goals. Intensity refers to the strength of the goal and is influenced by factors such as perceived goal importance and goal commitment.

Most goal-setting research has focused on the effects of assigned goal content attributes on task performance. In such research, the effects of difficulty and specificity are often studied by comparing performance in a nonspecific goal assignment condition (e.g. "Do your best") with performance obtained in a specific and difficult assigned goal condition (e.g. "Process 100 orders this month"). Goal difficulty is typically manipulated through the assignment of performance goals associated with different objective probabilities of attainment, where the probability of attainment is based on mean performance levels obtained by some reference sample. Thus, difficult goal assignments refer to performance levels attained by relatively few persons, and easy performance goals refer to standards attained by most persons. Goal specificity is typically operationalized as the extent to which the goal assignment is made explicit with respect to the target of action (Locke et al., 1981). Few researchers have manipulated goal specificity independently of goal difficulty (for exceptions, see Locke, Chah, Harrison, & Lustgarten, 1989; Klein, Whitener, & Ilgen, 1990).

Social Learning/Social-Cognitive Theories of Self-Regulation

Social learning and social cognitive theories of self-regulation have their roots in clinical-experimental psychology (see R. Kanfer, 1990). In these approaches, goals represent a critical feature of self-regulation. As described by Bandura (1986), goals provide the individual with a cognitive representation of desired outcomes. Attainment of difficult and specific goals is accomplished through self-regulation activities involving three major components: self-observation (self-monitoring), self-evaluation, and self-reactions (e.g. dissatisfaction, self-efficacy expectations) (see Bandura, 1982; F. Kanfer, 1970). Self-monitoring refers to the direction and quality of attention. Self-monitoring of activities corresponding to one's goal is viewed as an essential prerequisite for effective self-regulation. Self-evaluation refers to the comparison of one's behavior or condition with the goal state. Comparisons of the goal and current state yield self-reactions. Self-reactions, including affective responses and self-efficacy expectations for future goal attainment, depend upon the size and direction of the discrepancy in self-evaluation. A large negative discrepancy between one's goal and current level of performance, for example, is posited to result in dissatisfaction and lowering of one's self-efficacy expectations for goal attainment. Person and situation characteristics are further posited to mediate the impact of self-evaluation on satisfaction and self-efficacy expectations. Because self-regulation processes are posited to foster goal-directed effort through feedforward as well as feedback processes, self-regulation may sustain effort through self-development of new, more difficult goals (Bandura, 1988).

Numerous studies have examined the influence of self-regulatory components on task performance in the context of goal-directed action (see Bandura, 1986; F. Kanfer, 1977). Results of these studies provide support for each component of self-regulation. Recent studies have aimed at understanding the conditions that foster and sustain high levels of performance motivation in achievement contexts (e.g. Bandura & Schunk, 1981). Bandura and Cervone (1983), for example, examined the roles of goals and feedback on performance of a stationary bicycling task. They found that the combination of moderately difficult and specific goals along with performance feedback resulted in higher levels of performance than either goal assignments or feedback alone. Studies investigating the influence of self-reactions on performance motivation indicate that the pattern of self-reactions that maximizes motivation depends in part on specific features of the situation (see R. Kanfer, 1990, for a review). For example, when the task is novel, or the goal is difficult, the optimal pattern of self-reactions appears to be one of dissatisfaction and high self-efficacy expectations. When the task is well-practiced, however, high self-efficacy expectations may diminish on-task effort.

In the organizational domain, the social learning perspective has recently been applied as a motivational intervention to enhance performance in both training and job contexts. For example, Gist, Schwoerer, & Rosen (1989) demonstrated the beneficial effects of self-management methods used with trainees learning new computer software. Frayne and Latham (1987; Latham & Frayne, 1989) examined the effects of self-management training in reducing absenteeism among government employees. They found that employees who received training in self-regulatory procedures demonstrated less absenteeism over a period of 9 months, compared to a no training control condition.

Cybernetic Control Theories of Self-Regulation

Another perspective on self-regulation stems from theorizing by Carver and Scheier (1981). Similar to some aspects of social-learning/social-cognitive theories, Carver and Scheier (1981) posited a theory of self-regulation based on the notion of a negative (discrepancy-reducing) feedback loop. In this perspective, comparison between one's standard (or goal) and perceived performance (the products of self-monitoring) results in cognitive and behavioral output directed toward the reduction of discrepancies between the goal and the perceived state of affairs.

Building from Powers' (1973) notions of a hierarchical goal structure, Carver and Scheier (1981) also specified the process by which various types of goals become salient. According to Carver and Scheier (1981), difficulty in execution of a higher-order goal is posited to shift attention to a lower-order subgoal that is currently not being achieved. As the subgoal goal-performance discrepancy is reduced, attention is posited to shift back up the goal hierarchy. The inclusion of a hierarchical goal principle enables the self-regulation model to account for sequential behaviors related to attainment of long-term goals.

Control theories of work motivation have been posited by Lord (Campion & Lord, 1982; Lord & Hanges, 1987) and Klein (1989). These theories extend the Carver and Scheier framework to consider the influence of various work conditions on discrepancy-reduction processes and patterns of motivation over time. Empirical research testing predictions of behavior derived from the model have generally been supportive (see e.g. Lord & Kernan, 1989).

Resource Allocation Perspectives

Resource allocation perspectives on self-regulation and goal-setting have been provided by R. Kanfer and Ackerman (1989) and Naylor and Ilgen (1984), respectively. Naylor and Ilgen (1984) suggested that the benefits of difficult and specific goal assignments on task performance stem from the influence of the goal assignment on perceptions of the cognized utility functions linking effort to performance and performance to evaluation. Derived from the Naylor, Pritchard, and Ilgen (1980) resource allocation theory of behavior in organizations, the Naylor and Ilgen analysis provides a theoretical explanation for how specific attributes of a goal assignment affect allocation of cognitive effort and task performance. In particular, this analysis suggests that the provision of non-specific goals and extremely difficult goals may dampen performance through their influence on the perceived utility of various allocations of cognitive effort.

Another resource allcoation perspective on the influence of goal assignments on performance is provided by R. Kanfer and Ackerman (1989). These researchers proposed that the beneficial effects of difficult and specific goal assignments depend on the cognitive demands of the task and individual differences in cognitive abilities. In the R. Kanfer and Ackerman (1989) model, self-regulatory processes associated with goal assignments are proposed to require cognitive/attentional resources. When engaged in novel and complex tasks, the provision of difficult goal assignments was posited to impede performance due to the diversion of critical resources away from task processing. Empirical results reported by R. Kanfer and Ackerman (1989) provided support for the model and indicated detrimental effects of difficult and specific goal assignments during the early phase of skill acquisition, and in particular for persons of lower ability levels.

Goal Orientation

Recent investigations in the educational domain have focused on the influence of the individual's purpose for task engagement; namely the type of goal adopted by the individual. Motivational orientation theorists suggest that goal type affects the character of information-processing and self-regulatory activities during learning (see Dweck & Leggett, 1988; Nicholls, 1978, 1984). Several theorists have proposed a basic distinction between two forms of goal orientation, referred to by Dweck and Leggett (1988), as learning goals versus performance goals. Persons who adopt learning goals are posited to engage in the task for the purpose of increasing personal mastery or competence. In contrast, the adoption of performance goals is posited to reflect the individual's orientation toward performing the task as a means of demonstrating one's superior ability relative to others. Several studies involving children provide support for the influence of goal orientation on pattern of self-regulatory processing as well as task performance (e.g. Nolen, 1988; Elliott & Dweck, 1988). Evidence for this influence on adult performance was also obtained in a recent study by Wood and Bandura (1989).

Theoretical Comparisons

Overall, the various conceptualizations of goals and self-regulation provide complementary, rather than contradictory, perspectives on goals and self-regulation. Locke's goal-setting model concentrates almost exclusively on the influence of goal content attributes on performance, whereas goal-orientation approaches focus on the influence of goal type on patterns of self-regulation. Social-learning/social-cognitive and control theory perspectives focus on the cognitive and affective mechanisms underlying the goal–performance relation, but are relatively silent about the influence of specific goal characteristics on performance. Resource allocation perspectives provide theoretical explanations of goal-setting research that consider goal and self-regulation processes in the broader context of learning and information-processing. These perspectives suggest several important boundary conditions for the effectiveness of goal assignments on performance in work settings. Social-cognitive and cybernetic control theories posit similar mechanisms of self-regulation, with one exception. Bandura (1988) has noted that the principle of discrepancy reduction in cybernetic control models limits the analysis of motivational processes to contexts in which the individual seeks to rectify inadequate performance. In an attempt to explain motivational processes assoicated with higher-order motives, such as challenge, Bandura (1988) argued that greater attention be given to feedforward mechanisms by which persons adjust goals upward following successful discrepancy reduction.

Recent elaborations of the goal-setting model by Locke and his colleagues (see Locke & Latham, 1991) have incorporated self-efficacy expectations as important determinants of assigned goal acceptance and commitment. Studies from the social-cognitive perspective also typically investigate self-regulatory processing in the context of moderately difficult and specific goal assignments. In the cybernetic control paradigm, for example, organizational researchers have integrated cybernetic control and goal-setting perspectives to address topics such as the process and factors affecting feedback-seeking in the work setting (e.g. Ashford, 1989).

Differences between the perspectives described above pertain primarily to the topics that have received the most empirical attention. In goal-setting paradigms, researchers have focused largely on issues that appear to affect the strength of the goal assignment–performance relation: namely, (a) goal commitment, and (b) task complexity. Empirical progress on these topics is discussed next.

Goal commitment

Locke's original goal-setting model focused on the goal–performance relation; the model did not specify the process or factors that influence acceptance and commitment to externally-imposed goals (see Locke, 1968). Locke indicated, however, that goal assignments will only influence performance if they are accepted by the individual. Erez, Earley, and Hulin (1985) showed the necessity of goal acceptance for subsequent demonstration of the goal–performance relation. Given the critical importance of goal acceptance for enhancing performance using goal-setting procedures, it is not surprising that researchers have focused considerable recent attention in this issue.

Empirical research on goal commitment has bifurcated into two lines of inquiry: (1) assigned versus participative goal-setting; and (2) person-situation determinants of goal commitment. One line of inquiry focused on the process of goal assignment, and more specifically, on the influence of participative versus assigned goal-setting on commitment and performance. In goal-setting research, participative goal-setting refers to situations in which the individual aids or independently establishes his/her performance goal. In assigned goal-setting procedures, individuals typically do not provide input or help to establish their performance goal. Locke's model posits that participatively-set goal assignments should enhance performance through their effects on the difficulty level of the goal that the individual adopts. According to this model, the method of goal-setting (participative versus assigned) should not differentially affect performance as long as the procedures used result in goal acceptance and commitment to similar goal levels. A series of studies by Latham and his colleagues (e.g. Latham & Saari, 1979a,b) provided support for this hypothesis and showed that goal-setting method had no effect on goal commitment or performance when level of goal difficulty was held constant.

Other studies, however, indicated a differential effect of goal-setting method. Studies by Earley and R. Kanfer (1985), Erez and Arad (1986), Hollenbeck and Brief (1987), and Hollenbeck, Williams, and Klein (1989) found that participative goal-setting procedures did affect goal commitment, which in turn affected performance. These researchers proposed that personal involvement in the goal-setting process, provision of an opportunity to express one's opinions about the goal, and enhanced sense of personal control achieved through participative procedures enhanced goal commitment and performance (also see Erez & F. Kanfer, 1983; Austin, 1989).

In an attempt to resolve this inconsistency, Latham, Erez, and Locke (1988) conducted three experiments designed to test five possible methodological explanations for the conflicting findings. The results obtained in these experiments led the researchers to suggest that the critical difference between assigned and participatively-set goal procedures was the extent to which participants were provided with a rationale for the goal assignment. When goal assignments were modified to include a rationale for the goal assignment, no differences on goal commitment and performance were obtained between assigned and participative procedures.

The second line of inquiry in this area pertains to broader person–situation characteristics that may affect commitment to an assigned goal. Hollenbeck and Klein (1987) integrated expectancy value and goal-setting perspectives to propose how task, ability, and person characteristics may affect commitment to assigned performance goals. Evidence to support the Hollenbeck and Klein (1987) model was subsequently obtained in a study by Hollenbeck, Williams, and Klein (1989). In this study, individual differences in need achievement and goal publicness were found to interactively affect goal commitment and task performance in a study of course grade assignments.

The systematic research comparing participative and assigned goal-setting methods is consistent with theory and research in other domains suggesting the critical importance of goal orientation for mobilization of self-regulatory processes. Investigations of person–situation influences on goal commitment provide further support for the general notion that the process of transformation also depends on dispositional tendencies and the precise circumstances surrounding goal assignments.

Task complexity

Another issue that has received considerable recent attention in the organizational literature pertains to the potential moderating effects of task complexity on the goal–performance relation. Studies by R. Kanfer and Ackerman (1989), and Huber (1985) found small or negative effects of goal assignments on performance in a variety of complex tasks. In a meta-analysis of goal-setting studies, Wood, Mento, and Locke (1987) found that task complexity mediated the goal–performance relation. R. Kanfer and Ackerman (1989) provide a theoretical explanation of this effect from a resource allocation perspective. According to this theory, goal assignments made during the initial, cognitively-demanding phases of skill acquisition may exert little positive or negative effect on performance due to the lack of cognitive resources available for self-regulation. Empirical findings by R. Kanfer and Ackerman (1989) and Kanfer, Dugdale, Nelson, and Ackerman (1990) provide support for this explanation in the context of performance on a complex air traffic controller simulation task. Results obtained in the R. Kanfer *et al.* (1990) study further suggest that negative effects of goal assignments may be compensated by the beneficial influence of goal-setting on mental rehearsal during periods of off-task activity. That is, although self-regulatory processing during initial learning may be detrimental, these negative effects may be overriden by goal assignments that promote covert rehearsal and planning when persons are not engaged in the task. These results have implications for the development of motivational interventions in simulations and other high-technology training programs.

Summary and Implications for Work Motivation

The results of goal-setting research generally indicate that difficult and specific goal assignments facilitate task performance in many, but not all, situations. Numerous studies have been directed toward investigation of the process and factors that produce, or fail to produce benefits to performance. Many of these studies have focused on explanations derived from social-learning/social-cognitive and cybernetic control theories of self-regulation. A few studies have examined the goal–performance relation from motivational orientation and resource allocation perspectives. The products of this research activity provide convergent evidence for the joint importance of goals and self-regulation in work motivation.

To date, organizational research in this area has concentrated largely on topics that represent challenges to Locke's goal-setting model. However, theoretical advances in this area suggest a number of other potentially fruitful avenues for applied research and practice. For example, the positive results obtained by Frayne and Latham (1987; Latham & Frayne, 1989) and Gist, Schwoerer, and Rosen (1989) in self-regulation training warrant further attention. An interesting question raised by this research and by research on the effects of goal orientation is whether self-regulation training may be used to reduce dependence on performance goal assignments made by a superior.

Another relatively unexplored area pertains to identification of the influence of affective states on goal commitment and self-regulatory processing. Several studies indicate that strong affective states may influence performance through their effects on self-regulation processes (e.g. Kavanagh & Bower, 1985; Wright & Mischel, 1982). In organizations, various procedures and goals may induce a variety of affective states, such as anger, guilt, or pride. Investigation of how various forms of affect associated with performance goals affect self-regulation may help in the design of more effective motivational interventions.

AN INTEGRATIVE PERSPECTIVE

The coordination of distal and proximal constructs has proven to be quite difficult, and the mechanisms linking these systems will remain poorly understood (cf. Nuttin, 1984). The difficulties associated with integrating these portions of the motivational domain are further complicated by the use of different terminologies across the domains, and by the current lack of precision relating dispositional tendencies, motives, choice processes, goals, and affect to motivational processes in each domain.

Recent attempts to link these approaches have used advances in personality and cognitive, information-processing psychology as a foundation upon which to build the integration (e.g. Gollwitzer, Heckhausen, & Steller, 1990; Heckhausen & Kuhl, 1985; Hollenbeck & Klein, 1987; Humphreys & Revelle, 1984; R. Kanfer & Ackerman, 1989; Naylor, Pritchard, & Ilgen, 1980). Since the connection between choice and volitional theories provides the context for most contemporary challenges to the field, a brief overview of the prevailing view is presented next.

One approach that has generated substantial attention derives from theorizing by Heckhausen and his colleagues (e.g. Heckhausen and Kuhl, 1985). In this perspective, articulated by Heckhausen and Kuhl (1985) and Gollwitzer (1990), a fundamental distinction is made between goal-setting and goal-striving phases of action. The goal-setting phase, in which persons deliberate about which course of action to take, is often termed the predecisional phase of action. Typically, this phase is characterized by cognitive choice processes that yield intentions. Intentions and goals share the characteristic of providing persons with a cognitive representation of a future situation. Intentions and goals may relate to one's own behavior (e.g. an intention to work overtime for three hours) or to a desired outcome (e.g. an intention to obtain a salary increase). Consistent with expectancy-value theories, the Heckhausen and Kuhl (1985) framework suggests that the precise product of choice processes depends on two key determinants: (1) the individual's expectations; and (2) the individual's valuation of the expected consequences stemming from alternative outcomes. Person and situation characteristics influence expectations and valences, as well as the level of specificity at which outcomes are conceptualized.

The exact process by which intentions become goals that are infused with sufficient potency to enable cognitive control over action, is the least well understood, and perhaps the most important of all processes in motivation/ volition. This process is the focus of substantial organizational research on goal commitment. Several researchers have proposed that intentions gain currency as self-regulatory goals only when the strength of the intention passes one or more critical thresholds (e.g. Carver & Scheier, 1981; F. Kanfer & Hagerman, 1981; Kuhl, 1985). Again, both person and situation factors have been suggested as influencing the conversion of intentions into goals. Heckhausen and Kuhl (1985), for example, view the conversion of intentions into goals as a two-stage process. In the first stage, individuals become committed to the product of choice processes following the successful transaction of the intention through a mental check of various anticipated future conditions (e.g. opportunity for action, time for accomplishment, etc.). In Heckhausen and Kuhl's (1985) model, a choice product that passes this mental filter is termed an intention. Although intentions of this type may serve as goals for future cognized representations of desired outcomes, they do not activate or guide self-regulatory activities until they have passed a second mental filter (Heckhausen & Kuhl, 1985). Cognitive activities at this point are aimed toward assessment of the feasibility of acting on the intention at the present. Following this line of reasoning, activated goals are posited to influence the initiation and focus of self-regulatory, or volitional activities.

The Heckhausen and Kuhl model suggests that further processing of an intention is required before it assumes an active role in the self-regulatory system. This is consistent with organizational theories based on cybernetic control principles (e.g. Lord & Hanges, 1987), resource allocation theories (e.g. R. Kanfer & Ackerman, 1989; Naylor, Pritchard, & Ilgen, 1980), and goal-setting models (e.g. Locke, et al., 1981). In R. Kanfer and Ackerman's resource-allocation model, for example, the endpoint of the transition of an intention to a goal is indicated by the deliberate allocation of some portion of one's total available attentional resources (i.e. cognitive effort) toward accomplishment of a cognized goal. That is, when an individual establishes a goal, he/she devotes a portion of his or her total available attentional resources to goal accomplishment. This dedication of a substantial portion of one's total intentional resources differentiates goals from intentions. For example, an individual's intention to achieve a high score on a test remains a weak influence on action until the individual commits attentional effort to the desired outcome. This process of resource allocation is posited to underlie the beneficial effects of commitment on task persistence.

Gollwitzer (1990) described the phase in which an individual focuses on goal implementation as the goal-striving phase of action. Recent empirical work by Gollwitzer and his colleagues provides evidence demonstrating differential information-processing activities associated with goal setting (deliberative) and goal-striving (implemental) phases of action (Gollwitzer, Heckhausen, & Ratajczak, 1990; Gollwitzer, Heckhausen, & Steller, 1990; Gollwitzer & Kinney, 1989). In these experiments, deliberative or implemental mind-sets are induced by having subjects consider a personally relevant problem and then either thinking about making a decision (goal-setting) or thinking about a plan of action for execution of a decison (goal-striving). Results obtained indicate that subjects contemplating a decision (i.e. deliberative mind-set) tend to process information differently and to recall different types of information. For example, Gollwitzer, Heckhausen, and Steller (1990) found that subjects engaged in the deliberative condition recalled more decision-related information about the problem than subjects in the implemental condition.

SUMMARY AND FUTURE DIRECTIONS

In their 1986 review of the work motivation literature, Locke and Henne (1986) concluded that the most valid theories of work motivation are those aimed at proximal constructs and that the validity of theories decreases as one moves toward the distal construct portion of the continuum. The current review of the literature indicates that proximal theories, such as Locke's goal-setting model, continue to capture substantial theoretical and empirical attention. At the same time, however, this review shows that conceptualizations of the work motivation domain are undergoing fundamental change. Extant theories, such as Maslow's Need Hierarchy Theory, Adams' Equity Theory, organizational versions of Expectancy Theory, and even Locke's Goal-Setting Theory are rapidly giving way to new, more complex conceptualizations that build upon advances in information processing, personality, and self-regulation. New formulations, such as organizational justice theories, goal-orientation approaches, resource-allocation theories, and social-cognitive theory often incorporate elements of older theories, but do so in ways that reduce the sharp distinctions between various approaches. During this recent period of theory integration and consolidation, the exercise of organizing theories in terms of their superiority has become unnecessary and perhaps even counterproductive. As new approaches attempt to address enduring questions, evaluation of these theories ultimately lies in the extent to which they aid our understanding of the portion of the nomological network of motivation and volition constructs they seek to address. For example, although need fulfillment models may provide relatively poor prediction of behavior and job performance, few scholars would argue that dispositions play no role in motivation or volition. Current research investigating dispositional determinants of work behavior in both goal-setting and goal-striving suggest that new conceptualizations may more successfully address this issue than outmoded, yet well-known, theories.

As stated by Ryan and Smith (1954): "The motivation of work cannot be considered independently of other problems of motivation, and the industrial psychologist must work with others in searching for an adequate *general* theory of the initiation and control of activity" (pp. 353–354). During the past decade, it appears that organizational researchers have finally heeded this call. The recent broadening of work motivation theorizing and research may be directly mapped to advances in related disciplines and to the renewed interest in the topic of motivation among psychologists of many persuasions. Interest in the role of dispositions and emotions corresponds to continuing progress in the personality domain. New directions in organizational justice stem from analyses of psychological processes in the negotiation and legal domain. Recent emphasis in the intrinsic motivation domain on the role of goal structures that shift an individual's task orientation from intrinsic to extrinsic closely relates to the growing literature on this topic in educational psychology. The recent focus by expectancy theory researchers on factors that affect judgment and decision processes corresponds to advances in decision theory and cognitive, information-processing psychology. Finally, the recent focus on the role of self-efficacy expectations among goal-setting researchers capitalizes on new advances in social-cognitive theory. Although some may view the relative absence of new, unique work motivation theories as a signal of stagnation, I agree with Ryan and Smith (1954) that such an approach is less useful, particularly given the high level of current interest in motivation among so many scholars.

This review highlights another important feature of the current scene; namely, the growing influence of scholars from the international community. The general decline of interest in the topic of motivation during the 1940s in the United States was accompanied by a division of the broad construct domain into disparate research traditions. Although researchers in the United States made substantial progress in more narrowly defined approaches to the topic, a number of difficult problems were left largely unattended. During the past decade, researchers from several countries have written extensively about these and other issues related to work motivation (e.g. Erez & Arad, 1986; Feather, 1982; Frese & Sabini, 1985; Halisch & Kuhl, 1987; Heckhausen & Kuhl, 1985; Humphreys & Revelle, 1984; Kleinbeck et al., 1990; Matsui, Okada, & Mizuguchi, 1981; Nuttin, 1984; Von Cranach et al., 1982; Weinert & Kluwe, 1987). For example, Heckhausen and his colleagues have brought attention and developed research paradigms to address a central question, namely, the relationship between motivation and volition. Kuhl and his colleagues have pursued this issue from a state-trait perspective by demonstrating the correspondence between individual differences in action/state orientation and execution of goal-directed action. From a related perspective, Gollwitzer and his colleagues have shown the differential information-processing activities associated with decision-oriented and implementation-oriented frames of reference. The steady growth of writings by international scholars on these topics suggests the field is entering a period of rapid growth to be marked by even greater diversity in perspectives.

As stated at the onset, the objective of this chapter was not to provide a comprehensive summary of work motivation theory and research, but rather to highlight new trends that offer evidence for addressing old and new problems in the psychology of work motivation. Two points may be noted about these new trends. First, the greatest growth has taken place in areas that relate to the proximal or volitional portion of the motivation system. Theoretical developments and empirical research in dispositions and motives, cognitive-choice, and goal-setting paradigms have all moved in this direction. Although cognitive-choice models occupied center stage in work motivation research during the 1970s, continued research in this domain has led to the development of new, integrative models of motivation.

Second, many of the recent advances in work motivation have been theory-driven. Clearly, the products of this activity aid our understanding of motivational processes in the workplace. Nonetheless, a consideration of the uniqe properties of the workplace suggests several additional topics that deserve further attention (see Kanfer, 1990). Three topics suggested by this review of the literature are discussed below.

1. *Motivation and cognitive abilities.* Most organizational scientists view performance as a joint function of abilities and motivation. Until recently, however, little attention has been given to investigation of motivational processes in the context of individual differences in cognitive abilities. Empirical research by Revelle and his colleagues suggests that motivationally-related dispositional tendencies have specific effects on cognitive information processing. Theoretical conceptualizations of cognitively-based motivation processes accord perceptions of self-efficacy expectations and perceived abilities a central role in self-regulatory activities. Additional research is needed to understand the extent to which these perceptions and expectations derive from actual and perceived individual differences in cognitive abilities. Dweck and Leggett (1988), for example, suggest that perceived differences in cognitive abilities may dampen motivation in long-term endeavors.

A second, related, question pertains to the relationship between individual differences in cognitive abilities and effectiveness and use of cognitively-based motivational processes, such as self-regulation. For example, in an investigation involving school-age children, Kuhl and Kraska (1989) found an association between cognitive developmental processes and the development of effective self-regulatory skill. R. Kanfer and Ackerman (1989) found that among adults performing a complex learning task, persons of lower general cognitive ability consistently demonstrated less effective self-regulatory skill compared to persons of higher cognitive ability. These results were obtained even when self-efficacy expectations between the groups were similar. These studies suggest that individual differences in cognitive abilities may importantly affect efficiency in planning and implementation of goals. Research is needed to determine the extent to which skill deficits in this portion of the motivation system may be remediated through environmental or cognitive restructuring. Such research has potential implications for the development of job training programs.

2. *Motivation in the social milieu.* A fundamental difficulty in application of theories of work motivation to the workplace pertains to the fact that most theories of motivation tend to neglect the social, interpersonal context of job performance. However, a steadily increasing number of researchers have begun to focus on the social determinants of action. Ashford's (1989) analysis of feedback-seeking in organizational contexts, for example, posits that feedback seeking is influenced by the perceived potential costs to self-esteem associated with asking others for feedback. Similarly, results obtained by Hollenbeck, Williams, and Klein (1989) on the influence of goal publicness on commitment and performance have indicated that persons may exert more effort when personal goals are made in a public context. Research on the role of

interpersonal motives for task engagement is needed. Cross-cultural investigations would be quite informative for ascertaining the extent and strength of these motives in team contexts.

3. *Typical versus maximum performance.* Motivation researchers have not paid sufficient attention to the distinction between typical and maximum measures of job performance (Ackerman, in press; Fiske & Butler, 1963). Sackett, Zedeck, and Folgi (1988) examined the performance of supermarket cashiers under typical (non-reactive) and maximum ("test") conditions. They found relatively low performance correlations between these two conditions in two samples, and suggest that motivational factors may play a stronger role in prediction of typical performance than maximum performance. The bulk of recent work motivation research has examined the effects of motivational interventions in contexts more aptly characterized as eliciting maximum rather than typical performance. Further attention should be given to investigation of motivational interventions in settings that elicit typical performance. It may be that motivational strategies, such as goal-setting, have their strongest impact in the training context or in repetitive jobs where the individual has not learned the job to a high level of skill. In such conditions, substantial increases in effort aid learning and performance. However, when the job is inconsistent or already well learned, strategies designed to elicit maximum effort are likely to yield proportionately smaller increases in performance. In essence, it may be practically useful to think of matching motivational interventions in terms of their strength to the objective demands of the job.

In summary, the past decade has witnessed the steady growth of new conceptualizations in the psychology of work motivation. These developments illustrate the breadth of the motivation domain, the considerable progress that has been made in the proximal portion of the domain, the comparative paucity of contemporary theory and research directed at personality and motive portions of the domain, and the need for far more careful attention to both the interface between goal-setting and goal-striving and the criterion domain.

ACKNOWLEDGMENTS

Preparation of this chapter was supported by the National Science Foundation grant (SES-8910748). The author wishes to thank Phillip L. Ackerman and Robert Schneider for their helpful comments on earlier drafts.

REFERENCES

Ackerman, P. L. (in press) Intelligence, attention, and learning: Maximal and typical performance. In D. K. Detterman (ed.), *Current Topics in Human Intelligence*, vol. 4. Norwood, NJ: Ablex.

Adams, J. S. (1963) Toward an understanding of inequity. *Journal of Abnormal and Social Psychology*, **67**, 422–436.

Adams, J. S. (1965) Inequity in social exchange. In L. Berkowitz (ed.), *Advances in Experimental Social Psychology*, vol. 2. New York: Academic Press, pp. 267–296.

Ajzen, I. (1985) From intentions to actions: A theory of planned behavior. In J. Kuhl & J. Beckmann (eds), *Action Control. From Cognition to Behavior*. New York: Springer-Verlag, pp. 11–39.

Alderfer, C. P. (1969) An empirical test of a new theory of human needs. *Organizational Behavior and Human Performance*, **4**, 142–175.

Arvey, R. D., Carter, G. W., & Buerkley, D. K. (1991) Job satisfaction: Dispositional and situational influences. In C. L. Cooper & I. T. Robertson (eds), *International Review of Industrial and Organizational Psychology*, vol. 6. Chichester, England: Wiley, pp. 359–383.

Ashford, S. J. (1989) Self assessments in organizations: A literature review and integrative model. In L. L. Cummings & B. M. Staw (eds), *Research in Organizational Behavior*, vol. 11. Greenwich, CT: JAI Press, pp. 133–174.

Atkinson, J. W., & Birch, D. (1974) The dynamics of achievement-oriented activity. In J. W. Atkinson & J. O. Raynor (eds), *Motivation and Achievement*. Washington, DC: Winston & Sons.

Atkinson, J. W., & Feather, N. T. (eds) (1966) *A Theory of Achievement Motivation*. New York: Wiley.

Austin, J. T. (1989) Effects of shifts in goal origin on goal acceptance and attainment. *Organizational Behavior and Human Decision Processes*, **44**, 415–435.

Austin, J. T., & Bobko, P. (1985) Goal setting theory: Unexplored areas and future research needs. *Journal of Occupational Psychology*, **58**, 289–308.

Bandura, A. (1982) The self and mechanisms of agency. In J. Suls (ed.), *Psychological Perspectives on the Self*, vol. 1. Hillsdale, NJ: Erlbaum, p. 3–39.

Bandura, A. (1986) *Social Foundations of Thought and Action: A Social Cognitive Theory*. Englewood Cliffs, NJ: Prentice-Hall.

Bandura, A. (1988) Self-regulation of motivation and action through goal systems. In V. Hamilton, G. H. Bower, & N. H. Fryda (eds), *Cognition, Motivation, and Affect: A Cognitive Science View*. Dordrecht, Holland: Martinus Nijholl, pp. 37–61.

Bandura, A., & Cervone, D. (1983) Self-evaluative and self-efficacy mechanisms governing the motivational effects of goal systems. *Journal of Personality and Social Psychology*, **45**, 1017–1028.

Bandura, A., & Cervone, D. (1986) Differential engagement of self-reactive influences in cognitive motivation. *Organizational Behavior and Human Decision Processes*, **38**, 92–113.

Bandura, A., & Schunk, D. (1981) Cultivating competence, self-efficacy, and intrinsic interest through proximal self-motivation. *Journal of Personality and Social Psychology*, **41**, 586–598.

Barrick, M. R., & Mount, M. K. (1991) The big five personality dimensions and job performance: A meta-analysis. *Personnel Psychology*, **44**, 1–26.

Beach, L. R. (1990) *Image Theory: Decision Making in Personal and Organizational Contexts*. Chichester, England: Wiley.

Beach, L. R., & Mitchell, T. R. (1987) Image Theory: Principles, goals and plans in decision making. *Acta Psychologica*, **66**, 201–220.

Beach, L. R., & Mitchell, T. R. (1990) Image Theory: A behavioral theory of decision making in organizations. In B. Staw & L. L. Cummings (eds), *Research in Organizational Behavior*, vol. 12. Greenwich, CT: JAI Press, pp. 1–41.

Beckmann, J., & Kuhl, J. (1984) Altering information to gain action control: Functional aspects of human information processing in decision-making. *Journal of Research in Personality*, **18**. 223–237.

Berylne, D. E. (1966) Curiosity and exploration. *Science*, **153**, 25–33.

Blum, M. L. (1949) *Industrial Psychology and its Social Foundations*. New York: Harper & Brothers.

Broadbent, D., & Broadbent, M. (1988) Anxiety and attentional bias: State and trait. *Cognition and Emotion*, **2**, 165–184.

Campbell, J. P. (1986) Labs, fields and straw issues. In E. A. Locke (ed.), *Generalizing from Laboratory to Field Settings*. Lexington, MA: Lexington Books, pp. 269–279.

Campbell, J. P. (1990) An overview of the Army Selection and Classification Project (Project A). *Personnel Psychology*, **43**, 231–239.

Campbell, J. P., & Pritchard, R. D. (1976) Motivation theory in industrial and organizational psychology. In M. D. Dunnette (ed.), *Handbook of Industrial and Organizational Psychology*. Chicago: Rand McNally, pp. 63–130.

Campion, M. A., & Lord, R. G. (1982) A control system conceptualization of the goal setting and changing process. *Organizational Behavior and Human Performance*, **30**, 265–287.

Carver, C. S., & Scheier, M. F. (1981) *Attention and Self-Regulation: A Control Theory Approach to Human Behavior*. New York: Springer-Verlag.

Cellar, D. F., & Barrett, G. V. (1987) Script processing and intrinsic motivation: The cognitive sets underlying cognitive labels. *Organizational Behavior and Human Decision Processes*, **40**, 115–135.

Cellar, D. F., & Wade, K. (1988) Effect of behavioral modeling on intrinsic motivation and script-related recognition. *Journal of Applied Psychology*, **73**, 181–192.

Condry, J. C. (1977) Enemies of exploration: Self-initiated versus other-initiated learning. *Journal of Personality and Social Psychology*, **35**, 459–477.

Cosier, R. A., & Dalton, D. R. (1983) Equity theory and time: A reformulation. *Academy of Management Review*, **8**, 311–319.

Costa, P. T., Jr, & McCrae, R. R. (1988) From catalog to classification: Murray's needs and the five-factor model. *Journal of Personality and Social Psychology*, **55**, 258–265.

Csikszentmihayli, M. (1975) *Beyond Boredom and Anxiety*. San Fransicso, CA: Jossey-Bass.

Csikszentmihayli, M. (1978) Intrinsic rewards and emergent motivation. In M. R. Lepper and D. Greene (eds), *The Hidden Costs of Reward*. Hillsdale, NJ: Erlbaum, pp. 205–216.

Csikszentmihayli, M., & LeFevre, J. (1989) Optimal experience in work and leisure. *Journal of Personality and Psychology*, **56**, 815–822.

Day, D. V., & Silverman, S. B. (1989) Personality and job performance: Evidence of incremental validity, *Personnel Psychology*, **42**, 25–36.

deCharms, R. (1968) *Personal Causation*. New York: Academic Press.

Deci, E. L. (1975) *Intrinsic Motivation*. New York: Plenum Press.

Deci, E. L., & Ryan, R. M. (1980) The empirical exploration of intrinsic motivational processes. In L. Berkowitz (ed.), *Advances in Experimental Social Psychology*, vol. 13. New York: Academic Press, pp. 39–80.

Digman, J. M., & Takemoto-Chock, N. K. (1981) Factors in the natural language of personality: Re-analysis and comparison of six major studies. *Multivariate Behavioral Research*, **16**, 149–170.

Dweck, C. S. (1986) Motivational processes affecting learning. *American Psychologist,* **41**, 1040–1048.

Dweck, C. S., & Leggett, E. L. (1988) A social-cognitive approach to motivation and personality. *Psychological Review,* **95**, 256–273.

Earley, P,. C., & Kanfer, R. (1985) The influence of component participation and role models on goal acceptance, goal satisfaction, and performance. *Organizational Behavior and Human Decision Processes,* **36**, 378–390.

Elliott, E. S., & Dweck, C. S. (1988) Goals: An approach to motivation and achievement. *Journal of Personality and Social Psychology,* **54**, 5–12.

Erez, M., & Arad, R. (1986) Participative goal setting: Social, motivational and cognitive factors. *Journal of Applied Psychology,* **71**, 591–597.

Erez, M., Earley, P. C., & Hulin, C. L. (1985) The impact of participation on goal acceptance and performance: A two step model. *Academy of Management Journal,* **28**, 50–66.

Erez, M., & Kanfer, F. H. (1983) The role of goal acceptance in goal setting and task performance. *Academy of Management Review,* **8**, 454–463.

Feather, N. T. (ed.) (1982) *Expectations and Actions: Expectancy-Value Models in Psychology.* Hillsdale, NJ: Erlbaum.

Fenigstein, A., Scheier, M. F., & Buss, A. H. (1975) Public and private self-consciousness: Assessment and theory. *Journal of Consulting and Clinical Psychology,* **43**, 522–527.

Fishbein, M., & Ajzen, I. (1975) *Belief, Attitude, Intention, and Behavior: An Introduction to Theory and Research.* Reading, MA: Addison-Wesley.

Fisher, C. D. (1978) The effects of personal control, competence, and extrinsic reward systems on intrinsic motivation. *Organizational Behavior and Human Performance,* **21**, 273–288.

Fiske, D. W., & Butler, J. M. (1963) The experimental conditions for measuring individual differences. *Educational and Psychological Measurement,* **23**, 249–266.

Fogler, R., & Bies, R. J. (1989) Managerial responsibilties and procedural justice. *The Employee Responsibilities and Rights Journal,* **2**, 79–90.

Ford, D. H. (1987) *Humans as Self-Constructing Living Systems: A Developmental Perspective on Behavior and Personality.* Hillsdale, NJ: Erlbaum.

Frayne, C. A. & Latham, G. P. (1987) The application of social learning theory to employee self-management of attendance. *Journal of Applied Psychology,* **72**, 387–392.

Frese, M., & Sabini, J. (1985) *Goal Directed Behavior: The Concept of Action of Psychology.* Hillsdale, NJ: Lawrence Erlbaum.

Gardner, D. G. & Cummings, L. L. (1988) Activation theory and job design: Review and reconceptualization. In B. M. Staw & L. L. Cummings (eds), *Research in Organizational Behavior,* vol. 10. Greenwich, CT: JAI Press, pp. 81–122.

Gist, M. E., Schwoerer, C., & Rosen, B. (1989) Effects of alternative training methods on self-efficacy and performance in computer software training. *Journal of Applied Psychology,* **74**, 884–891.

Gollwitzer, P. M. (1990) Action phases and mind-sets. In E. T. Higgins & R. M. Sorrentino (eds), *Handbook of Motivation and Cognition,* vol. 2. New York: Guilford Press, pp. 53–92.

Gollwitzer, P. M., Heckhausen, H., & Ratajczak, H. (1990) From weighing to willing: Approaching a change decision through pre- or postdecisional mentation. *Organizational Behavior and Human Decision Processes,* **45**, 41–65.

Gollwitzer, P. M., Heckhausen, H., & Steller, B. (1990) Deliberative and implemental mind-sets: Cognitive tuning toward congruous thoughts and information. *Journal of Personality and Social Psychology,* **59**, 1119–1127.

Gollwitzer, P. M., & Kinney, R. F. (1989) Effects of deliberative and implemental mind-sets on illusion of control. *Journal of Personality and Social Psychology*, **56**, 531–542.

Graen, G. (1969) Instrumentality theory of work motivation: Some experimental results and suggested modifications [Monograph]. *Journal of Applied Psychology*, **53**, 1–25.

Greenberg, J. (1982) Approaching equity and avoiding inequity in groups and organizations. In J. Greenberg & R. L. Cohen (eds), *Equity and Justice in social Behavior.* New York: Academic Press, pp. 389–436.

Greenberg, J. (1987) A taxonomy of organizational justice theories. *Academy of Management Review*, **12**, 9–22.

Greenberg, J. (1990) Employee theft as a reaction to underpayment inequity: The hidden costs of pay cuts. *Journal of Applied Psychology*, **75**, 561–568.

Greenberg, J., & Ornstein, S. (1983) High status job title as compensation for underpayment: A test of equity theory. *Journal of Applied Psychology*, **68**, 285–297.

Guion, R. M., & Gottier, R. F. (1965) Validity of personality measures in personnel selection. *Personnel Psychology*, **18**, 135–164.

Guzzo, R. A. (1979) Types of rewards, cognitions, and work motivation. *Academy of Management Review*, **4**, 75–86.

Hackman, J. R., & Oldham, G. R. (1980) *Work Redesign.* Reading, MA: Addison-Wesley.

Halisch, F., & Kuhl, J. (eds) (1987) *Motivation, Intention, and Volition.* New York: Springer-Verlag.

Harackiewicz, J. M. (1979) The effects of reward contingency and performance feedback on intrinsic motivation. *Journal of Personality and Social Psychology*, **37**, 1352–1363.

Harackiewicz, J. M., & Larson, J. R. (1986) Managing motivation: The impact of supervisor feedback on subordinate task interest. *Journal of Personality and Social Psychology*, **51**, 547–556.

Harackiewicz, J. M., Sansone, C., & Manderlink, G. (1985) Competence, achievement orientation, and intrinsic motivation: A process analysis. *Journal of Personality and Social Psychology*, **48**, 493–508.

Heckhausen, H. (1977) Achievement motivation and its constructs: A cognitive model. *Motivation and Emotion*, **1**, 283–329.

Heckhausen, H., & Kuhl, J. (1985) From wishes to action: The dead ends and short cuts on the long way to action. In M. Frese and J. Sabini (eds), *Goal Directed Behavior: The Concept of Action in Psychology.* Hillsdale, NJ: Erlbaum, pp. 134–160.

Heckhausen, H., Schmalt, H. D. & Schneider, K. (1985) *Achievement Motivation in Perspective.* New York: Academic Press.

Helmreich, R. L., Swain, L. L., & Carsrud, A. L. (1986) The honeymoon effect in job performance: Temporal increases in the predictive power of achievement motivation. *Journal of Applied Psychology*, **71**, 185–188.

Hollenbeck, J. R. (1989) Control theory and the perception of work environments: The effects of focus of attention on affective and behavioral reactions to work. *Organizational Behavior and Human Decision Processes*, **43**, 406–430.

Hollenbeck, J. R., & Brief, A. P. (1987) The effects of individual differences and goal origin on the goal setting process. *Organizational Behavior and Human Decision Processes*, **40**, 392–414.

Hollenbeck, J. R., & Klein, H. J. (1987) Goal commitment and the goal-setting process: Problems, prospects, and proposals for future research. *Journal of Applied Psychology*, **72**, 212–220.

Hollenbeck, J. R., & Williams, C. R. (1987) Goal importance, self-focus, and the goal setting process. *Journal of Applied Psychology*, 72, 204–211.

Hollenbeck, J. R., Williams, C. R., & Klein, H. J. (1989) An empirical exmaination of the antecedents of commitment to difficult goals. *Journal of Applied Psychology*, 74, 18–23.

Hough, L. M., Eaton, N. K., Dunnette, M. D., Kamp, J., & McCloy, R. A. (1990) Criterion-related validities of personality constructs and the effects of response distortion on those validities [Monograph]. *Journal of Applied Psychology*, 75, 581–595.

Huber, V. L. (1985) Effects of task difficulty, goal setting, and strategy on performance of a heuristic task. *Journal of Applied Psychology*, 70, 492–504.

Humphreys, M. S., & Revelle, W. (1984) Personality, motivation, and performance: A theory of the relationship between individual differences and information processing. *Psychological Review*, 91, 153–184.

Hunt, J. McV. (1965) Intrinsic motivation and its role in psychological development. In D. Levine (ed.), *Nebraska Symposium on Motivation*, vol. 13. Lincoln, NE: University of Nebraska Press, pp. 189–282.

Ilgen, D. R., & Klein, H. J. (1988) Individual motivation and performance: Cognitive influences on effort and choice. In J. P. Campbell, R. J. Campbell, and Associates (eds), *Productivity in Organization*. San Francisco: Jossey-Bass, pp. 143–176.

Isen, A. M., Means, B., Patrick, R., & Nowicky, G. (1982) Some factors influencing decision-making and risk-taking. In M. S. Clark & S. T. Fiske (eds), *Affect and Cognition: The 17th Annual Carnegie Symposium on Cognition*. Hillsdale, NJ: Lawrence Erlbaum, pp. 243–261.

James, W. (1890) *Principles of Psychology*. New York: Holt.

Kanfer, F. H. (1970) Self-regulation: Research, issues and speculations. In C. Neuringer and K. L. Michael (eds), *Behavior Modification in Clinical Psychology*. New York: Appleton-Century-Crofts.

Kanfer, F. H. (1977) The many faces of self-control, or behavior modification changes its focus. In R. B. Stuart (ed.), *Behavioral Self-Management*. New York: Brunner/Mazel, pp. 1–48.

Kanfer, F. H., & Hagerman, S. M. (1981) The role of self-regulation. In L. P. Reh, (ed.), *Behavior Therapy for Depression: Present Status and Future Directions*. New York: Academic Press, pp. 143–179.

Kanfer, R. (1986) Toward a unified theoretical framework of performance motivation: Situational and self-regulatory determinants. Paper presented at the 21st International Congress of Applied Psychology, Jerusalem, Israel.

Kanfer, R. (1987) Task-specific motivation: An integrative approach to issues of measurement, mechanisms, processes, and determinants. *Journal of Social and Clinical Psychology*, 5, 237–264.

Kanfer, R. (1990) Motivation theory and industrial/organizational psychology. In M. D. Dunnette and L. M. Hough (eds), *Handbook of Industrial and Organizational Psychology*, 2nd edition, vol. 1. Palo Alto, CA: Consulting Psychologists Press, pp. 75–170.

Kanfer, R., & Ackerman, P. L. (1989) Motivation and cognitive abilities: An integrative/aptitude-treatment interaction approach to skill acquisition [Monograph]. *Journal of Applied Psychology*, 74, 657–690.

Kanfer, R., Dugdale, B., Nelson, L., & Ackerman, P. L. (1990) Goal setting and complex task performance: A resource allocation perspective. Paper presented at the annual meeting of the Society of Industrial and Organizational Psychology, Miami Beach, FL.

Kanfer, R., Sawyer, J., Earley, P. C., & Lind, E. A. (1987) Fairness and participation in evaluation procedures: Effects on task attitudes and performance. *Social Justice Research*, 1, 235–249.

Katzell, R. A., & Thompson, D. E. (1990) Work motivation: Theory and practice. *American Psychologist*, 45, 144–153.

Kavanagh, D. J., & Bower, G. H. (1985) Mood and self-efficacy: Impact of joy and sadness on perceived capabilities. *Cognitive Therapy and Research*, 9, 507–525.

Klein, H. (1989) An integrated control theory model of work motivation. *Academy of Management*, 14, 150–172.

Klein, H., Whitener, E. M., & Ilgen, D. R. (1990) The role of goal specificity in the goal setting process. *Motivation and Emotion*, 14, 179–193.

Kleinbeck, U., Quast, H-H., Theirry, H., & Hacker, H. (1990) *Work Motivation*. Hillsdale, NJ: Lawrence Erlbaum.

Klinger, E. (1975) Consequences of commitment to and disengagement from incentives. *Psychological Review*, 82, 1–25.

Klinger, E. (1987) Current concerns and disengagement from incentives. In F. Halisch & J. Kuhl (eds), *Motivation, Intention, and Volition*. New York: Springer-Verlag, pp. 337–347.

Klinger, E., & Murphy, M. D. (in press) Action orientation and personality: Some evidence on the construct validity of the Action Control Scale. In J. Kuhl & J. Beckmann (eds), *Volition and Personality: Action- and Sate-oriented Modes of Control*. Göttingen, Germany: Hogrefe.

Kuhl, J. (1982) The expectancy-value approach within the theory of social motivation: Elaborations, extensions, and critique. In N. T. Feather (ed.), *Expectations and Actions: Expectancy-Value Models in Psychology*. Hillsdale, NJ: ERlbaum, pp. 125–160.

Kuhl, J. (1984) Volitional aspects of achievement motivation and learned helplessness: Toward a comprehensive theory of action control. In B. A. Maher (ed.), *Progress in Experimental Personality Research*, vol. 13. New York: Academic Press, pp. 99–171.

Kuhl, J. (1985) Volitional mediators of cognition-behavior consistency: Self-regulatory processes and action vs. state orientation. In J. Kuhl & J. Beckmann (eds), *Action Control: From Cognition to Behavior*. New York: Springer-Verlag, pp. 101–128.

Kuhl, J., & Atkinson, J. W. (1984) Perspectives in human motivational psychology: A new experimental paradigm. In V. Sarris & A. Parducci (eds), *Perspectives in Psychological Experimentation: Toward the Year 2000*. Hillsdale, NJ: Erlbaum, pp. 235–252.

Kuhl, J., & Beckmann, J. (eds) (1985) *Action Control: From Cognition to Behavior*. New York: Springer-Verlag.

Kuhl, J., & Beckmann, J. (eds) (in press) *Volition and Personality: Action- and State-oriented Modes of Control*. Gottingen, Germany: Hogrefe.

Kuhl, J., & Geiger, E. (1986) The dynamic theory of the anxiety-behavior relation: A study of resistance and time allocation. In J. Kuhl & J. W. Atkinson (eds), *Motivation, Thought, and Action*. New York: Praeger, pp. 76–93.

Kuhl, J., & Koch, B. (1984) Motivational determinants of motor performance: The hidden second task. *Psychological Research*, 46, 143–153.

Kuhl, J., & Kraska, K. (1989) Self-regulation and metamotivation: Computational mechanisms, development, and assessment. In R. Kanfer, P. L. Ackerman, & R. Cudeck (eds), *Abilities, Motivation, and Methodology: The Minnesota Symposium on Learning and Individual Differences*. Hillsdale, NJ: Erlbaum, pp. 343–374.

Kuhl, J., & Wassiljew, I. (1985) An information-processing perspective on intrinsic task-involvement problem-solving and the complexity of action plans. In G. d'Ydewalle (ed.), *Cognition, Information Processing, and Motivation*. Amsterdam: North-Holland, pp. 505–522.

Kuhl, J., & Weiss, M. (1985) Performance deficits following uncontrollable failure: Impaired action control or generalized expectancy deficits? (Paper No. 5/84). Munich: Max Planck Institute for Psychological Research.

Landy, F. J., Barnes, J. L., & Murphy, K. R. (1978) Correlates of perceived fairness and accuracy of performance evaluation. *Journal of Applied Psychology*, **63**, 751–754.

Landy, F. J., Barnes-Farrell, J., & Cleveland, J. N. (1980) Perceived fairness and accuracy of performance evaluation: A follow-up. *Journal of Applied Psychology*, **65**, 355–356.

Landy, F. J., & Becker, W. S. (1987) Motivation theory reconsidered. In L. L. Cummings & B. M. Staw (eds), *Research in Organizational Behavior*. vol. 9. Greenwich, CT: JAI Press, pp. 1–38.

Latham, G. P., Erez, M., & Locke, E. A. (1988) Resolving scientific disputes by the joint design of crucial experiments by the antagonists: Application to the Erez-Latham dispute regarding participation in goal setting [Monograph]. *Journal of Applied Psychology*, **73**, 753–772.

Latham, G. P., & Frayne, C. A. (1989) Self-management training for increasing job attendance: A follow-up and replication. *Journal of Applied Psychology*, **74**, 411–416.

Latham, G. P., & Lee, T. W. (1986) Goal setting. In E. A. Locke (ed.), *Generalizing from Laboratory to Field Settings*. Lexington, MA: Lexington Books, pp. 101–118.

Latham, G. P., & Saari, L. M. (1979a) The effects of holding goal difficulty constant on assigned and participatively set goals. *Academy of Management Journal*, **22**, 163–168.

Latham, G. P., & Saari, L. M. (1979b) Importance of supportive relationships in goal setting. *Journal of Applied Psychology*, **64**, 151–156.

Lepper, M. R., & Greene, D. (eds) (1978) *The Hidden Costs of Reward*. Hillsdale, NJ: Erlbaum.

Leventhal, G. S. (1980) What should be done with equity theory? New approaches to the study of fairness in social relationships. In K. Gergen, M. Greenberg, & R. Willis (eds), *Social Exchange: Advances in Theory in Research*. New York: Plenum, pp. 27–55.

Levin, I., & Stokes, J. P. (1989) Dispositional approach to job satisfaction: Role of negative affectivity. *Journal of Applied Psychology*, **74**, 752–758.

Lewin, K. (1938) *The Conceptual Representation and the Measurement of Psychological Forces*. Durham, NC: Duke University Press.

Lind, E. A., & Tyler, T. R. (1988) *The Social Psychology of Procedural Justice*. New York: Plenum.

Locke, E. A. (1968) Toward a theory of task motivation and incentives. *Organizational Behavior and Human Performance*, **3**, 157–189.

Locke, E. A., Chah, D-O., Harrison, S., & Lustgarten, N. (1989) Separating the effects of goal specificity from goal level. *Organizational Behavior and Human Decision Processes*, **43**, 270–287.

Locke, E. A., & Henne, D. (1986) Work motivation theories. In C. L. Cooper & I. Robertson (eds), *International Review of Industrial and Organizational Psychology*. Chichester, England: Wiley, pp. 1–35.

Locke, E. A., & Latham, G. P. (1984) *Goal-Setting: A Motivational Technique that Works*. Englewood Cliffs, NJ: Prentice-Hall.

Locke, E. A., & Latham, G. P. (1991) *A Theory of Goal Setting and Task Performance*. New York: Prentice-Hall.

Locke, E. A., Motowidlo, S. J., & Bobko, P. (1986) Using self-efficacy theory to resolve the conflict between goal-setting theory and expectancy theory in industrial/organizational psychology. *Journal of Social and Clinical Psychology*, **4**, 328–338.

Locke, E. A., & Schweiger, D. M. (1979) Participation in decision-making: One more look. In B. M. Staw (ed.), *Research in Organizational Behavior*, vol. 1. Greenwich, CT: JAI Press, pp. 265–340.

Locke, E. A., Shaw, K. N., Saari, L. M., & Lantham, G. P. (1981) Goal setting and task performance: 1969–1980. *Psychological Bulletin*, **90**, 125–152.

Lord, R. G., & Hanges, P. J. (1987) A control systems model of organizational motivation: Theoretical development and applied implications. *Behavioral Science*, **32**, 161–178.

Lord, R. G., & Kernan, M. C. (1989) Application of control theory to work settings. In W. A. Herschberger (ed.), *Volitional Action*. Amsterdam: Elsevier, pp. 493–514.

Luthans, F., & Kreitner, R. (1985) *Organizational Behavior Modification and Beyond: An Operant and Social Learning Approach*. Glenview, IL: Scott, Foresman.

Malone, T. W., & Lepper, M. R. (1987) Making learning fun: A taxonomy of intrinsic motivations for learning. In R. E. Snow and M. J. Farr (eds), *Aptitude, Learning, and Instruction: Conative and Affective Process Analyses*. vol. III. Hillsdale, NJ: Erlbaum, pp. 223–253.

Manderlink, G., & Harackiewicz, J. M. (1984) Proximal versus distal goal setting and intrinsic motivation. *Journal of Personality and Social Psychology*, **47**, 918–928.

Maslow, A. H. (1943) A theory of human motivation. *Psychological Review*, **50**, 370–396.

Maslow, A. H. (1954) *Motivation and personality*. New York: Harper & Row.

Matsui, T., Okada, A., & Mizuguchi, R. (1981) Expectancy theory predictions of the goal theory postulate, "The harder the goals, the higher the performance." *Journal of Applies Psychology*, **66**, 54–58.

McClelland, D. C. (1985) *Human Motivation*. Glenville, IL: Scott Foresman.

McCrae, R. R., & Costa, P. T., Jr. (1990) *Personality in Adulthood*. New York: Guilford Press.

McHenry, J. J., Hough, L. M., Toquam, J., Hanson, M. A., & Ashworth, S. (1990) Project A validity results: The relationship between predictor and criterion domains. *Personnel Psychology*, **43**, 335–354.

Mento, A. J., Steel, R. P., & Karren, R. J. (1987) A meta-analytic study of the effects of goal setting on task performance: 1966–1984. *Organizational Behavior and Human Decision Processes*, **39**, 52–83.

Miner, J. B. (1980) *Theories of Organizational Behavior*. Hillsdale, IL: Dryden Press.

Mischel, W. (1973) Toward a cognitive social learning reconceptualization of personality. *Psychological Review*, **80**, 252–283.

Mitchell, T. R. (1982a) Expectancy-value models in organizational psychology. In N. T. Feather (ed.), *Expectations and Actions: Expectancy-Value Models in Psychology*. Hillsdale, NJ: Erlbaum, pp. 293–312.

Mitchell, T. R. (1982b) Motivation: New directions for theory, research, and practice. *Academy of Management Review*, 7, 80–88.

Mitchell, T. R. (1986) *A Diagnostic Model for the Use of Motivational Strategies*. Paper presented at the 21st International Congress of Applied Psychology, Jerusalem, Israel, July.

Mitchell, T. R., & Beach, L. R. (1977) Expectancy theory, decision theory, and occupational preference and choice. In M. F. Kaplan and S. Schwartz (eds), *Human Judgment and Decision Processes in Applied Settings*. New York: Academic Press, pp. 203–226.

Mitchell, T. R., & Beach, L. R. (1990) "Do I love thee? Let me count . . ." Toward an understanding of intuitive and automatic decision making. *Organizational Behavior and Human Decision Processes*, **47**, 1–20.

Mossholder, K. W. (1980) Effects of externally mediated goal setting on intrinsic motivation: A laboratory experiment. *Journal of Applied Psychology*, **65**, 202–210.

Naylor, J. C., & Ilgen, D. R. (1984) Goal setting: A theoretical analysis of motivational technology. In B. M. Staw and L. L. Cummings (eds), *Research in Organizational Behavior*. vol. 6. Greenwich, CT: JAI Press, pp. 95–140.

Naylor, J. C., Pritchard, R. D., & Ilgen, D. R. (1980) *A Theory of Behavior in Organizations*. New York: Academic Press.

Nicholls, J. G. (1978) The development of the concepts of effort and ability, perception of academic attainment, and the understanding that difficult tasks require more ability. *Child Development*, **49**, 800–814.

Nicholls, J. G. (1984) Achievement motivation: Conceptions of ability, subjective experience, task choice and performance. *Psychological Review*, **91**, 328–346.

Nicholls, J. G., & Miller, A. T. (1984) Development and its discontents: The differentiation of the concept of ability. In J. G. Nicholls (eds), *Advances in Motivation and Achievement: The Development of Achievement Motivation*. vol. 3. Greenwich, CT: JAI Press, pp. 185–218.

Nolen, S. B. (1989) Reasons for studying: Motivation orientations and study stategies. *Cognition and Instruction*, **5**, 269–287.

Notz, W. W. (1975) Work motivation and the negative effects of extrinsic rewards: A review with implications for theory and practice. *American Psychologist*, **30**, 884–891.

Nuttin, J. (1984) *Motivation, Planning, and Action*. Hillsdale, NJ: Leuven University Press, and Lawrence Erlbaum Associates.

Nuttin, J. (1987) The respective roles of cognition and motivation in behavioral dynamics, intention, and volition. In F. Halisch & J. Kuhl (eds), *Motivation, Intention, and Volition*. New York: Springer-Verlag, pp. 309–320.

O'Reilly, C. A. III (1991) Organizational behavior: Where we've been, where we're going. In M. R. Rosenzweig & L. W. Porter (eds), *Annual Review of Psychology*. vol. 42. Palo Alto, CA: Annual Reviews, pp. 427–458.

Pervin, L. A. (1989) *Goal Concepts in Personality and Social Psychology*. Hillsdale, NJ: Lawrence Erlbaum.

Pervin, L. A. (1990) *Handbook of Personality*. New York: Guilford Press.

Peters, L. H., & O'Conner, E. J. (1980) Situational constraints and work outcomes: The influences of a frequently overlooked construct. *Academy of Management Review*, **5**, 391–397.

Peterson, N. G., Hough, L. M., Dunnette, M. D., Rosse, R. L., Houston, J. S., Toquam, J. L., & Wing, H. (1990) Project A: Specification of the predictor domain and development of new selection/classification tests. *Personnel Psychology*, **43**, 247–276.

Pritchard, R. D., Jones, S. D., Roth, P. L., Stuebing, K. K., & Ekeberg, S. E. (1988) Effects of group feedback, goal setting, and incentives on organizational productivity [Monograph]. *Journal of Applied Psychology*, **73**, 337–358.

Porter, L. W., and Lawler, E. E., III. (1968) *Managerial Attitudes and Performance*. Homewood, IL: Dorsey Press.

Powers, W. T. (1973) Feedback: Beyond behaviorism. *Science*, **179**, 351–356.

Raynor, J. O. (1969) Future orientation and motivation of immediate activity: An elaboration of the theory of achievement motivation. *Psychological Review*, **76**, 606–610.

Revelle, W. (1989) Personality, motivation, and cognitive performance. In R. Kanfer, P. L. Ackerman, & R. Cudeck (eds), *Abilities, Motivation, and Methodology: The Minnesota Symposium on Learning and Individual Differences*. Hillsdale, NJ: Erlbaum, pp. 297–341.

Rotter, J. B. (1954) *Social Learning and Clinical Psychology.* Englewood Cliffs, NJ: Prentice-Hall.

Ryan, T. A., & Smith, P. C. (1954) *Principles of Industrial Psychology.* New York: Ronald Press Company.

Sackett, P. R., Zedeck, S., & Folgi, L. (1988) Relations between measures of typical and maximum job performance. *Journal of Applied Psychology,* 73, 482–486.

Sansone, C. (1986) A question of competence: The effects of competence and task feedback on intrinsic interest. *Journal of Personality and Social Psychology,* 51, 918–931.

Sawyer, J. E. (1990) Effects of risk and ambiguity on judgments of contingency relations and behavioral resource allocation decisions. *Organizational Behavior and Human Decision Processes,* 45, 85–110.

Schweiger, D. M., & Leana, C. R. (1986) Participation in decision making. In E. A. Locke (ed.), *Generalizing from Laboratory to Field Settings.* Lexington, MA: Lexington Books, pp. 147–166.

Sniezek, J. A., May, D. R., & Sawyer, J. E. (1990) Social uncertainty and interdependence: A study of resource allocation decisions in groups. *Organizational Behavior and Human Decision Processes,* 46, 155–180.

Staw, B. M., Bell, N. E., & Clausen, J. A. (1986) The dispositional approach to job attitudes: A lifetime longitudinal test. *Administrative Science Quarterly,* 31, 56–77.

Switzer, F. S. III, & Sniezek, J. A. (1991) Judgment process in motivation: Anchoring and adjustment effects on judgment and behavior. *Organizational Behavior and Human Decision Processes,* 49, 208–229.

Tellegen, A. (1985) Structures of mood and personality and their relevance to assessing anxiety, with an emphasis on self-report. In A. H. Tumas and J. D. Maser (eds), *Anxiety and the Anxiety Disorders.* Hillsdale, NJ: Lawrence Erlbaum, pp. 681–714.

Thibaut, J., & Walker, L. (1975) *Procedural Justice: A Psychological Analysis.* Hillsdale, NJ: Erlbaum.

Thibaut, J., & Walker, L. (1978) A theory of procedure. *California Law Review,* 66, 541–566.

Tolman, E. (1932) *Purposive Behavior in Animals and Men.* New York. Appleton-Century-Crofts.

Triandis, H. C. (1979) Values, attitudes, and interpersonal behavior. In M. M. Page (ed.), *Nebraska Symposium on Motivation.* Lincoln, NE: University of Nebraska Press, pp. 195–259.

Tubbs, M. E. (1986) Goal setting: A meta-analytic examination of the empirical evidence. *Journal of Applied Psychology,* 71, 474–483.

Tyler, T. R. (1988) What is procedural justice? *Law and Society Review,* 22, 301–335.

Tyler, T. R., & Bies, R. J. (1990) Beyond formal procedures: The interpersonal context of procedural justice. In J. S. Carroll (ed.), *Applied Social Psychology and Organizational Settings.* Hillsdale, NJ: Lawrence Erlbaum, pp. 77–98.

Von Cranach, M., Kalbermatten, U., Indermühle, K., & Gugler, B. (1982) *Goal-Directed Action.* New York: Academic Press.

Vroom, V. H. (1964) *Work and Motivation.* New York: Wiley.

Watson, D., & Tellegen, A. (1985) Toward a consensual structure of mood. *Psychological Bulletin,* 98, 219–235.

Weiner, B. (1985) An attributional theory of achievement, motivation, and emotion. *Psychological Review,* 92, 548–573.

Weiner, B. (1986) *An Attributional Theory of Motivation and Emotion.* New York: Springer-Verlag.

Weinert, F. E., & Kluwe, R. H. (1987) *Metacognition, Motivation, and Understanding.* Hillsdale, NJ: Lawrence Erlbaum.

Weiss, H. M., & Adler, S. (1984) Personality and organizational behavior. In B. M. Staw & L. L. Cummings (eds), *Research in Organizational Behavior*, vol. 6. Greenwich, CT: JAI Press, pp. 1–50.

White, R. W. (1959) Motivation reconsidered: The concept of competence. *Psychological Review*, **66**, 297–333.

Wood, R. E., & Bandura, A. (1989) Impact of conceptions of ability on self-regulatory mechanisms and complex decision making. *Journal of Personality and Social Psychology*, **56**, 407–415.

Wood, R. E., Mento, A. J., & Locke, E. A. (1987) Task complexity as a moderator of goal effects: A meta-analysis. *Journal of Applied Psychology*, **72**, 416–425.

Woodworth, R. S. (1929) *Psychology: Revised Edition*. New York: Henry Holt & Co.

Wright, J., & Mischel, W. (1982) Influence of affect on cognitive social learning person variables. *Journal of Personality and Social Psychology*, **43**, 901–914.

Zedeck, S. (1977) An information processing model and apporoach to the study of motivation. *Organizational Behavior and Human Performance*, **18**, 47–77.

Zinbarg, R., & Revelle, W. (1989) Personality and conditioning: A test of four models. *Journal of Personality and Social Psychology*, **57**, 301–314.

Chapter 2

SELECTION METHODS

Mike Smith
Victoria University of Wellington, New Zealand
and
Dave George
KPMG Peat Marwick, New Zealand

INTRODUCTION

One of the interesting features of the development of selection methodology over the years is that a gradual picture is emerging which suggests there is an imperceptible movement occurring from a consideration of selection methods, to an underlying principle which is leading to integration, and an understanding that all methods have a common thread.

The first people to present this argument in a coherent way were Asher and Sciarrino (1974) in their matchless review of work sample tests. They accounted for the excellent results using this approach through a "point to point" validation theory. Put simply, their theory states that there must be, for good predictive validity, a strong relationship between the content of the job and the content of the selection method. The theory of course relates to performance-oriented criteria, but as will be argued later, a case can be made from recent work for this to be extended to criteria such as labour turnover and absenteeism.

Asher and Sciarrino (1974) were of course arguing the case solely for the success of work sample tests. In this review we intend to show, from recent and not so recent research, that this theory can be used as an explanation for the success and failure of most selection methods, which in turn leads to a conclusion that selection research is moving more to an understanding that practical recommendations for the implementation of selection methods will centre round a selection method, as opposed to methods.

An important issue in selection methods is the discrepancy that has been observed, on a number of occasions, between usage of various methodologies and their validity. Empirical evidence is available from Dakin and Armstrong

(1989) who distributed a questionnaire to a group of New Zealand personnel consultants. The questionnaire listed and defined eleven selection methods derived from Hunter and Hunter's (1984) review. Dakin and Armstrong found that there was a high correlation (0.87) between validity estimates of the various predictors as evaluated by the consultants and frequency of use, but a low correlation (0.06) between research evidence and consultants' beliefs about validity. They also found that the consultants' practice did not agree with the research evidence (–0.06). Moderate agreement amongst the consultants was also found with a coefficient of concordance of 0.41. Mills (1991) has supported this result. In his study of 30 personnel consulting firms in New Zealand he found that interviews, references, psychological tests (presumably of various sorts), resumés, assessment centres and what he described as "competency profiling" were used, but most firms still select managers on the basis of unstructured interviews.

It seems also that some practitioners are seduced by complex selection procedures which have little real relationship to the job, but do have an appeal for them. This might occur because of the belief that things like personality are important for competent job performance. Practitioners, however, generally, have little understanding of ways of assessing these factors, and they are often deluded by pseudo science. This perhaps helps to explain the substantial application of methods such as personality tests in organisations, when the validity of non-work-related personality tests is suspect.

Ryan and Sackett (1989) studied individual assessment practices of industrial and organisational psychologists; presumably taking the view that these people could be regarded as experts. While they stated that their work was an exploratory study, their results were disturbing. They discovered variability in the job and organisational material obtained, the tests used, the personal history information gathered, the interview, the report, and finally, and most significantly, the report generated. Only one-third of the raters agreed with the conclusions of the assessor whose protocols they were reviewing. If there is this sort of lack of agreement amongst industrial and organisational psychologists about selection methods, it is hardly surprising that non-psychologists fare poorly in terms of their understanding of selection processes, and their use.

In a contribution to the quest for greater theoretical emphasis in personnel psychology (defined as personnel selection), Binning and Barrett (1989) pursued a process of investigating linkages between psychological constructs and operational measures with a view to deriving a conceptual framework. Validation was seen by them as "the process of accumulating various forms of judgmental and empirical evidence to support these inferences". In essence, a large part of their argument calls not just for the unification of concepts within personnel selection, but also for researchers in the area to place their research more in the general area of psychology by considering work done by social psychologists and others outside the work environment, such as at home or activities pursued during leisure time. There is no doubt about the influence of these issues in determining the utility of a selection method, but in this review we approach personnel selection from a more practical perspective. This is because research already available has not been assimilated by practitioners, as shown by Dakin and Armstrong (1989). We believe that, at present, industrial and organisational psychology would be better served pursuing goals associated with the communication of research results on selection methods rather than with the development of a unified theoretical base. We do not deny however, that the latter is important.

This review covers each selection method in turn and shows how research is increasingly suggesting that Asher and Sciarrino's (1974) principle can be extended as a theory to explain the success and failure of all selection methods. We hope to show that valid selection methods will be seen to have one element in common — a relationship to job content.

INTERVIEWS

Interviews have been, and will continue to be, the most popular selection method. This popularity probably derives from the necessity employers have to see the staff they are hiring, and also from a belief that this meeting will allow them to make a valid assessment of their ability to do a particular job. Over the years, many reviews and meta-analyses have suggested that the interview, taken as a global method, has not shown much success in terms of its validity and its reliability (Ulrich & Trumbo, 1965; Wagner, 1949; Arvey & Campion, 1982; Wiesner & Cronshaw, 1988; Harris, 1989).

There have, however, been some researchers over the years, who despite the generally poor validity results from the interview, have expressed the view that the interview does have validity, and that the results obtained in the literature were based on a large number of studies which did not pay enough attention to the value of a well-structured, situational, or job-related interview. Rodger (1952), for example, in his criticism of Kelly and Fiske's (1951) work, believed that the poor validity results for the interview obtained in their study were a consequence of the lack of structure of the interview and the artificiality of the selection situation. Bayne (1977) in an attempt to retrieve some value for the interview, went on to say that the interview is "reactive" compared to other ways of trying to assess personal qualities. Here Bayne was suggesting that there were certain interactions between interviewers and interviewees which would have a positive effect on the selection process in terms of its validity. It may well be that Bayne's belief in the interview was not misplaced, but the issue of reactivity is not the reason why the interview is today regarded more positively than it was in the past.

The turning point for the interview, in terms of an understanding of its validity, has been the concentration in reviews of the literature on the type of interview used in studies where the interview has been evaluated. When structured situational interviews are isolated, the validity for this sort of interview improves considerably (Wright, Lichtenfels, & Pursell, 1989; Harris, 1989; Wiesner & Cronshaw, 1988). Harris's review is particularly telling, with its updated review of the literature on the interview since the work of Arvey and Campion (1982). Harris (1989) ended his review by suggesting that several areas of social psychology need to be examined; especially the literature on attitudes–intentions–behaviour; the elaboration likelihood model; and theories of discrimination. This would lead to an even better understanding of the dynamics of the interview, and would perhaps allow improvements in the objectivity of the procedure by proposing techniques which would prompt interviewers to concentrate on job elements which, in turn, would improve validity.

An interesting issue is why improved structure should enhance the validity of the interview. It is likely that the act of structuring interviews makes interviewers focus more on the job and makes the questions asked more likely to be job-related. In a sense, structured interviews provide the basis for situational interviews. This probably explains the growing evidence to show that just improving the structure of the interview improves its validity (Wright, Lichtenfels, & Pursell, 1989). Other explanations have been differences in standardisation, job relatedness, and an overlap with cognitive abilities (Campion, Pursell, & Brown, 1988). Job relatedness best fits the general theory of high validity being attributable to a "point to point" correspondence between selection methods and performance and is the explanation we believe to be most persuasive.

Recently, Robertson, Gratton, & Rout (1990) have shown that the situational interview can predict the future performance and ratings of potential for administrative jobs. They obtained corrected correlations between the mean of situational interview scores and performance of 0.38 and for potential of 0.43. These results provide further confirmation for the growing body of research which supports the efficacy of this approach (Latham, Saari, Pursell, & Campion, 1980; Latham & Saari, 1984; Weekly & Gier, 1987) and the effectiveness of the procedure in yet another job family.

The success of job-related questions in improving the validity of the interview goes some way to providing support for the "point to point" theory, because what happens when interviews are job-related is that the job becomes the focus of the selection process. The problem with this conclusion is that because the interview is one of, if not the most, popular techniques used in selection (Schneider & Schmitt, 1986; Robertson & Makin, 1986), the information will be misinterpreted and used by practitioners as a justification for the use of interviews of any sort. What is needed is a more incisive way to describe non-situational, unstructured interviews to distinguish them from their more valid counterparts.

One possible description which highlights the unthinking way interviews on many occasions seem to be practised is the "casual" interview. This describes perfectly interviews which have not taken due consideration of the job in the interviewing process, and also hints at the usually disorganised, poorly prepared nature of interviews done in this way. The use of an alternative terminology, such as ours, would also aid the increased use of the job-related, structured, situational interview by emphasising the difference between it and its less valid counterpart.

While evidence for the validity of the structured, situational interview continues to be found, other research, such as that of Phillips and Dipboye (1989), has examined the process of the selection interview. They investigated interviewers' pre-interview impressions and their relationship to the subsequent conduct of the interview and how processing of information seems to be biased in the direction of confirming initial impressions. They found that interviewers' pre-interview evaluations were positively related to post-interview evaluations of applicant qualifications and process variables predicted to mediate this relationship. Presumably, structured, situational interviews might diminish this effect, but this would have to be tested.

In some further work on pre-interview impressions, Macan and Dipboye (1990) explored possible mediators and moderators of the relationship of interviewers' pre-interview impressions of applicants to their post-interview impressions of the same applicants. They also studied the effects of recruiting success. The results from their work demonstrated the replicability and robustness of expectancy effects in the interview. They discovered that interviewers' pre-interview impressions were not significantly related to the applicant's intention to accept the job. Applicants' evaluations of the interviewer were strongly related to what they believed to be the interviewer's evaluation of them. They went on to show that the strong correlation between pre-interview and post-interview impressions was not an ephemeral finding. To obtain an estimate of this effect from the accumulated data from previous research (Dougherty, Ebert, & Callender, 1986; Herriot & Rothwell, 1983; Phillips & Dipboye, 1989; Russell, Persing, Dunn, & Rankin, 1988; Sharf, 1970; Springbett, 1958) and their study, they computed an average correlation weighted by sample size. The resulting correlation was 0.53, the same as in Macan and Dipboye's study, but less than that of the original research by Springbett (1958). The results provide some evidence, in our view, for why the casual interview may not have a high criterion-related validity. It may fail in circumstances where pre-interview impressions are not congruent with the content of the job. This could occur in situations where an overemphasis is placed on possible irrelevancies such as age and interests.

Singer and Sewell (1989) investigated age bias and showed that, with neutral information, managers preferred hiring young applicants for low-status jobs and students preferred old applicants for high-status positions. In the age-related information condition, which extolled the merits of older employees, managers shifted to favouring old candidates for low-status jobs, and students preferred young applicants for both low- and high-status positions. Results that could perhaps be anticipated. Since older managers do most of the selection in organisations these results would carry most weight for them as a group in a real-life setting.

Rynes and Gerhart's (1990) work on employability (fit) discovered that interpersonal skills, goal orientation, and physical attractiveness contributed to assessments of applicant employability, but objective qualifications such as grade point average, extracurricular offices, and years of experience, did not. A question they posed as a consequence of their research centred around whether the employability construct is functional or dysfunctional for organisations. In some ways they were asking whether this approach was valid. In terms of the general research on the importance of structure, and job relatedness in the interview, it could be concluded that because the feeling variables seem to be the very ones that are elminated by using these interviews, subjective assessments of employability could reduce the validity of the interview process. The whole point of structured, situational interviews is to focus attention on the job. Employability as an issue would tend to shift this focus.

Caldwell and O'Reilly (1990) examined fit in relation to work outcomes. The authors used a profile comparison process (Q methodology; Stephenson, 1953) that presented an isomorphic assessment of job requirements and individual competencies. They assessed person–job fit in an assortment of jobs and organisations. Their results showed that person–job fit was related to a number of outcomes, which included job performance and satisfaction. Correlations obtained ranged between 0.38 and 0.98, which in all cases were statistically significant, but some of the samples were small. The authors suggested their research could be used to aid in selection decisions, citing the work of Chatman (1988) as an example of how its predictive validity for this purpose had been shown. From our point of view, this recent research supports the consolidation process which we believe is slowly occurring in selection. Semantic differences between methodologies are perhaps suggesting that there are more selection methods than there really are. Person–job fit does not seem to us too different from "point to point" correspondence between selection content and job content.

Research by Tullar (1989) compared communication behaviours and patterns in successful and unsuccessful initial recruiting interviews. His research showed that unsuccessful interviews were approximately two-thirds as long as successful interviews, and that successful applicants dominated the conversation more. When interviewers attempted to structure the conversation, unsuccessful applicants tried to structure the conversation in return. Successful applicants tended to be submissive when the interviewer dominated, and to dominate when the interviewer was submissive. It does seem that Tullar has provided more evidence to show that if his work can be generalised to all jobs, including those which do not require a high verbal content, then acute diligence is required on the part of interviewers to remain unswayed by unconscious irrelevant variables when interviewing, which could result in poor selection decisions.

Martin and Nagao (1989) studied the effects of computerised interviewing on job applicant responses. They found in a laboratory study that subjects using computer or pencil and paper (non-social) interviews scored lower on social desirability and reported factual scholastic information more accurately (with less inflation) than in face-to-face interviews. The use of the non-social interview with high-status jobs caused resentment in the candidates, which was directly in proportion to the appropriateness of the interview for the level of the position.

Lautenschlager and Flaherty (1990), on the other hand, presented findings that ran counter to those of Martin and Nagao (1989). They found that computer administration led to greater levels of impression management (socially desirable responding) than when pencil and paper administration was used. They did not, however, use an interview for comparison. They went on to explain their results by suggesting that different procedures and questionnaires could account for them. Certainly the generalisability of their result would have to be tested, given the weight of opinion to the contrary (Evan & Miller, 1969; Koson, Kitchen, Kochen, & Stodolosky, 1970; Martin & Nagao, 1989; Rezmovic, 1977; Smith, 1963).

In some research on the process of the graduate selection interview, Anderson and Shackleton (1990) investigated the influence of candidate non-verbal behaviour upon interviewer impression formation. As well as reconfirming the existence of strong personal bias, similar to me bias, and prototype bias in the graduate interview, they questioned the validity of this form of selection for graduates, because they believed that it was being used as a form of quasi-personality test. Herriot (1985) concluded that there was a tendency for this to occur in this sort of selection interview and that it should be avoided. In the context of this review this is interesting because in most instances the graduate selection interview is used as a means of gauging general suitability for the organisation concerned, or perhaps as a means of entry into a graduate training scheme. There is usually not a specific job in mind when the interview is conducted. This illustrates quite well the sort of process that often occurs in the casual interview, where there is incomplete job information. Structured, situational interviews force a focus on a job and thereby prevent a degeneration of the interview into a quasi-personality test.

Kinicki, Lockwood, Hom, and Griffeth (1990) examined the effect of varied interviewee cues on line managers' hiring decisions. They focused on aggregate and individual levels of analysis and discovered that interviewers used cues diversely and had differing levels of predictive validity, which in turn implies that interviewers use different frames of reference, and differ in their ability to identify qualified employees. Again this research poses questions about the nature of the cue usage by interviewers. It could well be that more successful interviewers use cues based on job content but this needs to be explored.

While not strictly based on interviews, Hitt and Barr (1989) showed quite clearly in a study of managerial decision models that, job-irrelevant variables were used heavily in selection decisions, and that selection decision models were complex. They got 68 line and staff managers to rate 16 applicants for positions. The raters were instructed to view videotaped presentations, review the corresponding application, and evaluate the candidate for the job he or she was applying for. Race and sex had significant main effects on overall favourability ratings, and only experience as a job-relevant variable had significant main effects on overall positive ratings. The study showed how strong job-irrelevant variables are and how some of the error occurs in decision-making, using the casual interview. This study is significant because what is needed are techniques to force a focus on job-relevant variables and this is what structured, situational interviewing does. It also points to the fact that in terms of equity, salary determination, and selection, decisions should not be the responsibility of a single individual. There should be a race and gender balance in a group of people making these decisions. For countries like New Zealand, with its Maori population disproportionately represented in the unemployed and the relative lack of sophistication in this country in the use of selection procedures, Hitt and Barr's work presents a depressing picture of how this state of affairs will continue unless more job-related methods can be forced into use in the selection process.

PERSONALITY TESTS

Ng and Smith (1991) have recently updated a meta-analysis of personality tests. They justified their new attempt at this analysis on the selective use of the literature by Schmitt, Gooding, Noe, and Kirch (1984) in their meta-analysis. They also pointed out that the often cited review by Guion and Gottier (1965) also only used *Personnel Psychology* and the *Journal of Applied Psychology* as the source of information for their review. Their updated meta-analysis consisted of a comprehensive on-line search and manual search of seven journals (*Journal of Applied Psychology, Journal of Occupational Psychology, Personnel Psychology, Psychological Bulletin, Organizational Behavior and Human Decision Making, Applied Psychology: An International Review* and the *Journal of Personality*). Their meta-analysis also included research published from 1953 and up to 1990. This was not the case in the Schmitt *et al.* study. Unpublished reports were also sought.

The striking part of the results from the journal analysis was that only 4% of articles on the validity of personality tests came from journals other than the *Journal of Applied Psychology* and *Personnel Psychology*. It would seem that the narrow range of journals used in earlier reviews and meta-analyses can be justified because of the lack of published studies on the validity of personality tests that appear outside these journals. The overall results showed that personality tests had an overall validity of 0.25 and the variance due to sampling error was 10%. This result is corrected for criterion and predictor unreliability. As a consequence of their meta-analysis, Ng and Smith (1991) state: "From the Guion and Gottier (1965) review to the present study 25 years later, non work-related personality tests used as selection tools are poor predictors of job success and if used should be treated with caution."

Despite their poor validity the popularity of personality tests amongst practitioners seems to know no bounds. Over the years concern has been expressed by psychologists over the use of instruments which, in many cases, were designed to assess and counsel people suffering mental trauma. Smith and George (1986) expressed their concern over the indiscriminate use of personality tests for personnel selection in New Zealand, basing their views on the growing literature which showed the poor predictive validity of both pencil and paper and projective personality tests. They accused consultants of duping their clients because there was a suggestion that giving personality tests was a way of satisfying client demand for assessments of personality. They also charged the consultants with being fully aware of the limitations of these instruments. In the case of tests that are designed and marketed by consultants, it becomes increasingly difficult to find adequately reported validity data. The excuse often made is that commercial considerations prevent such detailed disclosure. There is, however, usually no reason to expect any different results for such instruments from the ones which are included in the reviews and meta-analyses in personnel selection, which show that, generally, non-work-related personality tests have low criterion-related validity (Guion & Gottier, 1965; Hunter & Hunter, 1984; Schmitt et al., 1984).

More recently this concern has been expressed again by Blinkhorn and Johnson (1990), who accused many consultants and practitioners of using personality tests inappropriately. Their article was prompted by the increasing use of "off the shelf" personality tests for selection in Britain. They not only criticised the use of personality tests but also focused on the claims made by developers of new tests and users of old tests to get business. One of the increasingly frequent techniques of validity delusion, as they called it, is brought about by the availability of statistical software packages for microcomputers which allow easy computation of multiple correlations "which may lead to the claim that a set of scales predict job performance" through a linear regression equation. "And indeed, large multiple correlations are frequently found." They go on to cite the example of "when the population correlation is zero, the expected value of the multiple correlation between 30 predictors and one criterion on a sample of 50 subjects is 0.77." It is our view that there is increasing evidence of worldwide abuse of personality tests, which psychology as a profession has yet to address.

There is no escaping the fact that personality tests are extremely popular from the beliefs people have of their usefulness, as shown in the research of Dakin and Armstrong (1989) and Ryan and Sacket's (1987) survey of the extensiveness of the use of individual assessment by industrial and organisational psychologists in the US. This confidence stems from the belief that personality is a critical feature for carrying out many jobs well, especially managerial positions. Managers, when solicited, can usually cite instances where a person's personality either conflicted with that of another individual or was just generally regarded as unsuitable for the job they were doing. Unfortunately non-work-related personality tests have not shown much evidence of being able to predict these behaviours in individuals.

Despite well-documented evidence concerning the low validity of non-work-related personality tests research continues to be conducted on their validity. For example Rice and Lindecamp (1989) correlated the business incomes of owner managers of small retail stores with their Jungian personality types, measured on the abridged version of the Myres–Briggs Type Indicator. It would appear that thinking extraverts did best as small retailers. Whether this result can be replicated would be instructive, and surprising, given the knowledge available of the validity of such instruments.

Psychologists have tried to come to a greater understanding of why the criterion-related validity of non-work-related personality tests is so poor. It has even been argued that the failure of standard personality tests to predict performance well was an indictment of psychology itself, because personality must be an important variable in good job performance for many sorts of work. Recently research has been focusing more on the relationship between the content of personality questionnaires and their relationship to the job. The theory is that if work-related questions appear in the test, then the test is more likely to display validity.

An example of this approach in New Zealand has been the development of the Sales Performance Indicator (SPI) by Assessment and Development Services Ltd (Anon, 1987). According to the manual for this instrument, the SPI is a personal style assessment, which has been designed specifically to predict the suitability of people for sales work. The instrument provides information on what the authors regard as three main aspects of sales performance: a person's drive to achieve results, their ability to relate to people, and their preferences in terms of independence and self-determination in their work. The manual would appear to be intended for non-psychologists, and is somewhat brief in its presentation of the test's psychometric properties. For example, although the research is not presented, or cited, the manual states that research has indicated that the dimensions which form the basis of the instrument are important in successful salespeople. When describing the design of the instrument, the authors state that the process consisted of three steps. Firstly a large bank of items was assembled to measure the three central traits of competition, cooperation, and conformity. Secondly, the items used in the SPI were selected from this item bank, based on their ability to discriminate and their contribution to the three main scales. Finally a series of validation studies were conducted to determine how well the SPI predicts sales success.

Validities ranging between 0.50 and 0.60 are then cited for the instrument but no details of sample sizes, reliability, or statistics used are given.

The interesting thing about the SPI is that it would appear to be an example of a work-related test which has some predictive power. The arresting feature about it is that the test claims to predict general sales performance, regardless of the type of product sold. The question arises concerning how general the area of work can be before validity coefficients for work-related personality instruments diminish. On the other hand, the lack of detail concerning the research conducted could be an example of Blinkhorn and Johnson's (1990) validity delusion.

Day and Silverman (1989) use a similar approach to that taken in the SPI. They start off with a premise that personality variables are significant predictors of job performance when carefully matched to the appropriate occupation. They go one step further, however, and state that there must also be a match with the organisation for these instruments to be valid. They found that three personality scales, orientation towards work, degree of ascendancy, and degree and quality of interpersonal orientation, were significantly related to important aspects of job performance. This was even the case when the effects of cognitive ability were taken into account. The results they obtained were encouraging. The highest correlation obtained was between interpersonal orientation and cooperation (e.g. demonstrates a positive and professional manner in working with personnel at all levels) of 0.42.

In a monograph in the *Journal of Applied Psychology*, Hough, Eaton, Dunnette, Kamp, and McCloy (1990) used six constructs that had, in the past, some proven ability to predict job-related criteria. They developed an inventory to measure the six constructs and four validity scales that were developed to measure accuracy of self-description. The scales were administered in three contexts: a concurrent criterion-related validity study, a faking experiment, and an applicant setting. Their results showed that validities were in the 0.20s; respondents successfully distorted their self-descriptions when instructed to do so; response validity scales were responsive to different types of distortion; applicants' responses did not reflect evidence of distortion and that validities remained stable regardless of possible distortion by respondents in either unusually positive or negative directions.

The implications of this study are important for the use of personality tests. It shows that intentional distortion of self-descriptions in an overly desirable way is not a serious problem because applicants mainly do not distort their responses. This may mean that obvious questions which tap important job-related personality dimensions may be asked in a straightforward way without the necessity of using subtle wording. The authors, however, recommended a conservative approach to the use of temperament measures in a selection setting, through using response validity scales to detect potentially inaccurate self-descriptions, warning applicants that inaccurate descriptions will be detected, and using additional or other information to make employment decisions about those persons who are identified as providing inaccurate self-descriptions. Perhaps the most disappointing aspect of this study is the low correlation between the personality tests used and performance, which is lower than that obtained in meta-analyses of personality tests in general. It could well be that an even more direct approach to tapping job-related personality dimensions than using presently available tests is needed if these validity coefficients are to improve.

A study with results that are common for the use of standard personality tests is that of Crawley, Pinder, and Herriot (1990). They correlated the results from personality inventories (the Myers–Briggs Type inventory and Saville and Holdsworth's Occupational Personality Questionnaire) and four aptitude tests (Raven's standard progressive matrices, Saville and Holdsworth's VPI, a test of verbal intelligence; Saville and Holdsworth's NP2, a test of numerical reasoning; and the ACER, a test of clerical speed and accuracy) with assessment-centre dimensions. The correlations between the personality attributes and assessment-centre dimensions were generally low. Correlations between intellectual aptitude and dimensions were higher with aptitude being related to the more cognitive dimensions. While assessment centres are generally regarded as selection methods, and they will be treated as such later in this review, their content usually contains a lot of job-related problems for candidates to solve. It can be argued, therefore, that if for this research the assessment centres are treated as dependent variables, the results for the personality tests parallel what has been observed in the literature over the years. The cognitive test results also concur with the general results for them found in the literature (Hunter & Hunter, 1984).

While integrity testing may not be personality testing in the way that it is usually recognised in industrial and organisational psychology, the methodology employed in paper and pencil integrity testing has similarities with the methods used in pencil and paper personality testing. Sackett, Burris, and Callahan (1989) reviewed recent developments since Sackett and Harris's (1984) review of integrity testing. The legal issues addressed by the authors considered integrity testing from the perspective of the United States, and concluded that there were few restrictions on the use of such tests, except in Massachusetts which prohibits the use of the polygraph for selection together with any other device "whether written or otherwise presented". The interesting thing about the Massachusetts Polygraph Act is that it makes illegal the interpretation of any selection instrument for the purpose of vetting integrity. This places any person using any selection instrument for assessing integrity in the position of contravening this Act, whether the procedure obviously measures integrity or not. This could include questions in interviews designed to assess integrity in an indirect way. Employers probably have some genuine need to assess integrity where positions of trust are concerned, but agreeing on the means will be a continuing source of debate.

Since the last review by Sackett and Harris (1984) two distinct types of integrity tests have emerged, called overt integrity tests and personality-oriented measures. Overt tests often have two sections. The first deals with attitudes towards theft, and other forms of dishonesty. The second deals with admissions of theft, and other illegal activities. Personality-based measures use empirical keying of standard personailty test items against a theft criterion. There has also been a broadening of the criteria used for test validation to include global performance, absence, turnover, and forms of sabotage. An increase in the use of external criteria, such as detected theft and turnover rather than self-report criteria, such as admissions of theft, has also occurred in validation research (Sackett, Burris, & Callahan, 1989). The authors, while discussing the results of validity studies, recount that high validity coefficients are reported for integrity tests when self-report criteria are used (ranging from 0.50 to 0.87), but that this decreases substantially when external criteria are used such as detected theft (0.33). They concluded that there were insufficient data for strong conclusions about the value of the tests in predicting external criteria.

Sackett, Burris, and Callahan (1989) also highlighted the practical problems associated with using integrity testing. They pointed to the fact that the typical passing rate for integrity tests is 40–70%. This means that an organisation proposing to use an instrument of this sort must be in a position to turn away a large proportion of applicants. In the present recession many employers will not have this problem. They also stated that, in the US at least, these sorts of tests are marketed in large part to non-psychologists, and are done so in a more aggressive way than for most psychological tests. This leads to what they described as "questionable if not blatantly deceptive, sales tactics". We wonder whether our experiences in New Zealand for the sale of personality tests are any different. At least in the US there does appear, to outsiders at least, a more sober view of the utility, not just of integrity testing, but of personality testing as a whole.

In conclusion it would seem that there is emerging evidence that the validity of job-related personality tests is promising. This provides further support for the theoretical approach presented by Asher and Sciarrino (1974). What is needed is a comprehensive attempt to assess work-related personality items to understand the value of such tests in selection. Some design innovation will be necessary to completely solve problems of candidates making socially desirable responses. Furthermore, the issue, which has not altogether been resolved, of adequate assessments of deliberate distortion on the part of candidates in real selection situations will need to be addressed.

ASSESSMENT CENTRES

Gaugler, Rosenthal, Thornton, and Bentson's (1987) meta-analysis answered some important questions concerning assessment centres. Only a few of the large number of moderators of potential assessment-centre validity they tested affected their corrected validity coefficient of 0.37. The main results appeared to be that validities seemed to be higher when the assessment centre included women, when peer ratings were included in the evaluation, and when psychologists instead of managers were used as assessors. They were lower with a high proportion of minority candidates. Future potential also seemed to be better predicted than performance in their current job.

The interesting feature of assessment centres is that they refer to a group-oriented, standardised series of activities that provides a basis for judgments or predictions of human behaviours believed, or known to be relevant, to work performed in an organisational setting (Finkle, 1976). The critical feature as far as this review is concerned is the difference between those assessment centres known to be job-related and those that are not. Assessment centres typically use multiple methods to gain information about individuals being considered for a position. These methods will not all be equally related to the job. The difference between the ability of psychologists, peers, and others in their judgments of performance could simply reflect the greater knowledge of the job the first two groups have compared to others. Peers have this knowledge because often they are carrying out the job, and psychologists will usually have this information because they have had to understand the job to design the work sample tests which are commonly a feature of this particular technique. In the assessment phase, it is possible that this knowledge is displayed through an internal weighting when assessments are made of the importance of different scores on the various assessments used in the centre. In short, the research on assessment centres provides some support for the general thrust made here, that it is job relatedness which aids the better than average validity of the assessment centre.

Recently Schmitt, Schneider, and Cohen (1990) have considered several validity coefficients for the same assessment centre designed for the selection of school administrators. There were shown to be significant differences between the validity coefficients for this same centre validated in different settings, despite correction for range restriction, criterion unreliability, and sampling error. Support was found for job knowledge having a great affect on validity, because they discovered that when principals were used as assessors for the school administration assessment centre, the validities obtained were higher. Schmitt, Schneider, and Cohen (1990) also found that centres which were used to serve one school district alone were less valid than those that served more than one. Also familiarity with candidates lowered the validity of assessments.

The authors go on to point out the importance of administrative competence in the design of the assessment centre. They would appear to work when they are operationalised as they were intended, such that raters are selected and trained appropriately, and efforts to maintain quality control in the implementation of the centre are made on a regular basis.

Gaugler and Thornton (1989) investigated the number of assessment centre dimensions and its effect on assessor accuracy. They used 131 trained assessors who evaluated performance of people in assessment centres on 3, 6, or 9 dimensions. As a consequence of subjects who used a small number of dimensions, classifying behaviours more accurately, and rating more accurately, they concluded that developers of assessment centres should limit the cognitive demands placed on assessors by limiting the number of dimensions used. If this is the case, some attention has to be paid to the nature of the dimensions of performance chosen.

Shore, Thornton, and Shore (1990) examined the construct validity of assessment centre final dimension ratings using a general framework of cognitive and personality measures. Performance style dimension ratings correlated more strongly with external cognitive ability measures than did the interpersonal style ratings. Given the known relationship between cognitive ability and performance, and personality tests and performance, it would seem, from this research, and that of Gaugler and Thornton (1990), that if performance is the most important criterion of success for managers, dimension design in assessment centres should be limited to performance dimensions. This is because interpersonal style may have a limited influence on performance.

Other research by Reilly, Henry, and Smither (1990) has suggested that by using behaviour checklists the construct validity of assessment centre dimensions may be improved. Assessor use of behaviour check lists increased the average convergent validity from 0.23 to 0.43, while decreasing the average discriminant validity from 0.47 to 0.41. Reilly, Henry, and Smither also believed that the use of behaviour checklists would reduce the cognitive demands on raters. It would seem, therefore, that about three performance-based dimensions aided by behaviour checklists could be a good research-based structure for the design of ratings in assessmsent centres.

Pynes and Bernardin (1989) reported the predictive validity of an entry-level police assessment centre. Their results displayed generally lower predictive validity than is generally the case for assessment centres as reported in the meta-analytic studies of the validity of this procedure. Assessment centre ratings on 275 police recruits correlated 0.14 ($p < 0.05$) with training academy performance and 0.20 ($p < 0.05$) with on-the-job performance. The reasons for the results are given as the difficulty of measuring police performance, the limited number of exercises used in the assessment centre, and the number of scale points used in the rating procedure.

The difficulties of measuring police performance are understandable because it would seem that being a police officer allows a number of very different paths to success, and often success may lie in the nature of the work a new recruit does, and their success at doing that particular work. The work of a police officer is possibly more varied than managerial work. For this reason, as the authors point out, their research was not helped by the smaller than usual number of exercises used in the assessment centre. They used only role play in which candidates interacted with distressed citizens. There were no exercises in which candidates interacted with each other (Pynes & Bernardin, 1989). It would seem also that other important aspects of police work were omitted, such as note-taking, and observational skills, and such things as dealing with court appearances. It would not be difficult to incorporate these into an assessment centre designed to assess the potential new police recruits. The true potential for using the assessment centre for the selection of police officers needs further investigation.

Brannick, Michaels, and Baker (1989) investigated the construct validity of In-Basket Scores. While the in-basket is an individual work sample test designed to test managerial ability, their research is considered at this point, because of their focus in their article on predicting management performance, which is typically the goal of assessment centres. Brannick, Michaels, and Baker used a randomised pre-test–post-test experimental design with two alternate in-basket forms. Results showed that there was little convergent validity and evidence of method bias both within and between alternate in-basket forms. It was also shown that brief training improved in-basket performance on the perceptiveness and delegation dimensions and on overall performance. As a consequence of their results the authors called into question the validity of inferring individual differences in managerial ability from in-basket scores. This does not affect the use of assessment centres for selection purposes, according to the authors, because construct validity is not required for this purpose. It does, however, affect the use of assessment centres for training, because used in this way assessments do require validity and reliability at the individual level. The subjects who participated in the research were students with only a small amount of managerial experience (only 41% had one or more year's management experience). It may well be that training would have had a negligible effect for a sample of experienced managers. The authors stated that managerial abilities are relatively enduring. The lack of opportunity, in the first instance, to practise these skills could affect performance markedly, and a small amount of training could substantially improve performance in a relatively inexperienced group such as they used.

Tett and Jackson (1990) designed an in-basket measure of managerial participative tendency. They said that their results supported the continued development of the in-basket measure, because they found that inter-rater correlations indicated that participative behaviours can be reliably measured using the in-basket exercise. Correlations with participative personality correlates were low, however, and what would make their views more convincing would be a positive relationship between the in-basket test and a job which contained a high degree of participative behaviour that was crucial for good performance in it. From a practical perspective, practitioners would start with the job, and only be concerned about participative behaviour, if it was a crucial part of the job.

Dobson and Williams (1989) examined the validation of the selection of male British army officers. As they said, the Regular Commissions Board is the main method of the selection of British army officers, and their study would appear to be the most comprehensive validation of their decisions. The selection procedure involves a number of group tasks, but as they explained, no assessments were made at the end of each task so that this information could be cumulated to make a final decision easier. In the case of written tests used this would not matter, but as far as group discussions are concerned, this could be an important variable compared to the more usual way of conducting assessment centres. The final board grade only was used in the predictive validity study, and the criteria used were both training and job criteria. Total group validity coefficients of 0.33, 0.31, and 0.31 were obtained for the prediction of regimental performance, general officer, and specialist training respectively. They concluded that the Regular Commissions Board is a fair, moderately valid, method for the selection of officers and that it has utility. When selection methods are validated, correlations of about 0.3 are regarded as moderate. It is often forgotten that this only accounts for 9% of the variance. Their statement that the procedure has utility is more accurate.

Schippmann, Prien, and Katz (1990) researched the reliability and validity of in-basket performance measures. As a rationale for their study they made the point that despite there being a large amount of research on the in-basket test, it has tended to be unique for the position researched. They went on to say that there is relatively little work that has been done which has focused on critical issues involved in their construction or evaluation. They presented the literature on the in-basket test and suggested that there was only modest support from it for the usefulness of the in-basket test as a measurement tool. In terms of our advocacy for the point to point approach to selection decision-making, the authors found that "evidence of validity is at best marginal and generally higher in settings where the in-basket was specifically constructed for a defined target job". They continued by bemoaning the fact that such in-baskets were not very common, and that off-the-shelf products were most commonly used. Despite this statement, they said that work still needs to be done on systematic, work sample test construction based on job analysis to discover whether such work samples positively affect reliabilities and criterion-related validities. In terms of our thrust in this review we believe that it would be profitable research.

Much work continues to be done on the dimensions used in assessment centre performance evaluation. It does seem that one of the problems may be the relationship between the precise content of the assessment centre to the job, or jobs, in question. There is little doubt that assessment centres predict work performance when constructed well. There does appear to be continuing difficulty in establishing why this is so. Two reasons are possible. Firstly, the time taken for decision-making in the assessment centre is longer than for other forms of selection. This will allow decisions to be made based on a larger amount of behaviour than is usual for the other selection methods. Secondly, because of the use of a number of procedures; there will undoubtedly be good validity for some of them. This is partly supported from the research of Gaugler *et al.* (1987) which shows that those people who know the job best of all appear to be the people who are best at making judgments about people undertaking the assessment process.

WORK SAMPLE TESTS

The main thrusts of our argument in this review is that selection methods are moving closer together, and we have been using Asher and Sciarrino's (1974) "point to point" correspondence theory as a basis for our argument. Essentially, researchers concentrating on improving the concurrent and predictive validity of a class of selection procedures are discovering that the more closely related to the job the procedure is, the higher its validity. Nowhere is the essential correctness of this principle better illustrated than with work sample tests. According to the literature, they are one of the better selection instruments (Asher & Sciarrino, 1974; Robertson & Kandola, 1982; Hunter & Hunter, 1984) and this is because they concentrate on the job which is implicit in their name.

Recently, Robertson and Downs (1989) in their meta-analysis of work sample tests of trainability, have described the differences between trainability assessments and more conventional work sample tests. The former incorporate training into the selection procedure, and assessment concentrates not just on actual task performance but also on applicant behaviour. This assesses to what degree test takers have paid attention to the training component of the test. When introduced, the tests have shown themselves to be popular, especially when Downs (1968) called them "practical interviews" in a successful attempt to enhance their acceptability to practitioners.

The results of Robertson and Downs' meta-analysis were based on independent samples for which information was available on sample size, validity coefficient, type of predictor, type of criterion and length of follow-up period. The results suggested that trainability assessments predict short-term success more accurately than longer term training success. The correlations obtained ranged between 0.20 and 0.57, with correlations over 0.40 for all sample sizes over 1000. The attenuation of the validity of these tests over time is of some concern but, as the authors stated, this is not unique to trainability assessments. Muchinsky (1987), for example, highlighted this issue for biodata validity coefficients, but as Rothstein, Schmidt, Erwin, Owens, and Sparks (1990) have shown very recently, this problem might be illusory, and in the case of trainability tests, attributable to the lack of long-term performance data.

Research on job samples continues to be published. Hattrup and Schmitt (1990) conducted a criterion-related validation study of four aptitude tests, and five tests of content taken directly from job tasks. Large validities for both sorts of tests were obtained which when corrected for range restriction in the predictor, approached 0.55. The results contradicted the meta-analytic work of Hartigan and Wigdor (1989) on aptitude tests, because of the higher than average validities found by Hattrup and Schmitt for aptitude tests in their study. The authors put this down to the nature of their criteria, which were Task Performance Measures, or job samples developed for each trade by an independent source. They were constructed by using job analysis data and feedback from journey-level employees. These criteria, the authors argued, citing the work of Sackett, Zedeck, and Fogli (1988), could more closely resemble maximum performance measures rather than typical performance measures. If true, the ability/performance relationship would be overestimated for this research because these criteria fail to account for motivational issues.

Motowildo, Dunnette, and Carter (1990) presented research on what they called an alternative selection procedure: the low-fidelity simulation. They argued that it was different from conventional work sample tests, because it sampled hypothetical work behaviour only. They designed the instrument by conducting critical incident analyses and using judgments by subject matter experts to develop the instrument for selecting entry-level managers for the telecommunications industry. The simulation presents descriptions to applicants of work situations, and five alternative responses for each situation. Applicants were asked to select two responses. One they would most likely make, and another they would least likely make. In a concurrent validity study of 120 managers the test correlated from 0.28 to 0.37 with supervisory ratings of performance. Again, here is evidence of the validity of the point to point correspondence approach. While the test does not focus on precise work content, an attempt has been made to make it generic for management jobs, so that management potential can be predicted. It is possible that if an attempt were made to derive precise job item content it might not reflect the job domain any better than the procedure used to construct this test. On the other hand, the job chosen in this study (entry-level manager) is capable of being simulated quite accurately using this methodology. It would be interesting to see if more focused job performance could be predicted too. Also a comparison of validity with more conventionally constructed work samples would be valuable.

Simulation was also the basis of Arthur, Barrett, and Doverspike's (1990) research in the petroleum industry. They were concerned with trying to improve the selection of petroleum product transport drivers. A laboratory study simulation was used to supplement a field study. A computer-based simulation of the task was made from a job analysis. The simulation and a test battery, which included measures of selective attention, field independence, and general cognitive ability, were given to 60 subjects. Measures of selective attention and field independence were given to 71 transport drivers in the field study. The criterion used was accidents, the data for which were obtained from company records. This study emphasises the difficulty of predicting a criterion such as number of accidents. The reason almost certainly lies in the infrequency of their occurrence, which leads to simulation difficulties, because of the improbability of such errors being observed in what is usually a short selection process in most situations.

Research by Peters, Servos, and Day (1990) provided an explanation for the superior performance of women on fine motor skill tasks. They showed that finger size was an important co-variate and when taken into consideration, sex differences in performance disappeared. Since anthropometrically, women have smaller hands than men, this research provides a reason for sex differences in fine motor tasks, but the sex differences are still there. Men are generally bigger in stature than women so can be expected, as a group, to perform less well in tasks which employ fine motor skills.

The evidence that work sample tests predict work performance well is now overwhelming, and supports the general approach advocated by Asher and Sciarrino (1974). Future work needs to concentrate on refining work sample test design techniques such that items are created that relate to particular job behaviours, as found in job analysis procedures such as the Position Analysis Questionnaire (McCormick, Jeanneret, & Mecham, 1972). In this way specific work sample tests can be designed, which will consist of items from a database of work sample behaviours. They would be selected on the basis of their relevance to the job in question.

LETTERS OF RECOMMENDATION AND REFERENCES

Research on letters of recommendation or references has been sparse in recent years. This is probably because they have fared badly as screening devices for pesonnel selection. They appear to be characterised by problems of leniency, restriction of range, low predictive validity, and inadequate inter-rater reliability (Anderson & Shackleton, 1986; Muchinsky, 1979; Reilly & Chao, 1982). This has led to recommendations that reference reports are not particularly valuable and that their use should be confined to factual checks of biographical information (Anderson & Shackleton, 1986).

While the literature on reference checks is not encouraging in terms of their validity, this is not reflected in the usage of the procedure by practitioners (Anderson & Shackleton, 1986; Robertson & Makin, 1986), or in their understanding of its value (Dakin & Armstrong, 1989). This is probably attributable to the ease of use of the procedure and its low cost. Practitioners may reason that there is nothing lost if the procedure is used. This highlights another important point about this selection method, and that is the lack of research on the possibilities of improving reference checks, or even why they are used. Studies range from the microanalytic (e.g. Knouse, 1983; Sleight & Bell, 1954) to the more general (e.g. Baxter, Brock, Hill, & Rozelle, 1981; Carroll & Nash, 1972). What is needed is a concerted, organised effort to assess how, if at all, letters of recommendation or references can contribute in any valid way to the selection process. A similar plea was made by Muchinsky (1979) for research focusing on innovations and alternative approaches, rather than routine validation studies. Since letters of recommendation and references are popular, attempts need to be made to boost the validity of reference reports for employee selection decisions rather than the *ad hoc* basis that has characterised research on this procedure up to now.

The fact that the concentration on job content has shown itself to be useful for improving the validity of various selection devices could be applied to reference checks. This approach would again be using the model of Asher and Sciarrino (1974), through concentrating on getting research to centre on presenting relevant job content to referees based on crucial elements extracted from a job analysis and asking them for their opinion concerning the suitability of the candidate to do the work. The accomplishment record approach advocated by Hough (1984) is a possibility in this area. She analysed job behaviours identifying important dimensions of job performance. She then gathered written accomplishments illustrative of competence in the critical job dimensions. Subsequently, rating principles and scales were developed to score the written protocols that had been submitted. Scores on accomplishment records were then related to job performance. The resulting correlation was low but significant, but more importantly, seemed to be accounting for variance not usually associated with other selection instruments. The development of this procedure for referees may be a fruitful way of pursuing research using this selection method, and may lead to an increased appreciation of directly relating selection methods to job content.

PROJECT A

Project A does not of course refer to any particular selection method but to an important study which took up the whole of the summer issue of *Personnel Psychology* in 1990. Due to what Shields and Hanser (1990) describe as its "size and its focus on an entire personnel system", it merits consideration here as a separate section in this review.

Campbell (1990) presented an introduction and background to the US army's Selection and Classification Project (Project A). He outlined the principal objectives, the methods used, and the basic research design of the project. The overall objective was to generate the instrumentation and validity information database needed to model, and develop, an organisation-wide selection and classification system. In the second article in the issue; Shields and Hanser (1990) described the designing, planning, and selling of Project A. It does seem that the basic questions concerning the nature of the selection and classification process into the US army needed to be evaluated. This was probably due to two main reasons. In the US in the early 1980s, the climate was unfavourable to testing, and Americans were questioning the fairness of tests. This climaxed in 1981 with the US congress issuing a directive that the Services must "develop a better database on the relationship between factors such as high school graduation scores and entrance test scores and effective performance". Secondly, in 1980 it was discovered that the Armed Services Vocational Aptitude Test Battery Forms 6/7 had been misnormed, which resulted in 50% of non-prior service army recruits being drawn from the bottom 30% of the eligible youth population. This was later rectified so that currently 60% of recruits come from the top 50% of the youth pouplation. Naturally enough, because of this influx of low-scoring recruits in the late 1970s, the army began to ask what difference test scores made to eventual peformance in military occupations. In other words, did it matter what people scored on these tests as far as work performance in the army was concerned?

In the third article in the issue, Peterson, Hough, Dunnette, Rosse, Houston, Toquam, and Wing (1990) described how the new battery of selection/classification tests were chosen and how they were developed. As a consequence of a structured literature search, an expert judgment study of expected true validities for a number of predictors for a number of performance measures, the development of a special methodology for computerised presentation of tests, evaluations of the predictors, and reviews by scientific advisers, a battery of tests was developed. The battery consists of six pencil and paper tests (Reasoning; Object Rotation; Assembling Objects; Orientation; Maze; and Map), ten computer-administered tests (Simple Reaction time; Choice Reaction Time; Memory; Target Tracking 1, control precision; Target Tracking 2, multi-limb coordination; Perceptual Speed and Accuracy; Number Memory; Cannon Shoot; Target Identification; and Target Shoot) and three paper and pencil inventories (Assessment of Background and Life Experiences, ABLE; Army Vocational Interest Career Examination, AVOICE; and the Job Orientation Blank). The rest of the paper presented a description of each of the tests with comprehensive reliability information about the instruments. Test-retest reliabilities ranged between 0.53 and 0.78 for the cognitive tests; 0.37 and 0.74 for the computerised psychomotor tests; and 0.02 and 0.73 for the computerised cognitive perceptual tests. In some cases these coefficients were surprisingly low for the tests to be acceptable and in some cases this must compromise validity. Split half reliabilities and uniqueness estimates were generally acceptable.

Campbell, Ford, Rumsey, Pulakos, Borman, Felker, De Vera, and Riegelhaupt (1990) described how the multiple measures of job performance in Project A were constructed such that they covered the total performance domain for a representative sample of entry level positions in the US army. This involved task analyses, critical incident analyses, generating the critical performance dimensions that constitute it, constructing measures for each dimension, and evaluating them using expert judgment and field data. Young,

Houston, Harris, Hoffman, and Wise (1990) described the data collection procedures and database preparation for Project A. They recount, in essence, how the sample of 9430 entry level personnel's results were collected, edited for missing variables, and stored.

Campbell, McHenry, and Wise (1990) described how the criterion data for the project were derived. They used multiple methods of job analysis and criterion development to assess the performance of the sample. Over 200 performance indicators were obtained from a subsample of nine jobs. This was reduced to 32 criterion scores for each job by content analyses and principal component analyses. The latent structure of performance in the population of jobs was obtained through goodness of fit tests using LISREL VI (Jöreskog & Sörbom, 1986). A five-factor solution was judged to be the best fit. The performance measures used in the project were therefore core technical proficiency, general soldiering proficiency, effort and leadership, personal discipline, physical fitness, and military bearing. The authors went on to describe these factors in detail.

McHenry, Hough, Toquam, Hansom, and Ashworth (1990) investigated the relationship between predictor and criterion domains in project A. They summarised the measures into 24 composite scores and the relationships between these scores and the five components of job performance established by Campbell, McHenry, and Wise (1990) were analysed. The cognitive and perceptual-psychomotor tests provided the best prediction of job-specific and general task proficiency (correlations corrected for range restriction between 0.53 and 0.65), while the temperament/personality composites were the best predictors of giving extra effort, supporting peers, and exhibiting personal discipline (correlations corrected for range restriction of between 0.33 and 0.37 were obtained). The interesting feature of this result is that the inventories used tended to be job-related, thus providing further support for the "point to point" correspondence approach advocated in this review. Composite scores from the interest inventory were correlated more highly with task proficiency than with demonstrating effort and peer support. It seems that vocational interests were among the best predictors of task proficiency in combat jobs. The authors concluded by saying that the US army can improve the prediction of job performance by adding non-cognitive predictors to its battery of predictor tests.

Wise, McHenry, and Campbell (1990) investigated optimal predictor composites in project A and tested for generalisability across jobs and performance factors. They found that different predictor equations were needed for each of the five criterion factors. As far as generalisation across jobs was concerned; one equation fitted the data for four of the five performance components. Proficiency on the technical tasks specific to each job required different prediction equations. Finally, Sadacca, Campbell, Difazio, Schultz, and White (1990) scaled performance utility to assess the gains from the new system of selection. They were able to produce estimates of utility for five different performance levels for each of 276 jobs in the enlisted personnel system. This study is considered in more detail in the section on utility analysis and criterion issues.

Project A is a large selection and assessment undertaking and its detailed reporting in *Personnel Psychology* has provided an excellent model for any other large organisation contemplating a similar venture. It is also significant that work-related selection procedures fare well in this large selection project.

BIOGRAPHICAL PREDICTORS

Biographical data are one of the two most valid selection methods available. Hunter and Hunter's (1984) quantitative review of the literature showed that general cognitive ability was estimated to correlate with supervisory ratings of overall job performance at 0.47 and cross-validated biodata validity against the same criterion was estimated at 0.37. Research on cognitive ability tests has also shown that they can be generalised across settings organisations and even different jobs (Pearlman, Schmidt, & Hunter, 1980; Schmitt *et al.*, 1984; Hartigan & Wigdor, 1989). The same has not been found to be true for empirically keyed biographical data scales, with a number of authors believing that they are situationally specific. These are notably Hunter and Hunter (1984) and Thayer (1977): the latter argued that age, organisational customs and methods, the criterion, time, and the job, all served to make validity results situationally specific.

Important research by Rothstein *et al.* (1990) has changed this view. They note that the pioneers of biodata research believed that appropriately developed biodata forms would have generalisable validity (e.g. Owens 1968, 1976), so they set out to test this belief. In the questionnaires used, items were originally screened for job relevance, and keying was based on large samples in a number of organisations. Items were only kept if they were valid across organisations. Cross-validations were done on about 11 000 first-line supervisors in 79 organisations. Validities were then meta-analysed across age levels, sex, levels of education, supervisory experience, and company tenure. In all cases the validities were generalisable, and stable over time. Neither were they derived from measurement of knowledge, skills, or abilities acquired through job experience. The authors concluded by saying that their research provided further evidence against the situational specificity hypothesis, and it was the first example of validity generalisation outside the cognitive domain. The implications for practice are profound. It suggests that carefully constructed biographical information keys can be designed which will provide a useful, practical input into the selection process. The research is also consistent with the "point to point correspondence" approach advocated in this review that job-relevant selection methods will result in optimal validity coefficients. Based on this principle we would advocate that good validity coefficients were obtained because of the screening used for job relevance in the design of the questionnaires.

In another example of the amassing evidence for the validity of biographical information for the prediction of performance, Russell, Mattson, Devlin, and Atwater (1990) used material from essays completed by first-year students in the US Naval Academy. The essays focused on four aspects of life experiences: individual accomplishments, group accomplishment, disappointing situations, and stressful situations. The essays were coded to generate biodata items which were then given to a large sample of midshipmen entering the US Naval Academy. It was possible from the results to show that military performance, academic performance, and peer ratings of leadership, could be predicted from scales developed from the biodata. The significant validity coefficients reported ranged between 0.14 and 0.28. It is noteworthy again that the biographical items were selected on the basis "that they might be related to these (job-related performance appraisal) dimensions", which illustrates the inherent job relatedness of the methodology used in this study.

While not quite the same as the standard biographical data research, research on background investigations for personnel screening does deal with the same type of data. McDaniel (1989) reviewed the differences between the application of background investigation in personnel screening and biodata applications used by psychologists. Major differences revolved around the method of application, the nature of the behaviour measured, method of scoring, and the criterion used. He then went on to describe a very large study using the Educational and Biographical Information Survey (EBIS). He factor analysed the questionnaire, and settled on a seven-factor solution. The factors were school suspension, drug use, quitting school, employment experience, grades and school clubs, legal system contacts, and socio-economic status. He also reported test retest reliabilities ranging between 0.46 and 0.86 and alpha reliabilities ranging between 0.49 and 0.81. When correlated with unsuitability discharges in a validity study, somewhat disappointing results were obtained. Correlations ranged from −0.01 to 0.20. Whether this constitutes useful levels of criterion-related validity, as McDaniel declares, is debatable. McDaniel concluded that although there are elements of background information methodology in his research, the fact that the EBIS is a self-report instrument means that it "does not include the diversity of information sources tapped in a typical investigation" McDaniel (1989). These would be sources such as law enforcement agencies, credit bureaux, and neighbours. it could be argued that the low criterion-related validity is due to the lack of job relatedness as defined by unsuitability in the EBIS.

The evidence for the validity of the use of biographical information in selection continues to be amassed. In terms of predicting labour turnover and absenteeism, as biographical selection procedures do (England & Patterson, 1960; Cascio, 1975), it again seems "point to point" theory works because data on such variables as geographical distance from work and domestic responsibilities are likely to predict absenteeism and turnover, because it is plausible that they would do so.

The work by Rothstein *et al.* (1990) now suggests that biographical scales could be generalisable. This could lead to increased use of this method of selection, which would be welcome. It remains to be seen whether in the final analysis these sorts of scales will be assessing anything different to work-related personality tests or other selection methods.

REALISTIC JOB PREVIEWS

Realistic job previews (RJPs) have now been researched for over 30 years and their validity has been established (Premack & Wanous, 1985). It appears that they lower initial expectations of the content of jobs and increase job survival. Interestingly, despite their proven validity little had been said about how to implement RJPs until Wanous (1989) raised ten issues concerning their initiation, development and implementation. He called these: Getting started—Reaction or Proaction?; Diagnosis—Structured or Unstructured?; Content—Descriptive or Judgmental?; Content—Extensive or Intensive?; Content—High or Medium Negativity?; Medium Used—Written or Audio-Visual?; Message Source—Actors or Job Incumbents?; Timing—Late or Early; Getting Started—Pilot Study or Policy?; Sharing Results—Proprietary or Disseminate Results? In attempting to answer these questions Wanous (1989) provides invaluable help for those intending to implement RJPs—the sort of help which should be more often provided in the formal academic literature for selection methods.

In an attempt to get a greater understanding of the processes involved in RJPs, Saks and Cronshaw (1990) conducted a laboratory experiment to investigate the role of three possible mediating variables: job attitude, job knowledge, and job acceptance intention on entry level results. They also compared the effectiveness of a verbal RJP given by a selection interviewer, and a written one. They used 60 students in their study, who were randomly assigned into one of three conditions. One group was given a verbal RJP by an interviewer during an interview, another was given a written RJP before a selection interview. The final group, which acted as a control, received general job information from the interviewer during their selection interview. The results showed that only knowledge was an important mediator of RJP effects on entry outcomes. Attitude and job acceptance intention were, however, strongly related to job acceptance decisions. It also appeared that the verbal RJP was more effective than the other two conditions in creating positive perceptions of interviewer, and organisation honesty. Lowered job expectations resulted from RJPs, as did increased role clarity. This did not, however, affect job acceptance or commitment to job choice. The authors then spent some time defending their study and argued that the criticisms that had been levelled at laboratory studies on RJPs of this type, because of their potential lack of generalisability, did not apply to their work. The criticism is based on the possibility that the potential effects of RJPs occur only after new employees have been in the organisation a good length of time. They justifiably said that they were concerned with pre-organisation entry variables rather than post-organisation entry outcomes which made the use of students more legitimate. They used this argument also to defend the use of students in their study, in the sense that naïve interviewees such as university students "are exactly the type of individuals who receive RJPs in 'real life' before entering an organisation" (Saks & Cronshaw, 1990). In terms of practical implications, they suggested that the interview is an effective means of RJP information. This also enhances the public relations role of the interview in that it seems there is now striking empirical evidence for the potential of the selection interview for this purpose, which in turn could result in more reliable and valid selection decisions. Despite their defence of their laboratory experiment it would be useful to have this research replicated in a field study.

Vandenberg and Scarpello (1990) also investigated the processes underlying RJPs, but in a field study using information systems and data processing personnel in the insurance industry. They assessed the validity of Wanous's (1980) matching model as a framework of the processes linking RJPs to employee adjustment and employee stability. Wanous's model is an adaptation to the Theory of Work Adjustment (TWA) (Lofquist & Dawis, 1969), which led the authors to assess the relationship of the TWA's applicability to RJP, and turnover research. LISREL VI (Jöreskog & Sörbom, 1986) was used to test the matching model on data from newcomers and less new employees. Differences between groups were also tested.

Vandenberg and Scarpello (1990) found support for the matching model with new employees, but not for those who had been with the organisation longer. The TWA was also found to be applicable to RJP and turnover research. The authors explained away the lack of fit of the matching model to less new employees as a reflection of the fact that as an employee spent more time with an organisation, work context variables not accounted for by the matching model were more important. Turnover is more associated with job-related experiences such as vacation time, superannuation arrangements, and job enrichment, that occur after the employee has adapted to the work environment. (McEvoy & Cascio, 1985; Premack & Wanous, 1985; Reilly, Brown, Blood & Malatesta, 1981).

The interesting characteristic of the matching model is its similarity of the Asher and Sciarrino (1974) model promoted in this review, though the latter is simpler. There is compelling evidence that RJPs present applicants with more information about jobs, thus aiding a matching and correspondence process and enhancing the validity of any selection procedure that uses it. Important questions which arise from this work, and from that of Saks and Cronshaw (1990) described earlier, are whether the results would stand up outside a North American environment. While there is no direct research on the issue in countries like New Zealand, using RJPs as a means of helping selection procedures to comply with the bicultural approach to Maori and Pakeha (European New Zealander) development could be a fruitful area for research in our country, and also in other countries where North American and European selection methods are not wholly acceptable.

Smith (1990), in a booklet intended for practitioners, summarised the efficacy of various selection techniques and described how work sample tests could be used as RJPs for the Maori community, who in their culture would provide the employer with the most suitable candidate for the job based on an Iwi (tribal) decision. The use of conventional selection procedures, in this context, has been made difficult because of the differences between Maori and Pakeha cultures. In Maori culture, when it is allowed, the Iwi often participates in the selection decision-making, and provides the employer with the best candidate from their perspective. The work sample test, if designed well, could provide the Maori community with the necessary information to help make a job-related decision. While work sample tests are not really RJPs, they do extract crucial elements of the job and cover part of the ground covered by RJPs. It could well be that selection processes in New Zealand could benefit from the full implementation of RJPs. This may also be true for other countries where a clash of cultures is a personnel selection issue.

Research on self-assessment as a selection method has been sparse in recent years. Mabe and West (1982) focused on the effects of individual characteristics and measurement conditions on the relationship between various ability and peformance measures and self-assessment. The accurate self-evaluator tended to be intelligent, high in achievement status, and an internal locus of control. George and Smith (1990) investigated whether self-assessment was a practical selection method by asking participants in an assessment centre, before and after the assessment, to judge how well they would do the jobs they were likely to be allocated. Despite age, gender, intelligence, social desirability, work experience, and education being used as moderators, self-assessment was not found to be related to organisational assessment of performance. It was also interesting that post-assessment centre self-assessments were significantly lower than self-assessments obtained before the centre. In this case self-assessment did not appear related to performance, but the authors cautioned that the "effect of an applicant's self-evaluative processes cannot be ignored". With good RJPs it seems to us that the accuracy of self-assessment must be enhanced and is almost certainly the process occurring when good RJPs are provided for applicants to jobs.

There are formal and informal ways of providing RJPs. In the former case an attempt is made to give applicants a preview of the job, but any policy that the organisation might have could produce an impact on those seeking a position in an organisation. Crant and Bateman (1990) investigated the impact of drug-testing programmes on potential job applicants' attitudes and intentions. Essentially they discovered that the existence of drug testing programmes had a negative effect on a potential employee accepting a position with the organisation in question. The subjects in their experiment had more positive attitudes and intentions toward companies that did not have a drug-testing programme and those that did not need a testing programme. The authors went on to suggest that organisations should consider the potential effect drug testing programmes might have on recruitment and that applicant responses to general policy needed further research. In New Zealand, where smoke-free policies are now commonplace, it may be that an optimal decision in terms of selection could be compromised because of a policy where worker opinion is not monitored often enough.

COGNITIVE TESTS AND VALIDITY GENERALISATIONS

The developments in the work on biographical data suggesting that they are now able to be generalised (Rothstein *et al.*, 1990) has long been accepted as far as cognitive tests are concerned, and has ceased to be an issue of great controversy in the literature (Pearlman, Schmidt, & Hunter, 1980; Schmitt *et al.*, 1984; Hartigan & Wigdor, 1989). Recently research has focused on the influence of moderators on cognitive test scores. Avolio and Waldman (1990), for example, have considered age and cognitive test performance in relation to job complexity and occupational types. They used the General Aptitude Test Battery (GATB) data base of scores for 21 646 people on the general, verbal, and numerical ability subtests of that battery. They found differences between age and cognitive ability tests scores across occuaptional types but not for different levels of job complexity. The occupational types least affected were clerical in nature. The authors proposed that this was the case because clerical work contained exercises which in some cases were not too dissimilar to those tested in the GATB. The largest drop off occurred in health-related occupations. Avolio and Waldman speculated that this occurred because of the burn-out that happens in these jobs. They hypothesised that the stress caused by burnout caused cognitive abilities to decrease with increasing age. The authors were surprised that job complexity was not related to the decrement in cognitive abilities and put this down to possible problems measuring this variable. Alternatively, it could be argued that job complexity is not an important variable as far as cognitive decrement in performance with age is concerned. They concluded by recommending that more research needed to be conducted on the relationship between life experiences and cognitive ability. In effect they are recommending a study of the effects of the environment on intelligence. An enormously difficult, but not impossible undertaking. It may, however, be beyond the scope of industrial and organisational psychology and perhaps should be considered by psychology as a whole.

Turban, Sanders, Francis, and Osburn (1989) described an approach to deal with the common practical problem of the security of selection tests, especially cognitive tests, in practical settings. Often tests are used by more than one organisation and have become available to job applicants. They call their approach construct equivalence, where valid tests currently in use are replaced by new experimental tests "that have been shown to measure the same constructs". In essence, the technique amounts to designing new tests in such a way that they can be regarded as new parallel forms of the old tests. They collected data from over 2000 applicants for four different positions in a large pectrochemical company by giving the applicants both versions of the tests. Analysis was conducted by correlations, structural modelling, and analysis of selection decisions. The results showed that the experimental and published tests measured the same constructs, and that construct equivalence was a feasible way to substitute tests.

One of the more important aspects of test taking, or any assessment task on the part of applicants, is their motivation to do the task demanded. In the past this has been likened to the concept of face validity where it has been assumed that if applicants can see the relevance of the selection procedure they will have a better attitude to it and will perform as well as possible. This in turn will provide the best possible indication of their ability to do the job. Research by Arvey, Strickland, Drauden, and Clessen (1990) has extended and formalised research in this area. They concentrated on testing and designing an instrument to directly measure the attitudes and opinions of test takers to the tests they took. The construct validity of the test was established and then they showed that applicants displayed significantly more effort and motivation than job incumbents, even with ability held constant. They also showed that some racial differences could be accounted for via the Test Attitude Survey (TAS). Holding TAS scores constant resulted in racial differences being reduced. The study serves to illustrate the importance of test-taking attitudes and how they can affect test scores. The implications of evaluating group attitudes to various selection methods have yet to be established. It would be gratifying, from our perspective, if this was related to the validity and job relatedness of the selection procedure.

Coward, Sackett, and Wilkinson (1989) conducted a Monte-Carlo study to assess the power of various approaches to detecting curvilinearity and discovered that the test of the significance of the difference between the Pearson correlation and the correlation ratio (eta) used in previous research has low power to predict non-linear relationships. They recommended a power polynomial approach as the best method for testing such relationships. As a consequence of this research, Coward and Sackett (1990) examined the issue of the linearity of ability/performance relationships because in the past the most commonly used statistic to test curvilinearity had been eta. They used 174 studies, with a mean number of subjects of 210, which dealt with the relationship between 9 scales of the General Aptitude Test Battery and job performance, using a power polynomial approach. This change of test, despite being more powerful than other approaches, showed clearly that there were no more curvilinear results in these studies than would be expected by chance. The authors went on to say that similar to Hawk (1970), linearity between ability performance relationships can be assumed unless there is an empirical or theoretical reason to believe otherwise.

Stone and Hollenbeck (1989) clarified some controversial issues surrounding statistical procedures for detecting moderator variables. Arnold (1982) had shown that moderated regression was unsuitable for assessing form of relationship and degree of relationship but Stone and Hollenbeck reanalysed Arnold's data and showed that the results reported by Arnold did not serve as a reasonable basis for continuing with the custom of assessing degree of relationship differences by using a subgrouping method. It seems that moderated regression is a suitable way of detecting moderator variables and that alternative statistical procedures are not required. This is important for validity research in personnel selection.

In terms of validity generalisation (VG) Thomas (1990) proposed a likelihood-based model for validity generalisation. He concluded that it had a number of conceptual and practical advantages over existing validity generalisation procedures. Amongst the advantages, he made the point that model-based inference brings with it the fact that estimation of optimality criteria is made clear. The number of different maximum likelihood estimates of the population values that can be supported by the data can be estimated, and point estimation of their values can be provided, along with the corresponding estimates of the component probability weights.

In reply to an earlier article by Thomas (1988), Osburn and Callender (1990) asserted that the criticisms made by Thomas concerning validity generalisation variance estimates were misleading. They went on to say that there was no "really convincing reason to doubt or abandon the estimate of true validity variance obtained from the Callender–Osburn and other closely related methods. On the contrary, there is strong evidence to indicate that populations of true validities with meaningful differences in mean and variance can be reliably distinguished providing a sufficient amount of base data is available." Recommendations for conducting validity generalisation studies are then presented.

Raju, Pappas, and Williams (1989) conducted an empirical test of the accuracy of the correlation covariance and regression slope models for assessing validity generalisation. The Monte-Carlo study had a large database ($n = 84\,808$) and the study resulted in three major conclusions. Firstly, the correlation between sampling errors and population parameters was close to zero. Secondly, when the sampling error was the only artifact, all three models did well in estimating relevant parameters across three sample sizes and ten different numbers of validity studies per VG study. Finally, when predictor reliability, criterion reliability, and range restriction were also included as artifacts, the accuracy of estimation depended on how closely the hypothetical and true distributions of artifacts matched. It seems that all models peformed poorly when the match between the two sets of distributions was poor.

Kemery, Mossholder, and Dunlap (1989) looked at the 90% credibility value advocated as a rule of thumb by Pearlman, Schmidt, and Hunter (1980) for the transportability of employment test validities. They investigated the ability of the rule to detect discretely defined moderator variables, that is, the ability of the rule to detect instances where transportability is inappropriate. An infinite sample size and mathematical proof showed that the transportability rule may produce erroneous inferences at rates higher than expected. Their results are important for practitioners contemplating transferring employment test validities, and need to be taken into consideration in meta-analytic studies of selection methods.

McIntyre (1990) addressed a different transportability issue of validity coefficients. He looked at the problems associated with transporting predictor/criterion data from different geographic locations, and forming a composite sample from them. In general terms, subsamples are treated as random partitions in the literature. What McIntrye showed was that predictor or criterion mean differences could lead to over or underestimation of the population validity coefficient depending on the profile of mean differences on both variables. He suggested a number of methods of remedying the problem, including standardisation of predictor and criterion within each subsample before analysis, and a direct equation which he derived in the paper.

Overall recent literature on validity generalisation and cognitive tests continues to provide support for the "point to point" correspondence theory used in this review. Cognitive tests work as predictors principally because most jobs require adequate cognitive ability to carry them out. The challenge lies in accounting for more performance variance through the combination of cognitive tests with other job-related predictors.

UTILITY ANALYSIS AND CRITERION ISSUES

The utility of a selection method has taken on a great importance since the standard deviation of job performance was calculated in a simplified form avoiding time-consuming cost accounting procedures by Schmidt, Hunter, McKenzie, and Muldrow (1979). The attractiveness of presenting the value of a selection technique, using the language of business (i.e. money), has continued to generate theory and controversy.

Raju, Burke, and Normand (1990) presented a new approach to utility analysis which does not require the direct estimation of the standard deviation of job performance in dollars. They assumed a linear relationship between true employer job performance (e.g. performance appraisal ratings), and the economic value of the performance. They went on to present the details of their method and how it could be used to evaluate in dollar terms not just personnel selection but other interventions such as training. The framework is a useful addition to the burgeoning utility analysis literature and promises simplified methodology for the implementation of utilty analysis.

Sadacca *et al.* (1990), as described earlier, assessed the utility of the army's Project A selection and classification programme. They argued that for the army, and perhaps also in other contexts, it is difficult to apply the dollar metric and estimates of the standard deviation in dollars used in most situations. They claimed that compensation practices differ significantly in the army because Military Occupational Specialties (MOS) do not differ in terms of their salaries, and as such cannot be used as an indication of the job's worth to the organisation. They further contended that the army is not in the business of providing goods and services to maximise profit, but of defence of the country, on which it is difficult to place a monetary value on success or failure. We would maintain, however, that a dollar value could be important in a situation where defence spending is to be cut, as is the case in the US and Britain now that the Gulf War is over, and that it is not wholly appropriate in this situation to dismiss dollar value as a measure of utility.

The aim of the army selection and classification project is to maximise preparedness for catastrophic events. What was needed according to the authors therefore was a utility metric to make comparisons between different personnel practices which affect this outcome. In the development of the methodology the authors conducted workshops with army officers. One of the interesting outcomes of the workshops was that participants did not believe that the relationship of performance to utility was linear, which contradicts the assumption made by Raju, Burke, and Normand (1990) in their development of their new theory of utility analysis described earlier.

Specifically, the feeling from the workshops was that for some jobs the gain from above average performance was greater than the loss from below average performance, and vice versa for other jobs. This led to the definition of performance in terms of a percentile scale of five levels. It also emerged that the dollar criterion was not supported and not felt to be relevant to the army situation by the participants. This supported the original views of the authors, but does not validate them. The workshops were also used to pilot test a wide variety of possible scaling methods and evaluate the methods that seemed most appropriate. As a consequence, a combined procedure using both interval and ratio estimation methods was used to estimate utility for the five different levels of performance for each of 276 MOS jobs. It was found that the reliability of a single judge was extremely high, and high reliability between judges was also found. The actual utility values were not disclosed for national security reasons.

Cascio and Morris (1990) reanalysed Hunter, Schmidt, and Coggin's (1988) article on the "Problems and Pitfalls in using Capital Budgeting and Financial Accounting Techniques in Assessing the Utility of Personnel Programs". Hunter, Schmidt, and Coggin had argued that many of the capital budgeting techniques were often conceptually and logically inappropriate, and that there was no correct definition of utility. Cascio and Morris (1990) argued that Hunter, Schmidt, and Coggins's presentation of capital budgeting methods was "inconsistent with widely recognised capital budgeting methods". They went on to say that they used unreasonable illustrations produced to expediate their analysis and that Hunter, Schmidt, and Coggin's, arguments promoted continued inaccurate measurement and exposition of the expense and merits of personnel programmes. Cascio and Morris (1990) concluded by arguing that if pesonnel specialists lacked breadth and perspective and were unwilling to adopt unfamiliar ideas and methods, they would be less able to compete for resources within organisations when they have to compete with other functional areas of a business. Given the tremendous savings that can be made from improving selection methodology in organisations, as shown from utility analysis research, this would be undervaluing the personnel function and in Cascio and Morris's (1990), and our view, would be a tragedy.

Hunter, Schmidt, and Judiesch (1990) focused on differences in output and how this could make selection more important for some levels of job compared to others. They investigated individual differences in output variability as a function of job complexity. They argued that the standard deviation of employee output as a percentage of mean output increases as jobs get more complex. They analysed data on the extent of individual differences in output based on 68 studies measuring work output on the job and 17 work sample studies with ratio scale measurement. For each study the standard deviation of output measured as a percentage of average output was calculated. Hunter, Schmidt, and Judiesch (1990) found that, moving from routine to medium complexity to professional work, output mean standard deviaions for applicants varied from 19.3% to 31.8% to 47.5% respectively. They found the differences to be largest for sales jobs where the average standard deviation for life insurance sales applicants was 120% with the average for other sales jobs being 47.7%. The implications are that large gains can be made by selecting better workers and this reinforces the seriousness of the problem of ignorance in countries like New Zealand, where practitioners often have little knowledge of the validity of different selection methods.

Nathan and Tippins (1990) discovered that halo, measured as the standard deviation across dimensions, consistently moderated the relationship between dimension ratings and scores on valid tests. It would seem that greater halo resulted in higher performance ratings. Poorer validation results were obtained when the effect of the overall rating on dimension ratings was statistically controlled. Dimension ratings in this case rarely added variance to that of overall ratings. The results support recent laboratory studies (Bernadin & Pence, 1980; Borman, 1979) which have found accuracy and halo positively related. Similar scores on different performance appraisal dimensions may therefore imply halo but, from the results of this study, it may not be error. It is quite possible for a single dimension to affect performance in all aspects of a job. An example is cognitive ability, as we have stated earlier. The authors used the example of verbal ability which "in particular may be necessary for acceptable performance in many different aspects of the same job". The implications are, we suppose, that halo should not be regarded as worrisome but as a natural part of performance appraisal. What is missing in this debate, however, is whether the elevated validity coefficients obtained are spurious, due to the inaccurate, exaggerated assumption of importance held for the dimension which covers all aspects of performance.

An issue of some controversy in the literature recently has been that of dynamic criteria. Barrett, Caldwell, and Alexander (1985) concluded as a consequence of a secondary analysis of data from published studies that dynamic criteria do not exist, and that the changes in criteria which occurred could be accounted for through methodological artifacts. Austin, Humphreys, and Hulin (1989) criticised Barrett, Caldwell, and Alexander's argument because many of the artifacts were listed in summary form, and this was done without thought to invoking artifacts as *post hoc* explanations. They concluded by stating that it might be more useful to understand criteria rather than searching for artifacts. In a rejoinder Barrertt and Alexander (1989) argued that the burden of proof still rested with those who advocate the existence of dynamic criteria. They presented evidence to show that validity coefficients are stable over time and even might increase. They concluded by saying that more evidence is needed before the concept of dynamic criteria can be accepted.

In an attempt to clarify the debate concerning the concept of dynamic criteria, Deadrick and Madigan (1990) provided data supporting a refined concept of dynamic criteria. Their results revealed a decline in performance stability coefficients as the interval between measures increased. This decline was independent of employees' prior job experience, cognitive abilities, or psychomotor ability. The results of their study further showed that the validity of cognitive ability increased, the validity of psychomotor ability was stable, and that of prior job experience decreased over time. The authors used their results to support the contention by Murphy (1989) that most jobs possess multiple transition stages that "occur at different times and last for different durations" for different people. The implications for selection methods are that the selection procedure would need to identify those critical factors which are important for the different stages of performance. While all the answers may not exist here concerning the improvement of predictor criterion relationships, the opportunity must be available to account for some variance previously unaccounted for in selection research if research on the job environment, citizenship behaviour, and their fit to worker characteristics is carried out as Deadrick and Madigan (1990) recommended.

SOME CONCLUSIONS

We have tried in this review to give the reader a perspective on selection methods as they stand in early 1991. There are two things that we believe from the literature. Firstly, many of the selection methods are becoming similar, and the concentration on such issues as job fit, person match, work-related personality tests, work sample tests and the whole panoply of what could be considered separate methods are all becoming a concentration on improving one approach: making the selection method congruent with the job. We have used Asher and Sciarrino's (1974) theory to support our case. Secondly, we also believe that there is a considerable discrepancy between what is recommended in the selection method literature, and the methods recommended by practitioners. Dakin and Armstrong (1989) highlighted this in their research. We maintain that the formal academic literature on selection needs to focus more on the application of selection methods, so that valid techniques get used more on a daily basis. This may be occurring in the United States, because of the high regard with which industrial and organisational psychologists are held in industry and commerce in that country. This is not the case in nations like New Zealand and we suspect many other countries around the world. More research needs to be conducted on the application of selection methods to heighten validity, ensure equity, and improve productivity, something all countries must be concerned with in a recession.

REFERENCES

Anderson, N., & Shackleton, V. (1986) Recruitment and selection: A review of developments in the 1980s. *Personnel Review*, **15**, 19–26.

Anderson, N., & Shackleton, V. (1990) Decision making in the graduate selection interview: A field study. *Journal of Occupational Psychology*, **63**, 63–76.

Anon (1987) *The Sales Performance Indicator*. Assessment and Development Services Ltd: Christchurch, New Zealand.

Arnold, H. J. (1982) Moderator variables: A clarification of conceptual, analytic, and psychometric issues. *Organisational Behavior and Human Performance*, **29**, 143–174.

Arthur, Jr W., Barrett, G. V., & Doverspike, D. (1990) Validation of an Information-Processing-Based Test Battery for the Prediction of Handling Accidents Among Petroleum-Product Transport Drivers. *Journal of Applied Psychology*, **75**, 6, 621–628.

Arvey, R. D., & Campion, J. E. (1982) The employment interview: A summary and review of recent research. *Personnel Psychology*, **35**, 281–322.

Arvey, R. D., Strickland, W., Drauden, G., & Clessen, M. (1990) Motivational components of test taking. *Personnel Psychology*, **43**, 695–715.

Asher, J. J., & Sciarrino, J. A. (1974) Realistic work samples: A review. *Personnel Psychology*, **27**, 519–534.

Austin, J. T., Humphreys, L. G., & Hulin, C. L. (1989) Another view of dynamic criteria: A critical reanalysis of Barrett, Caldwell, and Alexander. *Personnel Psychology*, **42**, 583–612.

Avolio, B. J., & Waldman, D. A. (1990) An examination of age and cognitive test performance across job complexity and occupational types. *Journal of Applied Psychology*, **75**, 43–50.

Barrett, G. V., & Alexander, R. A. (1989) Rejoinder to Austin, Humphreys, and Hulin: Critical reanalysis of Barrett, Caldwell, and Alexander. *Personnel Psychology*, **42**, 597–612.

Barrett, G. V., Caldwell, M. S., & Alexander, R. A. (1985) The concept of dynamic criteria: A critical reanalysis. *Personnel Psychology*, **38**, 41–56.

Baxter, J. C., Brock, B., Hill, P. C., & Rozelle, R. M. (1981) Letters of Recommendation: A question of value. *Journal of Applied Psychology*, **66**, 3, 296–301.

Bayne, R. (1977) Can selection interviewing be improved? *Journal of Occupational Psychology*, **50**, 161–167.

Bernadin, H. J., & Pence, E. C. (1980) Effects of rater training: Creating new response sets and decreasing accuracy. *Journal of Applied Psychology*, **65**, 60–66.

Binning, J. F. & Barrett, G. V. (1989) Validity of personnel decisions: A conceptual analysis of the inferential and evidential bases. *Journal of Applied Psychology*, **74**, 478–494.

Blinkhorn, S., & Johnson, C. (1990) The insignificance of personality testing. *Nature*, **348**, 671–672.

Borman, W. C. (1979) Format and training effects on rating accuracy and rater errors. *Journal of Applied Psychology*, **64**, 60–66.

Brannick, M. T., Michaels, C. E., & Baker, D. P. (1989) Construct validity of In-Basket scores. *Journal of Applied Psychology*, **74**, 6, 957–963.

Bronach, C., Pinder, R., & Herriot, P. (1990) Assessment centre dimensions, personality, and aptitudes. *Journal of Occupational Psychology*, **63**, 211–216.

Caldwell, D. F., & O'Reilly III, C. A. (1990) Measuring person–job fit with a profile-comparison process. *Journal of Applied Psychology*, **75**, 648–657.

Campbell, C. H., Ford, P., Rumsey, M. G., Pulakos, E. D., Borman, W. C., Felker, D. B., De Vera, M. V., & Riegelhaupt, B. J. (1990) Development of multiple job performance measures in a representative sample of jobs. *Personnel Psychology*, **43**, 277–300.

Campbell, J. P. (1990) An overview of the army selection and classification project (Project A). *Personnel Psychology*, **43**, 231–239.

Campbell, J. P., McHenry, J. J., & Wise, L. L. (1990) Modelling job performance in a population of jobs. *Personnel Psychology*, **43**, 313–333.

Campion, M. A., Pursell, E. D., & Brown, B. K. (1988) Structured interviewing: Raising the psychometric properties of the employment interview. *Personnel Psychology*, **41**, 25–42.

Carrier, M. R., Dalessio, A. T., & Brown, S. H. (1990) Correspondence between estimates of content and criterion-related validity values. *Personnel Psychology*, **43**, 85–100.

Carroll, S. J., & Nash, A. N. (1972) Effectiveness of a Forced-Choice Reference Check. *Personnel Administration*, **42–46**, March–April.

Cascio, W. F. (1975) Accuracy of verifiable biographical information blank responses. *Journal of Applied Psychology*, **60**, 767–769.

Cascio, W. F., & Morris, J. R. (1990) A critical reanalysis of Hunter, Schmidt, and Coggin's (1988), "Problems and pitfalls in using budgeting and financial accounting techniques in assessing the utility of personnel programs". *Journal of Applied Psychology*, **75**, 410–417.

Chatman, J. A. (1988) Matching people and organizations: Selection and socialization in public accounting firms. Unpublished doctoral dissertation, University of California, Berkeley.

Coward, W. M., & Sackett, P. R. (1990) Linearity of ability-performance relationships: A reconfirmation. *Journal of Applied Psychology*, 75, 297–300.

Coward, W. M., Sackett, P. R., & Wilkinson, L. (1989) A statistical poser study of tests for curvilinearity in bivariate relationships. Manuscript submitted for publication.

Crant, J. M., & Bateman, T. S. (1990) An experimental test of the impact of drug-testing programs on potential job applicants' attitudes and intentions. *Journal of Applied Psychology*, 75, 127–131.

Crawley, B., Pinder, R., & Herriot, P. (1990) Assessment centre dimensions, personality, and aptitudes. *Journal of Occupational Psychology*, 63, 211–216.

Dakin, S., & Armstrong, J. S. (1989) Predicting job performance: A comparison of expert opinion and research findings. *International Journal of Forecasting*, 5, 187–194.

Day, D. V., & Silverman, S. B. (1989) Personality and job performance: evidence of incremental validity. *Personnel Psychology*, 42, 25–36.

Deadrick, D. L., & Madigan, R. M. (1990) Dynamic criteria revisited: A longitudinal study of performance stability and predictive validity. *Personnel Psychology*, 43, 717–743.

Dobson, P., & Williams, A. (1989) The validation of the selection of male British Army officers. *Journal of Occupational Psychology*, 62, 313–325.

Dougherty, T. W., Ebert, R. J., & Callender, J. C. (1986) Policy capturing in the employment interview. *Journal of Applied Psychology*, 71, 9–15.

Downs, S. (1968) Selecting the older trainee: A pilot study of trainability tests. *National Institute of Industrial Psychology Bulletin*, 19–26.

England, G. W., & Patterson, D. G. (1960) Selection and placement: The past ten years. In H. G. Heneman, R. L. C. Brown, M. K. Chandler, R. Kahn, H. S. Parnes, & G. P. Shulz (eds), *Employment Relations Research: A Summary and Appraisal*. New York: Harper & Brothers, pp. 43–72.

Evan, W. M., & Miller, J. R. III (1969) Differential effects on response bias of computer vs. conventional administration of a social science questionnaire: An exploratory methodological experiment. *Behavioral Science*, 4, 216–227.

Finkle, R. B. (1976) Managerial assessment centres. In M. D. Dunnette (ed.), *Handbook of Industrial and Organisational Psychology*. Chicago: Rand McNally, pp. 861–888.

Gaugler, B. B., & Thornton, G. C. III (1989) Number of assessment center dimensions as a determinant of assessor accuracy. *Journal of Applied Psychology*, 74, 611–618.

Gaugler, B. B., Rosenthal, D. B., Thornton, G. C. III, & Bentson, C. (1987) Meta-analyses of assessment center validity [Monograph]. *Journal of Applied Psychology*, 72, 493–511.

George, D. I., & Smith, M. C. (1990) An empirical comparison of self assessment and organizational assessment in personnel selection. *Public Personnel Management*, 19, 175–190.

Guion, R. M., & Gottier, R. F. (1965) Validity of personality measures in personnel selection. *Personnel Psychology*, 18, 135–164.

Harris, M. M. (1989) Reconsidering the employment interview: A review of recent literature and suggestions for future research. *Personnel Psychology*, 42, 691–726.

Hartigan, J. A., & Wigdor, A. K. (eds) (1989) *Fairness in Employment Testing: Validity Generalisation, Minority Issues, and the General Aptitude Test Battery*, Washington, DC: National Academy Press.

Hattrup, K., & Schmitt, N. (1990) Prediction of trades apprentices' performance on job sample criteria. *Personnel Psychology*, 43, 453–466.

Hawk, J. (1970) Linearity of criterion-GATB aptitude relationships. *Measurement and Evaluation in Guidance*, **2**, 249–251.

Herriot, P. (1985) Give and take in graduate selection. *Personnel Management*, May, 33–35.

Herriot, P., & Rothwell, C. (1983) Expectations and impressions in the graduate selection interview. *Journal of Occupational Psychology*, **56**, 303–314.

Hitt, M. A., & Barr, S. H. (1989) Managerial selection decision models: Examination of configural cue processing. *Journal of Applied Psychology*, **74**, 53–61.

Hough, L. M. (1984) Development and evaluation of the "accomplishment-record" method of selecting and promoting professionals. *Journal of Applied Psychology*, **69**, 135–146.

Hough, L. M., Eaton, N. K., Dunnette, M. D., Kamp, J. D., & McCloy, R. A. (1990) Criterion-related validities of personality constructs and the effect of response distortion on those validities [Monograph]. *Journal of Applied Psychology*, **75**, 581–595.

Hunter, J. E., Schmidt, F. L., & Coggin, T. D. (1988) Problems and pitfalls in using capital budgeting and financial accounting techniques in assessing the utility of personnel programs. *Journal of Applied Psychology*, **73**, 522–528.

Hunter, J. E., Schmidt, F. L., & Judiesch, M. K. (1990) Individual differences in output variability as a function of job complexity. *Journal of Applied Psychology*, **75**, 28–42.

Hunter, J. E., & Hunter, R. F. (1984) Validity and utility of alternative predictors of job performance. *Psychological Bulletin*, **96**, 72–98.

Jöreskog, K. G., & Sörbom, D. (1986) *LISREL VI: Analysis of Linear Structural Relationships by Maximum Likelihood*. Chicago: National Education Resources.

Kelly, E. L., & Fiske, D. W. (1951) *The Prediction of Performance in Clinical Psychology*. Ann Arbor, Michigan: University of Michigan Press.

Kemery, E. R., Mossholder, K. W., & Dunlap, W. P. (1989) Meta-analysis and moderator variables: a cautionary note on transportability. *Journal of applied Psychology*, **74**, 168–170.

Kinicki, A. J., Lockwood, C. A., Hom, P. W., & Griffeth, R. W. (1990) Interviewer predictions of applicant qualifications and interviewer validity: Aggregate and individuals analyses. *Journal of Applied Psychology*, **75**, 477–486.

Knouse, S. B. (1983) The letter of recommendation: Specificity and favourability of information. *Personnel Psychology*, **36**, 331–341.

Koson, D., Kitchen, C., Kochen, M., & Stodolosky, D. (1970) Psychological testing by computer: Effect on response bias. *Educational and Psychological Measurement*, **30**, 803–810.

Latham, G. P., & Saari, L. M. (1984) Do people do what they say? Further studies on the situational interview. *Journal of Applied Psychology*, **69**, 469–573.

Latham, G. P., Saari, L. M., Pursell, E. D., & Campion, M. A. (1980) The situational interview. *Journal of Applied Psychology*, **65**, 422–427.

Lautenschlager, G. J., & Flaherty, V. L. (1990) Computer administration of questions: More desirable or more social desirability? *Journal of Applied Pscyhology*, **75**, 310–314.

Lofquist, L. H., & Dawis, R. V. (1969) *Adjustment to Work*. New York: Appleton-Century-Crofts.

Mabe, P. A., & West, S. G. (1982) Validity of self-evaluation of ability: A review and meta-analysis. *Journal of Applied Psychology*, **67**, 280–296.

Macan, T. H., & Dipboye, R. L. (1990) The relationships of interviewers' pre-interview impressions to selection and recruitment outcomes. *Personnel Psychology*, **43**, 745–768.

Martin, C. L., & Nagao, D. H. (1989) Some effects of computerised interviewing on job applicant responses. *Journal of Applied Psychology*, 74, 72–80.

McCormick, E. J., Jeanneret, P., & Mecham, R. C. (1972) A study of job characteristics of job dimensions as based on the position analysis questionnaire. *Journal of Applied Psychology*, 36, 347–368.

McDaniel, M. A. (1989) Biographical constructs for predicting employee suitability. *Journal of Applied Psychology*, 74, 964–870.

McEvoy, G. M., & Beatty, R. W. (1989) Assessment centers and subordinate appraisals of managers: A seven-year examination of predictive validity. *Personnel Psychology*, 42, 37–52.

McEvoy, G. M., & Cascio, W. F. (1985) Strategies for reducing employee turnover: A meta-analysis. *Journal of Applied Psychology*, 70, 342–353.

McHenry, J. J., Hough, L. M., Toquam, J. L., Hanson, M. A., & Ashworth, S. (1990) Project A validity results: The relationship between predictor and criterion domains. *Personnel Psychology*, 43, 335–354.

McIntyre, R. M. (1990) Spurious estimation of validity coefficients in composite samples: Some methodological considerations. *Journal of Applied Psychology*, 75, 91–94.

Mills, A. J. (1991) Personnel consulting firms' managerial selection methods. Unpublished Masters thesis, University of Waikato, Hamilton, New Zealand.

Motowildo, S. J., Dunnette, M. D., & Carter, G. W. (1990) An alternative selection procedure: The low fidelity simulation. *Journal of Applied Psychology*, 75, 640–647.

Muchinsky, P. M. (1979) The use of reference reports in personnel selection: A review and evaluation. *Journal of Occupational Psychology*, 52, 287–297.

Muchinsky, P. M. (1987) *Psychology Applied to Work*, 2nd edn. Chicago; Dorsey Press.

Murphy, K. R. (1989) Is the relationship between cognitive ability and job performance stable over time? *Human Performance*, 2, 183–200.

Nathan, B. R., & Tippins, N. (1990) The consequences of halo "Error" in performance ratings: A field study of the moderating effect of halo on test validation results. *Journal of Applied Psychology*, 75, 3, 290–296.

Ng, E., & Smith, M. C. (1991) An updated meta-analysis on the validity of personality tests for personnel selection. Submitted for publication and under review.

Osburn, H. G., & Callender, J. C. (1990) Bias in validity generalization variance estimates: A reply to Hoben Thomas. *Journal of Applied Psychology*, 75, 328–333.

Owens, W. A. (1968) Toward one discipline of scientific psychology. *American Psychologist*, 65, 782–785.

Owens, W. A. (1976) Background data. In M. D. Dunnette (ed.), *Handbook of Industrial and Organisational Psychology*. New York: Rand McNally, pp. 609–644.

Pearlman, I., Schmidt, F. L., & Hunter, J. E. (1980) Validity generalisation results for tests used to predict job proficiency and training success in clerical occupations. *Journal of Applied Psychology*, 65, 373–406.

Peters, M., Servos, P., & Day, R. (1990) Marked sex differences on a fine motor skill task disappear when finger size is used as co-variate. *Journal of Applied Psychology*, 75, 87–90.

Peterson, N. G., Hough, L. M., Dunnette, M. D., Rosse, R. L., Houston, J. S., Toquam, J. L., & Wing, H. (1990) Project A: Specification of the predictor domain and development of new selection/classification tests. *Personnel Psychology*, 43, 247–276.

Phillips, A. P., & Dipboye, R. L. (1989) Correlational tests of predictions from a process model of the interview. *Journal of Applied Psychology*, 74, 41–52.

Pinder, R., & Herriot, P. (1990) Assessment centre dimensions, personality, and aptitudes. *Journal of Occupational Psychology*, 63, 211–216.

Premack, S. L., & Wanous, J. P. (1985) A meta-analysis of realistic job preview experiments. *Journal of Applied Psychology*, 70, 706–719.

Pynes, J. E., & Bernardin, H. J. (1989) Predictive validity of an entry-level police officer assessment centre. *Journal of Applied Psychology*, 74, 831–833.

Raju, N. S., Pappas, S., & Williams, C. P. (1989) An empirical monte carlo test of the accuracy of the correlation covariance and regression slope models for assessing validity generalization. *Journal of Applied Psychology*, 74, 901–911.

Raju, N. S., Burke, M. J., & Normand, J. (1990) A new approach for utility analysis. *Journal of Applied Psychology*, 75, 3–12.

Reilly, R. R., Brown, B., Blood, M. R., & Malatesta C. Z. (1981) The effects of realistic previews: A study and discussion of the literature. *Personnel Psychology*, 34, 823–834.

Reilly, R. R., & Chao, G. T. (1982) Validity and fairness of some alternative employee selection procedures. *Personnel Psychology*, 35, 1–62

Reilly, R. R., Henry, S., & Smither, J. W. (1990) An examination of the effects of using behavior checklists on the construct validity of assessment center dimensions. *Personnel Psychology*, 43, 71–84.

Rezmovic, V. (1977) The effects of computerized experimentation on response variance. *Behavior Research Methods and Instrumentation*, 9, 1–147.

Rice, G. H. Jr, & Lindecamp, D. P. (1989) Personality types and business success of small retailers. *Journal of Occuapational Psychology*, 62, 177–182.

Robertson, I. T., & Downs, S. (1989) Work-sample tests of trainability: A meta-analysis. *Journal of Applied Psychology*, 4, 402–410.

Robertson, I. T., & Kandola, R. S. (1982) Work sample tests: Validity adverse impact and applicant reaction. *Journal of Occupational Psychology*, 55. 171–182.

Robertson, I. T., & Makin, P. J. (1986) Management selection in Britain: A survey and critique. *Journal of Occupational Psychology*, 59, 45–57.

Robertson, I. T., Gratton, L., Rout, U. (1990) The validity of situational interviews for administrative jobs. *Journal of Organisational Behavior*, 11, 69–76

Rodger, A (1952) The worthwhileness of the interview. *Journal of Occupational Psychology*, 26, 101–106.

Rothstein, H,. R., Schmidt, F. L., Erwin, F. W., Owens, W. A., & Sparks, C. P. (1990) Biographical data in employment selection: Can validities be made generalizable? *Journal of Applied Psychology*, 75, 175–184.

Russell, C. J., Mattson, J., Devlin, S. E., & Atwater, D. (1990) Predictive validity of biodata items generated from retrospective life experience essays. *Journal of Applied Psychology*, 75, 569–580.

Russell, J. S., Persing, D. L., Dunn, J. A., Rankin, R. J. (1988) A field study to determine which predictors influence selection decisions. Paper presented at the Annual meeting of the Academy of Management, Anaheim, CA.

Ryan, A. M., & Sackett, P. R. (1987) A survey of individual assessment practices by I/O psychologists. *Personnel Psychology*, 40, 455–488.

Ryan, A. M., & Sackett, P. R. (1989) Exploratory study of individual assessment practices: Inter-rater reliability and judgments of assessor effectiveness. *Journal of Applied Psychology*, 74, 568–579.

Rynes, S., & Gerhart, B. (1990) Interviewer assessments of applicant "fit": An exploratory investigation. *Personnel Psychology*, 43, 13–35.

Sackcett, P. R., Burris, L. R., & Callaghan, C. (1989) Integrity testing for personnel selection: An update. *Personnel Psychology*, 42, 491–529.

Sackett, P. R., & Harris, M. M. (1984) Honesty testing for personnel selection: A review and critique. *Personnel Psychology*, 32, 487–506.

Sackett, P. R., Zedeck, S., & Fogli, L. (1988) Relations between measures of typical and maximum job performance. *Journal of Applied Psychology*, 73, 482–486.

Sadacca, R., Campbell, J. P., Difazio, A. S., Schultz, S. R., & White, L. A. (1990) Scaling performance utility to enhance selection/classification decisions. *Personnel Psychology*, 43, 367–378.

Saks, A. M., & Cronshaw, S. F. (1990) A process investigation of realistic job previews: Mediating variables and channels of communication. *Journal of Organizational Behavior*, 11, 221–236.

Schippmann, J. S., Prien, E. P., & Katz, J. A. (1990) Reliability and validity of performance measures. *Personnel Psychology*, 43, 837–859.

Schmidt, F. L., Hunter, J. E., McKenzie, R. C., & Muldrow, T. W. (1979) Impact of valid selection procedures on work force productivity. *Journal of Applied Psychology*, 64, 609–626.

Schmitt, N., Gooding, R. Z., Noe, R. A., & Kirch, M. (1984) Meta-analyses of validity studies published between 1964 & 1982 and the investigation of study characteristics. *Personnel Psychology*, 37, 407–422.

Schmitt, N., Schneider, J. R., & Cohen, S. A. (1990) Factors affecting validity of a regionally administered assessment center. *Personnel Psychology*, 43, 1–12.

Schneider, B., & Schmitt, N. (1986) *Staffing Organisations*. Glenview. IL: Scott, Foresman.

Sharf, J. (1970) Decision making in the employment interview. Unpublished dissertation, University of Tennessee, Knoxville.

Shields, J. L., & Hanser, L. M. (1990) Designing, planning, and selling Project A. *Personnel Psychology*, 43, 241–245.

Shore, T. H., Thornton, G. C., & Shore, L. M. (1990) Cosntruct validity of two categories of assessment center dimension ratings. *Personnel Psychology*, 43, 101–115.

Singer, M. S., & Sewell, C. (1989) Applicant age and selection interview decisions: Effect of information exposure on age discrimination in personnel selection. *Personnel Psychology*, 42, 135–154.

Sleight, R. B., & Bell, G. D. (1954) Desirable content of letters of recommendation. *Personnel Journal*, 32, 421–422.

Smith, M. C. (1990) *Saving Money Through Good Selection*. Health Services Equal Employment opportunities Development Unit, Department of Health, Wellington, New Zealand.

Smith, M. C., & George, D. I. (1986) Stupid personality tests, who's conning who? *Management (New Zealand)*, 32, 26–27.

Smith, R. E. (1963) Examination by computer. *Behavioral Science*, 8, 76–79.

Springbett, B. M. (1958) Factors affecting the final decision in the employment interview. *Canadian Journal of Psychology*, 12, 13–22.

Stephenson, W. (1953) *The Study of Behavior: O Technique and its Methodology*. Chicago: University of Chicago Press.

Stone, E. F., & Hollenbeck, J. R. (1989) Clarifying some controversial issues surrounding statistical procedures for detecting moderator variables: Empirical evidence and related matters. *Journal of Applied Psychology*, 74, 3–10.

Tett, R. P., & Jackson, D. N. (1990) Organization and personality correlates of participative behaviours using an in-basket exercise. *Journal of Occupational Psychology*, 63, 175–188.

Thayer, P. W. (1977) Something old, something new. *Personnel Psychology*, 30, 513–524.

Thomas, H. (1988) What is the interpretation of the validity generalisation estimate $S^2_p = S^2_r - S^2_p$? *Journal of Applied Psychology*, 73, 679–682.

Thomas, H. (1990) A likelihood-based model for validity generalization. *Journal of Applied Psychology*, **75**, 13–20.

Tullar, W. L. (1989) Relation control in the employment interview. *Journal of Applied Psychology*, **74**, 971–977.

Turban, D. B., Sanders, P. A., Francis, D. J., & Osburn, H. G. (1989) Construct equivalence as an approach to replacing validated cognitive ability tests. *Journal of Applied Psychology*, **74**, 62–71.

Ulrich, L., & Trumbo, D. (1965) The selection interview since 1949. *Psychological Bulletin*, **63**, 110–116.

Vandenberg, R. J., & Scarpello, V. (1990) The matching model: An examination of the processes underlying realistic job previews. *Journal of Applied Psychology*, **75**, 60–67.

Wagner, R. (1949) The employment interview: A critical review. *Personnel Psychology*, **2**, 17–46.

Wanous, J. P. (1980) *Organisational Entry: Recruitment, Selection, and Socialisation of Newcomers*. Reading, MA: Addison-Wesley.

Wanous, J. P. (1989) Installing a realistic job preview: Ten tough choices. *Personnel Psychology*, **42**, 117–133.

Weekly, J. A., & Gier, J. A. (1987) Reliability and validity of the situational interview for a sales position. *Journal of Applied Psychology*, **72**, 484–487.

Wiesner, W. H., & Cronshaw, S. F. (1988) A meta-analytic investigation of the impact of interview format and degree of structure on the validity of the employment interview. *Journal of Occupational Psychology*, **61**, 275–290.

Williams, C. P. (1989) An empirical Monte-Carlo test of the accuracy of the correlation, covariance, and regression slope models for assessing validity generalization. *Journal of Applied Psychology*, **74**, 901–911.

Wise, L. L., McHenry, J., & Campbell, J. P. (1990) Identifying optimal predictor composites and testing for generalizability across jobs and performance factors. *Personnel Psychology*, **43**, 355–366.

Wright, P. M., Lichtenfels, P. A., & Pursell, E. D. (1989) The structured interview: Additional studies and a meta-analysis. *Journal of Occupational Psychology*, **62**, 191–199

Young, W. Y., Houston, J. S., Harris, J. H., Hoffman, G., & Wise, L. L. (1990) Large-scale predictor validation in Project A: Data collection procedures and data base preparation. *Personnel Psychology*, **43**, 301–311.

Chapter 3

LEADERSHIP THEORY AND RESEARCH: A REPORT OF PROGRESS

Fred E. Fiedler
Department of Psychology
University of Washington
USA
and
Robert J. House
Department of Management
University of Pennsylvania
USA

INTRODUCTION

This chapter discusses selected research and theories in two areas of the literature which are, in many respects, at opposite poles of the rational–emotional continuum in our conceptions of leadership: those which deal with cognitive aspects and those which deal with the affective and motivational aspects of leadership, that is, the highly affect-laden and motivational variables inherent in charismatic and transformational leadership.

We do not intend to duplicate the inclusive treatments of the field represented in the *Annual Review* series and similar works, but present a more extended discussion of certain recent developments in the two leadership topics mentioned above, and conclude with some general comments about the current status of the field.

DOMINANT TOPICS IN LEADERSHIP RESEARCH: 1970–1987

The topics that dominated the leadership field in the decades from 1950 to 1970 have been transactional theories and contingency theories. The transactional models of that era in large part dealt with the exchange and social contract between leader and group members, and the leader behaviors that enable group members to gain satisfaction and reward by performing the tasks mandated by the organization. The primary examples of this genre are: Hollander's (1978) work on idiosyncracy credits; Path Goal theory (House, 1971); the Normative Decision Model (Vroom and Yetton, 1973); Vertical Dyad Theory (Graen and Scandura,

1987); and the work of the University of Michigan group (e.g. Bowers and Seashore, 1966; Katz and Kahn, 1978). The contingency theories specify the situations in which certain leadership styles or behaviors will be most successful (e.g. Fiedler, 1964; 1967; House and Mitchell, 1974). These also imply that group members perform their jobs as part of the social contract. The interest in transactional approaches to leadership remains strong and is expected to continue to be so in the foreseeable future.

It is perhaps somewhat ironic that two concerns of the earliest years of empirical leadership (Terman, 1904) and the nature of charismatic leadership (Carlyle, 1910; 1917; Weber, 1946)—are now reemerging after many years of relative neglect. Since the late 1970s, leadership researchers have increasingly turned their attention to the role of such cognitive variables as the leader's judgement, perceptions, intelligence, competence, and experience, in determining leader–member relations and performance. In this respect they are in tune with the direction in which many other areas of psychology have turned in the last two decades (e.g. Jones, 1985). However, as we noted, researchers also returned to another early concern in leadership, namely, the nature of charismatic and the closely-related transformational leadership, and the effects of these phenomena on the cognitions and performance of followers.

COGNITIVE VARIABLES AND LEADERSHIP PERFORMANCE

A growing number of researchers have been asking how leaders perceive, think and judge, and how they make use of these cognitive processes (e.g. Calder, 1977). This is exemplified by the excellent collection of papers in Sims and Gioia's (1986) book, *The Thinking Organization*. Likewise, motivation theories have moved in the cognitive direction, following the early seminal work by Vroom (1964) on expectancy theory, and more recently the work by Locke and Latham (1984) on goal-setting. The present section deals mainly with developments related to cognitive approaches to leadership during the past decade.

Attribution Theory and Leadership

A number of studies have applied the principles of attribution theory to problems in the leadership area. One good example of this type, based on attribution theory, is by Mitchell, Green and Wood (1981). Their study showed that a leader's judgement of the followers' competence depends on the consequences of the subordinate's actions. This is true even when the behavior causing undesirables outcomes is identical to that not causing undesirable outcomes. Thus, Mitchell *et al.* found lower performance ratings for a nurse whose patient fell out of bed and sustained an injury because of her failure to raise a bed rail than for a nurse in the same situation whose behavior did not result in an injury to the patient.

A series of studies by Lord has shown that cognitive schemes and labeling strongly affect perceptions of leaders. Thus, Foti, Fraser and Lord (1982) found marked changes over time and across candidates in the percentage of respondents who believed that strong leadership qualities were possessed by the person whom they rated. The authors hypothesized that as these leadership perceptions changed, so would the perceptions of other characteristics that were strongly associated with leadership. Consistent with this expectation, correlational results clearly showed a greater change for more prototypical items when the leadership ratings given to the same person (e.g. President Carter) were compared at earlier and later times in his term of office, or when comparisons were made of leadership ratings given to different politicians (President Carter versus Senator Kennedy).

In another study, Phillips and Lord (1981) showed that the individual's focus affects the attributions made to the individual. The investigators had subjects view video tapes of the same group discussion with the TV camera focused either on the leader or on others in the group. The results showed that the saliency of the leader (as manipulated by focusing the camera on different persons) srongly affected leadership ratings.

Such findings as those by Mitchell, Green and Wood, as well as by Phillips and Lord, and Foti, Fraser and Lord, are of considerable importance in interpreting leader behavior and performance ratings. It is clear that the frame of reference of the rater and the nature of the outcomes play a significant role in how leaders are evaluated, and in turn, how they evaluate the behavior and performance of subordinates. On the other hand, we must not lose sight of the fact that the effects obtained by these studies do not account for more than a relatively small portion of the variance. That the single, one-shot rating of leader behavior or follower behavior has its problems has been apparent for some time (Epstein, 1975). The above studies based on attribution theory tell us more specifically what the causes of the distortions are, and perhaps, how to correct for them in the future.

Cognitive Resource Theory

A quite different direction has been taken in a 15-year research program by Fiedler and his associates (Blades, 1976; Blades and Fiedler, 1976; Fiedler, 1978; 1986; Fiedler et al., 1979; Potter and Fiedler, 1981; Fiedler and Garcia, 1987). The research has led to the development of 'Cognitive Resource Theory' (CRT). This theory provides an integration of the roles played by intellectual abilities, competence and experience, as well as leader behavior and stress, in determining leadership and group performance. CRT addresses the long-standing question of why the leader's intellectual abilities and experience correlate so poorly (.20 – .30) with performance (e.g. Bass, 1981). The question is of theoretical importance since such critical leadership functions as decision-making, planning or evaluating are intellectual in nature, and should, therefore, be related to leader intelligence.

There also is no consistent evidence that leader experience generally contributes to performance (e.g. Fiedler, 1970). In fact, there is so little research on the effects of leader experience that the term is not even listed in the index of *Stogdill's Handbook of Leadership* (Bass, 1981). The problem is of practical importance in organizational psychology since ability and experience probably are among the most important factors in determining managerial hiring and promotion decisions.

One component of cognitive resource theory deals with the effects of stress. It is based on the assumption that leader intelligence and technical knowledge determine the quality of the leader's plans, decisions and action strategies, and that these, in turn, are affected by interpersonal stress. In contrast to job stress, which often focuses the individual's intellectual abilities on the task, interpersonal stress with a boss or subordinates cannot be dealt with intellectually. It distracts the leader from the task and, like examination anxiety (Sarason, 1984), channels his or her thinking into worry, concerns about self-efficacy, or how to evade the boss or the stress-producing situation. Under these stressful conditions, intellectual ability will not contribute to the task, and the leader will fall back on previously learned behavior. Hence, experience rather than intellectual abilities will correlate with performance. In other words, under low stress, leaders use their intelligence but not their experience; under high stress they use their experience but not their intelligence.

A second aspect of this problem was pointed out by Blades (1986; Blades and Fiedler, 1976). Namely, leader plans, decisions and action strategies are communicated principally in the form of directive behavior, and are implemented only if the group is supportive. On the other hand, member abilities contribute to the task primarily if the leader is nondirective and the group is supportive.

Support for the theory comes from studies of military and nonmilitary line and staff personnel at various levels of the organizational hierarchy, volunteer public health teams, and college students in laboratory experiments (Fiedler *et al.*, 1979; Potter and Fiedler, 1981; Fiedler and Garcia, 1987). These show that correlations between leader intelligence and group performance are near zero for the entire sample. However, the correlations for army mess stewards, squad leaders, volunteer public health workers and leaders in two sets of experiments, averaged 0.58 for supportive groups with directive leaders, but .19, .14 and −.18 for nonsupportive groups or those which had nondirective leaders. In groups divided on the basis of stress rather than group support, the corresponding mean correlations showed a similar pattern (.57, .07, .00, .03).

As one would expect, mean performance scores showed that the directive leaders of supportive groups performed substantially better if they were relatively bright; they performed poorly if they were relatively less intelligent. However, the nondirective leaders who were relatively bright performed considerably *less well* than did nondirective leaders who were relatively dull, especially in nonsupportive groups. In other words, bright leaders should be directive and tell group members what to do; the relatively less bright leaders should be participative and listen to others.

The interesting question is, of course, why the more intelligent leaders should perform less well than do those with lower intelligence under the given conditions (e.g. high stress, low group support, or being nondirective). This is an important problem since it means that the individual, selected for his or her intellectual abilities, in fact performs much less well than one who lacks these abilities.

Several alternative explanations appear plausible. First, the more intelligent leaders probably have higher expectations of themselves which might lead them to seek exotic and more risky solutions than would their less able and less imaginative counterparts. Second, the more intelligent leaders might be more conscious of the consequences of failure and hence also more anxious than those of less intelligence. Third, the bright leaders might well introduce many new and original ideas into the discussion but provide no direction for integrating the ideas and arriving at an acceptable solution.

The question also arises of why leaders use their experience but not their intelligence in stressful situations. Fiedler bases the interpretation on social faciliation theory (Zajonc, 1965) which predicts that a critical audience leads to better performance of overlearned and simple tasks but to poorer performance on new and complex tasks. The results make sense if we equate the stressful boss with a critical audience and experience with overlearned behavior.

Several recent laboratory experiments extend the theory. One dissertation by Blyth (1987) examined the conditions in which technical training of leaders and group members is effectively utilized. The task consisted of ranking various objects in order of their survival value to a crew that supposedly crashed in the desert. The rankings were then compared with those of experts.

In one study, Blyth randomly assigned leaders to four conditions: leaders were either trained or untrained in the potential use of various survival gear, and they were instructed either to be directive or nondirective in the management of their groups. As predicted, only the directive leaders with training had groups that performed well. Nondirective leaders with training performed no better than those without training. In a second study, Blyth (1987) trained only the group members, and instructed leaders to be directive or nondirective. In this experiment, the groups with nondirective leaders performed better than those with directive leaders.

McGuire (Fiedler and McGuire, 1987) used an in-basket exercise to study the effect of stress on the responses of leaders with high or low 'fluid' or 'crystallized' intelligence. Horn (1968) defined fluid intelligence as the ability to deal with new and unusual problems, and crystallized intelligence as the ability to solve problems on the basis of information previously learned or acquired through knowledge of the culture.

The in-basket exercise was performed either under relatively relaxed or under stressful conditions. The results showed that fluid intelligence correlated highly with responses indicating good judgement, effective problem analysis, and decisiveness when stress was low. However, under high stress, fluid intelligence correlated *negatively* with frequency and effectiveness of these leader behaviors.

Finally, the theory suggests a partial explanation for the Contingency Model of Leadership Effectiveness (Fiedler, 1964), since this model predicts not only performance but also directive leader behavior. The prediction is complex: Relationship-motivated leaders are directive if they have high situational control; task-motivated leaders are directive if they have moderate or low situational control (Sample and Wilson, 1965; Fiedler, 1970; Larson and Rowland, 1974; Shirakashi, 1980; Fiedler and Garcia, 1987). These interactions are quite strong in some cases, and have been found in a broad variety of group and organizational settings (see Fiedler and Garcia, 1987). The contingency model thus seems to predict when the leader is directive; cognitive resource theory specifies the conditions under which the leader's cognitive abilities will be most effectively used.

CRT has major implications for leader selection which should be of particular interest to industrial and organizational psychologists. Selection procedures typically are based on the assumption that a person will be effective in direct proportion to his or her job-relevant abilities and competence. Cognitive resource theory demonstrates that this assumption holds true only under limited conditions. Thus, selection will be substantially improved if the conditions obtain under which intelligence or experience is effectively utilized. CRT specifies these conditions. There have been many calls for leadership theories that combine situational and personality variables. Contingency theory and CRT provide one such combination, as well as preliminary supporting evidence.

The findings related to the effect of boss stress also are of significance to the practice of leadership since stress management, relaxation exercises and cognitive self-instruction methods provide means for alleviating stress. Thus, through the management of stress it is possible to increase the effective use of intelligence by leaders and, in Simon's (1976) terms, to relax one of the major 'limits to bounded rationality' in organizations.

Concluding Comments

Cognitive theories are becoming increasingly dominant in the leadership area as in psychology in general. Research based on attribution theory has contributed important new insights about factors that partly determine leader behavior and performance ratings. Cognitive resource theory provides a more general framework for integrating previous theories. It suggests the underlying basis for the predictions made by the contingency model, it identifies the role of such cognitive attributes as intellectual ability, experience, technical knowledge and training in determining organizational performance.

CHARISMATIC AND TRANSFORMATIONAL LEADERSHIP THEORIES

The theories reviewed in the first part of this chapter focus on the leader: how his or her cognitions affect behavior and performance. Charismatic and transformational leadership theories focus on the followers: their emotional responses to the leader. They ask how the leader affects the followers' work-related stimuli—their self-esteem, trust, values and confidence in the leaders, and their motivation to perform above and beyond the call of duty. These theories describe leaders in terms of articulating a vision and mission, and creating and maintaining a positive image in the minds of followers and superiors. At least in theory, these leaders challenge their followers and provide a personal example by behaving in a manner that reinforces the vision and the mission of the leader (see Berlew, 1974; House, 1977; Burns, 1978; Bennis and Nanus, 1985; Sashkin and Fulmer, 1985; and Bass 1985). Charismatic leaders have their major effect on the emotions and the self-esteem of followers, that is, on the followers' affective motivational responses rather than their cognitions and abilities.

At the risk of some oversimplification, transactional theories describe how leaders make work behavior more instrumental for the followers to reach their own *existing* goals while concurrently contributing to the goals of the organization. Charismatic or transformational theories primarily address the actions of leaders that cause subordinates to *change* their values, goals, needs and aspirations.

Smith (1982) showed, for example, that reputedly charismatic leaders have significantly different effects on followers than successful but non-charismatic leaders. Followers of charismatic leaders were more self-assured, saw more meaning in their work, reported more back-up from their leaders and saw them as more dynamic, reported working longer hours, and had higher performance ratings than the followers of the non-charismatic but effective leaders.

Howell (1985) compared the effects of charismatic leader behavior on followers with the effects of directive and considerate leader behavior under experimentally induced high and low productivity-norm conditions. The findings showed that charismatic leader behavior specified by prior theory (House, 1977) had a stronger and more positive influence on the performance, satisfaction and adjustment of followers than did directive and considerate leader behavior.

It is perhaps most interesting that only the charismatic leader behavior was able to overcome the negative effects of the low productivity norm condition. That is, regardless of whether the subjects were in the high or low productivity-norm condition, those working under charismatic leaders had higher general satisfaction, higher specific task satisfaction and less role conflict than individuals working under structuring or considerate leaders. Under the latter the negative effects of the low productivity norm treatment persisted.

House, Woycke and Fodor (1985) examined the behavior and motivation of US presidents. They asked nine political historians to classify US presidents as charismatic or non-charismatic with respect to their cabinet members. A charismatic leader was defined as one who induces a high degree of loyalty, commitment and devotion to the leader; identification with the leader and his mission, emulation of his values, goals and behavior; a sense of self-esteem from relationships with the leader and his mission; and an exceptionally high degree of trust in the leader and the correctness of his beliefs.

At least seven of the nine historians agreed on classifying six presidents as charismatic (Jefferson, Jackson, Lincoln, Theodore Roosevelt, Franklin D. Roosevelt and Kennedy) and six as non-charismatic (Tyler, Pierce, Buchanan, Arthur, Harding and Coolidge). Inaugural addresses of these presidents were coded for achievement, power and affiliation motives, using the major theme statements developed by Donley and Winter (1970).

All six charismatic presidents were either re-elected, or assassinated during their first term. Only one of the six non-charismatic presidents was re-elected. Content-analysed biographies of their cabinet members showed twice as many expressions of positive affect toward the charismatic than non-charismatic presidents ($p < .006$).

Political historians viewed charismatic presidents (Maranell, 1970) as engaging in significantly stronger actions, being more prestigious, active, flexible and having accomplished more in their administrations. Further, content-analysis of the inaugural addresses clearly demonstrated that charismatic presidents, as a group, were rated significantly higher on *both* the need for achievement and the need for power ($p < .03$). This finding is consistent with longitudinal field research by McClelland and Boyatzis (1982), and laboratory research by Fodor (personal communication, 1987). (President Reagan also has the same motive pattern as the charismatic presidents identified by the expert panel but was not categorized by the expert panel as he had just gained office at the time of the study.)

McClelland and Boyatzis (1982) found that managers with a combination of high need for achievement and high need for power had significantly higher levels of advancement eight and sixteen years later. Fodor (personal communication, 1987) found this same motive pattern on the part of group leaders to be predictive of group decision quality in an experimental decision-making simulation in which college students were subjects. Thus, the high achievement/high power motive pattern appears to have wide generalizability across such diverse samples as US presidents (House et al., 1986), middle managers (McClelland and Boyatzis, 1984) and college undergraduate students (Fodor, personal communication). Correlational studies, as well as predictive studies, have yielded results consistent with the above findings (Cummin, 1967; Wainer and Rubin, 1969; Varga, 1975; McClelland and Burnham, 1976).

Another empirical study relevant to charismatic theory is presented by Yukl and Van Fleet (1982). These authors found in four separate military samples that 'inspirational leadership' was significantly related to leader effectiveness and high levels of follower motivation. These findings held under combat, noncombat and similated combat conditions. Thus, studies of charismatic (or inspirational) leaders demonstrated that the behaviors specified by prior theory (House, 1977) rather consistently have the effects predicted by that theory.

A second theory of the same genre is the transformational leadership theory advanced by James MacGregor Burns (1978). Burns defines transactional leadership as based on a bargain, struck by both parties to the transaction. Transactional leaders induce followers to behave in ways desired by the leader, in exchange for some good desired by the follower. Such relationships usually endure only as long as the mutual need of the leader and follower can be satisfied by continuing exchanges of goods for services. This exchange of goods is usually specific, tangible and calculable. Hollander's (1958) concept of idiosyncracy points; Vertical Dyadic Linkage Theory (Graen and Scandura, 1984) and Path–Goal Theory of Leadership (House and Mitchell, 1974) fit the Burns' definition of transactional theories of leadership.

Bass (1985) and Avolio and Bass (1985) argue that transactional skills are necessary but not sufficient for transformational leadership. According to Burns (1978), transformational leadership occurs 'when one or more persons *engage* with others in such a way that leaders and followers raise one another to higher levels of motivation and morality' (p. 20; emphasis original). Accordingly, transformational leaders address themselves to their followers' 'wants, needs, and other motivations, as well as their own and, thus, they serve as an independent force in changing the make-up of followers' motive base through gratifying their motives' (ibid.).

Burns (1978) argues that transformational leadership in its most effective form appeals to the higher, more general, and more comprehensive values that express the followers' fundamental and enduring needs: equality, freedom, a world of beauty, and the instrumental value of self-control. Bass and his associates have conducted a substantial amount of research testing hypotheses devised from Burns' theory of transformational leadership.

Bass (1985) found that managers who were seen by their followers as transformational could be characterized by three behavioral dimensions. The first dimension or factor, accounting for 66 per cent of the response variance, reflects the behaviors and effects as hypothesized by House's (1977) theory of charismatic leadership. This factor is concerned with faith in the leader, respect for the leader, and inspiration and encouragement provided by his or her presence. The remaining two dimensions were individualized consideration and intellectual stimulation, accounting for 6.0 per cent and 6.3 per cent of the response variance respectively. Two other factors consistently associated with transactional leadership were management by exception and contingent reward, accounting for 3.1 per cent and 7.2 per cent of the response variance respectively. These scales developed by Bass are collectively referred to as the Multifactor Leadership Questionnaire.

A number of studies have been conducted by Bass and his associates using the Multifactor Leadership Questionnaire. Managers who are rated by subordinates as high on the three transformational scales were compared to random samples of managers who are low on these three scales, and to those who are rated high on the transactional scales but low on the transformational scales. Those rated as transformational received higher ratings by superiors for performance, promotability, and ability to manage (Bass, 1985; Hater and Bass, 1986). Transformational leaders are more frequently classified as 'great or world class leaders' (Bass, 1985) by biographers and historians (although there is some question about the cause–effect relationship). Transformational leaders also have higher performing teams in a management simulation exercies. Furthermore, these leaders take greater strategic risks in the same management simulation (Avolio and Bass, 1985) and their subordinates report greater satisfaction and more or 'extra' work effort (Bass, 1985; Hater and Bass, 1986; Pereira, 1986), as well as having subordinates who, themselves, demonstrate transformational leader behaviors (Bass et al., 1986).

These findings are impressive because they have occurred in India as well as in the United States (Pereira, 1986), and because the correlations between transformational leader behavior, followers' peformance and satisfaction are significantly higher under transformational than transactional leaders. Finally, the correlations between transformational leader behaviors and ratings by followers and superiors are consistently above .5 and often as high as .7.

Conclusions: Charismatic and Transformational Leadership

Empirical studies lend support to the charismatic and transformational theories. Leaders who manifest charismatic or transformational behaviors produce the predicted charismatic effects and are viewed as more effective by their superiors and followers than transactional leaders. Further, the correlations between follower satisfaction and performance are consistently high compared with prior field study findings concerning leader behavior.

SOME REFLECTIONS ON THE STATE OF LEADERSHIP THEORY

It seems fashionable in some quarters to assert that the term 'leadership' has lost its meaning and that leadership research is all just so much dross. Thus, Calder (1977) doubts that 'the accumulation of research is really leading anywhere' and proposes that 'leadership is not a viable scientific construct'—a sentiment previously also voiced by Miner (1975) and Perrow (1972). And in the first chapter of the leadership symposia edited by Hunt *et al.* (1984), Quinn, (1984, p. 10) laments that 'Despite an immense investment in the enterprise, researchers have become increasingly disenchanted with the field [of leadership]'.

What is the basis for all this gloom? *Stogdill's Handbook of Leadership* (Bass, 1981) referenced about 5000 items in the bibliography, and Bass (personal communication, 1987) estimates that about 7000–10 000 bibliographic reference items might legitimately be included in the forthcoming version of the *Handbook*. And while not all of these items are world-shakers, a substantial number will be more than respectable. This volume of research does not indicate disenchantment with the field nor does it represent compelling evidence that we should stop talking about leadership.

The more specific critiques are equally unconvincing. To take but one example, Tsui (1984, pp. 28–9) prounounces that the 'literature on managerial effectiveness is as much in a state of dismay as the literature on leadership effectiveness' because:

> Existing theories and research have concentrated on the personal character
> istics of the managers..., The lack of attention to these environmental
> determinants is a major problem that has retarded progress in both
> leadership and managerial effectiveness research.

What has Tsui been reading? According to Kerr's (1984) survey of manage-ment texts, the most frequently cited theories are: the contingency model, Path–Goal Theory, Normative Decision Theory, Vertical Dyad Linkage Theory and Substitutes for Leadership. Not one of these ignores environmental deter-minants.

Another example of this kind is McCall and Lombardo's (1978, p. 3) scathing criticism of the field which states at one point that:

> Students of leadership—academics and practitioners alike—have no doubt
> discovered three things: (1) the number of unintegrated theories, prescrip-
> tions, and conceptual schemes of leadership is mind-boggling; (2) much of
> the leadership literature is fragmentary and trivial, unrealistic and dull; and
> (3) the research results are characterized by Type III errors (solving the
> wrong problems precisely) and by contradictions.

We have not discovered these supposed verities. There are today less than a dozen empirically-based theories that are taken seriously (e.g. Kerr, 1984), and we doubt that the area of leadership has a corner on trivial studies. Whether one considers other people's papers dull obviously is a matter of taste.

We share McCall and Lombardo's concern for realism, but have some reservations about the realism to be found in the six-hour management game on which McCall and Lombardo base most of their conclusions. This management simulation, called, Looking Glass, has twenty participating executives play at running a simulated glass manufacturing company. Is this real life? At this point we do not even know the reliability of management games. We know even less about how well behavior and performance in a management game would predict behavior and performance of a manager two or three years down the road.

In trying to support their claim that bottom-line criteria of leadership effectiveness are mostly worthless, McCall and Lombardo cite Pfeffer and Salancik's (1978) finding that individual mayors accounted for less than 10 per cent of the variance in leadership performance, and Simonton's (1979) statement that Napoleon accounted for 'only 15 per cent of the variance in French military success' (p. 85).

First of all, most generals and managers (not to mention football coaches) would give their eye teeth for this extra 10 or 15 per cent of the variance. More to the point, there is considerable evidence from other studies that the leader contributes a great deal to the success or failure of an organization. One recent example comes from a carefully conducted study of the 200 trawlers in the Icelandic fishing fleet (Thorlindsson, 1987). These ships, which are 100–200 feet in length and typically carry a crew of eleven men, operate under almost identical conditions in a highly competitive environment. An analysis of a three-year period showed that the skipper accounted for 35–49 per cent of the variation in the catch. The best skippers remained at the top of this highly competitive occupation year after year, and that the correlation of catch by skipper were substantial over a three-year period (.59, .66 and .70), controlling for such variables as size of boat and number of days spent in fishing during the season. This and similar studies of leadership provide convincing empirical evidence that the leader represents a major factor in an organization's success.

Based on our reading of the field we cannot agree with the authors who describe most leadership research (save their own) as meaningless drivel. We also find many of the harsh condemnations hard to reconcile with much that we see in current books and journals. Could it be that the more vocal critics have been too disenchanted to read the literature? Bernard Bass, who certainly has read the leadership literature, strongly shares our opinion that these blanket criticisms are more hypberbole than sound scholarly evaluations of the field (personal communication, 1987).

Several viable and empirically supported theories have emerged, and there has been a notable complementarity and convergence among theories in recent years (e.g. Yukl, 1981). Contrary to Rauch and Behling (1984) and others, we believe that leadership research and theory have had a significant impact on leadership development and managerial selection although the research does not provide one-minute answers to the many complex problems the field presents.

Several theories and research programs (e.g. on assessment centers, transformational leadership, goal-setting, behavior modeling) show that the field is far from facing imminent death. Moreover, two sets of meta-analyses have been reported which deal with the validity of leadership theories (happily our own!), and we briefly report their results as further evidence that obituaries of leadership theory are premature.

The Contingency Model

This theory postulates two main types of personality attributes important to leadership performance. These attributes are the primary motivation to accomplish assigned tasks or the motivation to develop and maintain close relations with others. The situational component of the theory is the degree to which the leadership situation provides control, power and influence. The theory states that the effectiveness of a leader or an organization is contingent on the match between the leader's task or relationship motivation and the degree to which the situation gives the leader control and influence. Task-motivated (low LPC) leaders perform best in situations of very high or relatively low control; relationship-motivated leaders (high LPC) perform best in situations of moderate control. (For a recent summary see Fiedler and Garcia, 1987).

Based on a review of the literature, *Psychological Abstracts* and the *Social Science Citation Index*, Strube and Garcia (1981) located 33 tests on which the model was based, and 145 subsequent tests of the validity of the model. They defined a test as a statistical analysis within any of the eight octants (i.e. degrees of situational control). A meta-analysis of these data, using Rosenthal's (1978; 1979) technique, overwhelmingly supported the validity of the basic hypothesis. Strube and Garcia report a combined probability of all octant-bound studies of 1.71×10^{-23}. For studies which could only be classified as having high, moderate or low situational control, they reported a combined probability of 1.58×10^{-6}.

A less extensive meta-analysis by Peters, Hartke and Pohlman (1985), using the Schmidt and Hunter method (1977), presents a more guarded endorsement, again noting (as did Strube and Garcia) that the theory does not predict results for Octant II. However, the authors concur with Strube and Garcia 'in concluding that considerable evidence exists in support of the Contingency Theory'.

Path–Goal Theory

This theory, based on early work by Evans (1970), was developed by House (1971) and extended by House and Mitchell (1974). It postulates that effective leader behavior facilitates the attainment of the followers' desires, contingent on effective performance. The leader's role is 'instrumental' in enabling followers to achieve their desires. The leader does this by (a) identifying the personal goals of each follower, (b) establishing a reward system that makes such goals contingent on effective performance, and (c) assisting followers in achieving effective performance. Thus, according to this theory, followers and leaders enter into a transaction of performance for rewards.

Some of the specific leader behaviors that are instrumental to follower's goal attainment are (a) providing support for followers, (b) alleviating boredom and frustration with work, especially in time of stress, (c) providing direction, and

(d) fostering follower expectations that effort will lead to successful task accomplishment. The leader uses rewards and punishment contingent on the followers' compliance with the leaders' directions and the followers' level of performance.

According to the theory, it is the role of the leader to complement that which 'is missing' to enhance follower motivation, satisfaction and performance. What is 'missing' is determined by the environment, the task, the competence and the motivation of followers. It is also the role of the leader to enhance follower competence by coaching and support.

A recent meta-analysis of 48 studies designed to test Path–Goal Theory has yielded very promising results. Indvik (1986) tested for the theoretically predicted moderator effects of situational variables on relationships between leader behavior, leader directiveness, participation and supportiveness, and followers' role clarity, satisfaction and performance.

The situational moderators tested were task structure, job level and organizational size. These three variables were considered sources of psychological structure for followers. The results supported most of the hypotheses proposed by the theory. Following is a brief summary of Indvik's findings.

Path-goal theory predicts that directive leader behavior positively influences the subordinate's affect level to the degree that structure is absent from the work environment. That is, when followers have ambiguous task demands and little policy and procedural guidance, directive leader behavior will provide guidance and reduce role ambiguity. This hypothesis was supported with respect to intrinsic and overall satisfaction, and with satisfaction with the superior, but not with role clarity. A related path–goal hypothesis predicts that directive leader behavior improves performance regardless of the level of work environment (when environmental structure is low, directive leader behavior enhances performance by increasing role clarity; when environmental structure is high, directive leader behavior prevents low motivation from decreasing performance). Although as predicted, performance was enhanced by directive leader behavior when task structure was high, the effect was minimal when task structure was low, contrary to the hypothesis.

The path–goal hypothesis for supportive leader behavior predicts that leader support enhances subordinate affect and behavior to the degree that the work environment is structured. This hypothesis was supported for intrinsic, extrinsic and overall satisfaction, performance and role clarity.

Path–goal theory also predicts that participative leader behavior will be most effective under conditions where the followers' tasks are unstructured and when subordinates have a preference for internal structure. When both of these variables are high, it is hypothesized that participative leader behavior will enhance subordinate affect and behavior. The only test of the moderating effect of task structure on the relationship between participative leader behavior and criterion variables that could be made concerned overall satisfaction. As predicted, task structure negatively moderated this relationship as predicted.

Indvik considered job level as a surrogate for task structure, and organizational size as a surrogate for organizational formalization. Consistent with the theory, the relationship between leader behaviors and criterion variables were moderated by organizational level and organizational size. Further, in the moderated groups which were predicted to show positive relationships between leader behaviors and criteria, the correlations were generally in the .3 to .5 range. While the direction and statistical significance of relationships were largely as predicted, the number of studies considered to test any specific prediction was small, ranging from 2 to 11, depending upon the specific predictions tested. We are not aware of any other meta-analyses of leadership theories at this time. We confidently expect, however, that meta-analyses supporting other theories will begin to appear in the course of the next few years.

Management Training

How seriously should we take Argyris's pronouncement (cited in Rauch and Behling, 1984) that 'the additivity of the findings [on leadership] is limited and...their implications for the central problems of leaders are minimal'? In other words, to what extent has work in the leadership area produced tangible results in managerial training and selection?

A meta-analysis of management training programs by Burke and Day (1986) speaks to this point. First, most of the 64 studies included in the Burke and Day meta-analyses indicated changes in ratings by self or others of leader behaviors or attitudes, or interpersonal values. Only 15 of the reported studies used performance ratings by supervisors or advancement in the company as criteria. On the basis of the latter, the authors conclude that lecture training methods have been effective, as well as singling out two management training methods, both based on leadership theory. They go on to say:

> The results [of the meta-analyses] suggest that the Leader Match training method [Fiedler and Chemers, 1984] with respect to subjective behavior criteria [i.e. superiors' ratings] generalizes across situations. On the basis of these results as well as cost-effectiveness of Leader Match training compared with that of other leadership training programs, this method of leadership training is encouraged... "The effectiveness of managerial behavioral modeling training with respect to subjective behavior criteria was also shown to generalize across settings. This finding is consistent with the impressive empirical support for social learning theory obtained from well-controlled studies in experimental situations (cf. Bandura, 1977), as well as previous findings in organizational settings (cf. Burnaska, 1976; Byham, Adams and Kiggins, 1976; Latham and Saari, 1979; Smith, 1979). The magnitude of the estimated true mean effect for behavioral modeling provides an indication of how useful this method of managerial training is likely to be in improving managerial behaviors.

The conclusions by Burke and Day speak for themselves. In addition, we point to the work on motivation by Locke and Latham (1984), McClelland (1985) and Miner (1978) which provides not only a contribution to our understanding of leadership phenomena, but also to the practice of leadership training. Several other applications of leadership research to management (e.g. on assessment centers, goal-setting) also have been extensively validated.

There is little doubt that leadership research has resulted in an accumulation of substantial knowledge and that we are well beyond the slough of despair in which some of our colleagues seem to wallow with such gusto. Moreover, a wholesale condemnation of all research that preceded the author's own particular study raises a natural expectation that the remainder of the chapter will now resolve the dire problems that beset the field. These expectations are rarely fulfilled. We therefore urge our disenchanted colleagues to moderate their sweeping denunciations unless they are prepared either to document their claims that the leadership field is a disaster area, or to provide an empirically supported remedy for the problems that lead to their utter despair. For the sake of the record, we list some well-established conclusions about leadership which have come to light since 1936 and constitute important contributions to our knowledge.

Some Solid Contributions of Leadership Research

1. The field has identified two major categories of leader behavior, one concerned with interpersonal relations (e.g. consideration), the other with task-accomplishment (e.g. structuring). While there are questions about substructures of the various scales, questions of halo effect and attribution, there is solid evidence that leaders are judged on these two aspects of behavior by their subordinates, (Misumi, 1985).

2. There is no one ideal leader personality. However, effective leaders tend to have a high need to influence others, to achieve, and they tend to be bright, competent and socially adept, rather than stupid, incompetent and social disasters.

3. Leader–follower relations affect the performance, satisfaction, motivation, self-esteem and well-being of followers. Therefore, the study of leadership is of substantial social, as well as organizational significance.

4. We know that different situations require different leader behaviors. These are the behaviors required to compensate for deficiencies in the followers' environment and abilities. Whether these behaviors can be called out at will is a question in dispute. There are no behaviors exclusively manifested by leaders. For example, Megargee, Bogart and Anderson (1966) showed that pro-social assertiveness is aroused by salient factors related to the leader's control and influence; McClelland (1985) and his associates have consistently shown that social cues arouse needs for achievement and power. Fiedler's (1987) research shows that intellectual abilities are effectively used only if the leader is not under stress, is directive, and has the support of group members.

5. Attributions play a substantial part in the leadership process. As in any other human interaction, the motivations attributed by leaders to group members in judging their behavior and performance determine in large part how leaders behave toward them (Mitchell and Wood, 1980).

6. Intellectual abilities and experience contribute highly to performance only under selected conditions. Research is very clear in showing that experience correlates with performance only under conditions of stress while intelligence tends to correlate with performance only when stress experienced by the leader is relatively low. Whether leader intelligence or experience is required is determined by the task and the environment.

7. Charismatic or transformational leadership is not a mysterious process,

but the result of such clearly identifiable behaviors as the articulation of transcendent goals, demonstration of strong self-confidence and confidence in others, setting a personal example for followers, showing high expectations for followers' performance, and the ability to communicate one's faith in one's goals.

8. We have considerable evidence in support of several leadership theories. While the details and specific interpretations of measures may be in dispute, and some of the initial theoretical propositions have been rejected, there can be little question that many of their principles are supported empirically. We would consider among the more prominent to be, roughly in order of date of publication, Fiedler's contingency model (1964), McClelland's need-achievement theory (1961), House's (1971) path–goal theory, Vroom and Yetton's (1973) theory of leader decision-making, Graen's (Graen and Cashman, 1975) vertical dyad linkage theory, Misumi's (1985) PM theory, as well as the more recent charismatic and transformational theories of leadership (House, 1977; Bass, 1985).

9. Several leadership training methods have been subjected to a rigorous evaluations. These include behavior modeling (Goldstein and Sorcher, 1974), leader match training (Fiedler and Chemers, 1984), motivation training (McClelland, 1985; Miner, 1978), and goal-setting (Locke, 1968; Latham and Saari, 1979).

The above list is illustrative rather than inclusive. We do not yet have a single overarching theory of leadership, and we are not likely to achieve one for some years. The same can, of course, also be said of theories of depression, motivation, schizophrenia, microbiology, tectonic plates, and the origin of the common cold, to mention but a few.

All this is to be expected in a field which is complex and challenging. It is not a place for those who are impatient to have quick solutions and final answers. Our current theories are not what they are likely to be in another 50 or 100 years; but 50 or 100 years ago our theories were not what they are today. The nine contributions to our knowledge of leadership we listed are ample evidence that our understanding of leadership phenomena continues to progress at a respectable rate. A considerable amount of work still remains to be done, and we hope that this happy state of affairs will continue.

ACKNOWLEDGMENTS

We would wish to express our thanks to Sarah Lehman for critically reading the manuscript as well as for her editorial assistance.

REFERENCES

Avolio, B. and Bass, B. M. (1985) Charisma and beyond. Paper presented at the Academy of Management, San Diego.

Bandura, A. (1977) *Social Learning Theory*. Englewood Cliffs, N.J.: Prentice-Hall.

Bass, B. M. (1981) *Stogdill's Handbook of Leadership*. New York: The Free Press.

Bass, B. M. (1985) *Leadership and Performance: Beyond Expectations*. New York: The Free Press.

Bass, B. M., Waldman, D. A., Avolio, B. J. and Bebb, M. (1987) Transformational leadership and the falling dominoes effect. *Group and Organization Studies*, **12** (1), 73–87.

Bennis, W. and Nanus, B. (1985) *Leaders: The Strategies for Taking Charge*. New York: Harper and Row.

Berlew, D. E. (1974) Leadership and organizational excitement. In D. A. Kolb, I. M. Rubin and J. M. Mcintyre (eds), *Organizational Psychology*, Englewood Cliffs, N.J.: Prentice-Hall.

Blades, J. W. (1976) The influence of intelligence, task ability, and motivation on group performance. Unpublished doctoral dissertation, University of Washington, Seattle.

Blades, J. W. (1986) *Rules for Leadership*. Washington, D.C.: National Defense University Press.

Blades, J. W. and Fiedler, F. E. (1976) *The Influence of Intelligence, Task Ability, and Motivation on Group Performance*, (Organizational Research Tech. Rep. No. 76–78) University of Washington, Seattle.

Blyth, D. E. (1987) Leader and subordinate expertise as moderators of the relationship between directive leader behavior and performance. Unpublished doctoral dissertation, University of Washington, Seattle.

Bowers, D. G. and Seashore, S. E. (1966) Predicting organizational effectiveness with a four-factor theory of leadership. *Administrative Science Quarterly*, **11**, 238–263.

Burke, M. J. and Day, R. R. (1986) A cumulative study of the effectiveness of managerial training. *Journal of Applied Psychology*, **71**, 232–245.

Burns, J. M. (1978) *Leadership*. New York: Harper and Row.

Byham, W. C., Adams, D. and Kiggins, A. (1976) Transfer of modeling training to the job. *Personnel Psychology*, **29**, 345–349.

Calder, B. (1977) An attribution theory of leadership. In B. H. Staw and G. R. Salancik (eds), *New Directions in Organizational Behavior*. Chicago: St Clair Press.

Carlyle, T. Lecture on heroes, hero worship and the heroic in history. P. C. Parr (ed.) (1910) Clarendon Press, Oxford. [Weber, M. (1917), *Gesammelte Aufsätze der Religionssoziologie*, Vol. 3, J. C. B. Mohr, Tübingen.]

Cummin, P. (1967) TAT correlates of executive performance, *Journal of Applied Psychology*, **51**, 78–81.

Donley, R. E. and Winter, D. G. (1970) Measuring the motives of public officials at a distance; an exploratory study. *Behavioral Science*, **15**, 227–236.

Epstein, S. (1975) Stability of behavior: On predicting most of the people much of the time. *Journal of Personality and Social Psychology*, **37**, 1097–1126.

Evans, M. G. (1970) The effects of supervisory behavior on the path–goal relationship. *Organizational Behavior and Human Performance*, **5**, 277–298.

Fiedler, F. E. (1964) A contingency model of leadership effectiveness. In L. Berkowitz (ed.) *Advances in Experimental Social Psychology*, Vol. 1, New York: Academic Press.

Fiedler, F. E. (1967) *A Theory of Leadership Effectiveness*. New York: McGraw-Hill.

Fiedler, F. E. (1970) Leadership experience and leader performance – another hypothesis shot to hell. *Organizational Behavior and Human Performance*, **5**, 1–14.

Fiedler, F. E. (1978) The contingency model and the dynamice of the leadership process. In L. Berkowitz (ed.) *Advances in Experimental Social Psychology*, **11**, New York: Academic Press.

Fiedler, F. E. (1986) The contribution of cognitive resources and behavior to organizational performance. *Journal of Applied Social Psychology*, **16** (6), 532–548.

Fiedler, F. E. (1987) The contribution of cognitive resources to organizational performance. In C. F. Graumann and S. Moscovici (eds), *Changing Conceptions of Leadership*. New York: Springer-Verlag.

Fiedler, F. E. and Chemers, M. M. (1984) *Improving Leadership Effectiveness: The Leader Match Concept*, 2nd edition. New York: John Wiley.

Fiedler, F. E. and Garcia, J. E. (1987) *New Approaches to Effective Leadership: Cognitive Resources and Organizational Performance*. New York: John Wiley.

Fiedler, F. E. and McGuire, M. A. (1987) *Proceedings of the Third Army Leadership Conference*. Kansas City.

Fiedler, F. E., Potter, E. H. III, Zais, M. M. and Knowlton, W. A. Jr (1979) Organizational stress and the use and misuse of managerial intelligence and experience, *Journal of Applied Psychology*, **64**, 635–647.

Foti, R. J., Fraser, S. L. and Lord, R. G. (1982) Effects of leadership labels and prototypes on perceptions of political leaders. *Journal of Applied Psychology*, **67**, 326–333.

Goldstein, A. P. and Sorcher, M. (1974) *Changing Supervisory Behavior*. New York: Pergamon.

Graen, G. and Cashman, J. F. (1975) A role-making model of leadership in formal organizations: A developmental approach. In J. G. Hunt and L. L. Larson (eds) *Leadership Frontiers*. Carbondale: Southern Illinois University Press.

Graen, G. B. and Scandura, T. A. (1986) Toward a psychology of dyadic organizing. In B. M. Staw and L. L. Cummings (eds) *Research in Organizational Behavior*. Greenwich, CT: JAI Press.

Hater, J. J. and Bass, B. M. (1986) Superiors' evaluations of subordinates' perceptions of transformational and transactional leadership. Working paper, State University of New York: Binghamton.

Hollander, E. P. (1958) Conformity, status and idiosyncrasy credit. *Psychological Review*, **65**, 117–127.

Hollander, E. P. (1978) *Leadership Dynamics: A Practical Guide to Effective Relationships*. New York: The Free Press.

Horn, J. L. (1968) Organization of abilities and the development of intelligence. *Psychological Review*, **75**, 242–259.

House, R. J. (1971) Path–goal theory of leader effectiveness. *Administrative Science Quarterly*, **16**, 321–338.

House, R. J. (1977) A 1976 theory of charismatic leadership. In J. G. Hunt and L. L. Larson (eds) *Leadership: The Cutting Edge*. Carbondale, Ill.; Southern Illinois University Press.

House, R. J. and Mitchell, T. R. (1974) Path–goal theory of leadership. *Journal of Contemporary Business*. **3**, 81–97.

House, R. J., Woyke, J. and Fodor, E. (1986) Research contrasting the motives and effects of reputed charismatic versus reputed non-charismatic U.S. Presidents. Presented at the Academy of Management, San Diego.

Howell, J. M. (1985) A laboratory study of charismatic leadership. Working paper, the University of Western Ontario.

Hunt, J. G. and Larson, L. L. (1984) *Leadership: The Cutting Edge*. Carbondale, Ill.: Southern Illinois University Press.

Hunt, J. G., Sekaran, U. and Schriesheim, C. A. (eds) (1981) *Leadership: Beyond Establishment Views*. Carbondale, Ill.: Southern Illinois University Press.

Indvik, J. (1986) Path–goal theory of leadership: A meta-analyses. *Proceedings*. Academy of Management, Chicago.

Jones, E. E. (1985) Major developments in social psychology during the past five decades. In G. Lindzey and E. Aronson (eds) *Handbook of Social Psychology*. New York: Random House, 47–108.

Katz, D. and Kahn, R. L. (1966) *The Social Psychology of Organizations*. New York: John Wiley.

Kerr, S. (1984) Leadership and participation. In A. Brief (ed.) *Research on Productivity*. New York: Praeger.

Larson, L. L. and Rowland, K. M. (1973) Leadership style, stress, and behavior in task performance. *Organizational Behavior and Human Performance*, **9**, 407–420.

Latham, G. P. and Saari, L.M. (1979) Application of social learning theory to training supervisors through behavioral modeling. *Journal of Applied Psychology*, **64**, 239–246.

Locke, E. A. (1968) Toward a theory of task motivation and incentives. *Organizational Behavior and Human Performance*, 3 157–189.

Locke, E. A. and Latham, G. P. (1984) *Goal Setting: A Motivational Technique that Works!* Englewood Cliffs, N.J.: Prentice-Hall.

Lord, R. G. (1985) An information processing approach to social perceptions, leadership, and behavioral measurement in organizations. In L. L. Cummings and B. M. Staw (eds) *Research in Organizational Behavior*, 7. Greenwich, CT.: JAI Press.

Maranell, G. M. (1970) The evaluation of presidents: An extension of the Schlesinger Polls. *Journal of American History*, 57, 104–113.

McCall, M. W. Jr and Lombardo, M. (eds) (1978) *Leadership: Where Else Can We Go?* Durham, N.C.: Duke University Press.

McClelland, D. (1961) *The Achieving Society*. Princeton, N.J.: Van Nostrand.

McClelland, D. (1985) *Human Motivation*. Glenview, Il: Scott, Foresman.

McClelland, D. C. and Boyatzis, R. E. (1982) Leadership motive pattern and long term success in management. *Journal of Applied Psychology*, **67**, 737–43.

McClelland, D. C. and Burnham, D. H. (1976) Power is the great motivator. *Harvard Business Review*, **54** (2), 100–110.

Megargee, E. I., Bogart, P. and Anderson, B. J. (1966) Prediction of leadership in a simulated industrial task. *Journal of Applied Psychology*, **50**, 292–295.

Miner, J. B. (1975) *The Uncertain Future of the Leadership Concept: An overview. Third Leadership Symposium*, at Southern Illinois University. Carbondale, Ill.: Southern Illinois University Press.

Miner, J. B. (1978) Twenty years of research on role-motivation theory of managerial effectiveness. *Personnel Psychology*, **31**, 739–760.

Misumi, J. (1985) *The Behavioral Science of Leadership: An Interdisciplinary Japanese Research Program*. Ann Arbor: University of Michigan Press.

Mitchell, T. R. and Wood, R. E. (1980) Supervisors' responses to subordinates' poor performance: A test of the attributional model. *Organizational Behavior and Human Performance*, **25**, 123–138.

Mitchell, T. R., Green, S. G. and Wood, R. E. (1981) An attributional model of leadership and the poor-performing subordinate: development and validation. In B. Shaw and L. Cummings. (eds) *Research in Organizational Behavior*, 3. Greenwich, CT.: JAI Press.

Pereira, D. F. (1987) *Factors Associated with Transformational Leadership in an Indian Engineering Firm*. Administrative Sciences Association of Canada, Toronto.

Perrow, C. (1972) *Complex organizations: A critical essay*. Glenview, Ill.: Scott, Foresman.

Peters, L. H., Hartke, D. D. and Pohlmann, J. T. (1985) Fiedler's contingency theory of leadership: An application of the meta-analysis procedures of Schmidt and Hunter. *Psychological Bulltein*, **97**, 274–285.

Pfeffer, J. and Salancik, G. R. (1978) *The External Control of Organizations*. New York: Harper and Row.

Phillips, J. S. and Lord, R. G. (1981) Causal attributions and perceptions of leadership. *Organizational Behavior and Human Performance*, **28**, 143–163.

Potter, E. H. and Fiedler, F. E. (1981) The utilization of staff member intelligence and experience under high and low stress. *Academy of Management Journal*, 24 (2), 361–376.

Quinn, R. E. (1984) Applying the competing values approach to leadership: Toward an integrative framework. In J. G. Hunt, D. Hosking, C. A. Schrieshiem and R. Stewart (eds) *Leaders and Managers: International Perspectives on Managerial Behavior and Leadership*. New York: Pergamon Press.

Rauch, C. F., Jr and Behling, O. (1984) Functionalism: Basis for an alternate approach to the study of leadership. In J. G. Hunt, D. Hosking, C. A. Schriesheim and R. Stewart (eds) *Leaders and Managers: International Perspectives on Managerial Behavior and Leadership*. New York: Pergamon Press.

Rosenthal, R. (1978) Combining results of independent studies. *Psychological Bulletin*, 85 (1), 185–193.

Sample, J. A. and Wilson, T. R. (1965) Leader behavior, group productivity, and ratings of least-preferred co-worker. *Journal of Personality and Social Psychology*, 266–270.

Sarason, I. (1984) Stress, anxiety, and cognitive interference: reactions to tests. *Journal of Personality and Social Psychology*, **46**, 929–938.

Sashkin, M. and Fulmer, R. M. (1985) A new framework for leadership: Vision, charisma, and culture creation. Paper presented at Biennial Leadership Symposium at Texas Tech University.

Schmidt, F. L. and Hunter, J. E. (1977) Development of a general solution to the problem of validity generalization. *Journal of Applied Psychology*, **62**, 529–540.

Shirakashi, S. (1980) The interaction effects for behavior of least preferred coworker (LPC) score and group-task situations: a reanalysis. *The Commercial Review of Seinan Gakuin University*, **27** (2).

Simon, H. A. (1976) *Administrative Behavior*, 3rd edition. New York: The Free Press.

Simonton, D. K. (1979) Was Napolean a military genius? Score: Carlyle 1, Tolstoy 1. *Psychological Reports*, **44**, 21–22.

Sims, H. P., Jr and Gioia, D. A. (1986) *The Thinking Organization*. San Francisco: Jossey-Bass.

Smith, B. J. (1979) Management, modeling, training to improve morale and customer satisfaction. *Personnel Psychology*, **29**, 351–359.

Smith, B. J. (1982) An initial test to a theory of charismatic leadership based on the responses of subordinates.

Strube, M. J. and Garcia, J. E. (1981) A meta-analytical investigation of Fiedler's contingency model of leadership effectiveness. *Psychological Bulletin*, **90**, 307–321.

Terman, L. (1904) A preliminary study of the psychology and pedagogy of leadership. *Pedagogical Seminary*, **11**, 413–451.

Thorlindsson, T. (1987) *The skipper effect in the Icelandic herring fishing Reykavik*. University of Iceland

Tsui, A. S. (1984) Multiple-constituency framework of managerial reputational effectiveness. In J. G. Hunt, D. Hosking, C. A. Schriesheim and R. Stewart (eds) *Leaders and Managers: International Perspectives on Managerial Behavior and Leadership*. New York: Pergamon Press.

Varga, K. (1975) N achievement, n power and effectiveness of research development. *Human Relations*, **23**, 571–590.

Vroom, V. H. (1964) *Work and Motivation*. New York: McGraw-Hill.

Vroom, V. H. and Yetton, E. W. (1973) *Leadership and Decision Making*. Pittsburgh: University of Pittsburgh Press.

Wainer, H. A. and Rubin, I. M. (1969) Motivation of research and development entrepreneurs: Determinants of company success. *Journal of Applied Psychology*, **53** 178–184.

Weber, M. (1946) The sociology of charismatic authority. In H. H. Mills and C. W. Mills (eds and trans.) fr. Max Weber, *Essays in Sociology*. New York: Oxford University Press.

Yukl, G. A. (1981) *Leadership in Organizations*. Englewood Cliffs, N.J.: Prentice-Hall.

Yukl, G. A. and Van Fleet, D. D. (1982) Cross-situational multi-method research on military leader effectiveness. *Organizational Behavior and Human Performance*, **30**, 87–108.

Zajonc, R. B. (1965) Social facilitation. *Science*, **149** (3681), 269–274.

Chapter 4

JAPANESE MANAGEMENT—A SUN RISING IN THE WEST?[1]

Peter B. Smith
School of Social Sciences
University of Sussex
UK
and
Jyuji Misumi
Department of Social Psychology
Tchikushi Women's University
Japan

Japanese management methods have evoked steadily increasing interest in the West over the past few decades. The changing quality of that interest is reflected in the contrast between Abegglen's (1958) classic observations of Japanese factories, and the same author's more recent discussion of the evolving *kaisha* or Japanese corporation (Abegglen and Stalk, 1984). During this period Western commentators have moved from an interest in a phenomenon seen as strange and unusual, to a realization that the consequences of Japanese management are, and increasingly will be, felt throughout the world. There has also been a wide divergence of views as to whether the essence of Japanese management lies in its structures or within the processes or styles with which those structures are operated. In this chapter we shall take the view that structure and process are yin and yang—that we shall understand little about organizational behaviour if we do not take account of both structures and processes. Nonaka and Johansson (1985) lament the lack of emphasis upon 'hard' as well as 'soft' aspects of management in earlier reviews, and we aim to heed their advice. With passing time, increasing numbers of Japanese researchers are publishing their work in English as well as in Japanese, and a further aim is to ensure

[1]Thanks are due to the Japanese Ministry of Education Science and Culture, the British Council and the Unit for Comparative Research in Industrial Relations at the University of Sussex for grants to the first author which made possible the writing of this review, and to Toshio Sugiman, Toshihiro Kanai, and Tadao Kagono for comments and assistance.

that their work is as fully represented here as is that authored by non-Japanese. Finally, we aim to highlight and consider more fully in the concluding section, areas where the research findings do not support the conventionally accepted view as to the nature of Japanese management.

Research methods have also evolved over time with the early preponderance of case studies giving way to more systematic surveys and studies using comparative measures collected in several countries. The literature has grown to the point where this review cannot hope to be comprehensive within the space available. Emphasis will be given to studies focusing upon human resource management, while studies of methods of production, marketing, and research will only be considered where their implications for human resource management are evident.

Our review will first consider the various characterizations of Japanese management which have been advanced and how well founded they may be. Later sections will consider the evidence as to whether Japanese management is changing over time and what happens when Japanese plants open in other parts of the world. Finally, we shall consider whether the current successes of Japanese management hold lessons for us all or whether we must be content with some form of cultural relativism.

THE CLASSICAL DESCRIPTIONS OF JAPANESE MANAGEMENT

Keys and Miller (1984) propose that the distinctive qualities of Japanese management may be summarized under three heads: long-term planning, life-time employment, and collective responsibility. Hatvany and Pucik (1981) distinguish the development of an internal labour market, definition of a unique company philosophy and identity, and intensive socialization of organizational participants. We prefer to use four, although the boundaries between the elements in such classifications are diffuse. These will be termed *time perspective, collective orientation, seniority system,* and *influence processes.* In each of these areas one may discern organizational structures, policies, and procedures which are said to be distinctive.

Time Perspective

Abegglen and Stalk (1984) propose that the strategy of the Japanese *kaisha* is to assure its long-term survival through the preservation of market share and growth in size, rather than the goals more strongly favoured by Western firms such as short-term profitability and high share values. A recently completed large-scale survey comparing Japanese, US, and European firms supports this view (Nonaka and Okumura, 1984; Kagono, Nonaka, Sakakibara, and Okumura, 1985). Responses were received from a general sample of firms in manufacturing and mining. The highest priority stated by the 277 US and 50

European firms responding was return on investment, whereas the 291 Japanese firms ranked increased market share more highly. Abegglen and Stalk suggest that the ability of the *kaisha* to take a longer term view has been partly due to the absence of a substantial threat of takeover bids. However, they make clear that this absence should be considered as much a symptom as a cause of Japanese industry's long-term perspective. If the preoccupation of Japanese management is with planning a long-term strategy which ensures the survival of the firm's organization, issues such as disposal of resources which are underutilized or the acquisition of ailing organizations are a low priority. More important is the recruitment of a loyal and skilled workforce, investment in long-term research, and the identification of distinctive markets. The data of Kagono *et al.* (1985) again support these assertions. The Japanese firms in their sample reported spending proportionately more on research into new technologies and development of new products, whereas American firms put more into improving and updating existing products. Nonaka and Johansson (1985) see extensive information search more generally as a key attribute of Japanese organizational behaviour. By continual scanning of the environment a capacity is developed to anticipate long-term developments. Information search is not simply greater, but also involves the seeking out of different types of information. For instance, Johannsson and Nonaka (1987) describe Japanese scepticism of Western market research and preference for talking to retailers and observing customers instead.

An emphasis upon long-term planning is also evident within the production technologies first popularized within Japan. Examples are the *kanban* and other just-in-time procedures which have accomplished such enormous cost savings within the automobile and electronics industries (Schonberger, 1982; McMillan, 1985). These instances, like many other recent advances in production management, have benefited from the development of increasingly sophisticated computers. As such techniques have become widely known, they have proved increasingly attractive to managements of Western firms. It remains to be seen in what way Western firms will implement just-in-time procedures. The time may come when they will not be thought of as distinctive to Japanese management.

Another aspect of time perspective which has been widely commented upon is the system of lifetime employment. By assuring employees that once they have joined the organization they are guaranteed continuing employment, it is argued that Japanese firms ensure the loyalty and security of their workforce. Research studies suggest, however, that is by no means so widespread as was once believed. Oh (1976) estimated that no more than 30 per cent of the Japanese labour force work for the same firm throughout their career, while Cole (1979) showed that rather more Americans than Japanese continue to work for their first employer. There are a number of reasons why this may be so. Most large Japanese firms utilize numerous subcontractors, and these do not enjoy security in time of cutbacks. Indeed, Oh makes it clear that lifetime employment can be effective only because of the existence of such a dual labour market, whereby the risks of recession are borne by the subcontractors—70 per cent of the goods and services required for the manufacture of a Nissan car are represented by orders to subcontractors. In textile machinery the figure rises to 90 per cent (Clark, 1979). However, it is an oversimplification to represent the labour market as a dual one. There is no definite boundary between the large first-rank companies and the others, but rather a series of hierarchical gradations (Nakane, 1970), which we shall explore in a later section.

Several other factors also restrict the extensiveness of lifetime employment. Many of the women recruited by the major firms work for only a few years before marriage. In addition, the age of retirement in Japan was most usually 55, although there is currently some tendency for it to increase. Hazama (1978) showed that within three years of first employment, 73 per cent had left small firms, many of whom would be subcontractors, while only 38 per cent had left the larger firms. Lifetime employment should therefore be thought of as a process affecting predominantly male workers within the larger corporations. We should also note that the oft-cited low figures for unemployment in Japan are computed in a different manner to those from other countries. Taira (1983) has estimated that if the US system were used, rates of unemployment in Japan would be more than doubled.

A further point of contrast is that those who stay with one firm for long periods in the West may well have exercised some choice to do so. For a Japanese within the lifetime employment system this choice is effectively absent. Lifetime employment is sometimes written about as though it were simply a guarantee of a permanent job. In understanding the system it is important to bear in mind that in exchange the employee may be expected to accept loss of the very substantial pay bonuses which Japanese firms pay when they are profitable, to work extra unpaid hours or forgo holiday entitlements, to accept an actual salary cut, to transfer to an entirely new type of work or to be assigned to another company within a related 'family' of companies. Hazama gives data from a comparative survey of workers in Japan and Britain. Asked why they took their present job, the most frequent Japanese responses were firstly the stability of the company, and secondly that there was no other suitable job. In Britain, workers cited the lack of other suitable jobs, wages, working conditions, and other reasons pertaining to the company. For British workers the stability of the company ranked ninth. The bases upon which employees are committed to a Japanese organization are thus different from those which are most frequent in the West. This has implications for the valid study of job satisfaction, and we shall return to this theme in the next section. For the present we should note that for the Japanese employee as for his employer a longer time perspective than that found in the West predominates.

Although few observational studies of Japanese managers have yet been reported, it appears that this difference in time perspective is evident even in the structuring of daily activities. Doktor (1983) found that in his observation sample, 41 per cent of Japanese managers undertook tasks which took more than one hour to carry through, compared to only 10 per cent of American managers. Conversely, 49 per cent of Americans but only 18 per cent of Japanese undertook tasks of less than nine minutes. Given that most Western observational studies of managers have shown the average transaction to last no more than three or four minutes, Doktor's data show a remarkable contrast.

Collective Orientation

The collective nature of Japanese society has been frequently discussed (Nakane, 1973). Individualistic behaviour has traditionally been seen as selfish, and within family and school it is discouraged. The work organization provides the principal locus of adult male Japanese identity, and identification with one's immediate work group of peers and superior is frequently very intense (Dore, 1973; Clark, 1979). Comparative studies reveal that Japanese employees see work as more central in their lives than do employees in ten other countries (Meaning of Working International Research Team, 1987). This study showed that it is not simply the case that Japanese employees identify more with their work, but that they draw the boundaries between what is considered to be work related and what is not in different ways. Thus, many Japanese would expect to spend substantial periods of time eating or drinking with their work-mates after work and before going home. Atsumi (1979) found in his survey that 62 per cent of white-collar workers did this on two or more evenings per week. Among those from smaller firms only 26 per cent went out with their workmates that often. Employees are likely also to participate in company-organized sports, holidays, and outings. All of these activities would be under-taken in the absence of one's spouse or children. The bond between the employee and his organization and most especially his work group may thus take on some of the qualities of village life in traditional Japanese life. However, Atsumi cautions against the assumption that employees necessarily participate in all these activities simply for their own pleasure. The Japanese concept of *tsukiai* specifies one's obligation to develop and maintain harmonious relations with one's work colleagues. As Atsumi points out, the fact that employees in large firms engage in much more after-hours socializing than do those in small firms means that one cannot simply attribute the phenomenon to Japanese culture. Its meaning must lie in the culture of the large firms, the commitment they require, and the individual needs which are met by such informal contact. Further support for this view comes from the findings of the Meaning of Working International Research Team's (1987) findings. Asked to define the nature of work, Japanese were more likely than those from other countries to refer to concepts related to duty, which appeared in the Japanese version of the questionnaire as *gimu*.

Many large Japanese firms devote substantial resources to encouraging the collective commitment of their workforce. Matsushita, for instance, expects that all employees will participate each morning in singing the company song and reciting the employees' creed and seven spiritual values (Pascale and Athos, 1981). The values in question are: national service through industry, fairness, harmony and cooperation, struggle for betterment, courtesy and humility, adjustment and assimilation, and gratitude. Many other companies emphasize similar values, with most frequent emphasis upon the importance of *wa* or harmony. Commitment to the company is also fostered by extensive training programmes for new recruits, and by the fact that employees are not recruited to do a specific task but to share overall responsibility for the work of their team. Over time, those destined for senior positions are assigned to teams in each of the various functions within the organization, thus ensuring a generalist rather than a specialist view of the work to be done.

Loyalty to the firm is also fostered by a distinctive set of personnel policies. Pascale and Maguire (1980) compared policies in operation at ten Japanese plants with a matched sample of US plants. As one might expect, expenditure on social and recreational facilities per employee was more than twice as high in the Japanese companies. Pascale and Maguire also attempted to compare job rotation by comparing numbers of jobs per year of employee tenure. They found no difference, but this is most probably due to the tendency of Japanese firms not to label distinctive jobs as separate positions. Other widespread practices which encourage identification with the firm include the wearing of company uniforms and the provision of communal eating facilities. The existence of company unions rather than trade unions also aligns the interests of union and management more closely, and it is not infrequent for union officials to achieve management positions later in their career.

The concept of 'groupism' in Japanese management has been the subject of a number of Japanese-language books, some giving it a central role (Iwata, 1978), while others see it as one element among several (Tsuda, 1977; Urabe, 1978). In evaluating the function of groupism within Japanese organizations it is important to acknowledge a further Japanese distinction, that between *tatemae* and *honne*: *tatemae* refers to what might be considered ideal or correct concerning relations between two persons or groups. *Tatemae* will frequently derive from long-past events which have defined the state of relationships between the two groups in question; *honne* is what happens in practice. It is clear that the ideal values espoused by many Japanese organizations favour harmony and collective action within the organization. Detailed case studies by, for instance Dore (1973) in an electrical plant, Rohlen (1974) in a bank, and Clark (1979) in a corrugated board manufacturing company indicate that the *honne* or what actually occurs is more complex. Clark suggests that: 'perhaps one could say that in the West decision making is presented as individualistic until adversity proves it collective. In Japan it is presented as collective until it is worth someone's while to claim a decision as his own' (p. 130). In other words the basic assumption within a Western organization would be individualistic, until such time as it was desirable to share the blame around for some setback, whereas in a Japanese organization the basic assumption would be collective, unless there was some specific incentive for claiming a success as one's own. Hazama (1978) also compares the relation of the individual and the group in Japanese and Western work teams. He suggests that the difference parallels that between certain types of team sports. In baseball, for instance, the group's task is differentiated between a series of individually defined roles. Each individual's separate performance may be recorded and evaluated. A collective enterprise is carried through by a series of individualized performances, just as is the work of organizations in Western countries. In the tug-of-war, by contrast, a collective sport is undertaken which has no clear demarcation of individual roles. The team either wins or loses and no one knows which individuals contributed more or less to the result. Hazama points to the parallel between the way in which Japanese work groups do not have clearly differentiated work roles. All members are equally responsible for the success of the team's efforts.

There is substantial debate as to whether the collective orientation of Japanese primary work groups arises from the personal preferences of those who join them, or whether it is more true to say that what occurs is a matter of conformity to existing norms of harmony and solidarity. The existence of the concept of *tsukiai* provides an indication that, at the least, personal preference is enhanced by social obligation. Wagatsuma (1983) argues that commentators have certainly overstated the occurrence of harmony in Japanese society. There is clear evidence of conflict both within and between organizations. For instance Clark (1979), as part of his case study, scrutinized questionnaires which the company required employees to complete annually. He found no lack of criticisms and complaints, particularly from those who had subsequently resigned from the company. Thus the harmony of the work group may to some degree be sustained by a sense of obligation rather than by inherent pleasure in harmony. There are times at which it is acceptable for such obligations to be relaxed, such as after having a few drinks together, and criticisms made on such an occasion are treated as off the record. Leaving such occasions to one side, it is much more likely that conflict within an organization will be between teams rather than within them.

Considerations as to how far the behaviour of Japanese work team behaviour is a matter of choice or of obligation provide a vantage point from which to examine studies of the job satisfaction of Japanese employees. Western writers have usually expected that the joint impact of lifetime employment and involvement in the work group would ensure that Japanese workers were more satisfied than those in Western organizations. There are now a sufficient number of published findings reporting that, on the contrary, Japanese workers are *less* satisfied than Western workers that some explanation is required. The reported studies cover two decades of research and a variety of industries. During the 1960s, Odaka (1975) completed five studies in Japanese organizations varying from manufacturing to department stores and electricity companies. In all of these, less than half the respondents declared themselves satisfied with their work, which compares with substantially higher figures from most Western countries. Only in West Germany were lower figures reported. Around 1970, Cole (1979) compared work satisfaction of workers in Detroit and Yokohama. The Japanese were again substantially less satisfied. The more recent studies are based on large heterogeneous samples and have all repeated the same finding (Azumi and McMillan, 1976; Pascale and Maguire, 1980; Naoi and Schooler, 1985; Lincoln and Kalleberg, 1985). In the most extensive and recent of these studies, Lincoln and Kalleberg compared the job satisfaction of 4567 US employees drawn from 52 plants in Indiana with 3735 Japanese employees at 46 plants in Kanagawa prefecture. Four work satisfaction items were used and the Japanese scored lower on all items, in excess of one standard deviation on three of them. The largest difference was on the question 'Does this job measure up to your expectations?'

Several explanations are possible of lower Japanese job satisfaction. The most obvious possibility is that many Japanese work extremely long hours and do not find their pay adequate. A recent survey by Sohyo (the Japanese General Council of Trade Unions) reported that of a sample of 26 800 respondents, 76 per cent stated that they worked too hard. Asked what would be necessary for an improved lifestyle, 70 per cent cited wage increases and 62 per cent cited shorter working hours (Japan Times, 1988). Although no more than one worker in four belongs to a trade union in Japan, these figures are likely to be representative of frequent sources of discontent among non-unionized workers also. Kamata's (1983) descriptive account of shopfloor work at Toyota is consistent with this explanation. Lincoln and Kalleberg's data showed age to be much more strongly related to dissatisfaction in Japan than in America. This accords with the view that a major source of dissatisfaction in Japan is low wages among younger workers.

Cole (1970) proposes that Japanese workers are dissatisfied because they have higher aspirations for their job. High involvement and commitment lead to expectations which the organization cannot satisfy and which workers in the West would not look to their employer to satisfy. Support for this view comes from the fact that in the Lincoln and Kalleberg study the largest difference found was on the item referring to expectations.

There are difficulties in concluding that the difference in satisfaction is due to different levels of organizational commitment. Additional data in the Lincoln and Kalleberg (1985) study indicate that the Japanese sample also scored lower than the Americans on the six-item Porter Scale of Organizational Commitment. A further study by Luthans, McCaul, and Dodd (1985), using the same measure, showed that broad samples of Japanese and Korean employees both scored lower than Americans on the scale. Since both Lincoln and Kalleberg and Luthans *et al.* sampled a very wide range of organizations, their respondents will have included both those having lifetime employment with first-rank companies and those without job security—41 per cent of respondents in the Sohyo survey reported that their jobs were 'precarious'. The surprising findings obtained by these two studies may be accounted for by their confounding together those with lifetime employment and those without. An alternative possibility is that those who feel low commitment to US organizations feel freer to leave than do those in Japanese organizations. These two factors could also account for the lower Japanese job satisfaction found in the various other studies.

There is a third possible explanation of the reported differences which has to do with the difficulty of comparing mean scores on questionnaires which have been translated into different languages. While at least some of the studies under discussion used back-translation procedures to assure equivalence of meaning, one cannot control for differences in cultural norms. Japanese norms favour a modest presentation of self, while those in the United States encourage a more assertive presentation. It is quite possible that Japanese respondents would show lower mean scores than Americans on *any* self-descriptive questionnaire to which they were asked to respond. Buckley and Mirza (1985) cite a European Productivity Agency survey which showed that in 1980 only 50 per cent of Japanese described themselves as satisfied with life, compared to 89 per cent of Americans and 91 per cent of British. Lincoln, Hanada, and Olson (1981) studied Japanese-owned plants in the United States and found that Japanese-Americans employed there were less satisfied than Americans *in the same plants*. Of the explanations discussed here only the response bias explanation can account for this last finding, since presumably the conditions of employment were similar for all workers in these plants. The study by Pascale and Maguire (1980) asked respondents to compare their satisfaction with that of others similar to themselves. This way of phrasing might be expected to reduce the response bias problem to some degree, but we have no way of knowing by how much.

It is probable that all three explanations of lower Japanese job satisfaction contribute to the findings which have been obtained. For this reason it is unlikely that a definitive conclusion can be reached as to whether or not the Japanese are more dissatisfied with their jobs. In any event what is of more interest in our discussion of Japanese management is not so much the absolute level of satisfaction, but what types of structures or processes cause it to increase or decrease. We shall return to this issue when we discuss influence processes.

Seniority System

Japanese society is not only collective, but is also based upon a hierarchical status system. This is difficult for many Westerners to envisage, since in the West hierarchy is often thought of as opposite to collective activities such as participation. The Japanese language incorporates a wide variety of 'respect language', whereby it is impossible to speak to someone without making it clear whether that person is regarded as superior or inferior to oneself. The distinctions to be made are far more complex than the *tu/vous* distinction, for example, in French. Modes of address are formal and frequently refer to a person by rank rather than by name. A first-line supervisor is likely to be addressed as Mr Foreman (*hancho-san*) or Foreman Tanaka, even after long periods of working together.

The bases upon which such hierarchy is determined are numerous, including education, age, gender, and the firm one works for. The position of institutions in society, such as the firms in a particular industry or the universities in Japan, is also ordered in terms of an agreed hierarchy. One's own status is determined by the institutions one is or has been associated with combined with personal attributes such as age and gender. Wives take on their husband's status among other women. All of the above contribute to the *tatemae* of one's position relative to others, but in addition there will be factors relating not to one's own lifetime experiences but to one's family of origin.

Such processes are clearly operative also among Western business organizations, but in much more covert ways. In a business meeting or in office layout in Japan, status positions are likely to be physically represented, with high status persons furthest from the door. Behavioural differences such as amount of speaking and depth of bowing will also reflect hierarchical rank.

The management of hierarchy is exemplified by promotion procedures used within the large firms. Employee recruitment typically occurs only from school-leavers and college graduates and is followed by a substantial period of in-company training. This serves to strengthen commitment to the firm and inculcate the firm's favoured values. For about the next fifteen years, salary increases are paid regularly to all employees, with only relatively minor differentiation between high performers and low performers. This is the *nenko* system. Payment of a salary increase does not necessarily entail a change in work, but those who are destined for further promotion may be given the more interesting assignments. Thus throughout this period status differences are minimized between the members of a particular intake. Promotion beyond this point is more related to accomplishment. At the point when it becomes clear which members of a cohort are to be appointed to very senior positions, their peers may be encouraged to move to a job with one of the organization's subcontractors. By these devices, a situation is accomplished where it is rare for someone's boss to be younger than himself. It is thus possible to maintain a hierarchy of deference without confusing incongruities of age or gender. One's prospects for promotion are strongly dependent upon links with a more senior 'mentor' within the company. Assignment to a particularly senior mentor will depend upon the strength of one's prospects on entry. Wakabayashi and Graen (1984) have shown just how predictable this system makes ultimate promotion. They showed that the evaluation of the mentor–recruit relationship on entry to one of Japan's largest department store chains was a strong predictor of promotions achieved within the subsequent seven years.

In considering studies of Japanese organizational structure, it is important to bear in mind the description given above. Japanese organizations have two types of hierarchy—a seniority system for individuals, and a hierarchy of organizational ranks. The two systems do not necessarily overlap, since an organizational rank may quite frequently be left vacant. At the same time more than one person may be promoted to a particular seniority level, if their age, expertise or *tatemae* requires it. For instance in Clark's (1979) case study, 43 out of 109 ranked management positions were vacant at the time of the research. Dore's (1973) study at Hitachi gave a similar finding.

Researchers into organizational structure have mostly made use of Western measures, even though it is doubtful how far some of these may capture the aspects of organization just described. Lincoln, Hanada, and McBride (1986) drew upon the same comparative sample of organizations in Indiana and Kanagawa as has been discussed above. As they had predicted, they found that Japanese organizations had less functional specialization, that is to say fewer duties which are assigned exclusively to one individual within the organization. They also had a significantly greater number of seniority levels and a higher proportion of clerical staff. The most interesting aspect of this study was its findings concerning decision making. Respondents were asked at what level in the organization did authority rest formally for the taking of each of 37 types of decisions. They were then asked at what level these decisions were actually taken in practice. It was found that formal authority was located at significantly *higher* levels in Japanese firms than American ones, but that in practice decisions were taken at significantly *lower* levels in the Japanese firms than in the American ones. In the US firms the formal and informal locus of decisions was thus not that far apart; but in the Japanese firms the mean difference was greater than one level in the seniority system. The data thus reflect the distinction between *tatemae* and *honne* and shed light on the manner whereby a Japanese organization might appear to Western eyes to be both autocratic and participative.

The survey by Kagono *et al.* (1985) also included questions about organization structure. Within Japanese organizations, job descriptions were shown to be more general and less concrete. Power was said to be more widely shared and less systematized, particularly in respect of horizontal relationships. This survey did not distinguish between formal and informal procedures, but its findings are more in accord with Lincoln *et al.*'s description of decision making in practice. In these two surveys there is probably less reason to worry about response bias as a source of erroneous findings, since respondents were required to describe not themselves but their organizations.

Most researchers with interests in organization structures are interested not so much in absolute differences between Japan and the West as in whether the relationships between different aspects of formal organizational structure are the same within Japan as has been found elsewhere. Horvath, McMillan, Azumi, and Hickson (1976) examined the degree of formalization, specialization, and centralization within twelve matched trios of firms in Britain, Japan, and Sweden. Size and the degree of an organization's 'internal dependence', that is its links to parent organizations, were found to be the strongest predictors within Japan. Azumi and McMillan (1979) compared a larger sample of 50 Japanese firms with a databank of 128 British organizations. The Japanese sample scored much higher on centralization and on number of vertical levels, and somewhat higher on formalization, a measure which reflects the number of written documents used. These authors found no relationship between scores on centralization, formalization, and specialization, a finding which differs markedly from studies in Western countries. The most likely explanation for this is that the measures used in this and the preceding study, which are those developed by researchers at the University of Aston in England, fail to detect crucial aspects of Japanese organizational behaviour. As the later study by Lincoln *et al.* shows, there is an important distinction to be made between formal and informal decision procedures. Furthermore, the measure of specialization is defined in terms of assignment of specialist duties to *individuals*, where such specialization is much more likely to be carried through by teams in Japan.

Marsh and Mannari (1981) also made use of the Aston measures among others, but their prime goal was to compare the relative impact of size and technology as determinants of organizational structure and processes within 50 Japanese factories. They found that the type of technology employed was a somewhat stronger predictor than was size, whereas the reverse had been found earlier in Britain. In a similar study, Tracy and Azumi (1976) found that plant size and task variability were predictors of the level of automation and formalization. Lincoln *et al.* (1986) also studied the effect of type of technology. They concluded that the effects of technology were not, on the whole, detectably different from those in their US sample. However, on certain variables, particularly the centralization of decision making, the effects do differ. The US data show strong effects of technology type on both the formal and informal decision measures, while the Japanese data do not. Lincoln *et al.* conclude that variables other than technology are more crucial in Japan in this area. However, they do point out that newly emerging technologies such as highly automated process industries are precisely those in which Japan is at the forefront, and these types of plant may be ones in which it is less crucial to link supervision to technological processes. Although this may well be true, the sample used by Lincoln *et al.* spanned a wide range of technologies, and the implication of their finding is that it is not technology but something intrinsic to Japan which determines the type of decision making used. The most plausible candidate for such a cultural explanation would be the deeply rooted seniority system.

Seror (1982) attempts to specify a firmer basis upon which comparisons may be made of Japanese organizational structures and those in other countries. She proposes that before conclusions may be reached which favour universal theories of organizational structure, studies must be made that span several clearly defined cultures and show how the structures studied affect organizational effectiveness. The only study which approaches these requirements is that by Lincoln and Kalleberg (1985). In addition to the analyses within their paper that have already been discussed, these authors examine the effects of different organizational parameters upon satisfaction and commitment of employees. These are clearly not unambiguous measures of organizational effectiveness, but a study of them is none the less a step forward. Commitment in Japanese firms was found to be lower in small firms and in firms with tall hierarchies. A large span of control and low formalization was linked to positive commitment and satisfaction in the United States, but not in Japan. The implication would be that in the United States close contact with the supervisor is aversive, while in Japan it is not. A number of other differences which the authors had anticipated did not emerge. For instance there was no linkage between tenure and commitment. However, it is not clear why there should be such an effect. An employee who enters the lifetime employment system already knows the nature of the commitment he has made: there is no reason why commitment should increase with the passage of time. Lincoln and Kalleberg conclude that the differences they found in the effects of organizational structure in the two countries were rather modest. A possible reason for this may be that the effects of structures are not inherent in those structures, but in how they are interpreted and utilized in a particular cultural setting. This is a theme which we take up in the next section.

Influence Processes

The attributes of Japanese management outlined thus far delineate a system with clear positive qualities, but what may appear also to be substantial disadvantages. Japanese employers are also agreed upon the nature of these disadvantages. Hazama (1978) reports a survey made in 1967 by the Japan Federation of Employers' Associations. Among those who responded, 92 per cent agreed that lifetime employment caused employers to retain workers with inferior ability and those who were not needed, thus causing a large loss due to labour costs. Similarly, 84 per cent agreed that the seniority system led to a loss in vitality within the establishment, and 72 per cent said that the system adversely affected the morale of able workers. Whether such disadvantages are outweighed by the benefits must depend upon the manner in which the structures so far described are operated in practice. Such evidence is crucial, since when one reads descriptions of, for example, the seniority system, it is inevitable that one's reactions to it are coloured by the way in which such a system would be evaluated within one's own national culture.

Most discussions of Japanese management gave substantial emphasis to the occurrence of upward influence, particularly through the *ringi* system of decision making and through the widespread use of quality control circles. While these are certainly important and we shall discuss them shortly, it is necessary first to consider the nature of superior–subordinate relations in Japanese society. *Ringi* and quality control circles may then be seen as particular instances of a more fundamental attribute. Within Western societies a rigidly hierarchical system would most likely be one in which influence flowed down the hierarchy rather than up it. Those in high power positions would at times need to protect themselves from threats to their status from more able persons below. In Japan the position of a senior person is relatively invulnerable to such attack, due both to lifetime employment and to the fact that status derives principally from attributes which cannot be changed by others. Thus the senior manager in Japan has less reason to be threatened by suggestions from below. The traditional pattern of superior–subordinate relations in Japanese society depends upon the *oyabun–kobun* system, which derives from the parent–child relationship and now means patron–client relationship. Within modern organizations this is represented by the *sempai–kohai* or senior–junior system. This is an intense relationship of mutual obligation. The superior is expected to protect the subordinate's interests, develop his skills through training and feedback, and advance his position. The subordinate is expected to show deference and loyalty, as expressed through commitment and hard work, as well as the making of suggestions and the giving of gifts on occasions such as the New Year. The subordinate's commitment may be expressed through working extra unpaid hours, or through not taking up holiday entitlements, although as Lincoln and Kalleberg's (1985) data suggest, this may be due not so much to commitment as to an unwillingness to fall out of favour with one's superior. The superior's obligations may well extend to such matters as helping the subordinate to find someone to marry, where this is desired. The superior will be given credit for the achievements of the work team, but this will be due to the need for deference, rather than as a distinction to be made between the supervisor and his team of subordinates. It also motivates the superior to look out for valuable suggestions from subordinates. This pattern of superior–subordinate relations derives from the traditional obligations of Japanese village life, which are known as *ie* (Nakane, 1970).

The survey by Kagono *et al.* (1985) also included a series of questions about leadership styles. Japanese leaders were reported by respondents to be significantly higher than those in America and Europe on the following behaviours: strictness in applying rewards and punishments; clarifying and gathering information; adherence to the values of the current chief executive officer (CEO) or founder; conflict resolution through the use of authority; exchange of information prior to meetings; sharing of information down the line; use of a control system based upon employee self-discipline and commitment to work; long-term performance evaluation; consensus decision making; frequent informal and social exchange; commitment to change; and promotion policies from within. Few of the differences reported are surprising in view of the preceding discussion, but since the respondents were asked to describe practices within their company as a whole, their responses probably reflect *tatemae* rather more than *honne*.

The principal organizationally structured mode of upward influence within the Japanese organization is that of *ringi*. This is a procedure whereby proposals for new policies, procedures or expenditures are circulated through the firm for comment. An initial proposal is written by a junior member of the organization. The paper is then sent to all those who might be affected if it were implemented, each of whom writes comments or indicates approval with his personal seal. The document is circulated in ascending order of seniority. The above description outlines what occurs in theory. In practice, with increasing size of modern Japanese organizations, such procedures become exceedingly time consuming and a number of modifications may be noted (Misumi, 1984). For instance, the organization may use *ringi* only for important decisions, and may authorize managers at particular seniority levels to commit expenditures up to a given level without such broad consultation. Less important decisions may be handled by *ringi* among middle managers and never submitted to the highest level. It will be noted that the success of *ringi* requires a high degree of consensus among those affected. Consultation documents circulated within Western organizations are frequently criticized, negotiated over, and amended. The preferred procedure within Japanese organizations is to engage in such consultations *before* the *ringi* proposal is circulated. This informal procedure is referred to as *nemawashi*, whose literal meaning is the trimming of a tree's roots prior to its being transplanted. Only when it is clear from *nemawashi* that a proposal is likely to succeed will a written *ringi* proposal be put forward. The nearest Western equivalents, grapevine or bush telegraph, have a different connotation, since they refer to dissemination of information rather than preparation for decision. Through *nemawashi*, harmony in the organization will be preserved, but rather than being a method of decision making, *ringi* has become more a method of recording and reporting decisions already reached (Misumi, 1984).

A *ringi* decision may be thought of as the nearest which a Japanese organization will come to issuing job descriptions. The decision which is recorded will specify that certain tasks will be carried out by a particular group or groups, but it differs from a formal system of job descriptions in two senses. Firstly, it will relate to a particular task and hence will lapse when that task is complete. Secondly, it will specify the task to be done by one or more teams rather than by individuals. In practice, differential abilities and influence processes within the team may mean that one member does much more of the work than others, but *tatemae* says that all are equally responsible. The individual who does more than his 'share' will know that such industry may in the end lead to slightly more rapid promotion, but in the meantime all are equally accountable for what is done.

A further issue concerning *ringi* is the question of where the initiative comes from for the formulation of a new policy. It is often implied that the new idea derives solely from the junior member of the organization, and no doubt many ideas do so. But it must also be remembered that within the seniority system, subordinates are obligated to take note of the wishes of their superiors. Thus a superior who favours a particular initiative may drop hints to subordinates, who will then formulate a proposal in that direction. Clark (1979) reports instances where this occurred—*ringi* is thus not something apart from the rest of organizational processes. It is the product of *nemawashi*, and the fostering of both *ringi* and *nemawashi* is an integral part of the leadership processes occurring within Japanese organizations. Just as *ringi* exemplifies upward influence within the ranks of management, so does the extensive use of quality control circles and allied procedures at shopfloor level. However, QC circles will not be extensively discussed here, since they are the subject of a separate review (Van Fleet and Griffin, 1989).

Detailed studies have been undertaken of the processes of leadership within Japanese organizations (Misumi, 1985). These have shown that leaders whose effectiveness is rated most highly are those whose behaviour is perceived as high on two functions termed P and M. These initials stand for performance and maintenance, and they parallel distinctions made by US leadership researchers between, for instance, task and socio-emotional behaviours. However, while US researchers have found that environmental contingencies require different leader styles, Misumi's studies have shown that effective leaders score high on P and M in a very wide range of organizational settings. Misumi emphasizes that although measures of P and M are factorially independent, they cannot be thought of in isolation. Within the actions of an effective manager, the exercise of the P and M functions interacts, so that the effect of each augments the other. Over a period of more than 30 years his studies have included laboratory studies, field surveys, and field experiments. Within the Nagasaki shipyards, for instance, leadership training emphasizing the need for a PM style led to very large decreases in the rate of accidents (Misumi, 1975). On the face of it, effective Japanese leader style is less environmentally contingent than are US styles, just as we reported earlier that Japanese organizational structures appear to be less driven by technology. However, in the case of leader styles, comparative studies are not yet complete which would test for alternative explanations, such as the use of different measures of leader style in different countries.

Comparative data are available from three studies which do test the linkage between various organizational processes and ratings of work satisfaction or performance. Pascale (1978a) compared matched samples of US and Japanese companies. He found that in the Japanese companies written communications were used more frequently, that there were more superior–subordinate interactions initiated from below, and that implementation of decisions was rated more highly. These last two variables were positively correlated, so that where there was more upward influence, decision implementation was better. Using the same sample, Pascale and Maguire (1980) report correlations between their one-item measures of leader style and work satisfaction which are generally low. The highest correlations with work satisfaction within the Japanese sample were for 'supervisor pitches in' ($+0.23$) and mean number of supervisor–worker interactions ($+0.30$). The equivalent correlations for the US sample were -0.15 and $+0.05$, but the significance of these differences is not tested. Strongly significant correlations between supervisor style and absenteeism were found in the US sample, but these were absent from the Japanese sample probably because absenteeism was very much lower there. Another relevant finding from the Lincoln and Kalleberg (1985) study was that participation in quality circles in the United States was positively linked to organizational commitment. In Japan this was less true but participation in *ringi* showed a stronger effect.

More direct tests will be required before a firm conclusion is possible, but there are certainly some grounds for the belief that the effects of leadership and of group processes more generally may differ within Japanese organizations from those found in the West.

This concludes our survey of the classical model of Japanese management. The different attributes which we have outlined are summarized in Table 1.

CHANGE AND STABILITY IN JAPANESE MANAGEMENT

In his earliest analysis of Japanese factory organization, Abegglen (1958) argued that the structures he described were derived from traditional Japanese society. It is now widely agreed that this was incorrect, not least by Abegglen himself (Abegglen, 1973). A more tenable view is that many of the distinctive qualities of Japanese management have in fact evolved over the past few decades (Dore, 1973; Odaka, 1975; Cole, 1979; Urabe, 1984). In the first section of this review Japanese management was discussed as though it were a fixed and static entity. In this section we shall consider evidence as to its diversity and rate of change. Such a type of analysis is replete with irony, since as we shall see, many of the aspects of Japanese management which have been 'discovered' by Western

Table 4.1 The classical model of Japanese management

Attribute	Effect	Source of vitality	Difficulties
Lifetime employment	Stable tenure Job rotation Simultaneous recruitment Future abilities unknown Internal promotion	All in the same boat Can devote self to work Whole person contributes Sense of belonging	Low job mobility Small incentives to develop self Small incentives to perform well No right of dismissal
Collective orientation	Put company first Multilateral flow of information	Wish to contribute to group Sense of belonging Interchangeability of jobs Power of the group	Stress from suppression of ego needs Group process problems Unclear powers and duties
Seniority system	Gradual promotion Equitable system of promotion Job rotation	Long-term incentive Boosts collective morale Sense of belonging	'Tepid' management Promotion of low ability persons to management Elite morale low
Influence processes	Responsibilities delegated Many views sought Participative management	Flexible structure Young employee vitality Free resources utilised Shared strategy formulation	No unified control No hard-line policy Diffusion of responsibilities Time consuming

writers in recent years, have their roots in the West as much as they do in the East.

The principal difficulty in the way of analysing what is stable and what is in process of change lies in the Japanese genius for searching out new approaches, wherever they may be found and adapting them to their own purposes. It is doubtful whether there is another country in the world which has devised a system of notation for the sole purpose of incorporating into its own language words and concepts from other countries. Such a practice may in itself be no more than symbolic of Japanese enthusiasm for the importation and adaptation of technologies and procedures. None the less, the cumulative impact of such openness may have profound implications for the future of Japanese organizations, as for many other aspects of Japanese society.

Cole (1979) summarizes three views of the development of Japanese organizations. The first of these proposes, in line with Abegglen's (1958) thesis, that Japanese organizations are a unique product of Japanese cultural history. The second proposes that there are inexorable consequences of the use of specific technologies and that the structures of the modern industrial organizations of all societies are therefore destined to converge. The third alternative, which Cole himself supports, is that there may in fact be several ways in which organizations can successfully cope with the problems of production and marketing which they face. Organizational structures may therefore be expected to show some convergence, but also some diversity which is explicable in cultural terms.

The first or culturalist view has something of the status of the null hypothesis. That is to say, if studies show no evidence of change in Japanese organizations over time, its merits are enhanced, but if change is found, it is weakened. A judgement as to whether or not the changes found would require dismissal of the culturalist view, would also entail an evaluation of whether the changes found were explicable simply as a developmental stage within a unique culture, or whether they showed convergence towards the culture of other advanced industrial countries. Such judgements are by no means easy to make.

Despite such difficulties, certain facts are now well established. For instance, the system of lifetime employment for those working in first-rank companies arose after the Second World War (Cole, 1979). Between the wars there was little security of tenure, and considerable industrial conflict, sometimes violent (Urabe, 1986). The system of lifetime employment evolved out of these conflicts. Cole points out that the system is not a legally formalized one, and that in a period of expansion such as Japan has experienced since the Second World War, it may be difficult to distinguish between those who are entitled to lifetime employment and those who have merely experienced continuous employment. In the current situation, where there are already, or soon will be, substantial cutbacks in employment opportunities in such industries as coal mining, shipbuilding and car manufacture, the distinction is likely to become more explicit. Cole's (1971) survey of workers in Yokohama certainly revealed some confusion among his respondents as to the nature of their conditions of service.

There is an equal degree of uncertainty about the *nenko* system. In Cole's study at Toyota Auto Body, he found that no more than 40 per cent of a worker's pay was based upon the seniority principle, while the remainder was based upon abilities and work content. He comments that the criteria for abilities and work content were sufficiently vague that, in practice, they might well prove to be correlated with seniority. Nevertheless, since the 1960s, this and many other firms sought to include a job-based wage system (*shokumukyu*) within their criteria for determining pay. The impetus for this came from study of the personnel practices of American firms and Japanese protagonists of such changes sought to justify them by emphasizing that they are more modern (Cole, 1979, p. 130). *Shokumukyu* was found to require precise job descriptions and most firms have replaced it by an element of *shokunokyu* or payment by ability within their payment system. No evidence is available as to whether such payments do in practice conflict with the seniority system.

The *ringi* procedure has also been frequently attacked as insufficiently modern, and as we have seen its function has been changing. Takamiya (1981) reports that in 1961, 82 per cent of corporations surveyed used *ringi* for making decisions, whereas by 1969 many of these regarded *ringi* as a method for recording decisions. The other side of this picture is given by the survey conducted by Takahashi and Takayanagi (1985). They asked 299 firms by what method they took their most recent decision on a location plan for a factory, branch or office. They found that 63 per cent of the decisions were taken through *nemawashi*, 30 per cent through decision by the superior, and the remainder by conference. The firms using group-based decision methods (*nemawashi* and conference) were more likely to employ what the authors call a 'fixed size' procedure, in other words the simultaneous evaluation of a range of options. These firms tended to be those who are listed on the Tokyo Stock Exchange, and particularly those whose share performance is high. Thus this study indicates that *nemawashi* is currently most widespread among the successful first-rank companies.

The picture presented above is certainly one of change, but there is little indication that the changes which have occurred simply represent the adoption of the practices of the United States or of other industrialized countries. Cole (1979) cites several further examples of the manner in which innovations derived from the United States have been substantially amended as they are incorporated within Japanese practice. A widely known example is the manner in which the ideas of Deming on statistical quality control by staff experts were transmuted into the group-based procedure known as quality control circles. A less familiar one is the rapid adoption in the early years of this century of F.W. Taylor's prescriptions for scientific management (McMillan, 1985). The notion of work study and of production management was enthusiastically adopted, while the associated idea of performance-related pay was completely ignored. Japanese writers point out that Taylor himself was an advocate, not simply of work study but equally of 'hearty brotherly cooperation' (Mito, 1983).

The view that convergence of Japanese and Western organizations is inevitable is advanced by Marsh and Mannari (1976). Their study examined three firms manufacturing ships, electrical appliances, and *sake*. Their analyses were based both upon detailed case studies and also upon questionnaire surveys completed by the workforce of the three plants. Data collection occurred between 1967 and 1970. They found that variables such as organizational rank and work satisfaction were actually more strongly associated with 'universal' factors than with variables which might be derived from distinctively Japanese practices. For instance it was found that extra-organizational variables, such as age, gender, and number of dependents had more effect upon reward system variables such as pay than did intra-organizational variables, such as education, seniority, and rank. Work satisfaction was related to rank, age, gender, promotion chances, and the cohesiveness of the work group. Marsh and

Mannari argue that since the variables which proved the strongest predictors are not distinctive to Japan, the convergence or 'modernization' theory is more strongly supported than the cultural theory. Such a reading of cultural theories exaggerates their claims. None of the proponents of cultural theories (e.g. Abegglen, 1958; Rohlen, 1974) put forward the view that Japanese organizations have *nothing* in common with Western organizations, only the more moderate view that there are unique processes within them that have substantial importance. Furthermore, as Cole (1979) points out, it is difficult to arrive at a valid reason for classifying some predictors as 'modern' and others as 'traditional'. Marsh and Mannari think of payment by ability as modern, in contrast to the *nenko* system. However, among their respondents 48 per cent who favoured *nenko* also considered that ability should be the prime determinant of pay. Thus their respondents appear to see no contradiction between what Marsh and Mannari consider to be traditional and modern. One possible resolution of such a puzzle is that advanced above in discussing Cole's (1979) study at Toyota Auto Body. It may be that ability payments are in practice correlated with seniority ranks. In the Marsh and Mannari data, job classification certainly correlated highly with seniority ($+0.77$ and $+0.51$ for the two companies in which it was computed).

Marsh and Mannari take their argument further by suggesting that those firms with traditional Japanese emphasis will experience increasing difficulty in surviving. They support this argument by devising an index of worker performance and showing that high performance is again linked more strongly to factors such as rank, gender, and work satisfaction. However, their measure of performance was based not on actual productivity records, but upon answers to five questions, three of which had to do with the submission of suggestions for improvements. The conclusions drawn from this study are thus rather more general than the data might justify. It is difficult to draw valid conclusions about cultural differences in the absence of comparative data from different cultures. Conclusions about changes over time ideally also require data collection over some extended time period. However, the study does provide an illustration of the way in which there were substantial differences between the three firms studied, and thus contributes to the reduction of the belief that there is a single unified system of Japanese management. It does also validly demonstrate that among the sample studied the various elements postulated to make up the Japanese management system were not correlated with one another in a linear fashion. There was no particular tendency for instance for those who scored high on their measure of paternalism to express more company concerns, to have had no other previous jobs with other firms, to live in company housing, to score high on group cohesiveness or to be committed to lifetime employment. Marsh and Mannari suggest that this means that these aspects of Japanese organizations do not comprise a unified whole, but that employees participate in each one of them where they see it to be advantageous to them. This seems highly plausible.

An alternative version of the modernization hypothesis is that put forward by Dore (1973). Basing his thesis upon comparative case studies of electrical plants in Japan and Britain, he proposes that far from being backward or traditional, Japanese company organization may illustrate a form of welfare corporatism towards which other countries will converge. He reasons that since Japanese industrialization has occurred more recently than in Western countries there have been opportunities for Japan to learn from Western errors and thereby to create more advanced organizational structures. We should therefore expect more future changes in Western organizations than in Japanese ones. Cole (1979) is sceptical that Japan qualifies for 'late-developer' status, given the openness to Western ideas from the beginning of the Meiji era onwards, but acknowledges a wide range of ways in which Japanese organizations have observed and learned from Western organizations during the past century. We have noted some of these above. What are required, but have not yet been fully described, are accounts of the degree to which such innovations have been rendered into distinctively Japanese forms.

Comparative case studies of sixteen matched pairs of companies in Japan and the United States are presented by Kagono et al. (1985). They conclude that the strategies of these firms differ in five ways. The Japanese companies compared to the US ones were found to define their domain more broadly; to emphasize continuous in-house resource accumulation and development; to emphasize human resource development; to distribute risk through organizational networks; and to use inductive methods of problem solving, particularly focused upon improvement in production strategy. They conclude that both US and Japanese strategies are well adapted to certain types of market, but that each will need to change in response to continuing market change.

The most authoritative account of how such gradual transformations in Japanese firms are being accomplished is provided by Urabe (1984, 1986), the doyen of Japanese management writers. He stresses the manner in which the human and the technological innovations accomplished have been interrelated. Lifetime employment has enhanced the growth of company-specific skills. The *tatemae* of seniority has been preserved, while in practice pay differentials between senior and junior members of the organization have declined, and non-working directors have become a rarity. These changes and the payment of substantial bonuses have facilitated the convergence of management and union interests. The shift to process production increases the power of workers to disrupt production, and the trust accorded to workers by allowing them to halt a production line when necessary enhances the responsibility of their actions.

Urabe considers the potential of Japanese and Western organizations for the creation of change. He concludes that Japanese firms are well adapted to a continuous process of small incremental changes. Such changes are more likely to be the focus of resistance and negotiation in the West. Western organizations, on the other hand, may be better at making radical changes, and Urabe concludes that in this area lies a major problem for the Japanese organizations of the future. Urabe's reasoning is neatly complemented by the recent research of Yoshihara (1986), who made case studies of five Japanese firms which did accomplish successful innovations. The innovations were mostly changes into radically different markets, of which the best known is Canon. Yoshihara reports that in contrast to the popular view of Japanese firms having a 'bottom-up' system of influence, each of these firms had a strong and visible leader at the top who actively directed the innovations made. Numerous examples of the developing business strategy of specific Japanese corporations are also discussed by Itami (1987).

A major source of innovation and change in Japan as elsewhere lies in the management of research and development, and some studies of this process are now available. Kono (1986), surveyed the research facilities of 244 Japanese firms. He found that three sources of new product ideas were more frequent in the more successful firms: top management, central research groups, and divisional development teams. Westney and Sakakibara (1985) compared research and development within three Japanese and three American firms in the computer industry. Japanese researchers identified more strongly with the research administrators of their group and with the manufacturing function within their firm. US researchers gave more weight to professional colleagues and family. Promotion in Japanese labs was based upon seniority and track record, while in the United States it was based upon technical expertise and track record. Japanese researchers worked longer hours. US researchers had more choice of assignment to their next project. Kanai (1987) surveyed 49 research teams within a Japanese firm. Strong correlations were found between the leader's personal style, his network of links with other parts of the organization, and the team's performance. These studies suggest Japanese research labs share the characteristics identified in earlier sections, but also indicate that within this function as elsewhere, influence flows down the hierarchy as well as up it.

The work of Urabe and of Yoshihara confirms that substantial changes continue to occur in Japanese management practices, even though they are not necessarily convergent with Western practices. Dunphy (1987) also favours the view that these changes are the product of thought-out strategy choices by Japanese managements, rather than the inevitable consequence of culture or of technology. The work of Okubayashi (1986a, 1986b, 1987) gives some pointers as to how this process will continue in the face of further automation. He showed that the introduction of robots had not led to job losses within the firms installing them, and that unions are generally favourable to their use. His survey of 167 companies showed that automation has accentuated the division between highly skilled workers and unskilled ones. It has also led to shorter hierarchies and more decentralized decision making on production, but greater centralization of financial and personnel functions. These changes are likely to threaten wage systems based upon seniority and to pose particular difficulties for women and for older workers.

Further studies of workers have been reported which also suggest that evidence for convergence between Japanese and Western organizations is much less than might be expected, given the increasing rate of intercultural contact. The most striking evidence is that provided by Whitehill and Takezawa (1968) and Takezawa and Whitehill (1981). In this unique pair of studies, the same set of questions was posed to comparable samples of 2000 Japanese and US workers employed by eight large companies, at an interval of thirteen years. The survey included 30 questions, and significantly different patterns of response were found on every single question. The differences detected were consistent with the portrayal of Japanese management presented earlier in this chapter. The repeat survey found remarkably little evidence of convergence. Indeed on the majority of questions the gap between the United States and Japan had widened. Japanese responses showed more change than did US ones, but the strongest effect was that the attitudes of younger workers were now more similar to those of older workers.

Opinion surveys of the Japanese population have been undertaken every five years since 1953. Hayashi (1987) reports that over this period there has been remarkably little change in expressed preference for a work supervisor who 'looks after you personally', rather than one who never does anything for you that is unconnected with work. In the most recent survey, 89 per cent preferred the first of these two types of supervisor.

One other source of evidence for lack of change over time lies in the series of studies of leadership by Misumi (1985). There has been no change in support for PM theory from the earliest studies conducted in coal mines in 1963 (Misumi, 1985, pp. 22–7) to the present day.

The studies reviewed in this section provide substantial evidence of change over time in the specific practices employed by Japanese organizations. At the same time, the evidence that these changes necessarily entail the decline of those aspects of Japanese organizations which are distinctive is scant. Completed academic studies necessarily lag somewhat beyond the day-to-day life of organizations, so that one might propose that such change is present and increasing. The most substantial study indicating lack of change (Takezawa and Whitehill, 1981) was completed almost a decade ago. More recent commentators (Taylor, 1983) suggest that some at least of the younger generation shows rather different attitudes to work. Taylor notes the recent appearance in the Japanese language of 'myhomeism', a phrase used to criticize those Japanese who choose to go home after work rather than work extra hours or participate in *tsukiai*. It is also indisputable that the proportion of young to old in the population is changing rapidly, and that disrespect for one's elders, as measured by such indices as reports of assaults on schoolteachers, is on the increase. These changes, in addition to the effects of automation, are likely to place the seniority system under increasing strain during the next two decades.

However, experience to date suggests that such changes will find a mode of expression which assimilates them to Japanese culture, as has happened with some regularity over the past century. Hayashi's survey data (1987, 1988) provide the best clues as to how this will occur. He notes a decline in both those whose views are compulsively traditionalist and those who are compulsively 'modern'. The increasing trend is for respondents to state that their response to a situation would depend on the circumstances. This change in attitude mirrors the increasing pragmatism of Japanese organizations which we have already noted.

THE JAPANESE ABROAD

In recent years, a variety of economic and political pressures have led many Japanese firms to establish both manufacturing plants and sales facilities abroad. Although this process has been quite rapid, the title of Trevor's (1983) book, *Japan's Reluctant Multinationals*, conveys the impression of many observers that recent developments have been more a matter of necessity than of preference. The reasons for it have been fully explored by Ozawa (1979). He distinguishes the move into neighbouring Asian countries, primarily in search of lower labour costs, from the more recent worldwide expansion. The move towards multinational operation has been possible even for Japanese firms which are quite small, due to the existence of the giant *sogo shosha* or trading companies.

Generalizations about the performance of Japanese firms abroad need to be made with considerable caution, since not only do the reasons for setting up operations in various parts of the world vary, but so also does the manner in which firms are then staffed. Ozawa cites figures issued by the Japanese Ministry of Trade and Industry in 1971, indicating that the *average* number of Japanese nationals working within each overseas venture varied between 20 in the United States and 1 in Asia. While such differences no doubt represent an amalgam of the needs of each type of venture, and the preferences of Japanese to be stationed in particular parts of the world, they are likely to very strongly affect the degree of 'Japaneseness' of each venture.

Some studies are available of Japanese plants within Asia, but their focus is mostly general rather than specific. Ozawa indicates that the dual labour market within Japan is increasingly being replaced by a pattern where Japanese firms in other Asian countries pay very low wage rates, while more skilled work is retained within Japan. This has been encouraged by governments in Asian countries who are keen to foster foreign investment.

The loyalties of the Japanese to their in-group pose considerable problems for the Japanese abroad. They find it difficult to make contact with non-Japanese, particularly in Asian countries (Nakane, 1972). Those Japanese who do enter local networks or marry local women are thought of as having ceased to be Japanese. A wish to hire those who do understand the ways in which Japanese do business has led to preferential hiring of Japanese who already live there, especially in Hawaii and southern California. Japanese speakers are also preferred in countries where these are available, such as Korea and Taiwan. The difficulties which Japanese firms in Asia face have also included the fact they have allied themselves with the élites in some countries where those élites are unpopular, particularly in Indonesia (Ozawa, 1979). Everett, Krishnan, and Stening (1984) studied the mutual perceptions of Japanese managers and local managers working in plants in six South-East Asian countries. Factor analyses of ratings yielded three dimensions, which were termed managerial, entrepreneurial, and congenial. Japanese managers were generally rated high on the managerial factor, which included adjectives such as industrious, cautious, and honest. On the entrepreneurial factor they were rated high by Thais, Indonesians, and Hong Kong Chinese, but low by Filipinos, Malays, and Singaporeans. This factor was centred on the adjectives assertive, extraverted, and ambitious. On the congenial factor, all but the Thais rated Japanese managers low. This factor was based upon the adjectives tolerant, flexible, and cooperative. This study thus supports the more qualitative account provided by Ozawa.

Yoshino (1976) studied 25 Japanese firms operating in Thailand, and conducted some interviews also in Malaysia and Taiwan. Contrary to the figures cited by Ozawa, he found many more Japanese expatriates in post than there were in European or American firms in this area. He found this to be a consequence of Japanese mistrust in the abilities of locals to follow Japanese methods of decision making. In some plants, management was Japanese right down to the level of first-line supervisor. This pattern of staffing has one of two effects upon locally recruited management trainees. Either the locals observe that only minimal promotion is going to be available, and they therefore put in the minimum possible level of work. Alternatively, they eagerly seek out opportunities for training, including extended periods in Japan. When this is accomplished, they then leave the firm, since their level of training makes them attractive to other local firms. In both of these patterns, Japanese mistrust of the possibility of promoting local managers is enhanced. They see little prospect that locals will develop the company loyalty which a Japanese firm would expect of its employees. Negandhi, Eshghi, and Yuen (1985) discuss similar problems faced by Japanese firms in Taiwan.

Negandhi and Baliga (1979) summarize an extensive survey of 124 multi-nationals operating in developing countries, including 27 which are Japanese. While agreeing with Yoshino's view that Japanese firms face some difficulties in internal decision making, they found that Japanese firms had less conflict with governments and official bodies than did American firms.

Published comparative studies, with more detail of actual procedures used, focus almost entirely upon Japanese multinationals operating within advanced industrial countries. In considering these studies we need to bear in mind that not all Japanese multinationals are necessarily successful ones, despite the massive media coverage suggesting that they are. McMillan (1985) cites the case of Come-by-Change oil refinery in Newfoundland, which resulted in the bankrupting of one of the big ten *sogo shosha* companies, and of Mitsubishi Rayon, which withdrew from Canada after a thirteen-month strike. Other Japanese firms in Britain have experienced strikes, while in the United States there have been court cases alleging discriminatory hiring practices (Sethi, Namiki, and Swanson, 1984). None the less, these instances are more than balanced out by documented examples where plants have accomplished productivity levels equivalent to that of comparable plants in Japan (McMillan, 1985; Sethi *et al.*, 1984).

Fruin (1983) analyses the development since the Second World War of the Kikkoman Corporation, manufacturers of soy sauce, including their establishment of a plant in Wisconsin in 1972. He concludes that throughout this period management paid much more attention to what would work in a particular circumstance than to principle as to how things should be. Such pragmatism has proved to be a frequent attribute of Japanese multinationals, and has spawned a flood of articles in which authors enquire whether Japanese management is really distinctive at all. Kobayashi (1980) has pursued this direction by surveying 80 Japanese multinationals in comparison with 23 European and American multinationals. Respondents were asked to describe their present overseas structure and to predict how it might change in the future. Most envisaged a movement towards some type of matrix organization within a multidivisional structure. Asked which aspects of the classical Japanese approach would survive, the most frequently endorsed were (in order): joint ventures with host country firms; emphasis on market share rather than profits; joint ventures with *sogo shosha*; location close to raw materials; paternalism; lifetime employment and *ringi*. In a similar type of survey, Negandhi (1985) compared 120 US, German, and Japanese multinationals. The Japanese firms reported considerably more autonomy from headquarters. In comparison with the other multinationals they indicated that the problems they faced most frequently concerned personnel, marketing, and sales. This may not mean that they had more problems in these areas, but that they gave them greater priority.

A series of studies by Pascale and colleagues tests how substantial are current differences between American and Japanese firms operating in both Japan and the United States (Pascale, 1978a, 1978b; Pascale and Maguire, 1980; Maguire and Pascale, 1978). Fourteen American-owned units were compared with thirteen Japanese-owned units within the United States. There was a predominance of manufacturing and assembly but retailing and banking were also represented. Surprisingly few significant differences emerged. Comparing ten measures, Pascale and Maguire (1980) found only two that differed. The Japanese-owned firms spent more than twice as much per head on social and recreational facilities and they did more than twice as much job rotation. Furthermore, a larger number of differences were found between the Japanese-owned units and the comparable units owned by the same firms back in Japan. The Japanese subsidiaries in the United States were found to do more job rotation, to have supervisors who were rated more likely to listen to subordinates, and workers who were more satisfied, but also a much higher rate of absenteeism.

Some differences were also noted between the firms in the United States at managerial levels (Maguire and Pascale, 1978). Managers in the American-owned firms held larger meetings and spent more time in them, saw themselves as initiating more downward communication and receiving more upward communication. Their method of decision making more frequently involved obtaining the facts from subordinates and then deciding the matter themselves. The managers of the Japanese-owned firms more often used written communication to confirm the outcome of meetings and to request time off. They interacted more with their boss and less with their subordinates. They were more oriented towards consensus decision making, both with their subordinates and through being involved with their own boss. The personnel practices of these managers were also surveyed (Pascale, 1978b). The Japanese-owned firms had a smaller span of control at supervisor level and were more willing to allow workers to talk to one another on the job. Workers in the Japanese units reported significantly less of each of eighteen counterproductive behaviours, such as taking tools home from work. They were also stated to be more satisfied, although this is contradicted by Maguire and Pascale's (1980) report of the same data.

In summary, Pascale's project did succeed in finding a number of attributes on which Japanese-owned firms in the United States differed from locally owned firms. Most of these differences are consistent with the portrayal of Japanese management as practised in Japan. The majority of differences noted were at shopfloor level, but this may simply be because these are easier to detect. However, an equally important outcome of the project was the detection of an equally large number of differences between Japanese firms at home and abroad. This should encourage us further in the view that Japanese management abroad does not simply consist in the transposition of Japanese practices to other settings. A more active process appears to be involved, as Fruin (1983) reported, in which managements seek out what does and what does not work in a particular location.

This process of search is likely to include both the selection of worksites which appear more congenial, and the hiring of employees who will feel familiar with Japanese procedures. Lincoln, Olson, and Hanada (1978) predicted that

Japanese managers and workers would prefer organizational structures with a tall hierarchy and less horizontal differentiation into specialized groups. They found that among a sample of 54 Japanese-owned firms in America, the larger the proportion of Japanese or Japanese-American employees, the more the organization took on this form. In a subsequent paper (Lincoln, Hanada, and Olson, 1980), they showed that Japanese and Japanese-Americans were also more satisfied in organizations which had this type of structure.

A further series of detailed studies has examined some of the Japanese firms in Britain. White and Trevor (1983) studied three manufacturing firms and three banks. They report that there were marked differences in the degree to which these organizations had become noticeably 'Japanese'. The plant which had gone furthest along this path had employees who were no more satisfied than employees of other British and American-owned firms in the locality, although they did feel more secure in their jobs. Their managers were not seen as particularly oriented towards human relations. However, management was more strongly concerned with timekeeping, quality control, and efficiency generally. More meetings were held. The workforce worked hard but was willing to accept management's standards. White and Trevor propose that this was because management worked the same hours. Managers were keen to impart their expertise and wore the same clothing. Further aspects of a related study which compared the personnel practices of four manufacturers of colour televisions are reported by Takamiya and Thurley (1985). The authors propose that generalizations about Japanese management are hazardous in the light of substantial differences they found between the culture of the different companies studied. Of the two Japanese firms in the study, one was markedly more 'people oriented' than the other. None the less, both firms had considerably better productivity than the matched non-Japanese firms. Other attributes shared by both Japanese firms included dealing with only a single union and a less differentiated personnel function. The conclusion drawn from this study, as from the one by White and Trevor (1983), is that what best accounts for the superior performance of the Japanese firms is their meticulous attention to production management, their superior coordination of different organizational functions, and the management of their relations with trade unions.

The evidence discussed above derives most directly from the shopfloor level of manufacturing plants. In other types of organization and at more senior levels, it appears that it may be less easy to create a distinctively Japanese organizational climate within Western countries. White and Trevor's (1983) study indicated that although the encouragement of collective responsibility was popular among assembly-line workers, there was more reservation among the white-collar employees of Japanese banks located in London. A similar contrast is evident in a detailed case study of the operations of the subsidiaries of the YKK manufacturer of zip-fasteners in Britain and France (Davis, 1979). Although good relations with the workforce are described, an instance of conflict with secretarial staff is included. It is likely that white-collar staff would wish to retain a stronger sense of their individual skills and possible career mobility.

Yoshino (1975) suggests that one of the principal difficulties to be faced by Japanese multinationals lies in the area of decision making. There are two principal sources of difficulty. Firstly, remoteness from head office is likely to make participation in *nemawashi* particularly difficult. Yoshino argues that the creation of autonomous international divisions at least reduces this problem. This position is consistent with the data collected by Kobayashi (1980) which we cited earlier. In a more recent work, Yoshino and Lifson (1986) propose that the strength of the *sogo shosha* lies precisely in their capacity to practice a worldwide network of *nemawashi*. The second problem of multinationals concerns unfamiliarity of non-Japanese managers with *nemawashi* and *ringi*. Studies in Britain by Kidd and Teramoto (1981) and Trevor (1983) confirm that some Japanese firms in Britain do use *ringi*. Instances were found, however, where this was restricted to Japanese employees and the British managers within the plant were unaware even that the system was in use. Similar barriers between Japanese and non-Japanese are said also to exist in some firms in relation to promotion, as Yoshino (1976) found in Asia. Above a certain level, only Japanese are appointed. This means that local managers with ambition for further promotion are likely to seek posts elsewhere. The same problems will occur in more acute form within joint ventures.

Such problems will only be overcome when Japanese management is able to trust local managers to the same degree that managers trust one another. Given the strength of organizational socialization processes within Japanese organizations in Japan, this is likely to be a continuing problem. Studies by Sullivan, Peterson, Kameda, and Shimada (1981) and Sullivan and Peterson (1982) have addressed the issue. In both these studies, managers were asked to complete a questionnaire concerning a hypothetical joint venture. Japanese managers expressed greater trust in the future of the enterprise when a Japanese was in charge, and where decision making was initiated by a Japanese. This held true whether the sample was in Japan or in the United States. Where an American was in charge, Japanese managers felt that disputes should be resolved through the use of binding arbitration, but when a Japanese was in charge mutual consultation was thought preferable. American respondents showed none of these differences in preference. Sullivan and his co-workers conclude that Japanese see themselves as expert in avoiding uncertainty and conflict, but that where they are not in charge they have no confidence that similar outcomes can be achieved. Such issues become particularly important within negotiations. Miyazawa (1986) analyses the multiple pressures surrounding the establishment of legal departments within Japanese firms in the United States, on the basis of a survey of 233 firms. Crucial issues are whether the department shall include US nationals and whether it may be headed by one, particularly when seniority indicates that this should be done. Tung (1984) surveyed 113 US firms which had experienced negotiations in Japan. The parties to negotiation were reported as frequently using different negotiation styles. Failures were most frequently attributed to these differences, while successes were strongly associated with adequate prior preparation by US negotiators as to Japanese methods. A study which also addresses differences in perceived styles is that by Miyajima (1986) who asked Japanese managers in Britain to complete a test of managerial orientation and to predict how their British colleagues might complete it. The Japanese managers saw themselves as focused upon task issues, while they saw the British as more concerned with power.

A final issue concerning the experience of Japanese multinationals has to do with the processes whereby managers are prepared for overseas assignments. Tung (1987) reports a survey of European, American, and Japanese multi-nationals. The Europeans and the Japanese were found to have much lower failure rates, whereby managers returned home before their term was complete. Japanese multinationals were shown to be particularly thorough in their preparation of those sent abroad, both in terms of language training and of provision of prior information and of resources on arrival. Such preparation shows the same meticulous attention to detail as does Japanese production management. For instance, YKK's managers in Europe are instructed not to drive Japanese cars (Davis, 1979), as a sign of willingness to integrate with the local community. The study by Negandhi and Baliga (1979) also found Europeans and Japanese better prepared for overseas assignments, partly because they thought in terms of longer postings.

This section has shown that the experiences of Japanese corporations abroad are many and various. Only the rhetoric of popular writing could have led us to expect a uniform Japanese style to emerge everywhere, when there are substantial divergences of organizational culture even within Japan. None the less we do have evidence that Japanese-owned organizations in many parts of the world appear to function differently from those with other types of ownership. In the final section we shall discuss further how sure we can be as to why this might be so.

CULTURE AND MANAGERIAL EFFECTIVENESS

The first three sections of this review have surveyed the studies which have been made at home and abroad. A number of discussion points have been made in passing, but in this section we shall consider more thoroughly what types of conclusion the research studies permit. The issues at stake are basically three. We need to evaluate the widely held view that Japanese management is both distinctive and effective. Assuming a positive answer to this question for the moment, we need to know why this is so. Finally, we need to consider what implications our conclusions might have for managements, both Japanese and non-Japanese.

Within Japan there exists a flourishing literature known as *nihonjinron*, which seeks to distil exactly what it is about the Japanese which makes them unique. It is a truism that all ethnic groups are unique, but many Japanese believe that they are more unique than other cultural groups. In evaluating studies of Japanese management we need to be sure whether what we are considering is a particular instance of the Japanese fascination with, and perhaps even exaggeration of, their differentness, or whether there are indeed categorical differences between Japanese management and all other types of management. The studies we have reviewed make it plain that it will become increasingly difficult to argue that Japanese management is distinctive and unique. We have noted its evolution over time within Japan, and the manner in which Japanese corporations have been adept at modifying procedures and structures to align with the local needs of subsidiaries in varying parts of the world. On a broader front also, *nihonjinron* has received substantial critique (Mannari and Befu, 1982; Dale, 1986).

However, a number of more recent commentators have gone further and suggest that what characterizes Japanese management is no different from the policies which are pursued by the more progressive American corporations (Pascale and Athos, 1981). A more moderate position is that of Abegglen and Stalk (1984) and Buckley and Mirza (1985), who assert that there is no reason why Western firms cannot adopt policies and practices similar to the Japanese, even if they have mostly not done so yet.

Buckley and Mirza (1985) point out that whether or not Westerners should be in awe of Japanese management skills depends very much upon the manner in which one chooses to make comparisons with the West. While some sectors of the Japanese economy are extremely efficient, others such as agriculture and retailing are not. Still other sectors, while they may be efficient, are none the less in decline, just as they are in the West. These are industries focused upon the extraction and processing of raw materials, such as coal mining and the processing of aluminium and steel. Thus we do better to enquire not why the Japanese are such skilled managers, but why they are skilled at the management of certain types of enterprises.

Abegglen and Stalk (1984) indicate their position rather concisely in the sub-title of their book: 'How marketing, money and manpower strategy, not management style, make the Japanese world pacesetters'. Abegglen and Stalk analyse the basis upon which Japanese firms have been able to create competitive advantage within particular markets. They show that the ratio of labour costs in American and Japanese firms is directly related to *the number of separate operations required during manufacture of a product*. Where the number of operations is as high as 1500, as in car assembly, Japanese labour costs are half those of American car manufacturers. Where the number of operations is no more than ten to twenty, as in steel or paper manufacture, there is little difference in labour costs. The implication of such statistics is that Japanese firms are superior in the coordination of complex tasks. They also secure competitive advantage by restricting product variety and using large-scale facilities, both of which render coordination easier.

Although Abegglen and Stalk's lengthy sub-title dismisses management style as a source of Japanese success, this appears largely addressed towards those who suggest that analysis of management style is by itself sufficient to account for Japanese successes. Abegglen and Stalk do in fact discuss traditional Japanese management practices and assign them considerable importance. A better summary of their position might therefore be that Japanese management style is a necessary but not a sufficient explanation of the successes of the *kaisha*. While it is undeniable that Japanese firms are good at devising systems for coordinating production such as kanban, just-in-time and the like, it may well be that the collective orientation of the workforce assists in the devising and implementation of these systems. The same point could be argued with regard to the collaborative arrangements which Japanese firms sustain with banks and with trading companies.

Those who favour technologically oriented explanations of Japanese success (McMillan, 1985; Takamiya and Thurley, 1985) point to the way in which Japanese firms in Western countries can achieve equally impressive productivity, even where the workforce is almost entirely non-Japanese. There are two weak points in such arguments. The first is that most Japanese plants in the West have been open for a few years at most. One might anticipate a 'honeymoon' period for any new organization, particularly where the workforce has been newly recruited, and the production system is already tried and tested elsewhere. The YKK plant in Britain which was opened in 1967, and has frequently been written about as a success story, recently experienced an extended strike. Only passing time can show how well other plants in the West can sustain their initial successes. The second point is that most Japanese plants in the West utilize production systems which have already been designed in minute detail by Japanese in Japan. Many of the large number of assembly plants opened in Europe during the past several years in response to Common Market protectionism have been referred to as 'screwdriver' plants, that is to say that their task is only to assemble and package materials which have been designed and manufactured in Japan. While many such plants intend to make greater use of locally manufactured components, the processes of research, production design, and control remain firmly located in Japan.

It may be that rather than debating the 'hardware' versus 'software' explanations of Japanese successes, we should see them as the two faces of the same coin. It could be that the cultural context of Japan makes possible and encourages certain patterns of government, financing, research, production control and marketing and that these patterns have advantage in contemporary conditions. The firmest position from which to discuss the value of such a 'culturalist' explanation is the work of Hofstede (1980). Hofstede compared the values of managers working within a single (non-Japanese) firm located in 40 countries around the world. His analysis of the Japanese responses in his sample showed them to be particularly distinctive on two of the four dimensions used. The Japanese ranked fourth out of 40 on 'Uncertainty Avoidance', and top out of 40 on 'Masculinity'. The remaining two dimensions, 'Power Distance' and 'Individualism–Collectivism' were not wholly separable, and the Japanese scored an average ranking upon them. Hofstede's findings have been criticized for possible unrepresentative sampling, but they are none the less of great value. The classical attributes of Japanese culture are frequently portrayed as collectivism and the seniority system. Yet on Hofstede's dimensions of Power Distance and Collectivism, Japan was no more than average. The study suggests that there are numerous other countries with a more strongly collective orientation and a more hierarchical structure. On the other hand, Hofstede's data imply that Japanese are very strongly oriented towards Uncertainty Avoidance. Many attributes of Japanese management are indeed readily interpretable as attempts to reduce uncertainty, including their management of time perspective, investment in research, production and quality control systems and extensive use of *nemawashi*. However, Japanese avoidance of uncertainty is a selective process. We have seen that job descriptions are deliberately left open, and the practice of negotiation and of conflict management is enhanced by preserving areas of ambiguity (Pascale and Athos, 1981). The labelling of Hofstede's final dimension of Masculinity has been criticized. High-scoring questionnaire items loading upon this factor emphasize the centrality of work goals in the life of the respondent. If we assume that the Japanese respondents were male, it need be no surprise that they scored high here also.

In evaluating this type of culturalist explanation, we need to take account of the 'ecological fallacy', which cross-cultural psychologists have noted. That is to say, we should avoid the assumption that because a mean score on one of Hofstede's dimensions is high for Japan, all Japanese individuals or all Japanese organizations are high on that scale. What we are discussing are population *means*. No doubt, there are many Japanese who enjoy the challenge of uncertainty or who hate work, just as there are those in Western countries who seek identity collectively or favour hierarchical authority. We also need to bear in mind that Hofstede's data derive from the late 1960s, and that many commentators see evidence of increasing individualism in Japan since that time.

Further evidence relevant to the culturalist model is provided by the rapid development of the Pacific rim economies, triggered by Japanese investment. While there is substantial cultural diversity in the area, there are some common elements not shared by Western cultures. Abegglen and Stalk point out that those nations in which growth has been particularly strong have more uniform ethnic groupings and low birth rates, while those with diverse populations and high birth rates have prospered less. The high growth nations—Korea, Taiwan, Hong Kong and Singapore—share a Confucian value system, with many elements in common with Japanese modal values. As Buckley and Mirza (1985) point out, Confucian values have a long history, and cannot plausibly be used to account for recent events on their own. However, they may provide a necessary though not sufficient basis for the optimal utilization of the types of production systems which the Japanese have pioneered. Low wage levels no doubt contribute also, but these are present equally in the low-growth South-East Asian nations.

Adler, Doktor and Redding (1986) propose that the modes of thought which predominate in Pacific Basin nations and Western nations differ in quite fundamental ways. If we are to understand the operations of firms within these countries we need to investigate not simply what is done, but how it is done and why. Such a proposition may at first sound close to the *nihonjinron* type of argument, except that it is generalized to the Confucian nations of the Pacific rim. However it is based upon a detailed review of comparative studies of management, and may be helpful in summarizing what our review has found. Their suggestion is that while Western thought tends to focus upon the study of causal relations between abstractly conceptualized entities, Eastern thought focuses more upon the achievement of harmony between practical, concrete performance criteria such as quality control or sales targets. The value of this distinction between the abstract and the concrete can be illustrated through reference to Misumi's (1985) theory of leadership.

The theory proposes a distinction between the general functions of groups and organizations and the specific behaviours by which those functions are accomplished. Such a distinction has not been advanced by Western theorists. Our review has covered a number of areas in which such a distinction may prove valuable. For instance, studies of the intercorrelations of dimensions of organizational structure have shown some differences between Japan and the West. It may be that aspects of organizational structure such as centralization or formalization are indeed universal attributes of organizations, but that these attributes serve different specific functions in each cultural setting according to the meanings which attach to them. Similarly, dimensions of leadership behaviour such as task structuring and maintenance of good working relations may be universals, but the specific behaviours required to implement them in varying cultures may be entirely different (Smith and Tayeb, 1988). Thus it may be that while organizations in all parts of the world are faced with the same general problems, culture patterns in East and West encourage different patterns of specific problem solving. Growing internationalization may then reveal to us that some of these specific problem solutions have value not just within their culture of origin but much more widely.

Our argument thus leads to the view that Japanese management may indeed have lessons for Western nations, but that those lessons will need to be translated into the specific idiom of Western cultures if they are to prove applicable there. The findings to date suggest that this may prove easier in blue-collar occupational groups, and in market sectors where it is possible to retain key functions to organizational success within Japan. More substantial efforts to transplant entire Japanese organizations to Western settings are likely to encounter substantial difficulties, particularly in the areas of management decision making and promotion.

Consideration of the success of Japanese firms in the West leads us to our final discussion point: the impact of Japanese methods upon the practices of Western firms. This is most readily apparent in firms that supply components to Japanese firms in the car and electronics industries. In order to win contracts, they have been required to satisfy quality standards and delivery schedules specified by the Japanese. There has been some movement towards the development of long-term contracts between manufacturers and suppliers, with consequent reduction in the numbers of suppliers. Just-in-time systems have been widely implemented in the United States and British car industries (e.g. Turnbull, 1986). The joint venture between Honda and Rover has led to enhanced emphasis on quality within Rover (Smith, in press). Quality circles have been introduced within a wide variety of firms. On the whole the magnitude of these changes is not large, so that substantial differences most probably remain between the practices of local firms and their Japanese neighbours in Western countries, as the studies by Pascale and his colleagues showed a decade ago.

Dispassionate analysis of Japanese management is hard to come by. Japanese writers have tended either to stress its uniqueness or to foresee convergence with American practice. Western authors, on the other hand, have preferred either the view that its essentials are readily applicable in the West, or the view that it is a coercive system which would never work in the West. We have sought a middle path between these views, but it is time which will show to what degree the varying industrial cultures of the world will converge upon one another.

REFERENCES

Abegglen, J.C. (1958) *The Japanese Factory: Aspects of its social organization.* Glencoe IL: Free Press.

Abegglen, J.C. (1973) *Management and Worker: The Japanese Solution.* Tokyo: Sophia University Press.

Abegglen, J.C., and Stalk, G. (1984) *Kaisha, The Japanese Corporation.* New York: Basic Books.

Adler, N.J., Doktor, R., and Redding, S.G. (1986) From the Atlantic to the Pacific century: cross-cultural management reviewed. *Journal of Management,* **12,** 295–318.

Atsumi, R.(1979) Tsukiai—obligatory personal relationships of Japanese white-collar employees. *Human Organization,* **38,** 63–70.

Azumi, K., and McMillan, C.J. (1976) Worker sentiment in the Japanese factory: its organizational determinants. In L. Austin (ed.), *Japan: The paradox of progress*. New Haven CT: Yale University Press, pp. 215–230.

Azumi, K., and McMillan, C.J. (1979) Management strategy and organization structure: a Japanese comparative study. In D.J. Hickson and C.J. McMillan (eds), *Organization and Nation: The Aston Programme IV*. Farnborough, UK: Gower, pp. 155–172.

Buckley, P.J., and Mirza, H. (1985) The wit and wisdom of Japanese management. *Management International Review*, 25, 16–32.

Clark, R.C. (1979) *The Japanese Company*. New Haven, CT: Yale University Press.

Cole, R.E. (1971). *Japanese Blue Collar: The Changing Tradition*. Berkeley: University of California Press.

Cole, R.E. (1979) *Work, Mobility and Participation: A comparative study of Japanese and American industry*. LosAngeles, CA: University of California Press.

Dale, P.N. (1986). *The Myth of Japanese Uniqueness*. London: Croom Helm.

Davis, S.M. (1979) *Managing and Organizing Multinational Corporations*. New York: Pergamon.

Doktor, R. (1983) Culture and the management of time: a comparison of Japanese and American top management practice. *Asia Pacific Journal of Management*, 1, 65–71.

Dore, R.P. (1973) *British Factory, Japanese Factory*. London: Allen and Unwin.

Dunphy, D. (1987) Convergence/divergence: a temporal review of the Japanese enterprise and its management. *Academy of Management Review*, 12, 445–459.

Everett, J.E., Krishnan, A.R., and Stening, B.W. (1984) *Through a Glass Darkly— South East Asian Managers: Mutual perceptions of Japanese and local counterparts*. Singapore: Eastern Universities Press.

Fruin, W.M. (1983) *Kikkoman: Company, clan and community*. Cambridge, MA: Harvard University Press.

Hatvany, N., and Pucik, V. (1981) An integrated management system: lessons from the Japanese experience. *Academy of Management Review*, 6, 469–480.

Hayashi, C. (1987) Statistical study on Japanese national character. *Journal of the Japan Statistical Society*, Special issue, 71–95.

Hayashi, C. (1988) The national character in transition. *Japan Echo*, 25, 7–11.

Hazama, H. (1978) Characteristics of Japanese-style management. *Japanese Economic Studies*, 6, 110–173.

Hofstede, G. (1980) *Culture's Consequences: International differences in work-related values*. Beverly Hills, CA: Sage.

Horvath, D., McMillan, C.J., Azumi, K., and Hickson, D.J. (1979) The cultural context of organizational control: An international comparison. In D.J. Hickson and C.J. McMillan (eds), *Organization and Nation: The Aston Programme IV*. Farnborough, UK: Gower, pp. 173–186.

Itami, H. (1987) *Mobilizing Invisible Assets*. Cambridge, MA: Harvard University Press.

Iwata, R. (1978) *The Environment of Management in Modern Japan* (in Japanese). Tokyo: Nihon Keizai Shimbun.

Japan Times (1988) Sohyo members complain about long hours, low pay. 17 January.

Johansson, J.K., and Nonaka, I. (1987) Market research the Japanese way. *Harvard Business Review*, 65, 16–22.

Kagono, T., Nonaka, I., Sakakibara, K., and Okumura, A. (1985) *Strategic vs Evolutionary Management: A US–Japan comparison of strategy and organisation*. Amsterdam: North-Holland.

Kamata, S. (1982) *Japan in the Passing Lane: An insider's account of life in a Japanese auto factory*. New York: Pantheon.

Kanai, T. (1987) Differentiation of contrasting cosmologies among R and D personnel:

subtlety in Japanese R and D management. *Annals of the School of Business Administration, Kobe University*, **31**, 109–141.

Keys, J.B., and Miller, T.R. (1984) The Japanese management theory jungle. *Academy of Management Review*, **9**, 342–353.

Kidd, J.B., and Teramoto, Y. (1981) Japanese production subsidiaries in the United Kingdom: a study of managerial 'decision-making'. Working paper no. 203. University of Aston Management Centre, UK.

Kobayashi, T. (1980) *Japan's Multinational Corporations* (in Japanese). Tokyo: Chuo Keizai.

Kono, T. (1986) Factors affecting the creativity of organization: an approach from the analysis of the new product development. First International Symposium on Management, Japan Society for the Study of Business Administration, Kobe University, pp. 271–326.

Lincoln, J.R., Hanada, M., and McBride, K. (1986) Organizational structures in Japanese and US manufacturing. *Administrative Science Quarterly*, **31**, 338–364.

Lincoln, J.R., Hanada, M., and Olson, J. (1981) Cultural orientations and individual reactions to organizations: a study of employees of Japanese-owned firms. *Administrative Science Quarterly*, **26**, 93–115.

Lincoln, J.R., and Kalleberg, A.L. (1985) Work organization and workforce commitment: a study of plants and employees in the US and Japan. *American Sociological Review*, **50**, 738–760.

Lincoln, J.R., Olson, J., and Hanada, M. (1978) Cultural effects on organizational structure: the case of Japanese firms in the United States. *American Sociological Review*, **43**, 829–847.

Luthans, F., McCaul, H.S., and Dodd, N.G. (1985) Organizational commitment: a comparison of American, Japanese and Korean employees. *Academy of Management Journal*, **28**, 213–219.

McMillan, C.J. (1985) *The Japanese Industrial System*. Berlin: de Gruyter.

Maguire, M.A., and Pascale, R.T. (1978) Communication, decision-making and implementation among managers in Japanese and American managed companies. *Sociology and Social Research*, **63**, 1–22.

Mannari, H. and Befu, H. (Eds) *The Challenge of Japan's Internationalization: Organization and Culture*. Tokyo: Kodansha.

Marsh, R.M., and Mannari, H. (1976) *Modernization and the Japanese Factory*. Princeton, NJ: Princeton University Press.

Marsh, R.M., and Mannari, H. (1981) Technology and size as determinants of the organizational structure of Japanese factories. *Administrative Science Quarterly*, **26**, 33–57.

Meaning of Working International Research Team (1987) *The Meaning of Working*. London: Academic Press.

Misumi, J. (1975) Action research on the development of leadership, decision-making processes and organizational performance in a Japanese shipyard. *Psychologia*, **18**, 187–193.

Misumi, J. (1984) Decision-making in Japanese groups and organizations. In B. Wilpert and A. Sorge (eds), *International Perspectives on Organizational Democracy*. Chichester, UK: Wiley, pp. 525–539.

Misumi, J. (1985) *The Behavioral Science of Leadership*. Ann Arbor, MI: University of Michigan Press.

Mito, T. (1983) Japanese management principles and seniority systems. *The Wheel Extended*, Special Supplement 12, 4–8.

Miyajima, R. (1986) Organization ideology of Japanese managers. *Management International Review*, **26**, 73–76.

Miyazawa, S. (1986) Legal departments of Japanese corporations in the United States: a study on organizational adaptation to multiple environments. *Kobe University Law Review*, **20**, 97–162.

Nakane, C. (1970) *Japanese Society*. London: Weidenfeld and Nicholson.

Nakane, C. (1972) Social background of Japanese in southeast Asia. *Developing Economies*, **10**, 115–125.

Naoi, A., and Schooler, C. (1985) Occupational conditions and psychological functioning in Japan. *American Journal of Sociology*, **90**, 729–752.

Negandhi, A.R. (1985) Management strategies and policies of American, German and Japanese multinational corporations. *Management Japan*, **18**, 12–20.

Negandhi, A.R., and Baliga, B.R. (1979) *Quest for Survival and Growth: A comparative study of Japanese, European and American multinationals*. New York: Praeger.

Negandhi, A.R., Eshghi, G.S., and Yuen, E.C. (1985) The management practices of Japanese subsidiaries overseas. *California Management Review*, **27**, 93–105.

Nonaka, I., and Johansson, J.K. (1985) Japanese management: what about the 'hard' skills? *Academy of Management Review*, **10**, 181–191.

Nonaka, I., and Okumura, A. (1984) A comparison of management in American, Japanese and European firms. *Management Japan*, **17**(1), 23–29; **17**(2), 20–27.

Odaka, K. (1975) *Toward Industrial Democracy: Management and workers in modern Japan*. Cambridge MA: Harvard University Press.

Oh, T.K. (1976) Japanese management: a critical review. *Academy of Management Review*, **1**, 14–25.

Okubayashi, K. (1986a) The impacts of industrial robots on working life in Japan. *Journal of General Management*, **11**, 22–34.

Okubayashi, K. (1986b) Recent problems of Japanese personnel management. *Labour and Society*, **11**, 18–37.

Okubayashi, K. (1987) Work content and organizational structure of Japanese enterprises under microelectronic innovation. *Annals of the School of Business Administration, Kobe University*, **31**, 34–52.

Ozawa, T. (1979) *Multinationalism Japanese Style: The political economy of outward dependency*. Princeton, NJ: Princeton University Press.

Pascale, R.T. (1978a) Communication and decision-making across cultures: Japanese and American comparisons. *Administrative Science Quarterly*, **23**, 91–109.

Pascale, R.T. (1978b) Personnel practices and employee attitudes: a study of Japanese and American managed firms in the United States. *Human Relations*, **31**, 597–615.

Pascale, R.T., and Athos, A.G. (1981) *The Art of Japanese Management: Applications for American Executives*. New York: Simon and Schuster.

Pascale, R.T., and Maguire, M.A. (1980) Comparison of selected work factors in Japan and the United States. *Human Relations*, **33**, 433–455.

Rohlen, T.P. (1974) *For Harmony and Strength: Japanese white-collar organization in anthropological perspective*. Berkeley, CA: University of California Press.

Schonberger, R.J. (1982) *Japanese Manufacturing Techniques*. New York: Free Press.

Seror, A.C. (1982) A cultural contingency framework for the comparative analysis of Japanese and US organizations. In S.M. Lee and G. Schwendiman (eds), *Management by Japanese Systems*. New York: Praeger, pp. 239–255.

Sethi, S.P., Namiki, N., and Swanson, C.L. (1984) *The False Promise of the Japanese Economic Miracle*. Marshfield, MA: Pitman.

Smith, D. (in press) *Management, Technology and Culture*. London: Macmillan.

Smith, P.B., and Tayeb, M.H. (1988) Organizational structure and processes. In M.H.

Bond (ed.), *The Cross-Cultural Challenge to Social Psychology.* Newbury Park, CA: Sage.

Sullivan, J., and Peterson, R.B. (1982) Factors associated with trust in Japanese–American joint ventures. *Management International Review*, **22**, 30–40.

Sullivan, J., Peterson, R.B., Kameda, N., and Shimada, J. (1981) The relationship between conflict resolution approaches and trust: a cross-cultural study. *Academy of Management Journal*, **24**, 803–815.

Taira, K. (1983) Japan's low employment: an economic miracle or statistical artefact. *Monthly Labour Review*, **106**.

Takahashi, N., and Takayanagi, S. (1985) Decision procedure models and empirical research: the Japanese experience. *Human Relations*, **38**, 767–780.

Takamiya, S. (1981) The characteristics of Japanese management. *Management Japan*, **14**(2), 6–9.

Takamiya, S., and Thurley, K.E. (eds) (1985) *Japan's Emerging Multinationals: An international comparison of policies and practices.* Tokyo: Tokyo University Press.

Takezawa, S.I., and Whitehill, A.M. (1981) *Workways: Japan and America.* Tokyo: Japan Institute of Labour.

Taylor, S.J. (1983) *Shadows of the Rising Sun: A critical view of the 'Japanese Miracle'.* Tokyo: Tuttle.

Tracy, P., and Azumi, K. (1976) Determinants of administrative control: a test of a theory with Japanese factories. *American Sociological Review*, **41**, 80–93.

Trevor, M. (1983) *Japan's Reluctant Multinationals.* London: Pinter.

Tsuda, M. (1977) *Theory of Japanese Style Management* (in Japanese). Tokyo: Chuo-Keizai.

Tung, R.L. (1984) How to negotiate with the Japanese. *Californian Management Review*, **26**, 62–77.

Tung, R.L. (1987) Expatriate assignments: enhancing success and minimizing failure. *Academy of Management Executive*, **1**, 117–126.

Turnbull, P.J. (1986) The Japanization of production at Lucas Electrical. *Industrial Relations Journal*, **17**, 193–206.

Urabe, K. (1978) *Japanese Management* (in Japanese). Tokyo: Chuo-Keizai.

Urabe, K. (1984) *Japanese Management Does Evolve* (in Japanese). Tokyo: Chuo-Keizai.

Urabe, K. (1986) Innovation and the Japanese Management System. Keynote address, First International Symposium on Management, Japan Society for the Study of Business Administration, Kobe University, 11–49.

Van Fleet, D.D., and Griffin, R.W. (1989) Quality circles: a review and suggested future directions. *International Review of Industrial and Organizational Psychology 1989* [*Volume 4*], Chapter 7, pp. 213–233. Chichester: Wiley.

Wagatsuma, H. (1982) Internationalization of the Japanese: group model reconsidered. In H. Mannari and H. Befu (eds), *The Challenge of Japan's Internationalization: Organization and culture.* Tokyo: Kodansha, pp. 298–308.

Wakabayashi, M., and Graen, G.B. (1984) The Japanese career progress study: a 7 year follow-up. *Journal of Applied Psychology*, **69**, 603–614.

Westney, D.E., and Sakakibara, K. (1985) The role of Japan based in global technology strategy. *Technology in Society*, **7**, 315–330.

White, M., and Trevor, M. (1983) *Under Japanese Management.* London: Heinemann.

Whitehill, A.M., and Takezawa, S.I. (1968) *The Other Worker: A comparative study of industrial relations in the United States and Japan.* Honolulu: East-West Center Press.

Yoshihara, H. (1986) Dynamic synergy and top management leadership: strategic innovation in Japanese corporations. First International Symposium on Management,

Japan Society for the Study of Business Administration, Kobe University, pp. 353–376.

Yoshino, M.Y. (1975) Emerging Japanese multinational enterprises. In E.F. Vogel (ed.), *Modern Japanese Organization and Decision-Making*. Berkeley, CA: University of California Press, pp. 146–166.

Yoshino, M.Y. (1976) *Japan's Multinational Enterprises*. Cambridge, MA: Harvard University Press.

Yoshino, M.Y., and Lifson, T.B. (1986) *The Invisible Link: Japan's sogo shosha and the organization of trade*. Cambridge, MA: MIT Press.

Chapter 5

JOB AND WORK DESIGN

Toby D. Wall and Robin Martin
MRC/ESRC Social and Applied Psychology Unit
Department of Psychology
University of Sheffield
UK

INTRODUCTION

Job design is an area of enduring interest within the broader field of industrial and organizational psychology. Research focuses on the charactistics of jobs and how these affect people's attitudes and behavior. Traditionally, the emphasis has been on lower-level jobs within organizations, such as clerical and shopfloor work.

Explicit psychological interest in job design can be traced back to the turn of the century, to the early days of the emergence of psychology as an academic and applied discipline in its own right. Since that time, as is typical of most areas of scientific endeavour, progress has been uneven. Periods of high research activity and rapid advance are followed by quiet times in which the momentum appears to be lost and the avenues for future inquiry are obscure. In reviewing the literature for this chapter we came to the conclusion that currently we are experiencing such a lull. There is a lower rate of publication on job design during the 1980s than there was during the 1970s.

It is clear, nevertheless, that the nature of jobs will remain an important influence over the quality of people's lives, and less research will not alter that fact. So we turned our thoughts to the kinds of influence that might serve to rekindle progress in the area. We decided to ask ourselves two questions. First, what are the major deficiencies in the literature as it stands? Second, what developments in the 'outside world' are likely to help us overcome those weaknesses and open up opportunities for innovative studies? Our tentative answers to these questions will emerge during the course of the chapter. For the present it is sufficient to signal that, with respect to the second question, we identified the application of information technology in work settings as an important stimulus. The diffusion of such microelectronic based technology into organizations is accelerating, and changing the nature of jobs in offices and on the shopfloor. It represents what some have called the 'second industrial revolution' (Halton, 1985), or the 'information technology revolution' (Forester, 1985). The diffusion of this technology raises numerous questions about how it can best be exploited, and what dangers are inherent in its use. Central among these are the implications of the technology for job design, and conversely, how psychological knowledge of job design can be deployed in the development of new technologies. It is these opportunities and challenges which should stimulate research and development studies.

This chapter is divided into four main sections. The first is a history of job design research up to the mid-1970s. This is followed by a summary of the more recent literature which is considered thematically. The third part outlines some of the weaknesses in the literature to date, by identifying important issues which are inadequately treated, and others which are neglected. Finally, the chapter concludes with a brief consideration of the implications of the 'information technology revolution' for research into job design.

A BRIEF HISTORY OF JOB DESIGN RESEARCH

It is useful to recap on some of the major early developments in job design for two reasons: first, this serves as a background against which to consider the research reviewed in the following section: second, aspects of this history have been recently revived to help analysis of the job and psychological implications of the application of information technology in work organizations. We begin this brief historical review at the usual starting point, the evolution of the 'traditional' approach to job design, that of work simplification.

Work Simplification

The major influences on traditional job design practices can be traced back to the writings of such theorists as Adam Smith (1776) and Charles Babbage (1835). A key idea in their arguments is the division of labour, which they saw as the vehicle for increasing output per man–hour. For Smith this would occur for three reasons: greater dexterity would arise when employees 'specialized' in a small part of the required work; time would be saved by not having to change from one task to another; and labour-saving inventions were more likely to appear when the focus had been narrowed in this way. Babbage added the rationale that learning times would be reduced by fragmentation of jobs and savings thus could be made both in training and by employing less skilled and therefore cheaper labour.

The writings and practical demonstrations offered by Taylor (1911) and Gilbreth (1911) contributed to the progression towards work simplification. Taylor's Scientific Management approach has many facets, but an important feature is that it built upon the principle of the division of labour and suggested that management should explicitly assume responsibility for the design of jobs, and exercise greater influence over the execution of work. This involved developing more efficient work methods and, through a combination of training, incentives, and control, ensuring these were put into practice. To the fragmentation of work into jobs comprising only a small range of the required tasks (a horizontal division of labour) was added the idea of a vertical division of labour. Here management assumed more regulation, and 'workers' less, over how and when work was to be completed. There was a separation between planning and control on the one hand, and 'doing' on the other.

The extent to which the ideas introduced by Smith, Babbage, and particularly Taylor influenced the evolution of job design is a matter of controversy among historians of the area (see, for example, Baritz, 1960; Kelly, 1982). It is certainly clear that a range of other developments, such as the moving assembly line introduced in 1914 at the Ford Motor Company at Highland Park in Michigan (Edwards, 1978) and the incorporation of the principles of the division of labour and Scientific Management into classical management theories (e.g. Gulick and Urwick, 1937), played an important part (see Davis, and Taylor, 1962; Kelly, 1982). It also seems likely that the principles of job design which emerged themselves reflected existing trends in industry. What is less in dispute is the conclusion that work simplification has been, and still is, the dominant job design paradigm. As Klein (1976, p. 14) describes:

> the choices made in the design and organization of work have tended to be in the direction of rationalization, specialization and the sub-division of tasks, and the minimizing and standardization of skills . . . first in manufacturing and later in administration, the knowledge and methods of the natural sciences have been put to the task of discovering new methods of working and organizing which would give economic and predictable results.

That work simplification has spread from shopfloor jobs in manufacturing to most other areas of work is an argument offered by many commentators (e.g. Braverman, 1974; Cherns and Davis, 1975; Kraft, 1977), and its continuing influence over job design practice has been documented by Davis, Canter, and Hoffman (1955), Hedberg and Mumford (1975) and Taylor (1979).

Though clearly neither a universal nor homogeneous phenomenon, work simplification is the reference point for contemporary I/O psychology approaches to job design. These attempt to reverse the trend by creating jobs which involve a wider range of tasks over which job holders exercise greater control. The term job redesign is thus often used as it signifies a change from the dominant paradigm. The productivity argument behind this alternative approach is that more complex, responsible jobs will engender better performance through promoting work motivation, which will compensate for gains otherwise obtained by the division of labour. It is also argued that job redesign leads to greater flexibility and, by enhancing satisfaction, to an improvement in the quality of working life—itself a benefit to which employees are entitled as major contributors to their employing organizations (Mohrman et al., 1986). Research into job design can be seen as the quest to test these assumptions empirically, to examine their general validity and determine the limits within which they operate.

Early Studies of Work Simplification

Early psychological interest in job design was mainly reactive to the horizontal aspect of work simplification. It sought to document the affective and behavioral consequences of creating jobs involving the repetition of a narrow range of tasks. The vertical division of labour was an issue left relatively untouched.

In the UK some of the earliest studies of repetitive work were undertaken under the auspices of the Industrial Fatigue Research Board, which evolved into the Industrial Health Research Board funded by the Medical Research Council. These involved intensive investigations of such jobs as bicycle chain assembly, soap wrapping, tobacco weighing and packing, cartridge case assembly, and pharmaceutical product packing (e.g. Burnett, 1925; Wyatt and Ogden, 1924). The results confirmed the now accepted view that repetitive work is dissatisfying and, if taken to extremes, is not necessarily more productive. Thus Wyatt, Fraser, and Stock (1928) reported 'operatives who have experience of both uniform and varied conditions of work generally prefer the latter' (p. 25). Similarly, the Board's eleventh annual report drawing on the results of the whole programme of research concluded, 'boredom has become increasingly prominent as a factor in the industrial life of the worker, and its effects are no less important than those of fatigue' (Industrial Health Research Board, 1931, p. 30).

A later Health Board report brought a new dimension to the area. Fraser (1947) examined the association between job (and social) factors and the incidence of neurotic illness in a large sample of over 3000 employees in engineering factories. Neurosis (independently assessed by clinicians) was found to be most prevalent among those who found work boring, were engaged in asssembly, bench inspection, and tool room work, or performed jobs requiring constant attention. He summarized the results as follows: 'It may still be less important to make jobs foolproof than to design them so that they will not be disliked, found boring, or demand long periods of close attention to unvarying detail. . . . More variety, and scope for initiative and interest, could be introduced without any fundamental alteration of production programmes' (Fraser, 1947, p. 10).

In the United States similar findings were obtained. Walker and Guest's (1952) classic study, *Man on the Assembly Line*, conducted in the car industry, confirmed the relationship between simplified jobs and negative work attitudes; and Kornhauser's (1965) investigation of mental health, in the same industrial sector, supported Fraser's findings. Kornhauser concluded that 'by far the most influential attribute [of jobs] is the opportunity work offers — or fails to offer — for the use of workers' abilities and for associated feelings of interest, sense of accomplishment, personal growth and self-respect' (1965, p. 363). Simplified jobs were seen as offering few such opportunities.

Overall, this early line of research served to establish the importance of job factors to psychological wellbeing. It confirmed the intuitively accepted view that simplified, repetitive jobs were less satisfying, and introduced mental health as a relevant outcome variable (which later investigators have largely ignored). However, it generally failed to address the issue of productivity, did not move effectively into a proactive mode involving the deliberate redesign of jobs (Walker's 1950 study is an exception), and focused on the horizontal aspect of the division of labour (the range of tasks carried out) to the relative exclusion of the vertical aspect as reflected by job autonomy, control, and responsibility.

Job Enrichment

During the 1950s and 1960s research into work design was guided by two largely independent developments. Both encouraged a more proactive, change-oriented research approach by describing how jobs should be redesigned; and both challenged work simplification not only by suggesting a wider range of tasks be included in jobs, but also by advocating that more autonomy and control be afforded to employees over the execution of work. The first of these was the notion of job enrichment. The second development was that of autonomous work groups (which is considered later).

Job enrichment has its origins in the work of Herzberg and associates (1959, 1966, 1968) in the United States. In his Two-Factor Theory, Herzberg (1966) distinguished between characteristics intrinsic to jobs, such as achievement, advancement, recognition, responsibility, and the nature of the work itself; and those extrinsic to the jobs, such as company policy and administration, supervision, interpersonal relations, and work conditions. He argued that the former ('motivators') are instrumental in promoting motivation and satisfaction, whereas the latter ('hygiene factors') are only important as sources of dissatisfaction. Thus the central proposition of the theory is that sources of job satisfaction and motivation are qualitatively different from the determinants of dissatisfaction.

Research failed to confirm the Two-Factor Theory as a whole (e.g. Locke and Henne, 1986; King, 1970; Wall and Stephenson, 1970), but the focus on the importance of intrinsic job factors for satisfaction and motivation provided impetus for subsequent studies. It was from this perspective that the idea of job enrichment arose, a proposal for redesigning jobs to provide employees with greater responsibility and control over their work activities.

Herzberg's theory was effectively superseded by Hackman and Oldham's (1976) Job Characteristics Model, which built upon earlier work by Turner and Lawrence (1965) and Hackman and Lawler (1971). The Job Characteristics Model specifies five 'core job dimensions' salient to job attitudes and behaviour. These are task variety, task identity, task significance, autonomy, and task feedback. By (differentially) affecting the 'critical psychological states' of experienced meaning, responsibility, and knowledge of results, the five job characteristics are predicted to promote work motivation, work performance, and job satisfaction, and to reduce labour turnover and absenteeism. The model (through the medium of the 'motivating potential score') ascribes particular importance to autonomy and feedback. In addition, the strength of the job characteristics–outcome relationship is predicted to be affected by individual differences, in particular the level of employees' 'growth need strength'. The attitudes and behavior of those who place greater importance on challenge, using their own judgement and the opportunity for achievement at work (high growth need strength), are held to be more strongly affected by the job characteristics than are the attitudes and behavior of those with less strong growth needs.

The Job Characteristics Model did not represent a major new departure in job design. Rather, it served to summarize a previous line of research stretching back more than 15 years and to present this in a commendably explicit and digestible form. Moreover, by developing a set of measures covering each of the key variables (the Job Diagnostic Survey, Hackman and Oldham, 1975) the authors provided an attractive research package. Together these properties account for the fact that it was to become a major theoretical influence on research from its inception to the present day.

Group Work Redesign

The second major development concerns the concept of the autonomous work group. This evolved within the more general socio-technical systems approach to organizational analysis and design developed at the Tavistock Institute in Great Britain (Trist and Bamforth, 1951; see also Trist, 1981, for a more recent review). Early work at Tavistock involved intensive studies of people engaged in functionally interrelated tasks. It is thus not surprising that the focus on work design which emerged took the work group as the main unit of analysis.

A key feature of autonomous work groups is that they provide for a high degree of self-determination by employees in the management of their everyday work. Typically this involves collective control over the pace of work, distribution of tasks within the group, and the timing and organization of breaks; also participation in the training and recruitment of new members (Gulowsen, 1972). Often it also requires little or no direct supervision (Emery, 1980). In recent years autonomous work groups have been given a variety of labels including, *inter alia*, 'semi-autonomous work groups,' 'self-managing work groups,' 'self-managing work teams,' and 'self-regulating work teams'. In practice this approach has much in common with job enrichment with regard to the recommended content of work since it emphasizes the provision of autonomy, feedback, and task completeness. The focus, however, is on the group level of design and analysis.

The early history of research into autonomous work groups is punctuated by carefully documented case studies and action research projects (e.g. Davis and Valfer, 1965; Rice, 1958; Trist and Bamforth, 1951). This approach to work design has also had considerable practical success, especially in Europe, and later in the United States. In the 1970s Volvo and Saab built new car production plants which eschewed conventional production lines and were based around autonomous work groups, as did General Motors in the 1980s. Along with job enrichment, the ideas behind autonomous work groups and socio-technical systems theory more generally have played a prominent role in the quality of working life (QWL) movement which emerged in almost all Western industrial societies in the 1960s and 1970s (Mohrman *et al.*, 1986; Wall, 1982).

The influence of the autonomous work group concept on empirical research, however, developed more slowly. During the 1960s it gave rise to few studies based on designs allowing causal inference, and was not systematically evaluated in terms of its effects on attitudes and behaviour. The literature was disparate, and no focused set of studies emerged. This in part was due to its origins in a more action research oriented environment dedicated to meeting client rather than 'scientific' needs. It was also a reflection of a lack of specificity, and considerable complexity, in the underlying socio-technical systems theory (Clark, 1975; Hill, 1972; McLean and Sims, 1978). As Cherns and Davis (1975) note, the approach requires the use of a 'number of nonexistent dictionaries' in order to be put into practice. Not until the mid-1970s did interest in the socio-technical approach take root in the United States. Nevertheless, because of its clear potential, and its compatibility with contemporary values (Davis, 1976; Hertog, 1976; Klein, 1976), the approach survives to influence the direction of more recent research.

Overview

The above four perspectives continue to structure contemporary research. Work simplification remains as the predominant job design influence in practice, against which I/O approaches are contrasted. There has persisted a line of inquiry focused on the horizontal aspect of the division of labour, that which is concerned with the psychological implications of short cycle, repetitive, and paced jobs. Through the Job Characteristics Model, job enrichment persists as an approach which also emphasizes the role of individual difference variables in the explanation of its effects. Finally, the original idea of autonomous work groups which is receiving renewed attention provides a starting point for group work redesign and, through its roots in socio-technical systems theory, reminds investigators that such developments should be considered in their organizational contexts. We turn now to consider how recent research has built and elaborated upon these guiding approaches.

CONTEMPORARY RESEARCH INTO WORK DESIGN

Research since the mid-1970s clearly reflects the issues central within the history of job design, but is also characterized by an increasing diversity of perspective. In this section we attempt to represent this diversity by briefly describing some of the main themes that have guided recent investigations.

Repetitive and Machine-paced Work

Early interest in job design reactive to the horizontal aspect of work simplification has been represented by recent research into the psychological effects of repetitive and machine-paced jobs. Cox and his colleagues have examined the effects of such work both in laboratory experiments and field settings (Cox and Mackay, 1979; Cox, 1980; Cox, Mackay, and Page, 1982; Cox, Thirlaway, and Cox, 1982; Cox and Cox, 1984). They found machine-paced repetitive work to be associated with higher levels of reported stress, but that high 'attentional demands' and socializing could serve to alleviate this effect.

In a similar vein Hurrell (1905) examined the moderating effect of the Type A behaviour pattern on the relationship between paced work and psychological mood disturbance. Using a sample of nearly 3000 machine-paced letter sorters, and an equivalent sized comparison group engaged in unpaced work, he found pacing to be associated with mood state (e.g. higher tension–anxiety, anger–hostility, and depression–dejection), but there was no differential effect for subjects with high Type A scores.

A provocative paper by Broadbent (1985) suggests a more differentiated view of the relationship between job characteristics and mental health. Using data from his own research and that of NIOSH reported by Caplan et al. (1975) and LaRocco, House, and French, (1980), and also drawing on Karasek's (1979) ideas, Broadbent argued that job demands (work load and pacing) have effects primarily on anxiety, social isolation operates on depression, and repetitive, unskilled work mainly affects job dissatisfaction. He also suggested that social support, instrumental attitudes (the extent to which people work for pay as opposed to job satisfaction), and leisure satisfaction either buffer or moderate such relationships.

Other recent work on repetitiveness and pacing is described by Broadbent and Gath (1979, 1981), Dainoff, Hurrell, and Happ (1981), Murrell (1978), Murphy and Hurrell (1980), Salvendy and Smith (1981), and Smith, Hurrell, and Murphy (1981).

This area of inquiry is promising, and Broadbent's ideas in particular warrant further attention. The focus on mental health is refreshing in a field which has traditionally been rather conservative in its choice of outcome variables (as we shall discuss later). It provides a clear link between I/O and clinical psychology which is worthy of pursuit. Nevertheless, this aspect of job design has received relatively little attention in recent years, and correspondingly its empirical base is less than impressive. Studies are predominantly cross-sectional and far from definitive.

The Job Characteristics Approach and Job Enrichment

Recent research into the design of individual jobs has been strongly influenced by Hackman and Oldham's (1975, 1976) Job Characteristics Model (JCM). Published studies based on this model increased dramatically in number up to the appearance of the thorough critical review of the job characteristics approach by Roberts and Glick (1981), since which time they have diminished. We shall not attempt to repeat and update that analysis, the main conclusions of which are equally valid today. Rather, we shall look more selectively at some of the issues of continuing interest.

Despite the general influence of the JCM over research, the full model has only rarely been investigated empirically. The feature which distinguishes the JCM most clearly from its predecessors is the inclusion of the critical psychological states as intervening variables (see p. 65 for a description of the JCM). Direct examination of this part of the model has confirmed neither the predicted differential pattern of relationships between the five job characteristics and the three critical psychological states, nor that these intervening variables are required to account for the relationship between the core job dimensions on the one hand and the outcome variables on the other (e.g. Wall, Clegg, and Jackson, 1978). It appears that the critical psychological states are an unnecessary elaboration which concern for parsimony would lead one to exclude. Generally, investigators have either ignored this aspect of the JCM (e.g. Oldham, 1976; Orpen, 1979) or treated the critical psychological states as dependent variables (e.g. Baghat and Chassie, 1980; Kiggundu, 1980).

In practice, therefore, the JCM has been simplified to an approach concerned with the direct causal links between job characteristics and outcome variables, with growth need strength specified as a moderator. Its considerable influence over the literature stems from its identification of a particular set of variables and the provision of instruments to tap these. This has given a consistency of focus to the literature which other approaches have failed to achieve. We shall consider the primary causal proposition here, and address the issue of individual differences afterwards.

The central component of the JCM, along with other approaches to work design is that the specified job characteristics are posited as determinants of employees' attitudes and behaviour. The natural progression of research effort is to move from weak but expedient cross-sectional research designs, which are sufficient to suggest whether the proposition deserves further attention, to change studies with designs capable of supporting causal inference. There has been much effort of the correlational exploratory type which supports the job characteristics approach (see, for example, the meta-analysis reported by Loher et al., 1985), and it seems generally agreed that little more is needed (Roberts and Glick, 1981).

Progress with respect to building up evidence based on change studies has been disappointing. Such investigations are few and far between, and in general exhibit important design weaknesses. One interesting trend in this area has been a particular variant of the 'naturally occurring field experiment'. Here investigators have homed in on instances of organizational change which are incidental to but may have (unknown) consequences for job design (e.g. the introduction of a 4-day week, Baghat and Chassie, 1980; job moves, Keller and Holland, 1981; and technological change, Hackman, Pearce, and Wolfe, 1978). The allocation of employees to enriched, no change, and impoverished 'conditions' has then been made *post hoc* on the basis of self-report measures of job characteristics obtained both before and after the change. In the absence of either a clear rationale for predicting the effects of the organizational change for job design, or the use of independent or objective measures of job characteristics, this approach seems to offer at best only a minor advance over cross-sectional research using perceptual measures, and provides a dubious base for causal inference.

Other field change studies have involved actual, and typically deliberate, theory-related job changes (e.g. Griffeth, 1985; Griffin, 1983; Locke, Sirota, and Wolfson, 1976; Orpen, 1979). Perceived job characteristics measures have been used to confirm that the manipulation had its expected experienced counterpart. Taken as a whole the evidence from this research, in common with laboratory experiments (e.g. White and Mitchell, 1979) and longitudinal field surveys (e.g. Griffin, 1981), supports predictions concerning attitudinal and (to a lesser degree) performance effects, but is neither unproblematic nor definitive. Performance effects without corresponding motivational or attitudinal ones, and vice versa, point to theoretical deficiencies, and suggest there may be unidentified factors which promote or inhibit particular outcomes. Methodological considerations also cloud the issue: only a small proportion of the few investigations is based on strong research designs; it seems likely that failures are under-represented in the literature (but see Frank and Hackman, 1975; Lawler, Hackman, and Kaufman, 1973); and it is often difficult to ascribe changes recorded to job design itself rather than to the various associated changes which the redesign may have necessitated. A particular weakness in change studies is that the effects of job redesign have only been pursued in the short term, a few weeks to 6 months. In the absence of clear theoretical specification of an appropriate time scale for job redesign effects to appear, it is unclear whether negative findings reflect an inappropriate measurement period, or indeed if positive ones are really only short-term rather than enduring.

The above criticisms are not intended as an indictment of particular studies or investigators. Indeed, those that have undertaken change studies are to be commended. Rather it is a comment on the area as a whole. There remains a need for still more field experimentation and longitudinal research using a variety of alternative designs and techniques. Only by creating such a large body of evidence can the inevitable weaknesses in individual studies, which arise because of the many constraints inherent in working in real-life settings, be compensated for by the strengths of others. As in other areas of I/O psychology there is a paucity of change studies (cf. Griffin and Bateman, 1986), and this presumably reflects the difficulties experienced in mounting such research. We consider this more general issue later.

Another aspect of research stemming directly from the JCM concerns the measurement of job characteristics. The large majority of studies have been based on the Job Diagnostic Survey (JDS, Hackman and Oldham, 1975), used in such a way that observations of the independent and dependent variables derive from the same source, the job incumbent. Examinations of this instrument have shown that whilst the scales to measure the five core job dimensions typically exhibit high internal reliability, multivariate analysis does not always confirm the theory specified separation among them. For example, Abdel-Halim (1978), Ferratt and Reeve (1977), and Katz (1978b) obtained confirmation of the five dimensions, but Dunham (1976, 1977) Dunham, Aldag, and Brief (1977), and Green et al, (1979) did not. Schnake and Dumler (1985) similarly obtained non-confirmatory results, but went on to show that partialling out intrinsic job satisfaction changed the findings to one of support for the hypothesized structure. They concluded that the measure can be contaminated by people's affective reactions (see also Ferratt, Dunham, and Pierce, 1981).

This latter point highlights the continuing concern about the validity of attempting to measure actual job characteristics through the medium of people's perceptions of their own jobs. Hackman and Oldham (1975), in their original report on the Job Diagnostic Survey, presented limited evidence to show that perceived scores were associated with ratings of job characteristics obtained from independent sources. More recently Kiggundu (1980) showed empirical support for the JCM when using independent ratings of job characteristics (from immediate supervisors and informed coworkers) and relating these to job incumbents' attitudes. It should be noted, however, that the support was stronger where the job incumbents' own ratings were used. Algera (1983) describes comparable results. These studies (along with field experiments involving actual changes to jobs) suggest that empirical support for the job characteristics approach as a whole cannot be dismissed as simply an artifact of the use of perceptual measures of job characteristics. However, they do not rule out the possibility that such measures are subject to attributional processes which could inflate or otherwise affect the nature of the evidence obtained (see p. 72), and these processes could be sufficient to account for the results of correlational studies based solely on self-report data.

In summary, research on the relationship between job characteristics and job reactions does not contradict the main predictions embodied within the JCM. Nevertheless, it is far from satisfactory. Two particular areas of weakness are: the lack of a sufficiently substantial body of field experiments examining the effects of job redesign over appropriate periods of time; and inadequate measurement of the objective job characteristics. These weaknesses were highlighted by Roberts and Glick in 1981, and little progress is evident since then. It should also be noted that researchers have paid considerably more attention to the predicted attitudinal outcome variables (job satisfaction and intrinsic motivation) than to the behavioural ones (performance and absence). Another area of research activity promoted by the JCM, that concerned with the role of individual differences in moderating the relationships between job characteristics and outcome variables, is considered next.

Individual Differences and Other Moderator Variables

One consequence of the JCM was to promote interest in individual differences as moderators of the relationship between job characteristics and employee responses. Initially, reflecting the particular variables specified by the JCM, the focus was predominantly on growth need strength (GNS), or related constructs such as higher-order need strength.

Much research effort has gone into examining the moderating role of GNS, either as an issue in its own right, or as part of investigations into the job characteristics approach to job design more generally (e.g. Champoux, 1980; Farr, 1976; Ganster, 1980; Griffin, 1982; Hackman, Pearce, and Wolfe, 1978; Jackson, Paul, and Wall, 1981; Kemp and Cook, 1983; Lawler, Hackman, and Kaufman, 1973; Orpen, 1979; Umstot, Bell, and Mitchell, 1976; Zierden, 1980).

Recently, two meta-analyses have been published which serve to integrate empirical research in this area. Loher et al. (1985) limited their analysis to the five job dimensions specified by the JCM and the single outcome variable of job satisfaction. They concluded that 'we can now state with some confidence that growth need strength acts as a moderator of the relationship between job characteristics and job satisfaction' (p. 287), but also noted that the main effect was still in evidence among employees with low GNS scores. Spector (1985) examined a wider range of outcome variables, including different dimensions of work satisfaction, motivation, performance, and absenteeism, and reached an equivalent conclusion for all these variables except the last.

The underlying tendency within the research as a whole thus lends support to the moderating effect of GNS. Nevertheless, it should be noted that the meta-analyses were based on subgroup correlations, rather than the more appropriate moderated regression (Zedeck, 1971) or analysis of covariance (Jackson, Paul, and Wall, 1981). Moreover, they encompassed a substantial proportion of negative findings. It thus remains unclear if there exists a generalizable GNS effect, or whether its discovery has been obscured by the use of inadequate measurement instruments, insensitive statistical techniques (Morris, Sherman, and Mansfield., 1986; Peters and Champoux, 1979), or other factors (cf. O'Connor, Rudolf, and Peters, 1980). Once again, the bulk of investigations have been based on cross-sectional data with independent, moderator, and dependent variables all measured through self-report data. There are few investigations examining whether high GNS employees respond more positively to actual job enrichment than do their lower GNS counterparts.

The inconclusiveness of investigations into GNS no doubt encouraged the search for other individual differences and contextual variables which moderate employees' responses to job characteristics. Among those examined have been work values such as need for achievement, need for autonomy, self-esteem, and the Protestant work ethic (Ganster, 1980; Mossholder, Bedeian, and Armenakis, 1982; O'Reilly and Caldwell, 1979; Steers, 1975; Steers and Spencer, 1977; Stone, Mowday, and Porter, 1977); job longevity (Katz, 1978a, 1978b; Kemp and Cook, 1983); role stress (Abdel-Halim, 1978, 1981; Beehr, 1976; Keller, Szilagyi, and Holland, 1976); extrinsic satisfaction (Abdel-Halim, 1979; Champoux, 1980; Oldham, 1976); and organizational climate and setting (Ferris and Gilmore, 1984; Walsh, Taber, and Beehr, 1980). As for GNS, the outcome has been an inconsistent rather than a coherent pattern of findings.

It would seem inappropriate to dismiss the issue of individual differences in job design or other areas of psychological research, as some would have us do (e.g. White, 1978). Yet research to date makes it clear that no strong and consistent moderating effect is apparent. Perhaps, as Kemp and Cook (1983) observe, rather than ask the question 'Which moderators are replicable across situations?' we should be attempting to 'specify the conditions under which moderators are important' (p. 896). It is also the case that the emphasis on moderator effects has distracted attention from other contributions of individual differences to people's work attitudes and behaviours.

The Social Information Processing Approach

The central role of perceived job characteristics in the literature provided the springboard for the recent growth of interest in the social information processing (SIP) approach to work design. In its most general form the SIP approach is based on the premise that job attitudes and perceptions are socially construed, and reflect information provided by others in the workplace. In some respects this can be seen as complementing the job characteristics approach, by offering the prospect of explaining additional variance with regard to the relationship between job perceptions and reactions. In other respects, the SIP approach can be seen as an alternative and invalidating perspective, which explains the relationship between the salient variables as caused by social factors rather than by objective job differences, which job design models assume (Griffin and Bateman, 1986).

Interest in the SIP approach was fostered by two theoretical papers by Salancik and Pfeffer (1977, 1978; see also Shaw, 1980). Subsequent empirical research has been mainly in the form of laboratory experiments in which informational cues (e.g. others' views of job characteristics, and their satisfactions) were manipulated and the effects on job perceptions, attitudes, and performance observed (e.g. Adler, Skov, and Salvemini, 1985; Mitchell, Liden, and Rothman, 1985; O'Reilly and Caldwell, 1979; Shaw and Weekley, 1981; Slusher and Griffin, 1980; White and Mitchell, 1979).

Field studies, using indirect indices of social influence (e.g. professional attitudes, work-group membership and affiliation), have been reported by Oldham and Miller (1979), O'Reilly, Parlette, and Bloom (1980), Griffin (1983, a field experiment), and O'Reilly and Caldwell (1985). Within the SIP framework attention has also been paid to individual difference effects on task perceptions and other reactions (e.g. O'Connor and Barrett, 1980; O'Reilly, Parlette, and Bloom, 1980; Weiss and Shaw, 1979). A difficulty with these studies is that the nature of the social cues from the indirect sources remains undefined.

Useful reviews of the SIP literature are provided by Blau and Katerberg (1982) and Thomas and Griffin (1983). Overall, it is clear that social factors do affect people's job perceptions, attitudes, and behaviour, much as would be expected. But it also appears that these influences complement rather than invalidate the job characteristics approach. Where objective job characteristics and social cues have been examined together they have been shown to affect employee reactions independently. Much remains to be done to take the SIP approach beyond its current exploratory status, not least of which is to develop direct measures of social cues in field settings.

The Socio-technical Systems Approach and Work-group Design

Although comparisons are difficult, it seems that autonomous work groups have been more widely implemented in practice than individually oriented job design approaches. Certainly, many observers have commented on their increasing use, along with that of socio-technical analysis more generally (e.g. Cummings, 1978; Kerr, Hill, and

Broedling, 1986; Pasmore *et al.*, 1983). Paradoxically, this practical interest does not appear to be fully reflected by the recent research literature. Nevertheless, academic interest has been growing, and this is evident in three respects. First, a number of authors have attempted to make more explicit, and develop, early theoretical thinking. The work of Susman (1976) and Cummings (1978, 1982) drew wider attention to the potential of this approach to work design, and its relevance to the design of jobs for advanced manufacturing technology has been made clear by Cummings and Blumberg (1987). Second, attempts have been made to adapt the job characteristics approach to make it applicable at the level of group work design. Hackman (1977) went so far as to suggest that autonomous work groups are likely to prove more powerful than individual forms of job design since they can encompass much larger and more complete pieces of work. Hackman (1983) subsequently extended the Job Characteristics Model to apply at the group level. Similarly, Rousseau (1977) and Cummings (1982) argued for a synthesis of the two approaches. Finally, there has been a number of reviews of empirical research in the area which point to the potential benefits of autonomous work groups whilst calling for initiatives in conducting field studies with strong research designs (e.g. Cummings, Molloy, and Glen, 1977; Pasmore *et al.*, 1983).

The response to the plea for more adequate empirical examination of autonomous work groups, however, has been disappointing. Case studies and general accounts continue to describe how change agents could or have set about undertaking socio-technical systems design, and provide valuable, but nevertheless circumstantial, evidence concerning the psychological and organizational benefits (and some costs) to be expected (e.g. Walton, 1977; Lawler, 1978; Emery, 1980; Kolodny and Kiggundu, 1980; Manz and Sims, 1982; Ciborra, Migliarese, and Romano, 1984). But this literature is mainly illustrative. The move towards a more adequate empirical base has been slow. Two comparative studies have been reported by Denison (1982) and Kemp *et al.*, (1983); a longitudinal investigation by Wall (1980) and Wall and Clegg (1981); and a field experiment (examining effects over 30 months) by Wall *et al.*, (1986). All these provide evidence in support of the attitudinal and performance benefits of autonomous group work, but the latter study also suggests costs with regard to labour turnover and managerial stress.

The above research only begins to scratch the surface with respect to the effects and implications of autonomous work groups. It is sufficient to encourage greater effort in the area, but does not provide a substantial enough base from which to generalize. It is even less adequate with regard to empirical evidence on the processes which take place within autonomous work groups, and how these may account for attitudinal and behavioural effects. It should also be pointed out that whilst socio-technical theory emphasizes the joint optimization of technical and social subsystems, empirically based research has almost entirely focused only on the social dimension (Denison, 1982; Pasmore *et al.*, 1983). It is to be hoped that recent initiatives encourage more systematic, comprehensive, and extensive investigation of autonomous work groups in field settings.

Context in Theory and Practice

A general criticism of the job characteristics approach to work design was that it encouraged a narrow theoretical perspective (e.g. Roberts and Glick, 1981). Certainly, until around the 1980s work in this area paid scant attention either to other relevant theories, or to contextual factors which may affect job properties and their effects on attitudes and behaviour. In principle research on autonomous work groups is less open to such a charge, since it is axiomatic to the underlying socio-technical systems theory that interdependence among a range of variables is considered. In practice, however, even studies emanating from this background showed little systematic consideration of organizational variables.

Recent investigations have shown signs of moving towards a broader perspective. We have already noted the introduction of social information processing theory to the job design area (p. 72), and the attempt to integrate job characteristics and socio-technical systems approaches (p. 73). This diversification is apparent in a number of other respects. Several investigators have examined the link between technology and the design of jobs. Technological uncertainty and its relationship with job characteristics has been considered by Brass (1985), Clegg (1984), Jones and James (1979), Pierce (1984), and Slocum and Sims (1980). The job design implications of technological interdependence (e.g. pooled, sequential, and reciprocal) and technological type (e.g. long-linked, mediating, and intensive) have been explored by Abdel-Halim (1981), Kiggundu (1981, 1983), Rousseau (1977), and Slocum and Sims (1980). Others have considered the relationship of job design to organizational structure (Aldag and Brief, 1979; Fry and Slocum, 1984; Pierce, Dunham, and Blackburn, 1979; Porter, Lawler, and Hackman, 1975; and Vecchio and Keon, 1981); managerial and leadership practices (Cordery and Wall, 1985; Ferris and Rowland, 1981; Hulin and Roznowski, 1985; Ovalle, 1984; Zierden, 1980); functional speciality (Dunham, 1977); staffing levels (Greenberg, Wang, and Dossett, 1982; Vecchio and Susman, 1981); turbulence (Williams, 1982); goal setting (Umstot, Bell, and Mitchell, 1976; Umstot, Mitchell, and Bell, 1978); management information systems (Clegg and Fitter, 1978); and organizational climate (Ferris and Gilmore, 1984).

Another consideration to receive attention is that concerned with the implementation of new forms of work design. Although Nicholas (1982) found that job enrichment has been based largely on 'top-down' approaches, the normative position taken by many investigators, and especially socio-technical theorists, is that employees should participate in the design or redesign of their own jobs. Empirical evidence for this view is scarce. Seeborg (1978) described an experimental study which provides some support for employee involvement in the design process (see also Huse and Cummings, 1985), but a recent field experiment reported by Griffeth (1985) showed that participation did not enhance the effects of job enrichment. Neither of these studies is without interpretational difficulty, and the effectiveness of alternative approaches to implementation remains largely undocumented. More generally, as Clegg (1979) has pointed out, the process of job redesign is a 'theoretical orphanage'.

The literature relating work design to organizational context is at present fragmented. It suggests a range of factors it is plausible to take into account, but as yet there is insufficient empirical evidence to identify the most salient among these. It does, however, hold out the prospect of leading to a more realistic perspective. Here the questions posed concern the conditions under which alternative approaches to job design will be successful and, conversely, the kinds of adjustment required in organizational structures and practices in order to effectively introduce a chosen form of work design.

ISSUES FOR THEORY AND RESEARCH

The aim of this section is to highlight issues of general relevance to the development of research and theory in job and work design. Some of these are elaborations of deficiencies already touched upon in the review so far. Others concern areas for development largely neglected in the contemporary literature. We have selected five we consider to be among the most important.

A Restriction of Focus

In an earlier review of the job design literature Roberts and Glick (1981, p. 210) noted: 'Investigations have become narrower over time. A restricted set of task characteristics and moderator variables have been focused on.' This remains a feature of contemporary research, as does concentration on a severely limited range of outcome variables.

In one sense this narrowness of focus is a testimony to the appeal of existing theory and its success in bringing coherence to the research effort. In this respect the Job Characteristics Model has been a dominant influence. In another sense, however, it is an indictment of the area, and of the absence of competing theoretical perspectives. Taking the independent variables first, there is clearly more to jobs than skill variety, task identity, task significance, autonomy, and feedback. Jobs can be characterized at different levels of analysis, and in different respects. Cycle time, physical load, attentional demand, memory load, cognitive demand, time span of discretion, level and mix of responsibility, time pressure, and a range of other variables seem likely to be important in themselves as well as potential determinants of employee job attitudes and behaviour. Little attention has been paid to such factors. It is not that they have been investigated and found wanting as salient job properties, but that they have been largely ignored. The inclusion of such variables would not only open up the prospect of a more comprehensive characterization of jobs, but also offers the opportunity for job design to more adequately cover a wide range of jobs, and particularly those at higher organizational levels which have been customarily neglected (cf. Wood, 1986).

In a similar way, the job design area is characterized by concentration on a very narrow range of dependent variables. Satisfaction, motivation, attendance behaviour, and performance are undoubtedly important aspects of work experience. But so, too, are other factors, such as industrial relations attitudes, grievances, stress, accidents and safety, and health. All these, and many others, are likely to be affected by the nature of jobs. A particular dependent variable which has periodically surfaced in relation to job design, but never been systematically integrated theoretically, is that of mental health (e.g. Kornhauser, 1965; Karasek, 1979; Wall and Clegg, 1981; Broadbent, 1985). A difficulty here, however, is that most existing conceptualizations and measures of mental health focus on the absence of mental illness. Since mental illness is evident in only small proportions of typical work populations, research is hampered by the lack of adequate variance in the dependent measure. However, re-emergent interest in the notion of positive mental health and the resultant creation of more sensitive instruments (e.g. Warr, 1987) makes it possible to pursue this area of inquiry. The same point about restricted focus can be made with regard to moderator variables, although recent research has shown greater diversity in this respect (see pp. 70-72).

The general point is that theory and research are currently very narrowly conceived. This may have been functional at one stage, but the time is now ripe for a wider perspective both in substantive terms and with regard to levels and types of measurement. The particular variables suggested above are introduced only as illustrations of what might be considered. If a broader base were to be adopted, especially within single studies, then empirical evidence could contribute to the selection of relevant variables. In this way theory could be built more explicitly on factors of demonstrable significance rather than being based on content by theoretical fiat.

The Theoretical Status of Motivation

The concept of motivation is logically central to all approaches to job design. It is required in order to explain why job characteristics affect performance and other behaviour. Nevertheless, the role of motivation is poorly articulated within existing theory. In the context of autonomous work groups it is rarely explicitly considered. In the Job Characteristics Model, motivation is ascribed the status of an outcome variable and its relationship with performance (and other dependent variables) is left unspecified. This is perhaps no more than a reflection of the ubiquitous yet unsatisfactory role of motivation within I/O psychology more generally (Locke and Henne, 1986), but nonetheless requires attention.

In practice there appears to be a large number of implicit assumptions within the literature concerning how and why job design affects performance. Perhaps the most conventional yet nebulous interpretation, based on need theory, is that enriched jobs lead to feelings of wanting to exert effort and this leads to higher performance (job enrichment→motivation→performance). A second, stemming from goal-setting theory (Umstot, Mitchell, and Bell, 1978), is that the provision of autonomy requires clear performance objectives and feedback, and it is this which motivates performance (target setting/feedback→motivation→performance). A third is that people in enriched jobs feel satisfied when they perform well (Hackman and Oldham, 1980). Thus the link is performance (given complex jobs)→motivation. A fourth explanation, most closely associated with the socio-technical systems approach, focuses on 'the control of variance at source'. Here the argument is that performance benefits accrue because with control over work being in the hands of operators they can respond more rapidly and flexibly to presenting circumstances than if being directed by supervision. The explanation thus lies in the logic of the work situation (but also assumes that employees wish to deploy their effort to performance ends). Here the assumption is: autonomous work groups→rapid and flexible response to production needs→ performance. Other explanations abound (e.g. labour intensification, Kelly, 1982).

It is clearly important to explore the validity of these several explanations, since they can have very different practical implications. For example, under the first explanation above there would be little benefit from enriching jobs if either the incumbents had insufficient ability to translate their enhanced motivation into performance, or the technology itself so constrained output that performance could not be raised. Similarly, performance benefits under the fourth explanation would be expected to be positively related to the amount of variance inherent in the work system. For reliable and predictable systems with little variance to control, minimal advantage would accrue from introducing autonomous work groups. More generally, the need is for research to come to grips with this issue of motivation, and to explain how job design affects performance. This implies more clearly articulated theory, closely monitored longitudinal field studies, and research designed to assess competing (or complementary) propositions.

The Dynamics of Redesigning Work

The above criticism of the status of motivation in work design theory is in fact a special case of a more general problem in the area. Too little attention has been paid to the questions of why and how the principles of work design operate with regard to each of the dependent variables. Empirical work has focused on outcome evaluations to the exclusion of documenting and explaining the processes within enriched jobs or autonomous work groups. In the latter approach to work design, for example, numerous intra-group and inter-group processes seem likely to affect both employees' attitudes and behaviour. Group cohesiveness, procedures for handling interpersonal conflict, the emergence of group norms and inter-group conflict are among the many factors which could influence the effects of this approach. Understanding of these factors may account for apparently conflicting results. Moreover, such a perspective is interesting in its own right and has important implications for the selection and training of employees for this form of work design.

Occasionally investigators have commented on such aspects of work design. Manz and Sims (1982) considered the potential for 'groupthink' in autonomous work groups; and Hackman (1983) introduced a number of group process issues in his theoretical approach to the design of work teams. One of the few empirical studies was reported by Blumberg (1900) who examined job switching within autonomous work groups in relation to job satisfaction and absenteeism. In general, however, the way in which individuals and groups respond and adapt to the challenge of redesigned work has not been on the research agenda. It ought to be, along with the related issue (introduced earlier, p. 74) concerning the process of implementing new forms of work design.

Theoretical Integration

So far our critique of job design research has applied largely within the parameters existing theory has set for itself. Here we broaden the focus by suggesting that the area might expand its boundaries and could benefit by taking on board ideas and propositions from traditionally separate areas of inquiry.

We have already drawn attention to emerging initiatives in relating work design to organizational context, and attempts to integrate the two areas both theoretically and empirically (pp. 73–74). It may be advantageous to extend this cross-fertilization into other fields. Implicit in the previous account of the dynamics of redesigned work is an integration with social psychological studies of small-group behaviour and processes. Personality theory and clinical psychology have contributions to make with regard to explanations of why job characteristics may have particular psychological effects, and clinical psychology could underpin the development of mental health as a dependent variable. Microeconomics offers the prospect of more adequate treatment of performance issues, particularly where the economic effects of work redesign appear to arise from altered labour costs rather than changed individual performance. Industrial relations perspectives are relevant, and are currently almost entirely neglected by psychologists.

A particular approach which has not been effectively adopted is open systems theory. Despite the support from within the work design area, as represented by socio-technical systems theorists, and the influential work of Katz and Kahn (1966, 1978) promoting this approach for I/O psychology more generally, it remains little more than a perspective. Its potential for guiding theory development and empirical research has not been realized. Part of the reason for this lies in the nature of the approach itself. As Klein (1976, p. 76) observed, 'It is easy to agree that the enterprise is a socio-technical system; it is a little hard to know what to do next, if one's own learning and experience is not within this tradition.' Similarly, Clark (1975, p. 184) concludes that 'socio-technical analysis is one of the best known, highly relevant, least understood and rarely applied perspectives'. Systems theory requires development both outside and inside the work design area to a level where it provides explicit and refutable predictions concerning the relationships between variables measured at different levels of analysis. Progress in this respect could be a vehicle for achieving wider theoretical integration, and provide the requisite breadth for work design theory to reflect more fully the complexities it necessarily involves.

A final issue, relevant to theory at all levels of development and integration, concerns the treatment of time. To our knowledge no established framework of work design attempts to specify even the order in which predicted effects occur, let alone the time it takes for them to be observable, or their duration. If attitudes and behaviours at work are the product of cumulative experience, how long will it take for these to be altered by changes in job characteristics? And how long will effects persist? The inclusion of such predictions would make theory much more testable and, where empirically supported, would have immense practical value. Consideration of time in this way would also underscore the need for longitudinal and experimental research designs, the general issue with which we conclude this critique.

Research Design for Causal Interpretation

In a recent review Cummings (1982) foresaw increased use of experimental and longitudinal research designs within organizational behaviour by the mid-1980s. Unfortunately, such development does not appear to have materialized, either within the field generally or in the work design area in particular. The lack of a substantial empirical base derived from field studies using designs which allow for causal inference remains a major weakness. This is not a new criticism, but one which has been raised in almost all major reviews over the last decade or more. Since the repeated call for more change studies is largely unanswered it is worthwhile considering why this is so.

A common explanation for the lack of field experiments focuses on the acceptability of work redesign within organizations. It is suggested that because such change is of unproven value (hence the research) it is not worth the risk and disruption to normal working practices. This undoubtedly is an important part of the explanation, but it cannot be the whole story. There are numerous examples of enterprises implementing new forms of work organization on their own account, within the more general QWL paradigm. As Mohrman *et al.* (1986, p. 191) concludes: 'since the mid-1970s the QWL movement has had a life of its own. There has been rapid diffusion of it and a growing body of literature, much of it in the popular and business press. Indeed, one of its most striking aspects has been the degree to which practice recently has outpaced theory and research.'

If the nature of work redesign is acceptable in practice, then maybe the lack of experimental and longitudinal research reflects that such forms of investigation place unacceptable demands on organizations. This is surely a large part of the explanation, and points to the need both to create strong research designs which minimize the intrusiveness of the research process, and to develop approaches which ensure that research is carried out in such a way that it is of evident and more immediate benefit to the organization itself. Attention should also be given to 'naturally occurring' developments within organizations which both have clear implications for the design of work and open up opportunities for access and creative research design.

Problems of access of the kind considered above clearly exist, and will remain as a greater obstacle to change studies than to correlational ones. However, they do not seem entirely sufficient to account fully for the lack of field experiments and longitudinal studies. There is a danger of externalizing in looking for explanations. Perhaps one should also look closer to home, and ask whether our own institutional structures and practices are likely to discriminate against such research. Here we can see some impediments. Long-term change studies are high risk for the individual researcher in that they can be aborted for reasons outside his or her control. Compared with correlational, survey, and laboratory research they also offer the prospect of a poor effort-to-publication ratio. With academic career prospects so strongly affected by publication rates many individuals may have reservations about committing themselves to change studies where other kinds of research offer more certain rewards. More team-based research, longer-term funding, and ascribing additional weight to field experimental studies might be ways of promoting the much needed commitment to this form of investigation. It is an issue on which to ponder!

WORK DESIGN AND THE 'INFORMATION TECHNOLOGY REVOLUTION'

By way of conclusion to this review we turn to consider the implications of information technology for future research into job and work design. As mentioned in the introduction, it appears from the literature that research in the area is in need of fresh impetus. If history is anything to go by then general critiques, such as we have just provided, are insufficient in themselves to foster major changes in emphasis. Criticism concerning the scarcity of change studies, narrowness of perspective, lack of theoretical integration, or the absence of competing conceptual frameworks will at best only exert a mild influence over future development. For more rapid change to be achieved one needs external conditions which offer new opportunities and perspectives. We believe that new technology as applied in work settings presents such an opening.

Let us look first at the implications of new technology for the nature of jobs. It currently appears that one of the effects of implementing new technology, particularly in the case of manufacturing applications, is to polarize jobs with regard to the dimensions central to work design theory. Some applications lead to much more repetitive and simplified jobs, others require operators to think, plan, and take much more responsibility for machine operation and product quality. Moreover, this polarization sometimes affects only some aspects of the job, with others remaining largely unaltered. It is worthwhile briefly considering the emerging literature in the area to illustrate the new technologies in question and how this divergence of effect arises.

One current perspective on new technology is that it will lead to deskilled or simplified shopfloor work. The argument is a general one, but has been most clearly articulated in the context of new manufacturing technology. For example, Braverman (1974), and later Shaiken (1979, 1980), considered the job content implications of the now most prevalent form of new manufacturing technology, the computer numerically controlled (CNC) machine tool. This replaces hand-controlled, general purpose machine tools which, in precision engineering companies, are traditionally operated by time-served skilled employees. Conventionally, the operator uses his or her knowledge of the properties of different metals, cutting tools, cutting and feed speeds, and so on, to translate the information on a drawing into the required end-product. With CNC technology all this information is incorporated into a program which guides the machine tool through the entire cycle, without the need for skilled human intervention. The technical advantage is that by loading different programs a whole range of different products can be made on one machine within tolerances which are less variable than those which can be achieved when direct human operation is involved.

In a similar way robots can be programmed to carry out skilled operations previously performed by human operators, such as paint spraying and spot welding. Here the technlgoy has been developed so that the robot can be programmed by copying operator movements. A skilled paint sprayer, for instance, can guide a robot arm through the physical movements necessary to achieve a given finish, and the entire sequence can be recorded on its program. The whole sequence can then be reproduced on demand.

The argument behind the deskilling prediction is basically simple. It is evident by their nature that many new manufacturing technologies can simplify existing jobs by absorbing traditional skills and knowledge into computer programs. Where previously reliance was placed on direct manual work, or the operation of general purpose machine tools in real time, the new technology allows one to distil relevant knowledge and motor skills into a program which replaces human control. Operators, if required (as is usually the case), can be left to load, unload and monitor the new technology. Where malfunctions occur they call the experts (computer programmers, tool setters, electronics engineers, etc.). The operator thus experiences reductions in task variety, task feedback, autonomy, and other salient job characteristics.

Proponents of the deskilling perspective suggest that this new technical opportunity will be grasped by organizations in order to enhance management control over production and reduce manning costs (through the hiring of less skilled labour). In this way the opportunity arises to deskill jobs which hitherto have been relatively immune from simplication, and for new technology to be used to extend the historical trend towards work simplification. The same effects have been predicted for a variety of other applications of information technology, such as computer-aided design (CAD) systems (Cooley, 1984).

Empirical support for the above work simplification argument has been forthcoming from a number of sources (see, for example, the collection of case studies reported in Butera and Thurman, 1984; also Blumberg and Gerwin, 1984; Burns *et al.*, 1983; Scarborough and Moran, 1985). At the same time, however, investigations have shown that simplification is not a necessary outcome of the application of new technology. Many cases have been documented in which CNC and other new technology has been implemented in such a way as to enhance operator responsibility and feedback, and the loss of regular use of traditional skills has been replaced by the acquisition of new computing and engineering related skills and knowledge.

To some extent this divergence of effect reflects differences in technology, but more often arises from different strategic choices of how to manage and organize the new work (Buchanan and Boddy, 1982, 1983; Clegg and Kemp, 1986; Clegg, Kemp, and Wall, 1984; Nicholas *et al.*, 1983; Sorge *et al.*, 1983). Evidence is also accumulating that in uncertain production environments enriching jobs by enskilling operators and giving them control over the new technology is the better alternative with regard to productivity. By dealing with variances at source they can improve utilization and promote quality (Clegg and Wall, 1987; Cummings and Blumberg, 1987). More generally, it is evident that new technology is not being applied solely to skilled jobs, but also to ones which are inherently repetitive and short cycle and involve little discretion, as for example on assembly lines. The technologies selected, and often customized to local needs, are varied, as are the forms of implementation. One thus sees diverse effects of new technology not only between organizations but also within them, and often opposite job design effects are associated with equivalent forms of new technology.

The important general point is that new manufacturing technology is being implemented in diverse ways and this is having a polarizing effect in terms of job design. This means that more extreme differences are being created between jobs; these are towards both simplification and enrichment, and often they emphasize particular job dimensions. Add to this the fact that implementation is typically incremental and takes place alongside unaltered traditional job designs, and it becomes clear that the opportunity to mount experimentally oriented and comparative studies is improving. Also, such differences are occurring not only between organizations but also within them. This means investigations can be carried out where context is relatively constant.

Our argument, therefore, is that there is evolving, as a result of the introduction of new technology, a set of circumstances particularly conducive to experimentally oriented field studies of job design. We are now witnessing the beginnings of a move towards substantial changes in job dimensions occurring at a rate and to an extent that permits the use of strong research designs. The fact that such change arises for reasons internal to organizations, rather than being inspired by researchers or others, means they are there to be exploited. Over the next decade, and probably longer, these conditions will become more common, as more and more manufacturing organizations begin their piecemeal adoption of new technology. The rate of adoption is demonstrably accelerating (Child, 1984; Northcote and Rogers, 1984). This offers the opportunity to overcome one of the major practical impediments which has historically hampered research, the difficulty of implementing and sustaining major change in work design.

The existence of conditions which allow experimental field research into work design are not sufficient to ensure that it will occur. Also important is the question of access. Why should managements, trade unions, and others welcome the attention of researchers? This will remain somewhat of a problem. Nevertheless, there appears to be more opportunity than previously. It results from the needs of organizations. Most managements and trade unions now believe that they must follow the path of introducing new technology in order to remain competitive and survive (Mueller et al., 1986). They set out on this road driven by technical possibilities, and reach a point where they feel they can handle this side of the issue. In so doing, however, they soon realize the implications of the technology for jobs. In the light of the substantial changes that are necessary for technical reasons, their attitudes are to some extent unfrozen. They are willing to put on the agenda issues which before were not negotiable. There is, in short, a readiness to change and experiment. What is missing, however, is a conceptual framework to handle the human and organizational side of the change. Here psychologists can play a part, for the framework offered by job design theory provides a way of highlighting some of the issues and options available. Increasingly, organizations are looking beyond their own boundaries for such ideas.

The opportunity the introduction of new technology offers for revitalizing research into work design has so far been considered from the standpoint of current applications of information technology on the shopfloor. These are predominantly stand-alone systems. The next stage of development of such technology (already operating in a few hundred organizations worldwide) is flexible manufacturing systems (FMS). This application involves the integration of stand-alone systems through shared information processing. In such systems materials can be passed from one machine to another, to complete the operations required, through the use of robots, automated guided vehicles, and conveyors, with the entire sequence under the control of micro-processing technology. The further integration of FMS with production control, inventory, stock, and other organization-wide information systems offers the prospect of large-scale computer-integrated manufacturing (CIM) (see Cummings and Blumberg, 1987; Sharlt, Chang, and Salvendy, 1986).

The advent of such larger-scale applications of information technology in manufacturing is of considerable relevance to research into work design. In addition to having implications for the content of operator jobs, they will make clearer than ever the interrelationship between job design on the one hand and the larger organization on the other. Such technical systems incorporate and symbolize many features of systems theory, and provide a springboard from which a broader theoretical perspective may be easier to develop. Along with their now current stand-alone predecessors, FMS and CIM also draw attention to the narrow range of job dimensions covered by existing job design theory. It is, for example, extremely difficult to encapsulate the jobs of operators of new manufacturing technology without paying attention to the planning, problem solving, diagnostic, and system understanding aspects of their work. In other words, a job characteristic which such technology requires one to take into account is that of cognitive demand, which is overlooked by current theory in work design. In these and many other ways the introduction of new technology on the shopfloor provides a stimulus to broaden and improve the theoretical base of research into work design.

The discussion to date has been based predominantly on manufacturing applications of information technology. It may be that the opportunities foreseen turn out to be somewhat overstated, and that for other areas of application prospects for work design research and practice are less marked. Nevertheless, opportunities clearly exist. As Walton (1982) observes, there is much scope for the application of job design and social criteria more generally in understanding the effects and contributing to the design of a range of systems for clerical, managerial, and professional use.

This brings us to our concluding point. Our emphasis has been on exploiting technically induced change in work organizations in order to upgrade empirical research and theoretical development in job and work design. Such advance will be of little consequence unless it feeds back into practice. The parallel challenge is to apply current knowledge of work design to the design of new technology itself. Initiatives are already being taken in this respect, often under the banner of 'human-centred systems' (e.g. Corbett, 1985; Rosenbrock, 1983, 1985). Work on this dual front offers the prospect of providing those concerned with the psychological implications of the design of jobs with a source of ideas, and research opportunities, from which the field as a whole should benefit.

REFERENCES

Abdel-Halim, A. A. (1978). Employee affective responses to organizational stress: Moderating effects of job characteristics. *Personnel Psychology*, **31**, 561–579.

Abdel-Halim, A. A. (1979). Individual and interpersonal moderators of employee reactions to job characteristics: A re-examination. *Personnel Psychology*, **32**, 121–137.

Abdel-Halim, A. A. (1981). Effects of role stress–job design–technology interaction on employee work satisfaction. *Academy of Management Journal*, **24**, 260–273.

Adler, S., Skov, R. B., and Salvemini, N. J. (1985). Job characteristics and job satisfaction: When cause becomes consequence. *Organizational Behaviour and Human Decision Processes*, **35**, 266–278.

Aldag, R. J., and Brief, A. P. (1979). *Task Design and Employee Motivation*. Scott, Foresman: Glenview, Ill..

Algera, J. A. (1983). 'Objective' and perceived task characteristics as a determinent of reactions by task performers. *Journal of Occupational Psychology*, **56**, 95–107.

Babbage, C. (1835). *On the Economy of Machinery and Manufacturers*. Charles Knight: London.

Baghat, R. S., and Chassie, M. B. (1980). Effects of changes in job characteristics on some theory-specific attitudinal outcomes: Results from a naturally occurring quasi-experiment. *Human Relations*, **33**, 297–313.

Baritz, L. (1960). *The Servants of Power*. Wiley: New York.

Beehr, T. A. (1976). Perceived situational moderators of the relationship between subjective role ambiguity and role strain. *Journal of Applied Psychology*, **61**, 35–40.

Blau, G. J., and Katerberg, R. (1982). Toward enhancing research with the social information processing approach to job design. *Academy of Management Review*, **7**, 543–550.

Blumberg, M. (1980). Job switching in autonomous work groups: An exploratory study in a Pennsylvania coal mine. *Academy of Management Journal*, **23**, 287-306.

Blumberg, M., and Gerwin, D. (1984). Coping with advanced manufacturing technology. *Journal of Occupational Behaviour*, **5**, 113-130.

Brass, D. J. (1985). Technology and the structure of jobs: Employee satisfaction, performance, and influence. *Organizational Behavior and Human Decision Processes*, **35**, 216-240.

Braverman, H. (1974). *Labour and Monopoly Capital*. Monthly Review Press: New York.

Broadbent, D. E. (1985). The clinical impact of job design. *British Journal of Clinical Psychology*, **24**, 33-44.

Broadbent, D. E., and Gath, D. (1979). Chronic effects of repetitive and non-repetitive work. In C. J. Mackay and T. Cox (eds.), *Response to Stress: Occupational Aspects*. Independent Publishing: London.

Broadbent, D. E., and Gath, D. (1981). Symptom levels of assembly line workers. In G. Salvendy and M. Smith (eds.), *Machine Pacing and Occupational Stress*. Taylor & Francis: London.

Buchanan, D. A., and Boddy, D. (1982). Advanced technology and the quality of working life: The effects of word processing on video typists. *Journal of Occupational Psychology*, **55**, 1-11.

Buchanan, D. A., and Boddy, D. (1983). Advanced technology and the quality of working life: The effects of computerised controls on biscuit-making operators. *Journal of Occupational Psychology*, **56**, 109-119.

Burnett, I. (1925). *An Experimental Investigation into Repetitive Work*. Report no. 30, Industrial Fatigue Research Board. HMSO: London.

Burns, A., Feickert, D., Newby, M., and Winterton, J. (1983). The miners and new technology. *Industrial Relations Journal*, **14**(4), 7-20.

Butera, F., and Thurman, J. E. (1984). *Automation and Work Design*. Amsterdam: North-Holland.

Caplan, R. D., Cobb, S., Frech, J. R. P., Van Harrison, R., and Pinneau, S. R. (1975). *Job Demands and Worker Health*. NIOSH Research Report, USHEW. US Government Printing Office: Washington, DC.

Champoux, J. E. (1980). A three sample test of some extensions to the job characteristics model of work motivation. *Academy of Management Journal*, **23**, 466-478.

Cherns, A. B., and Davis, L. E. (1975). Assessment of the state of the art. In L. E. Davis and A. B. Cherns (eds.), *The Quality of Working Life* (vol. 1). Free Press: New York.

Child, J. (1984). New technology and developments in management organization. *Omega International Journal of Management Science*, **12**, 211-223.

Ciborra, C., Migliarese, P., and Romano, P. (1984). A methodological inquiry of organizational noise in sociotechnical systems. *Human Relations*, **37**, 565-588.

Clark, P. A. (1975). Intervention theory: Matching role, focus and context. In L. E. Davis and A. B. Cherns (eds.), *The Quality of Working Life* (vol. 1). Free Press: New York.

Clegg, C. W. (1979). The process of job redesign: Signposts from a theoretical orphanage? *Human Relations*, **32**, 999-1022.

Clegg, C. W. (1984). The derivation of job designs. *Journal of Occupational Behaviour*, **5**, 131-146.

Clegg, C. W., and Fitter, M. J. (1978). Information systems: The Achilles heel of job redesign? *Personnel Review*, **7**, 5-11.

Clegg, C. W., and Kemp, N. J. (1986). Information Technology: Personnel where are you? *Personnel Review*, **15**, 8-15.

Clegg, C. W., Kemp, N. J., and Wall, T. D. (1984). New Technology: Choice control and skills. In G. C. Van der Veer, M. J. Tauber, T. R. G. Green, and P. Gorny (Eds.), *Readings in Cognitive Ergonomics—Mind and Computers*. Springer-Verlag: Berlin.

Clegg, C. W., and Wall, T. D. (1987) Managing factory automation. In F. Blackler and D. Oborne (eds.), *Information Technology and People: Designing for the Future*. British Psychological Society: Leicester.

Cooley, M. (1984). Problems of automation. In T. Lupton (ed.), *Proceedings of the 1st International Conference on Human Factors in Manufacturing*. North-Holland: Amsterdam.

Corbett, J. M. (1985). Prospective work design for a human-centred CNC lathe. *Behaviour and Information Technology*, **4**, 201-214.

Cordery, J. L., and Wall, T. D. (1985). Work design and supervisory practices: A model. *Human Relations*, **38**, 425-441.

Cox, T. (1980). Repetitive work. In C. L. Cooper and R. Payne (eds.), *Current Issues in Occupational Stress*. Wiley: London.

Cox, T., and Cox, S. (1984). Job design and repetitive work. *Employment Gazette*, **92**, 97-100.

Cox, T., and Mackay, C. J. (1979). The impact of repetitive work. In R. Sell and P. Shipley (eds.), *Satisfaction in Work Design: Ergonomics and Other Approaches*. Taylor & Francis: London.

Cox, T., Mackay, C. J., and Page, H. (1982). Simulated repetitive work and self-reported mood. *Journal of Occupational Behaviour*, **3**, 247-252.

Cox, T., Thirlaway, M., and Cox, S. (1982). Repetitive work, well-being and arousal. In R. Murison (ed.), *Biological and Psychological Basis of Psychomatic Disease*. Pergamon: Oxford.

Cummings, L. L. (1982). Organizational behavior. In *Annual Review of Psychology* (vol. 33). Annual Reviews Inc.: Palo Alto, Calif.

Cummings, T. G. (1978). Self-regulating work groups: A socio-technical synthesis. *Academy of Management Review*, **3**, 625-634.

Cummings, T. G., and Blumberg, M. (1987). Advanced manufacturing technology and work design. In T. D. Wall, C. W. Clegg, and N. J. Kemp (eds.), *The Human Side of Advanced Manufacturing Technology*. Wiley: Chichester, Sussex.

Cummings, T. G., Molloy, E. S., and Glen, R. (1977). A methodological critique of fifty-eight selected work experiments. *Human Relations*, **30**, 675-708.

Dainoff, M., Hurrell, J. J., and Happ, A. (1981). A taxonomic framework for the description and evaluation of paced work. In G. Salvendy and M. J. Smith (eds.), *Stress in Machine Pacing*. Taylor & Francis: London.

Davis, L. E. (1976). Developments in job design. In P. D. Warr (ed.), *Personal Goals and Work Design*. Wiley: London.

Davis, L. E., Canter, R. R., and Hoffman, J. (1955). Current job design criteria. *Journal of Industrial Engineering*, **6**, 5-11.

Davis, L. E., and Taylor, J. C. (1962). *Design of Jobs*. Penguin: Harmondsworth, Middx.

Davis, L. E., and Valfer, E. S. (1965). Intervening responses to changes in supervisors' job designs. *Occupational Psychology*, **39**, 171-189.

Denison, D. R. (1982). Sociotechnical design and self-managing work groups: The impact of control. *Journal of Occupational Behaviour*, **3**, 297-314.

Dunham, R. B. (1976). The measurement and dimensionality of job characteristics. *Journal of Applied Psychology*, **62**, 760-763.

Dunham, R. B. (1977). Reactions to job characteristics: Moderating effects of the organisation. *Academy of Management Journal*, **20**, 42-65.

Dunham, R. B., Aldag, R., and Brief, A. (1977). Dimensionality of task design as measured by the Job Diagnostic Survey. *Academy of Manufacturing Journal*, **20**, 209-223.

Edwards, R. C. (1978). The social relations of production at the point of production. *Insurgent Sociologist*, **8**, 109-125.

Emery, F. E. (1980). Designing socio-technical systems in 'greenfield' sites. *Journal of Occupational Behaviour*, **1**, 19-27.

Farr, J. L. (1976). Task characteristics, reward contingency, and intrinsic motivation. *Organizational Behavior and Human Performance*, **16**, 294-307.

Ferratt, T. W., Dunham, R. B., and Pierce, J. L. (1981). Self-report measures of job characteristics and affective responses: An examination of discriminant validity. *Academy of Management Journal*, **24**, 780-794.

Ferratt, T. W., and Reeve, J. M. (1977). The structural integrity of the JDS and JDI when examined together. *Proceedings of the Mid-West Division of the Academy of Management*, **20**, 144-155.

Ferris, G. R., and Gilmore, D. C. (1984). The moderating role of work context in job design research: A test of competing models. *Academy of Management Journal*, **27**, 885-892.

Ferris, G. R., and Rowland, K. M. (1981). Leadership, job perceptions, and influence: A conceptual integration. *Human Relations*, **34**, 1069-1077.

Forester, T. (ed.) (1985). *The Information Technology Revolution*. Blackwell: Oxford.

Frank, L. L., and Hackman, J. R. (1975). A failure of job enrichment: The case of the change that wasn't. *Journal of Applied Behavioural Science*, **11**, 413-436.

Fraser, R. (1947). *The Incidence of Neurosis among Factory Workers*. Report no. 90, Industrial Health Research Board. HMSO: London.

Fry, L. W., and Slocum, J. W. (1984). Technology, structure, and workgroup effectiveness: A test of contingency model. *Academy of Management Journal*, **27**, 221-246.

Ganster, D. C. (1980). Individual differences and task design: A laboratory experiment. *Organizational Behavior and Human Performance*, **26**, 131-148.

Gilbreth, F. B. (1911). *Brick Laying System*. Clark: New York.

Green, S. B., Armenakis, A. A., Marber, L. D., and Bedeian, A. G. (1979). An evaluation of the response format and scale structure of the job diagnostic survey. *Human Relations*, **32**, 181-188.

Greenberg, C. I., Wang, Y., and Dossett, D. L. (1982). Effects of work group size and task size on observers' job characteristics ratings. *Basic and Applied Social Psychology*, **3**, 53-66.

Griffeth, R. W. (1985). Moderation of the effects of job enrichment by participation: A longitudinal field experiment. *Organizational Behaviour and Human Decision Processes*, **35**, 73-93.

Griffin, R. W. (1981). A longitudinal investigation of task characteristics relationships. *Academy of Management Journal*, **24**, 99-113.

Griffin, R. W. (1982). Perceived task characteristics and employee productivity and satisfaction. *Human Relations*, **35**, 927-938.

Griffin, R. W. (1983). Objective and social sources of information in task design: A field experiment. *Administrative Science Quarterly*, **28**, 184-200.

Griffin, R. W., and Bateman, T. S. (1986). Job satisfaction and organizational commitment. In C. L. Cooper and I. T. Robertson (eds.), *International Review of Industrial and Organizational Psychology*. Wiley: Chichester, Sussex.

Gulick, L., and Urwick, L. (eds.) (1937). *Papers on the Science of Administration*. Institute of Public Administration: New York.

Gulowsen, J. (1972). A measure of work group autonomy. In L. E. Davis and J. C. Taylor (eds.), *Design of Jobs*. Penguin: London.

Hackman, J. R. (1977). Work design. In J. R. Hackman and J. L. Suttle (eds.), *Improving Life at Work: Behavioral Science Approaches to Organizational Change*. Goodyear: Santa Monica, Calif..

Hackman, J. R. (1983). The design of work teams. In J. Lorsch (ed.), *Handboook of Organizational Behavior*. Prentice-Hall: Englewood Cliffs, NJ.

Hackman, J. R., and Lawler, E. E. (1971). Employee reactions to job characteristics. *Journal of Applied Psychology*, **55**, 259-286.

Hackman, J. R., and Oldham, G. (1975). Development of the Job Diagnostic Survey. *Journal of Applied Psychology*, **60**, 159-170.

Hackman, J. R., and Oldham, G. (1976). Motivation through the design of work: Test of a theory. *Organizational Behavior and Human Performance*, **16**, 250-279.

Hackman, J. R., and Oldham, G. (1980). *Work Redesign*. Addison-Wesley: Reading, Mass..

Hackman, J. R., Pearce, J. L., and Wolfe, J. C. (1978). Effects of changes in job characteristics on work attitudes and behaviors; A naturally occurring quasi-experiment. *Organizational Behavior and Human Performance*, **21**, 289-304.

Halton, J. (1985). The anatomy of computing. In T. Forester (ed.), *The Information Technology Revolution: The Complete Guide*. Blackwell: Oxford.

Hedberg, B., and Mumford, E. (1975). The design of computer systems. In E. Mumford and H. Sackman (eds.), *Human Choice and Computers*, North-Holland: New York.

Hertog, F. J. den (1976). Work structuring. In P. B. Warr (ed.), *Personal Goals and Work Design*. Wiley: London.

Herzberg, F. (1966). *Work and the Nature of Man*. World Publishing: Cleveland, Ohio.

Herzberg, F. (1968). One more time: How do you motivate employees? *Harvard Business Review*, **46**, 53-62.

Herzberg, F., Mausner, B., and Snyderman, B. (1959). *The Motivation to Work*. Wiley: New York.

Hill, C. P. (1972). *Toward a New Management Philosophy*. Gower: London.

Hulin, C. L., and Roznowski, M. (1985). Organizational technologies: Effects on the organisations' characteristics and the individuals' responses. *Research in Organizational Behavior*, **22**, 350-365.

Hurrell, J. J. (1985). Machine-paced work and the Type A behaviour pattern. *Journal of Occupational Psychology*, **58**, 15-25.

Huse, E., and Cummings, T. (1985). *Organization Development and Change*. West Publishing: St Paul, Minn..

Industrial Health Research Board (1931). *Eleventh Annual Report*. HMSO: London.

Jackson, P. R., Paul, L. J., and Wall, T. D. (1981). Individual differences as moderators of reactions to job characteristics. *Journal of Occupational Psychology*, **54**, 1-8.

Jones, A. P., and James, L. R. (1979). Psychological climate: Dimensions and relationships of individual and aggregated work environment perceptions. *Organizational Behavior and Human Performance*, **23**, 201-250.

Karasek, R. A. (1979). Job demands, job decision latitude, and mental strain: Implications for job redesign. *Administrative Science Quarterly*, **24**, 285-308.

Katz, D., and Kahn, R. L. (1966). *The Social Psychology of Organizations*. Wiley: New York.

Katz, D., and Kahn, R. L. (1978). *The Social Psychology of Organizations* (2nd edn). Wiley: New York.

Katz, R. (1978a). The influence of job longevity on employee responses to task characteristics. *Human Relations*, **31**, 703-725.

Katz, R. (1978b). Job longevity as a situational factor in job satisfaction. *Administrative Science Quarterly*, **23**, 204-223.

Keller, R. T., and Holland, W. E. (1981). Job change: A naturally occurring field experiment. *Human Relations*, **34**, 1053-1067.

Keller, R. T., Szilagyi, A., and Holland, W. E. (1976). Boundary spanning activity and employee reactions: An empirical study. *Human Relations*, **29**, 699-710.

Kelly, J. E. (1982). *Scientific Management, Job Redesign and Work Performance*. Academic Press: London.

Kemp, N. J., and Cook, J. D. (1983). Job longevity and growth need strength as joint moderators of the task design-job satisfaction relationship *Human Relations*, **36**, 883-898.

Kemp, N. J., Wall, T. D., Clegg, C. W., and Cordery, J. L. (1983). Autonomous work groups in a greenfield site. A comparative study. *Journal of Occupational Psychology*, **56**, 271-288.

Kerr, S., Hill, K. D., and Broedling, L. (1986). The first-line supervisor: Phasing out or here to stay? *Academy of Management Review*, **11**, 103-117.

Kiggundu, M. N. (1980). An empirical test of the theory of job design using multiple job ratings. *Human Relations*, **33**, 339-351.

Kiggundu, M. N. (1981). Task interdependence and the theory of job design. *Academy of Management Review*, **6**, 499-508.

Kiggundu, M. N. (1983). Task independence and job design: Test of a theory. *Organizational Behavior and Human Performance*, **31**, 145-172.

King, N. A. (1970). A clarification and evaluation of the two-factor theory of job satisfaction. *Psychological Bulletin*, 74, 18-30.

Klein, L. (1976). *New Forms of Work Organisation*. Cambridge University Press: Cambridge.

Kolodny, H. F., and Kiggundu, M. N. (1980). Towards the development of a sociotechnical systems model in woodlands mechanical harvesting. *Human Relations*, **33**, 623-645.

Kornhauser, A. (1965). *Mental Health of the Industrial Worker*. Wiley: New York.

Kraft, P. (1977). *Programmes and Managers*. Allen Lane: London.

LaRocco, J. M., House, J. S., and French, J. R. P. (1980). Social support, occupational stress, and health. *Journal of Health and Social Behaviour*, **21**, 202-218.

Lawler, E. E. (1978). The new plant revolution. *Organizational Dynamics*, **6**, 2-12.

Lawler, E. E., Hackman, J. R., and Kaufman, S. (1973). Effects of job redesign: A field experiment. *Journal of Applied Social Psychology*, **3**, 49-62.

Locke, E. A., and Henne, D. (1986). Work motivation theories. In C. L. Cooper and I. T. Robertson (eds.), *International Review of Industrial and Organizational Psychology*. Wiley: Sussex.

Locke, E. A., Sirota, D., and Wolfson, A. (1976). An experimental case study of the successes and failures of job enrichment in a government agency. *Organizational Behavior and Human Performance*, **5**, 484-500.

Loher, B. T., Noe, R. A., Moeller, N. L., and Fitzgerald, M. P. (1985). A meta-analysis of the relation of job characteristics to job satisfaction. *Journal of Applied Psychology*, **70**, 280-289.

McLean, A. J., and Sims, D. B. P. (1978). Job enrichment from theoretical poverty: The state of the art and directions for future work. *Personnel Review*, **7**, 5-10.

Manz, C. C., and Sims, H. P. (1982). The potential for 'groupthink' in autonomous work groups. *Human Relations*, **35**, 773-784.

Mitchell, T. R., Liden, R. C., and Rothman, M. (1985). Effects of normative information on task performance. *Journal of Applied Psychology*, **70**, 48-55.

Mohrman, S. A., Ledford, G. E., Lawler, E. E., and Mohrman, A. M. (1986). Quality of worklife and employee involvement. In C. L. Cooper and I. T. Robertson (eds.), *International Review of Industrial and Organizational Psychology*. Wiley: Chichester, Sussex.

Morris, J. H., Sherman, J. D., and Mansfield, E. R. (1986). Failures to detect moderating effects with ordinary least squares-moderated multiple regression: Some reasons and a remedy. *Psychological Bulletin*, **99**, 282-288.

Mossholder, K. W., Bedeian, A. G., and Armenakis, A. A. (1982). Role perceptions, satisfaction and performance: Moderating effects of self-esteem and organizational level. *Organizational Behavior and Human Performance*, **28**, 224-234.

Mueller, W. S., Clegg, C. W., Wall, T. D., Kemp, N. J., and Davies, R. (1986). Pluralist beliefs about new technology within an organization. *New Technology, Work and Employment*, **1**, 127-139.

Murphy, L. R., and Hurrell, J. J. (1980). Machine pacing and occupational stress. In R. Schwartz (ed.), *New Developments in Occupational Stress*. DHHS (NIOSH) Publication no. 81-102. US Government Printing Office: Washington, DC.

Murrell, H. (1978). Work stress and mental strain. Occasional Paper no. 6. Work Research Unit, Department of Employment: London.

Nicholas, J. (1982). The comparative impact of organization development interventions on hard criteria measures. *Academy of Management Review*, **7**, 531-542.

Nicholas, J., Warner, M., Sarge, A., and Hartman, G.(1983). Computerised machine tools, manpower training and skill polarisation: A study of British and West German manufacturing firms. In G. Winch (ed.), *Information Technology in Manufacturing Processes*. Rossendale: London.

Northcote, J., and Rodgers, P. (1984). *Micro-electronics in British Industry: The Pattern of Change.* Policy Studies Institute: London.

O'Connor, E. J., Rudolf, C. J., and Peters, L. H. (1980). Individual differences and job design reconsidered: Where do we go from here? *Academy of Management Review,* **5**, 249-254.

O'Connor, G. J., and Barrett, G. V. (1980). Informational cues and individual differences as determinants of subjective perceptions of task enrichment. *Academy of Management Journal,* **23**, 697-716.

Oldham, G. (1976). Job characteristics and internal motivation: The moderating effect of interpersonal and individual variables. *Human Relations,* **29**, 559-569.

Oldham, G., and Miller, H. E. (1979). The effect of significant other's job complexity on employee reactions to work. *Human Relations,* **32**, 247-260.

O'Reilly, C. A., and Caldwell, D. F. (1979). Informational influence as a determinant of perceived task characteristics and job satisfaction. *Journal of Applied Psychology,* **64**, 157-165.

O'Reilly, C. A., and Caldwell, D. F. (1985). The impact of normative social influence and cohesiveness on task perceptions and attitudes: A social information processing approach. *Journal of Occupational Psychology,* **58**, 193-206.

O'Reilly, C. A., Parlette, G., and Bloom, J. (1980). Perceptual measures of task characteristics: The biasing effects of differing frames of reference and job attitudes. *Academy of Management Journal,* **23**, 118-131.

Orpen, C. (1979). The effects of job enrichment on employee satisfaction, motivation and performance: A field experiment. *Human Relations,* **32**, 189-217.

Ovalle, N. K. (1984). Organizational/managerial control processes: A reconceptualization of the linkage between technology and performance. *Human Relations,* **37**, 1047-1062.

Pasmore, W., Francis, C., Haldeman, J., and Shani, A. (1983). Sociotechnical systems: A North American reflection on the empirical studies of the seventies. *Human Relations,* **35**, 1179-1204.

Peters, W. S., and Champoux, J. E. (1979). The use of moderated regression in job design decisions. *Decision Sciences,* **10**, 85-95.

Pierce, J. L. (1984). Job design and technology: A sociotechnical systems perspective. *Journal of Occupational Behaviour,* **5**, 147-154.

Pierce, J. L., Dunham, R. B., and Blackburn, R. S. (1979). Social systems structure, job design, and growth need strength: A test of congruency model. *Academy of Management Journal,* **22**, 223-240.

Porter, L. W., Lawler, E. E., and Hackman, J. R. (1975). *Behavior in Organizations.* McGraw-Hill: New York.

Rice, A. K. (1958). *Productivity and Social Organization.* Tavistock: London.

Roberts, K. H., and Glick, W. (1981). The job characteristics approach to job design: A critical review. *Journal of Applied Psychology,* **66**, 193-217.

Rosenbrock, H. H. (1983). Robots and people. *Work and People,* **66**, 193-217.

Rosenbrock, H. H. (1985). Designing automated systems: Need skill be lost? In P. Marstrand (ed.), *New Technology and the Future of Work and Skills.* Pinter: London.

Rousseau, D. M. (1977). Technological differences in job characteristics, employee satisfaction motivation: A synthesis of job design research and socio-technical systems theory. *Organizational Behavior and Human Performance,* **19**, 18-42.

Salancik, G., and Pfeffer, J. (1977). An examination of need-satisfaction models of job attitudes. *Administrative Science Quarterly,* **22**, 427-456.

Salancik, G., and Pfeffer, J. (1978). A social-information processing approach to job attitudes and task design. *Administrative Science Quarterly,* **23**, 224-253.

Salvendy, G., and Smith, M. J. (1981). *Stress in Machine Pacing.* Taylor & Francis: London.

Scarborough, H., and Moran, P. (1985). How new tech. won at Longbridge. *New Society,* **71**, 207-209.

Schnake, M. E., and Dumler, M. P. (1985). Affective response bias in the measurement of perceived task characteristics. *Journal of Occupational Psychology,* **58**, 159-166.

Seeborg, I. (1978). The influence of employee participation in job redesign. *Journal of Applied Behavioral Science*, **14**, 87-98.

Shaiken, H. (1979). Impact of new technology on employees and their organizations. Research report. International Institute for Comparative Social Research: Berlin.

Shaiken, H. (1980). Computer technology and the relations of power in the workplace. Research report. International Institute for Comparative Social Research: Berlin.

Sharlt, J., Chang, T. C., and Salvendy, G. (1986). Technical and human aspects of computer-aided manufacturing. In G. Salvendy (ed.), *Handbook of Human Factors*. Wiley: New York.

Shaw, J. B. (1980). An information processing approach to the study of job design. *Academy of Management Journal*, **1**, 41-48.

Shaw, J. B., and Weekley, J. A. (1981). The effects of socially provided task information on redesigned tasks. *Proceedings, Southern Management Association*, 64-66.

Slocum, J. W., and Sims, H. P. (1980). A typology for integrating technology, organization and job design. *Human Relations*, **33**, 193-211.

Slusher, E. A., and Griffin, R. W. (1980). Social comparison processes and task design. Working Paper. University of Missouri: Columbia, Mo.

Smith, A. (1776). *The Wealth of Nations*. Republished in 1974 by Penguin: Harmondsworth, Middx.

Smith, M. J., Hurrell, J. J., and Murphy, R. K. (1981). Stress and health effects in paced and unpaced work. In G. Salvendy and M. J. Smith (eds.), *Stress in Machine Pacing*. Taylor & Francis: London.

Sorge, A., Hartman, G., Warner, M., and Nicholas, T. (1983). *Microelectronics and Manpower in Manufacturing: Applications of Computer Numerical Control (CNC) in Great Britain and West Germany*. Gower Press: London.

Spector, P. E. (1985). Higher-order need strength as a moderator of the job scope-employee outcome relationship: A meta-analysis. *Journal of Occupational Psychology*, **58**, 119-127.

Steers, R. M. (1975). Problems in the measurement of organizational effectiveness. *Administrative Science Quarterly*, **20**, 546-558.

Steers, R. M., and Spencer, D. (1977). The role of achievement motivation in job design. *Journal of Applied Psychology*, **62**, 472-479.

Stone, E. F., Mowday, R. T., and Porter, L. W. (1977). Higher-order need strengths as moderators of the job scope-job satisfaction relationship. *Journal of Applied Psychology*, **62**, 466-471.

Susman, G. (1976). *Autonomy at Work*. Praeger: New York.

Taylor, F. W. (1911). *The Principles of Scientific Management*. Harper: New York.

Taylor, J. C. (1979). Job design criteria twenty years later. In L. E. Davis and J. C. Taylor (eds.), *Design of Jobs* (2nd edn). Goodyear: Santa Monica, Calif.

Thomas, J., and Griffin, R. W. (1983). The social information processing model of task design: A review of the literature. *Academy of Management Review*, **8**, 672-692.

Trist, E. L. (1981). The sociotechnical perspective: The evolution of sociotechnical systems as a conceptual framework and as an action research program. In A. H. Van de Ven and W. F. Joyce (eds.), *Perspectives on Organizational Design and Behavior*. Wiley: New York.

Trist, E. L., and Bamforth, K. W. (1951). Some social and psychological consequences of the long-wall method of coal-getting. *Human Relations*, **4**, 3-38.

Turner, A. N., and Lawrence, P. R. (1965). *Individual Jobs and the Worker*. Harvard University Press: Cambridge, Mass.

Umstot, D. D., Bell, C. H., and Mitchell, T. R. (1976). Effects of job enrichment and task design goals on satisfaction and productivity: Implications for job design. *Journal of Applied Psychology*, **61**, 379-394.

Umstot, D. D., Mitchell, T. R., and Bell, C. H. (1978). Goal setting and job enrichment: An integrated approach to job design. *Academy of Management Review*, **2**, 867-879.

Vecchio, R. P., and Keon, T. L. (1981). Predicting employee satisfaction from congruency among individual need, job design, and system structure. *Journal of Occupational Behaviour*, **2**, 283-292.

Vecchio, R. P., and Sussman, M. (1981). Staffing sufficiency and job enrichment: Support for an optimal level theory. *Journal of Occupational Behaviour*, **2**, 177-187.

Walker, C. R. (1950). The problem of the repetitive job. *Harvard Business Review*. **28**, 54-58.

Walker, C. R., and Guest, R. H. (1952). *Man on the Assembly Line*. Harvard University Press: Cambridge, Mass.

Wall, T. D. (1980). Group work redesign in context: A two-phase model. In K. D. Duncan, M. Gruneberg, and D. Wallis (eds.), *Changes in Working Life*. Wiley: Chichester, Sussex.

Wall, T. D. (1982). Perspectives on job redesign. In J. E. Kelly and C. W. Clegg (eds.), *Autonomy and Control in the Workplace*. Croom Helm: London.

Wall, T. D., and Clegg, C. W. (1981). A longitudinal field study of group work redesign. *Journal of Occupational Behaviour*, **2**, 31-49.

Wall, T. D., Clegg, C. W., and Jackson, P. R. (1978). An evaluation of the Job Characteristics Model. *Journal of Occupational Psychology*. **51**, 183-196.

Wall, T. D., Kemp, N. J., Clegg, C. W., and Jackson, P. R. (1986). An outcome evaluation of autonomous work groups: A long-term field experiment. *Academy of Management Journal*, **29**, 280-304.

Wall, T. D., and Stephenson, G. M. (1970). Herzberg's two-factor theory of job attitudes: A critical evaluation and some fresh evidence. *Industrial Relations Journal*, **1**, 41-65.

Walsh, J. T., Taber, T., and Beehr, T. A. (1980). An integrated model of perceived job characteristics. *Organizational Behavior and Human Performance*, **25**, 252-267.

Walton, R. E. (1977). Work innovations at Topeka: After six years. *Journal of Applied Behavioural Science*, **13**, 422-433.

Walton, R. E. (1982). New perspectives on the world of work. *Human Relations*, **35**, 1073-1084.

Warr, P. B. (1987). *Work Unemployment and Mental Health*. Oxford University Press: Oxford.

Weiss, H. M., and Shaw, J. B. (1979). Social influences on judgements about tasks. *Organizational Behavior and Human Performance*, **24**, 126-140.

White, J. K. (1978). Individual differences and the job quality–worker response relationship: Review, integration, and comments. *Academy of Management Review*, **3**, 267-280.

White, S. E., and Mitchell, T. R. (1979). Job enrichment versus social cues: A comparison and competitive test. *Journal of Applied Psychology*, **64**, 1-9.

Williams, T. A. (1982). A participative design for dispersed employees in turbulent environments. *Human Relations*, **35**, 1043-1058.

Wood, R. E. (1986). Task complexity: Definition of the construct. *Organizational Behavior and Human Decision Processes*, **37**, 60-82.

Wyatt, S., Fraser, J. A., and Stock, F. G. L. (1928). *The Comparative Effects of Variety and Uniformity in Work*. Report no. 52, Industrial Fatigue Research Board. HMSO: London.

Wyatt, S., and Ogden, D. A. (1924). *On the Extent and Effects of Variety and Uniformity in Repetitive Work*. Report no. 26, Industrial Fatigue Research Board. HMSO: London.

Zedeck, S. (1971). Problems with the use of moderator variables. *Psychological Bulletin*, **76**, 295-310.

Zierden, W. E. (1980). Congruence in the work situation: Effects of growth needs, management style, and job structure on job related satisfactions. *Journal of Occupational Behaviour*, **1**, 297-310.

Chapter 6

DECISION MAKING IN ORGANIZATIONS

Paul L. Koopman
Department of Work and Organisational Psychology
Free University, Amsterdam
The Netherlands
and
Jeroen Pool
Dutch National Hospital Institute
The Netherlands

INTRODUCTION

Research on decision making in organizations does not yet have a long tradition in industrial/organizational psychology, although the Nobel Prize winner Herbert Simon laid the foundations for what would come to be called the 'behavioral approach' as long ago as 1947. The 'Carnegie School', where people such as March, Cyert and others worked alongside Simon, played a key role in this early period. Theories were founded on concepts such as 'bounded rationality' and 'satisficing objectives'. Interest in this topic gradually grew in the 1950s and early 1960s, when case studies also began to appear (e.g. Ansoff, 1965; Cyert and March, 1963; Lindblom, 1959). Aspects of decision making such as politics and conflict received more attention. Starting in the early 1970s, the scope of the growing stream of publications clearly widened; for example the research of Pettigrew (1973), in which the power line was elaborated, that of Cohen, March, and Olsen (1972), in which decision making was described by the metaphor of the 'garbage can', that of Janis (1972) on the phenomenon of 'group-think', and that of Mintzberg, Raisinghani and Théorêt (1976) comparing 25 strategic decisions.

Starting in the mid-1970s, decision making in organizations became a permanent subject in the handbooks of industrial/organizational psychology (Heller, 1976; Koopman, Broekhuysen, and Meijn, 1984; MacCrimmon and Taylor, 1976). Many studies comparing decision making in various organizations, in various countries, and on various topics were published (e.g. Hickson *et al.*, 1986; Heller *et al.*, 1988). Contingency factors turned out to play an important role in the course of the process.

The main results of this and other research are summarized in this chapter, which is structured as follows. First of all, the context in which decision making takes place is sketched. We turn our attention to variables at the level of the individual decision maker, the organization, the environment, and to the subject of the decision. All these factors have a share in determining the course of decision making. Then we look at the building blocks of the actual decision making process as indicated in four basic dimensions: centralization, formalization, information and confrontation. Based on these dimensions, four decision making models can be formulated: the neo-rational model, the bureaucratic model, the arena model and the open-end model. It is postulated that management has a certain freedom of choice ('strategic choice') in the design of the decision making process. However, with a view to effectiveness, it is wise to take some contingencies into account. Next, specific issues and research results for each of the models are discussed in more detail. Finally, directions for future research are indicated.

CONTEXT AND SUBJECT MATTER OF DECISION MAKING

Decision making does not take place in a vacuum, but in a certain context. This context can be described at various levels. From low to high aggregation level, we can distinguish the decision maker(s), the group, the organization and the environment. Each of these context levels makes up part of decision making and influences it. Furthermore, decision making is not a neutral exercise, but it is about something. Subjects of decision making can differ in complexity, in controversiality, in political import. Both of these factors (i.e. context and subject) are of importance for the manner in which the decision making processes can be structured and controlled and for the course that they ultimately take.

The Decision Maker(s): the Individual Level

Decision making in organizations is done by people. Although we will see later in this chapter that the individual leeway of decision makers is often very limited (see also Koopman, Broekhuysen, and Wierdsma, 1988), each actor nevertheless tries to keep a hand on the controls whenever possible. The participants in the process continually make decisions, both in a substantial and in a strategic-political respect. Their decisions are often based on their own positions in the force field and their preferences for certain solutions. How successful they are at this will depend on the structural context in which they find themselves. For instance, in a small organization with a simple production process, the influence of the director will be more evident than in a conglomerate with complex production processes, many hierarchical levels and highly skilled personnel. In the former case, personal characteristics of the decision maker(s) greatly influence the manner in which problems and opportunities are approached, and the choices that result.

Traditional management and decision making theories often base their approach to decision making on a normative model (Koopman and Pool, 1990).

Such a model assumes that the decision maker strives for a decision with a maximum yield. It also makes the rather simplistic assumption that the decision maker is aware of all alternatives and their possible consequences, at least the short-term ones. This model's usefulness is thus largely limited to situations with the following characteristics:

1. There is only one decision maker.
2. The decision maker has only one goal.
3. The goal can be described in quantitative terms.
4. There is a limited number of solutions and they are known to the decision maker.
5. The best alternative can be 'calculated'.

Many managers are trained in such a version of decision making (Schwenk, 1988). However, it has become clear that the assumptions that lie at the foundation of this view are too optimistic. In the following sections we shall see how group processes, organizational characteristics and environmental characteristics can make the decision making situation so complex that the rational model has little practical value. But even if we assume that there is one decision maker who can exert a dominant influence, two factors still subtract from the validity of the model: cognitive and perceptual limitations of decision makers (March and Simon, 1958; Nutt, 1984; O'Reilly, 1983; Schwenk, 1984; 1988; Simon, 1947, 1957) and more or less stable personality traits (Kets de Vries and Miller, 1984; Larson et al., 1986; Miller, Kets de Vries, and Toulouse, 1982; Miller and Toulouse, 1986).

Simon (1947, 1957) and March and Simon (1958) focused attention on several restrictions with which decision makers are faced. For instance, because of their limited cognitive capacity, decision makers utilize only part of the relevant information. Time and money considerations also play a role in determining if there will be a search for more information and how long it will last. The search process generally stops when a 'satisficing solution' has been found: alternatives are not studied exhaustively. Only when old recipes and rules of thumb turn out not to work does one start to look for new possibilities.

Simon went on to state that the goals are often fairly broad, that there are limited and subjective chance estimates, that not all alternatives are known and that the process is often poorly structured and short-sighted. The 'administrative man' makes do with the alternative that gives him just enough satisfaction with respect to his aspirational level, while he avoids making unnecessary investments in time as much as possible.

Other researchers have pointed out more specific limitations of human decision making (Tversky and Kahneman, 1974). Laboratory research has shown that, under time pressure, decision makers pay more attention to negative information and weigh fewer aspects of a decision (Wright, 1974).

Connolly (1977) distinguished information processing in decision making into individual processes and 'diffuse' processes. Diffuse processes involve several persons, the decision is of concern at several organizational levels and there may be disagreement or conflict. Ungson, Braunstein, and Hall (1981) referred to these cases as 'ill-structured' problems requiring a different manner of solution than well-structured problems. For example, there is a distinct preference for salient, concrete and preferably oral information (cf. Mintzberg, 1973), and for working with causal models based on previous experiences.

Simplification processes occur primarily in the more complex, ambiguous decision situations. Schwenk (1984) inventoried a number of these mechanisms, which primarily occur in strategic decision making. Fundamentally, it appeared that decision makers commit themselves at an early stage to one solution and take insufficient consideration of other alternatives (Payne, 1976). Schwenk (1984, 1988) described existing prejudices, fixed assumptions and cognitive schemata and the use of analogies and metaphors as background processes. These processes lead to a biased approach to decision situations, in which choices are made on the basis of existing assumptions, expected causal connections and comparison with previous experiences of themselves and of others.

Based on an intensive analysis of the working and thinking of 12 top managers, Isenberg (1984, 1986) described how senior managers make decisions. His main conclusion was that managers do not act according to the phases of the rational model, but rather rely on intuition. According to Isenberg, managers often decide on the basis of a 'Gestalt' of data, experience and feeling.

Janis and Mann (1977) described the concept of 'bolstering', a form of reduction of cognitive dissonance in which an unrealistically optimistic view of the progress of a project or decision occurs. Following Staw (1976), 't Hart (1988) discussed the related concept of 'entrapment'. This is the phenomenon that decision makers, when faced by set-backs, ignore negative signals and continue on a road taken earlier. They are thus drawn into a negative spiral, which ends as a fiasco.

The extent to which managers are subject to limitations and are susceptible to processes of diminished rationality varies from person to person. Below we discuss a number of studies in which data were collected on such individual differences.

One of the personal characteristics of managers that may play a role is reactivity versus proactivity (Larson et al., 1986). Managers can differ in the manner in which they perceive problems and opportunities, or at least in how they react to them. Miller, Kets de Vries, and Toulouse (1982) used the locus of control concept of Rotter (1966) to make a distinction between internal and external orientation. Internal managers were said to be more proactive and innovative, more willing to take risks and to work more systematically. Externally oriented managers, on the other hand, were termed submissive, showing risk avoidance and reactivity. Miller *et al.* (1982) reported data from 33 companies (and managers) which lent strong support to these expectations. When a distinction was made between large and small companies (averaging 5000 and 450 employees respectively), all relationships between locus of control and the strategy factors noted above turned out to be very high in small companies. In large companies only the relationship with proactivity was observed. In small companies, an internally oriented manager can thus more clearly leave his mark on policy than in more complex companies.

In a follow-up study, Miller and Toulouse (1986) investigated two other personality characteristics in addition to locus of control: flexibility and need for achievement. It was expected that an internal orientation would be associated with informal, long-term oriented, proactive and risk-neutral decision making; need for achievement with analytical, systematic, proactive, but risk-avoiding decision making; and flexibility with intuitive, short-term oriented, reactive but risk-taking decision making. Data from 97 small companies (with an average of 100 employees) showed that flexibility and need for achievement in particular showed a relationship with decision making. These relationships were significantly stronger for the smaller companies, as they were for companies in a more dynamic environment.

Another approach was taken by Hambrick and Mason (1984). These authors assumed that organizations are a reflection of characteristics of the top management. The 'objective' situation of an organization is perceived by the top management. Perceptions thus become important (Anderson and Paine, 1975; Duncan, 1972). The prevailing values and cognitive orientations, linked to a limited view of the environment, selective observation and interpretation, lead to certain strategic choices. Because these intermediate psychological variables are difficult to measure, Hambrick and Mason assumed that more easily measurable 'objective characteristics' of management such as age, seniority, education, socio-economic background and such would show relationships to strategic and organizational structure choices. They formulated 21 hypotheses, but reported no empirical data.

Taylor (1975) reported data on the relationship of the age and experience of 70 managers to their information processing and decison making in personnel decisions. He found a relationship to age in particular. On average, older managers took more time for their decisions, assessed the value of information better, had less confidence in the decision made and showed more flexibility.

Gupta and Govindarajan (1984) also studied the relationship of personal characteristics of managers to the strategy they pursued. Data from 58 business units of eight concerns confirmed the assumption that experience, willingness to take risks and tolerance for ambiguity were associated with the effectiveness of an expansion strategy (aimed at developing and expanding the market share).

The same personality characteristics precisely countered the effectiveness of a 'harvest' strategy, and because of this the authors favoured matching managers (by means of selection) to the task awaiting them.

Pickle and Friedlander (1967) studied the relationship of skills (critical thinking and verbal comprehension) and personality characteristics (authority, responsibility, sensitivity, sociability, caution, originality, willingness to make efforts and personal relationships) of management to criteria for organizational success. Organizational success was measured by a satisfaction measurement among seven groups in and around the organization. Data from 97 organizations showed a number of relationships between skills (primarily critical thinking) and a few success variables. There were few relationships with the personality characteristics. The drawback of this study, however, is that it did not measure the intermediate processes such as the decision making approach and the strategy adopted, and so no statements could be made about them.

Altogether, it may be stated that there are indications that certain characteristics of managers influence the manner of decision making and the resulting strategies. Cognitive and perceptual skills exert the primary influences. In addition, personality characteristics such as willingness to take risks, flexibility and an internal orientation seem to be associated with preferences for certain strategies and tactics. This is in agreement with MacCrimmon and Taylor (1976), whose review of the literature named four characteristics of decision makers that they felt were of influence on the decision making method used: perceptual skill, information processing capacity, risk tendency and aspirational level.

The influence of such personal characteristics depends on the extent to which managers can leave their mark on the organization: for example, when the organization is relatively small in size or operates in a dynamic environment. Hickson et al. (1986) stated that this relationship might be U-shaped.

Hambrick and Mason (1984), cited above, stated that we should not look to the characteristics of a single top manager, but to the more general characteristics of the top management team, or rather the dominant coalition. Donaldson and Lorsch (1983) discussed a number of psychological factors that they felt were important in decision making at the top. These factors, which they termed 'belief systems', are more or less generally shared convictions that serve to guide decisions. They distinguished three belief systems: risk tendency, independence and distinctive competence. These belief systems act as stabilizing factors in organizations when newcomers are being inaugurated by means of socialization. Donaldson and Lorsch felt that discontinuity in belief systems would be possible only sporadically; for example, if a new top manager was hired from outside the company. This suggests that managers do leave their mark on the organization they head.

Similarly, Beyer (1983) described the influence of ideologies and values on decision making in organizations. Her description makes it clear that a strongly felt and shared ideology has a directional effect. Decision making in such situations is much more transparent (Brunsson, 1982). This bears a resemblance to Mintzberg's (1983) description of the missionary organization, in which a strong ideological system is present.

The Organizational Context of Decision Making

Complex decisions are usually not made by individuals, but—after the necessary preliminary work—by boards of directors, project teams, management teams and so on. By virtue of their specific expertise or position in the organization, various people take part in discussions of proposals, consider alternatives, present arguments for and against, in short participate in the decision making.

Ideally, this yields a well-considered and well-analysed decision, with sufficient acceptance in the organization. But there are situations in which the course of decision making and the effects of decisions are less optimal, even disastrous. Janis (1982, 1985) and Janis and Mann (1977) gave a large number of examples of group processes that led to calamities on a world-wide scale, such as the Bay of Pigs crisis, Pearl Harbor, or more recently, the Watergate affair. Decision making groups around the American president charged with preparing, analysing and advising on these (and other) decisions overlooked some matters, made unrealistic estimates of chances, risks and consequences. This resulted in fiascos. Janis termed this phenomenon 'group-think', and his analysis of the composition and manner of working of decision making groups provides insight into the causes. The primary reason for the occurrence of 'group-think' is the presence of a closely-knit homogeneous group whose members show much resemblance in norms, values, ideas and backgrounds. The result is decisions with a low probability of successful outcomes. Although Janis and Janis and Mann analysed large-scale fiascos which took place in very specific circumstances, this type of process also occurs in more day-to-day decision making situations. Jick and Murray (1982) and Staallekker (1984) applied this model to decisions to close down units in companies.

More generally, Hambrick and Mason (1984) stated that the effectiveness of management teams depends on the prevailing situation. In their view, a homogeneous team would be faster and more effective in a stable situation, while in a turbulent, emergency-like situation a heterogeneous team would be more successful.

In addition to characteristics of the group, the organization as the context in which decisions are made influences the manner in which decisions take place.

The organizational context is, as Hickson *et al.* (1986) put it, 'the rules of the game'.

Fredrickson (1986a) reversed the traditional statement of Chandler that 'structure follows strategy'. In his view, strategic decison making processes are largely determined by structural characteristics of the organization in which they take place. Fredrickson cited centralization, formalization and complexity as variables of structure. In his view, these characteristics were best represented by three of Mintzberg's (1979) structural configurations, the simple structure, the machine bureaucracy and the professional bureaucracy. Fredrickson assumed that decision making processes would take different courses in the different types of organizations. Decision making in the centralist, simple structure would be more proactive and innovative, in the formalized machine bureaucracy it would be more problem-oriented and incremental, while in the complex professional bureaucracy it would be of a political nature. Unfortunately, no research results on these assumptions are available.

Miller (1987) expanded on Fredrickson's work. In almost one hundred small and medium-sized companies, Miller studied the relationship between organizational structure (formalization, integration, centralization and complexity) and characteristics of decision making processes (rationality, interaction and assertiveness). Rationality here stands for the amount of attention paid during the decision making process to an analysis of the problem and of alternatives, and the extent to which there is explicit policy, a future orientation and an active attitude towards the environment. Interaction stands for the extent to which decision making is individual or by consensus and the leeway for negotiation. Assertiveness refers to how far behaviour is proactive and how far risks are taken in decisions.

From Miller's study it appeared that formal integration (formalization and integration together turned out to form a single structural factor) was primarily associated with the rationality characteristics and to a lesser extent with interaction and assertiveness. The presence of liaison devices (committees, project groups and liaison officers) showed a particularly strong positive correlation with the rationality characteristics. Furthermore, centralization was positively associated with risk level and individual decision making, and negatively with future orientation and planning.

Horvath and McMillan (1979) also linked organizational characteristics to strategic decision making processes. The authors primarily saw the prevailing power system as an important organizational characteristic. To determine the power system, they used a forerunner of Mintzberg's typology of power configurations (1977), which contained five configurations at the time (later six). The authors selected three configurations (the bureaucracy, the autocracy and the meritocracy) which they felt were especially applicable to larger organizations. In a 'clinical analysis' of four companies, Horvath and McMillan found confirmation of their expectation that the power constellation influences strategic processes. However, some of their results were contrary to Fredrickson's expectations. In an autocratic organization they found a reactive pattern with incomplete phasing and an informal approach, which differs from the proactive, rational pattern that Fredrickson expected for the simple structure. Horvath and McMillan found this pattern more in meritocracies, while Fredrickson had expected this type of organization to exhibit the most incremental, politicized decision making. In the bureaucratic configuration, the results of Horvath and McMillan showed decision making to be reactive and standardized, which was in reasonable agreement with Fredrickson's expectations.

Shrivastava and Grant (1985), too, found a relationship between the type of organization and the dominant types of decision making processes. They worked with the structural typology of Greiner (1972) (entrepreneurial, functional, divisionalized and conglomerate). 'Managerial Autocracy' processes, characterized by a personal, intuitive and result-oriented approach, turned out to occur frequently in small companies, but were not found in any of the other organizational types. The 'Adaptive Planning Model', a structured, systematic decision making model aimed at intensive analysis of the problem and of solutions, was in the majority in functional organizations. In the two remaining organizational types (divisionalized and conglomerate), the 'Adaptive Planning Model' occurred along with the 'Systemic Bureaucratic Model' (highly regulated) and the 'Political Expediency Model' (mainly aimed at the achievement of self-interests) with approximately equal frequency. The political model chiefly occurred in the conglomerate structure (in three out of four cases).

Indications were also found in the study by Hickson et al. (1986) that the type of organization has a determining effect on the course of decision making. The 30 organizations studied were classified on the dimensions of profit versus non-profit, production versus service and private versus state-owned. Combinations of these dimensions were also considered. Production companies (as opposed to service companies) turned out to have more sporadic processes and fewer fluid ones. State-owned companies (as opposed to private) also showed more sporadic and fewer fluid and restricted processes. The much-cited distinction of profit/ non-profit yielded no significant differences. Production organizations in state ownership turned out to have the most sporadic processes, while private service companies (banks, insurance companies) showed the most fluid processes. Private producers (industry) and government services (hospitals, universities) occupied an intermediate position.

Koopman (1983) discussed a number of situational factors that influence the strategy to be followed in rationalization decisions. At the level of the organization, he distinguished the nature of relations between the groups involved (primarily the mutual trust), the decision making structure (centralized or decentralized), the expertise present among those involved and the power position of top management. These factors turned out to be of influence on the choice between a consultative approach with possibilities for compromises, or a more compelling 'tell-and-sell' approach.

Taking stock of these studies, the prevailing power system and the power relations appear to be especially important. The fact that the power configuration is one determinant of the course of decision making processes also came forward from the Decision-making in Organizations (DIO) studies (DIO, 1983; Heller et al., 1988; Koopman, 1980). Factors such as meta power (the extent to which the top of the organization is subjected to outside influences) and status power (formal positional power) turned out to influence the course of complex decision making processes. Research by Blankenship and Miles (1968) also showed the importance of hierarchical position for decision making behaviour.

The organizational context apparently exerts an important influence on decision making processes. In strategic decision making, however, standard procedures may well be inadequate. Wilson et al. (1986) named four factors that make routine decisions impossible:

1. Unusual facts.
2. Conflicts between players.
3. New topics.
4. Unusual source from which the problem arises.

In such cases the standard procedures are set aside, and the participants are relatively free to try to achieve their interests and goals via the power game.

The fact that the organizational structure influences the choices made in determining a strategy is often recognized by managers and theoreticians. Manipulation of the structural context is one of the elements in the power game (Bower, 1970). The strategy is not only influenced directly, but also via earlier structural changes. The structure of the organization and the existing power configuration are not fixed, but can be influenced (Pool, Koopman, and Kamerbeek, 1986). A manager will, for instance, invest energy in restructuring the organization, and especially in collecting his 'own' people around him. Seen in this way, strategy and structure are interdependent, interacting parameters (Burgelman, 1983).

Environmental Characteristics and Influences

Contingency theory (Hazewinkel, 1984; Lawrence and Lorsch, 1969) is widely accepted in the organizational sciences. This approach is based on the assumption that there must be a certain degree of harmony between the organization and the environment. A changeable environment, for example, demands a flexible structure, while stability opens the way to a bureaucracy (Hedberg, Nystrom, and Starbuck, 1976). So the environment can influence the more permanent pattern of positions and relations which, as described in the previous section, influence the course of decision making processes that take place within that context. Dirsmith and Covaleski (1983) reasoned along similar lines. In interaction with their environment, organizations develop 'reality maps, language, strategies and organizational and environmental values'. This can be compared with the 'belief systems' of Donaldson and Lorsch (1983). These factors contribute to the formation of 'strategic norms', which have a directive influence on the decisions that are made in and by the organization.

Child (1972) has shown that this relationship is not deterministic, but that harmony must be obtained through strategic choices of management (Bobbitt and Ford, 1980). Miller, Dröge and Toulouse (1988) and Montanari (1978) further elaborated the choice process in respect of organizational structuring as influenced by environmental characteristics. This internal adaptation is one way of achieving a certain organizational–environmental fit. A second way is active intervention in the environment. Pfeffer and Salancik (1978) gave a large number of examples of both kinds of adaptive mechanisms.

What part or what aspects of the environment are important to the course of decision making processes? In general terms, the relevant environment for the organization can be termed the 'task environment' (Thompson, 1967), or those parts of the environment that 'are relevant or potentially relevant for setting and achieving goals' (Dill, 1958, in Thompson, 1967, p. 69). The task environment has four main sectors: (1) customers (large and small); (2) suppliers (capital, labour, materials, etc.); (3) competitors; and (4) regulatory bodies (governments trade unions, employers' organizations, etc.). Here the environment is viewed from the groups that are its building blocks.

Murray (1978) gave a practical elaboration of this point of view. He analysed two decision making processes in an electricity company, one of which was substantially influenced by a group of residents living near a site where a nuclear power plant was planned, and the other by several regulatory bodies which, with a concern inspired by the oil crisis in 1973, managed to block the switch to oil-fired plants by means of their permit policy. These two cases showed that external parties can exert a very substantial influence on the course of the process and on the ultimate decision.

The results of Hickson et al. (1986) confirmed this picture. They measured the amount of influence by external parties in 150 decision-making processes. External influence varied from zero to 90% of the total influence exerted, with a mean of 28%. In decreasing order, customers, regulatory bodies, suppliers, governmental agencies, competitors and trade unions appeared to influence the internal decision making in organizations.

Another approach was taken by Stein (1981a, 1981b). He classified the environment on general characteristics such as volatility, complexity, change, competition and restrictiveness, in explicit relation to the course of decision making processes, which were measured based on four dimensions; explicitness of analysis, comprehensiveness of search process, flexibility and what was termed group behavour. This was intended to measure something like negotiating, interest groups and diffusion, and may be interpreted as political activity. Stein's study, based on a postal enquiry among 64 companies, showed relationships between complexity of the environment and analysis activity; between volatility, changeability and restrictiveness of the environment and search activity; between complexity and restrictiveness of the environment and flexibility; and finally, between volatility of the environment and political activity. The multitude of relationships makes it clear that the environment has an influence on elements of decision making processes, even though the author made no statements about the meaning of the relationships found.

Miller and Friesen (1983) also studied the relationship between environment and decision making or strategy formulation. Following Child (1972), Dess and Beard (1984), Mintzberg (1979) and others, they took as environmental variables: dynamics, hostility and complexity. As elements of strategy Miller and Friesen distinguished: (1) analysis (amount of analysis activity, number of aspects of a decision that are considered, integration of decisions and the extent to which long-term expectations are included) and (2) innovation (introduction of new products and production techniques, new solutions to marketing and production problems, proactivity and willingness to take risks). Miller and Friesen's research comprised two studies, one of which was a survey among 50 Canadian companies, and a second among 36 American companies. The total sample was divided into high and low 'performers'. Analysis showed that in the more successful companies, a dynamic environment was associated with more analysis and innovation, a hostile environment with more analysis, and a complex environment with more innovation.

Fredrickson (1984) and Fredrickson and Mitchell (1984) studied the importance of comprehensiveness of decision making processes in organizations in stable and variable environments respectively. Comprehensiveness was viewed as the amount of search and analysis activity (analytical comprehensiveness) and the extent to which decisions were integrated in a more general strategy (integrative comprehensiveness); it was defined by the author as 'the extent to which an organization attempts to be exhaustive or inclusive in making and integrating strategic decisions'. A scenario was written for a common problem situation for the companies in both types of environment. Top managers answered a questionnaire indicating how they would deal with this standardized stimulus. In the stable industries, comprehensiveness of decision making was positively related to effectiveness of the company (Fredrickson, 1984). In the dynamic industries, however, Fredrickson and Mitchell (1984) found a negative relationship. It would seem that, depending on the stability of the environment, different decision making procedures are needed.

Miles and Snow (1978) proposed a typology of strategies distinguishing three functional types (prospectors, analysers and defenders) and one dysfunctional type (reactors). Prospectors actively seek renewal, they usually function in a dynamic environment and often show an 'organic' structure. Defenders, on the other hand, seek stability in an environment conducive to the status quo, and they usually exhibit a more 'mechanistic' structure. Analysers occupy an intermediate position, while reactors are an unstable and dysfunctional type. It is clear that the type of strategy chosen must be adjusted to environmental characteristics.

Hrebiniak and Joyce (1985) classified strategies into four types (natural selection, differentiation, strategic choice and undifferentiated choice), depending on the extent to which organizations were subject to influences from the environment, and the extent to which the environment was open to influence. The authors regarded these two variables as independent of each other.

An international study of 217 complex organizational decisions in England, Yugoslavia and the Netherlands (Heller *et al.*, 1988) showed that meta power— that is, external influence on the decision making process, e.g. by the parent company—was one of the most important determinants of the structure of the process; another was national legislation. Dutch and English companies, for instance, showed the lowest amount of participation (by the various groups within the organization) in the first and the third phases (start-up and finalization), and the highest in the second and the fourth phases (development and implementation). In Yugoslavia, the reverse was true: the greatest amount of participation was found in the first and third phases. This suggests that, where decision making is more formalized and public (Yugoslavia), it more closely follows the classical phase model, since this offers a stronger guarantee of the legitimization of the process.

The relationship between environment and decision making or strategy is not a direct one. It is not the objective environmental factors that are important, but how they are perceived by the relevant decision makers (Child, 1972; Hambrick and Snow, 1977; Weick, 1979). Duncan (1972) held the view that two environmental factors, complexity and instability, contributed to the perception of environmental uncertainty. Anderson and Paine (1975) stated that what was experienced by one manager as uncertainty would not necessarily be perceived as such by others, and that this perceptual difference affected the formulation of decisions. A factor such as tolerance of ambiguity was felt to be of importance here (Duncan, 1972).

Topics of Decision Making

In the previous sections we have discussed how the context influences the course of decision making processes. In this section we will go into the determining influence of the topic, or the substance of the decision. It is known, for example, that rationalization decisions generally take an entirely different course from expansion or innovation decisions (Jick and Murray, 1982; Staallekker, 1984;

Koopman, 1983). The ten topics used by Hickson *et al.* (1986) as a classification framework for the subjects of decision making (such as reorganizations, new products or services, location decisions, new production technologies, acquisitions) exhibited widely different processes. These authors stated that not only decisions on different topics, but also decisions in one and the same topic category, can take different courses. This raises the question of what factors are behind this.

As long ago as 1959, Thompson and Tuden classified decisions into four types based on two criteria: whether or not there was agreement on the goals to be achieved and whether or not there was agreement on the means to achieve them. If there is agreement both on the goals to be achieved and the means, then a decision can be made in a routine manner. If people agree on the goals, but not on the means, then it is up to experts to make a majority decision. In the opposite case, when people do know how they want to achieve some desired end, but they disagree on what that situation is, then a compromise is needed. Finally, disagreement on both goals and means implies quite a predicament, and only an approach based on inspiration can offer a way out.

Several researchers have since presented a similar classification (Axelsson and Rosenberg, 1979; Grandori, 1984; Koopman, Kroese, and Drenth, 1984; McMillan, 1980). With different emphases here and there and with different names for the dimensions, all these authors use a 2 × 2 matrix containing a classification into decision making processes. The cell in which Thompson and Tuden had to call upon inspiration always causes the most difficulties. There is reasonable consensus about the aspects that are difficult to make manageable and solvable: the technical complexity of the subject matter and the socio-political import.

The terms technical complexity and socio-political import are borrowed primarily from the results of the aforementioned study of strategic decision making (Hickson *et al.*, 1986). Their analysis of 150 decision making processes in 30 organizations yielded a classification into three types: sporadic (lengthy, muddled), fluid (not as lengthy, but continual) and constricted processes (fewer participants, shorter duration). Further analysis of the contents of these processes yielded a classification based on two dimensions, complexity and politicality. Combination of these dimensions led to three sorts of decisions: vortex decisions (highly complex and highly political), tractable decisions (less political, but complex) and familiar decisions (less complex, but more political than the tractable decisions). The fourth possible type, low on complexity and political import, was quite logically not found, because the study was aimed at the strategic level, where such simple decisions seldom or never take place (Koopman *et al.*, 1988). Comparison of the classification based on process characteristics to that on subject matter characteristics showed an overlap of 66%. That is, highly complex and political topics (vortex) took a sporadic course in two out of three cases. The same is true of tractable decisions, which were often fluid, and familiar decisions, which were usually constricted. These results are a further confirmation of the importance of the topic for the manner in which decision making processes take place.

Although the distinction into complexity–politicality is conceptually useful, and is used by several authors, in our view it oversimplifies matters, primarily with respect to the complexity aspect. Under complexity, Hickson *et al.* (1986) included a number of substantial aspects of decisions: their frequency, how serious, how far-reaching, and how radical the consequences were, as well as how long they lasted, precedent setting and the number of parties involved. They distinguished four aspects of politicality: pressure exerted, the amount of external involvement, inequality of the distribution of influence and contention (or divergence) of objectives.

Stein (1981b) described a total of 13 aspects of the subject matter and divided them into four main elements: (1) crisis/opportunity (the extent to which a subject is seen as new opportunity or possibility, the extent to which there is a clear vision of future goals and the presence of time pressures); (2) intensity (significance, complexity, extent to which the consequences are measurable, and potential consequences for career); (3) solvability (initial difficulty of problem, insufficiency of information and amount of information collection); and (4) ramifications (problem is part of larger problem, relatedness to other decisions, number of aspects of the problem that can be distinguished).

Beach and Mitchell (1978) described the task of decision makers, distinguishing between characteristics of the problem and characteristics of the 'environment of the decision'. In the second category the authors included irreversibility, importance, accountability, and time and money contingencies in that order. The former category of characteristics involved unfamiliarity, ambiguity, complexity and instability.

It is remarkable that the categories of Stein and Beach and Mitchell pay no attention to the presence or absence of contrasting interests. This was taken into account by MacCrimmon and Taylor (1976), whose rough classification distinguished three aspects: uncertainty, complexity and conflict. These aspects, said the authors, contributed to the 'ill-structuredness' of decisions. Pinfield (1986) considered whether or not there was agreement between participants on the goals as the primary factor that determined whether decision making processes were more structured or more chaotic.

Koopman (1983) identified a number of situational characteristics important in rationalizations. In addition to characteristics of organizational structure, he named the following characteristics of the decision: available time and room to manoeuvre, the percentage of dismissals, the future prospects and the nature of the arguments. The greater the urgency, seriousness and magnitude of the decision and the poorer the prospects, the more resistance was to be expected and the smaller the possibilities for arriving at a solution through consultation.

Based on this summary, we have made a classification of relevant substantial aspects of problems or decisions. The first aspect is the newness of the problem (Simon, 1957). When a problem situation is dealt with for the first time, new ways will have to be found to solve it (Butler *et al.*, 1979). This implies that new problems are perceived as more complex than problems which have been dealt with before, because in the latter case methods of solving are known (Fahey, 1981; Hickson *et al.*, 1986). If certain problems come up regularly, then standard solutions (standard operating procedures, March and Simon, 1958) will be developed. In addition to the availability of solutions, the insight into their effectiveness plays a role: it decreases the uncertainty (MacCrimmon and Taylor, 1976). Mintzberg *et al.* (1976) called unstructured decisions 'decision processes that have not been encountered in the same form and for which no predetermined and explicit set of ordered responses exists in the organization'.

A second factor is the ambiguity of a problem (Butler *et al.*, 1979; March and Olsen, 1976). Some problems are fairly clear, while in other cases there is much less insight into the nature of the problem (Beach and Mitchell, 1978). If the problem is the expiry of a contract for the rent of a building, then either the contract will have to be renewed or new premises sought. If the problem is a gradually declining market share, then the cause is much less clear, and so is the remedy to be applied. It will depend on the analysis of the problem (relative lack of quality, inadequate marketing, price too high, etc.). The more ambiguous the problem, the more must be invested in a diagnosis of the situation to obtain insight in the direction in which the solution must be sought.

A third factor is the size or scope of a problem (Beach and Mitchell, 1978; MacCrimmon and Taylor, 1976). A large-scale problem has all kinds of aspects that will have to be seen and discussed from different points of view and disciplines (Butler *et al.*, 1979). This also brings up the issue of agreement. Clearly, as the scope of the problem increases, so does the number of assessment aspects. The nature of the desired change is also important. One aspect of this is the extent to which the new situation differs from the old one. Small, step-by-step alterations are easier to grasp and to implement than more fundamental changes (Miller and Friesen, 1980). The magnitude of a decision is a related factor, in the sense that as the time span of a decision increases, so does uncertainty about its correctness. Whereas a short-term or medium-term estimate can be made of the probable changes, it becomes more and more difficult in long-term decisions.

A fourth factor is the importance of a decision, or how basic it is to policy (Beach and Mitchell, 1978; Fahey, 1981). Mintzberg *et al.* (1976) stated that 'strategic simply means important', referring to the action undertaken, the resources allocated and the precedents set by the decision. The closer a problem lies to the heart of the organization and the more it affects its survival, the greater are the risks linked to it (Butler *et al.*, 1979). This means that the choices made will have to be made more cautiously, more will have to be invested in analysing information collected, and the involvement of top management will be more constant (Pool, Koopman, and Kamerbeek, 1986). In this way, the complexity increases with the importance.

Another factor is the seriousness or urgency of the problem (Beach and Mitchell, 1978; Koopman, 1983). If rapid action is called for and there are clear deadlines, then opportunities for extensive consultation and deliberation are usually limited (Pool and Koopman, 1987). If the organization's survival is seriously threatened by the problem, however, the willingness of other parties to place their fate in the hands of the manager will be greater. The legitimacy of the decisions to be made is questioned less. This factor is related to how a decision is perceived: as a crisis that must be faced, a problem to which a solution must be found, or as an opportunity to obtain advantage from a situation (Fahey, 1981; Mintzberg et al., 1976).

A following factor is the extent to which a problem or decision is strategically embedded, the extent to which it fits within a policy framework. If previous decisions have been made in the organization that set parameters for further development, then a part of the uncertainty or leeway for later decisions has been eliminated with them. If this is not the case, more freedom of choice remains, and there is less control by past experience. Decision making will demand more attention in this case, the more so since it may influence later decisions, thus setting a precedent (Hickson et al., 1986; Mintzberg et al., 1976).

The final factor here is the degree to which the parties involved in the decision making process have contrasting interests in the decision, or support different alternatives. Generally speaking, parties may try to achieve contrasting objectives, or attach different values to possible outcomes (Hickson et al., 1986; MacCrimmon and Taylor, 1976; Thompson and Tuden, 1959). Lastly, it is important not only to look at internal differences of opinion. Particularly in strategic decision making processes, various external parties can also make themselves heard (Hambrick, 1981; Jemison, 1981). The extent to which external parties influence the decision making process forms a complicating factor, because it limits the internal leeway (Hickson et al., 1986).

DIMENSIONS AND MODELS OF DECISION MAKING

'Strategic Choice'

Several decision making models will be discussed in this section. But first it will be explained what concepts, in our view, play a central role in the conceptualization of the decision making processes (Pool and Koopman, 1989). On the whole, research results in this field show that decision making processes can vary primarily on four dimensions: centralization, formalization, information and confrontation. These dimensions are further elaborated below. Different arrangements of processes in terms of their scores on the dimensions are linked to the contingencies of topic and context (persons, organization and environment) discussed in the previous section.

However, a decision making process does not only come about as the result of interaction of several forces. Often one or more central actors (usually termed the 'dominant coalition' (Thompson, 1967), although it need not always be a coalition) manage to give a strong personal accent to the decision making process. It should be kept in mind that this does not take place in complete freedom. As noted above, the primary criticism of the normative decision making theory concentrates on the fact that a number of factors escape the control of management. Another important factor that limits regulatory possibilities is that, with a few exceptions, no single party has complete control of the steering wheels, even if a coalition is dominant. Other actors or parties will also try to influence the direction the process takes. Nevertheless a certain amount of leeway remains to give intentional form to decision making processes, within the contingencies formed by the topic and the context.

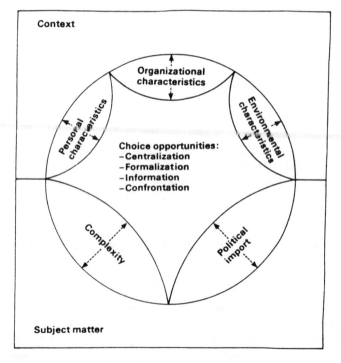

Figure 6.1 Schematic representation of opportunities and leeway for choice in the structuring of strategic decision making (from Pool and Koopman, 1989)

A similar line of thought is used in the discussion of organizational structure: Child's (1972) concept of 'strategic choice'. The presence of leeway for strategic choices implies that, in addition to the determining effects of environmental factors and technology, opportunities still remain for personal accents. As opposed to a complete determinism, it is stated, there are opportunities for the management of a company to choose, without altering the determining influence of the contingency factors mentioned.

The same can be said of decision making processes: although they are partly determined by their substance and the context in which they take place, the decision makers still have the necessary leeway for choice (Miller et al., 1988). The amount of leeway can differ per case and per organization (see Figure 6.1). How this leeway is used largely determines how effective and efficient the decision making process will be.

Dimensions of Decision Making Processes

Decision making processes come about in the context of the organization and its environment, and as a result of the perception and the behaviour of decision makers and other participants. Within this context, certain control options are available to management which they can use in the design and control of problem solving. We will discuss these options in this section. In our view, they constitute the chief process characteristics in decision making.

The classification is based on an inventory of strategy and decision making techniques that have been described by other authors and researchers, and on our own previous research of the manageability of decision making (Koopman and Pool, 1990).

Centralization

The amount of centralization is one of the most important parameters of decision making. Much research has been done on the manner in which decentralization and participation take place in decision making and on the question of how far participation is effective. This dimension involves the extent to which top management keeps decision making to itself, or involves other groups, parties or hierarchical levels in it (Butler et al., 1979; Duncan, 1973; Fredrickson, 1986a; Hickson et al., 1986; Mintzberg et al., 1976; Shrivastava and Grant, 1985). Aspects of this concept are the openness with which the top approaches the rest of the organization (Hickson et al., 1986), the extent to which parts of the decision making process are delegated (Stagner, 1969; Vroom and Yetton, 1973), and the way in which the participation of organization members takes concrete shape (Duncan, 1973; Heller et al., 1988; Koopman, 1980; Vroom and Yetton, 1973).

This dimension is related to models of decision making which emphasize power and influence relations (Abell, 1975; Bacharach and Lawler, 1980; Heller *et al.*, 1988; Mintzberg, 1983; Pfeffer, 1981). In some studies the centralization dimension is viewed as the primary source of variance (Heller *et al.*, 1988; IDE, 1981). Decision making processes can however also differ to a large extent on other dimensions.

Formalization

A second important dimension is the extent to which the decision making is formalized (Allison, 1971; Duncan, 1973; Fredrickson, 1986a; Hickson *et al.*, 1986; Stagner, 1969; Stein, 1981a). This indicator comes from previous research of bureaucratic and organizational models of decision making (Allison, 1971; Klootwijk and Wagenaar, 1983; Lindblom, 1959; Perrow, 1972). Decisions can take place according to an established procedure set down in advance, as in governmental decision making, or they can proceed more flexibly, according to informal considerations of what is required or desirable (Stein, 1981a). Other aspects of formalization are whether the decision takes place within the fixed communication and consultation structure, or whether a separate, temporary structure is set up, how many committees need to discuss the decision (Hickson *et al.*, 1986), and whether prescriptive contingencies (in terms of money or resources) are set in advance within which the process or the decision must remain (Koopman and Pool, 1986). If this is the case, the extent to which control is exercised is important in determining whether or not these contingencies are met. Finally, in addition to formal consultation, the extent to which the decision is discussed informally ('off the record') is also an aspect of formalization (Hickson *et al.*, 1986).

Information

Third, the way in which the substance of a decision comes about is important. The information dimension comes from the classical decision making theory, in which it is assumed that decision makers not only have access to all necessary information but can also process it (see, for example, Harrison, 1987). In practice this is not feasible and perhaps even undesirable; this has been argued by many authors (Janis, 1982; Nutt, 1984; O'Reilly, 1983; Schwenk, 1984, 1988; Simon, 1947, 1957). On the basis of what information is a decision made? What alternatives are developed or sought, and from where do they come? Have important possibilities or consequences been overlooked? These questions involve the extent to which the requirements assumed by the traditional rational perspective of decision making are met (Butler *et al.*, 1979; Mazzolini, 1981; Mintzberg *et al.*, 1976; Miller, 1987; Nutt, 1984; O'Reilly, 1983; Shrivastava and Grant, 1985; Stein, 1981a; Witte, 1972). Fredrickson (1984, 1986a) spoke of the comprehensiveness of decision making processes.

Aspects of this dimension are the number of alternatives that are considered (Fredrickson, 1984; Hickson *et al.*, 1986; Nutt, 1984; Stein, 1981a), where the information is sought (internally or externally) (Hickson *et al.*, 1986; Mintzberg *et al.*, 1976; Miller, 1987), whether the solution found can be implemented directly or whether further synthesis is needed (Mintzberg *et al.*, 1976; Nutt, 1984), what confidence people have in it (Hickson *et al.*, 1986) and whether consultants are enlisted (Koopman and Pool, 1986; Nutt, 1984).

Confrontation

The fourth and final dimension is the extent to which there is confrontation and conflict in the decision making process. This last dimension comes from models of decision making as a political process, in which parties try to achieve their own interests on the basis of their power positions (Allison, 1971; Hickson *et al.*, 1971; Mintzberg *et al.*, 1976; Pettigrew, 1973). Especially in strategic decisions, different parties often have different interests in certain outcomes (see above). In order to articulate this, it must be possible to find some way to balance preferences (Allison, 1971; Etzioni, 1967; Lindblom, 1959; Quinn, 1978; Thompson and Tuden, 1959). The amount of negotiation that turns out to be necessary to arrive at a decision gives an indication of the amount of confrontation. The way in which conflicts of interest are dealt with is also important. A person may prefer a clash followed by pushing through his own preference, or a compromise, in which a solution is found by consultation and negotiation; he may choose to convince the opposite party on the basis of arguments, or to postpone or sidestep the decision until the subject of conflict has died down or disappeared (MacCrimmon and Taylor, 1976; Wrapp, 1988).

These dimensions are the basis for a description of decision making processes. However, they are not exhaustive specifications of the complete process. Strategic decisions often take a long time, and go through several phases (Heller *et al.*, 1988; Mintzberg *et al.*, 1976; Witte, 1972). The time aspect is an underlying characteristic of decision making processes, together with the social space in which they take place. Time and space serve as a pair of axes along which decision making processes in organizations can be set out (Heller *et al.*, 1988). This is also expressed in the research by Hickson *et al.* (1986). Their analysis of 150 strategic decisions led to a classification on the basis of two dimensions, dispersion and discontinuity, in which the space and time elements are also evident.

Characteristics of the course taken by decision making are the 'skeleton' of the decision making process. Of first importance here are the phasing and the total duration. In addition, decision making processes are often characterized by delays and by feedback loops to earlier phases. Decision making processes that show much retracing and many delays become turbulent or even chaotic, while other processes can remain more fluent.

Decision Making Models

Depending on various context factors, the topic of decision making and the policy of management, the decision making process can assume very different shapes. Decision making can show much or little centralization, but also formalization, for centralization and formalization do not always go together (Robbins, 1987). Sometimes information plays an important role in the decision preparation, sometimes power processes determine the contents of the decision and information primarily serves the purpose of legitimating after the fact.

Combination of the four above-described dimensions (centralization, formalization, information and confrontation) leads to a typology of four basic models of decision making which can reasonably accommodate most literature in this field (see Table 6.1). We distinguish in this order:

—The neo-rational model.
—The bureaucratic model.
—The arena model.
—The open-end model.

Theoretically, classification based on the four dimensions would yield sixteen different models. In our view, such diversity is not wise, nor can it be defended

Table 6.1 Four models of decision making and their relationships with the process dimensions

	Neo-rational model	Bureaucratic model	Arena model	Open-end model
Characteristics of decision making process				
Centralization	high	moderate/ high	low	low
Formalization	low	high	moderate/ high	low
Information	high/ low	high	low	high/ low
Confrontation	low	low	high	high

empirically. In addition, the dimensions are not completely independent. A high score on one dimension frequently implies a low score on another. Within the neo-rational model, highly centralized processes are often also fairly informal and show little conflict. In an organization with one clear and accepted power centre, there will be a larger role for factual information and arguments, at least as far they are in keeping with the goals of the top. The room for factual arguments will come under pressure when semi-autonomous groups with different preferences must reach agreement. Sometimes, however, the dimensions are more independent. One and the same centralized process can be allowed to operate fairly intuitively, or management can adopt a broad, comprehensive information strategy. What we then see are actually two subforms of the neo-rational model.

The models are not typified by a single dimension, although this seems to occur sometimes. Decision making processes of the neo-rational type, for instance, are primarily centralized, while those of the bureaucratic type are primarily characterized by a high degree of formalization. They often show a large degree of information processing and relatively little conflict. The arena model is chiefly determined by conflict and negotiation, which implies that the leeway for an objective assessment of the available information is often slight. Often several relatively autonomous parties are involved, which makes the centralization low. Lastly, the open-end model, entirely in the nature of its open character, can be organized in different ways, and differences can occur with each step in the process. So, while one phase can come to concentrate on information collection, in the next one a confrontation may take place about the alternatives generated. Characteristic of the open-end model is the flexible adaptation to the requirements of the situation, which can always change. The interdependence of the dimensions means that the models are defined by certain profiles of positions on the four dimensions. The degrees of freedom that are still present in the four models may be regarded as ways to further specify the main models.

The classification proposed here attempts to include as much empirical research as possible, and models based upon it. To exemplify, Hickson et al. (1986) distinguished sporadic, fluid and limited processes. Schwenk (1988), following Allison, discussed the rational choice perspective, the organizational perspective and the political perspective. Thompson and Tuden (1959) distinguished decisions through computation, majority judgement, compromise and inspiration. Axelsson and Rosenberg (1979) and McMillan (1980) used similar typologies. Fahey (1981) reduced reality to two contrasting types of decision making: rational–analytical versus behavioural–political. McCall and Kaplan (1985) spoke of quick versus convoluted action. Our classification most clearly corresponds to that of Shrivastava and Grant (1985). As mentioned above, these authors distinguished the managerial autocracy model, the systemic bureaucratic model, the political expediency model and the adaptive planning model.

Another more or less related classification is that of Quinn and Cameron (1983), who described the rational goal model, the internal process model, the human relations model and the open systems model (see also Quinn, 1988; Quinn and Rohrbaugh, 1983).

Context-Model Configurations

The models as sketched above are not only configurations of dimensions; there is often also a clear relationship between the various models and the context in which they take place. The various characteristics of the context have been extensively described above (in the section on context and subject matter of decision making). Here we will discuss how the context and the topic of decision making align with the various models. We have summarized the expected configurations in Table 6.2.

The *neo-rational model* is characterized by strong centralization, combined with low formalization and confrontation. Here we should think of not very complex decision making processes that are guided and controlled from one point: the top management. There is little power distribution in the organiza-

Table 6.2 The four decision making models and their hypothetical relationships with various context factors

	Neo-rational model	Bureaucratic model	Arena model	Open-end model
Context factors:				
Environment:				
complexity	low	low	high	high
dynamics	high	low	low	high
hostility	high	low	high	low/high
Organization: power				
distribution	low	low	high	high
type of organization (Mintzberg)	autocracy	machine bureaucracy	professional bureaucracy	adhocracy
type of culture (Harrison)	power culture	role culture	person culture	task culture
Characteristics of decision maker	proactive, intuitive	reactive, analytic	autonomous, intrapreneur	innovative, willing to take risks
Type of subject:				
complexity	low	high	low/high	high
dynamics	high/low	low	high	high

tion. According to Fredrickson (1986a) and Shrivastava and Grant (1985), this type of decision making process may primarily be expected in the organizational type that Mintzberg (1979, 1983) termed a 'simple structure' or 'autocracy'. In terms of organizational culture, Harrison's (1972) 'power culture' would be most conducive to this type of decision making process. The model is rational in the sense that decision making aims to maximize the goals of top management. Like a spider in its web or like Zeus in Greek mythology (Handy, 1985), the top manager leaves his personal mark on decision making, and in so doing, strives to maximize his goals. Intuition and quick decisions are more typical of this model than extensive analysis and study of alternatives (Shrivastava and Grant, 1985). We speak of the neo-rational model because it takes account of some fundamental characteristics relating to human cognitions and emotions. Because of this, the behaviour of decision makers is characterized by 'bounded rationality' and 'satisficing' (as opposed to maximal) goal achievement (Simon, 1976). A dynamic and/or threatening environment can lead decision making processes to follow the neo-rational model (McCall and Kaplan, 1985; Pettigrew, 1986; Pounds, 1969): they demand quick reaction (see Figure 6.2).

Characteristic of the *bureaucratic model* is that decision making is 'constricted' by rules and regulations. They may be rules of the organization itself, such as job descriptions, tasks and competencies, meeting rules, etc., but also rules that are laid down outside the organization, as by legislation or by directives from the head office. The decision making comes to be formalized by all manner of rules and methods of planning and control. Different actors or groups are expected to make their contribution at various stages, even if it merely means initialling a document. Various alternatives are explored and officially documented. The selection of the best solution is conducted by way of existing procedures (Shrivastava and Grant, 1985). In contrast to the neo-rational model, the bureaucratic model usually involves fairly complex decision making processes. Its counterpart in Mintzberg's structural typology is the 'machine bureaucracy' or the 'closed system'. Its counterpart in Harrison's culture typology is the 'role culture'. As in these counterparts, the environment is characterized by stability and predictability. When time pressure or external threats increase, decision making increasingly leans to the neo-rational model (temporary centralization, Mintzberg, 1983). If innovation requirements are central, then characteristics of the open-end model still to be discussed gain the upper hand.

Decision making in the *arena model* is dominated by negotiations between various interested parties, which form coalitions around certain sub-interests. These groups defend a point of view or alternative as the only correct and legitimate view of reality (Shrivastava and Grant, 1985). Power in the organization is relatively distributed; power differences are small. There is no central machinery that can easily impose its will. Although there is a certain degree of coordination (primarily through professional training, Mintzberg, 1983), the organization must constantly contend with the problem of acquiring sufficient consensus and acceptance for decisions. Mutual contention and lack of cooperation threaten the quality of the decision making. This type of decision making, with controversial topics, is primarily found in organizations that are composed of relatively independent units, such as universities or other 'conglomerates'. The decision making sometimes takes place at two levels: at the first level a small group of insiders arrives at the critical choices, which are subsequently legitimized for the constituency by the official bodies and by means of arguments which are accepted by these bodies (Koopman *et al.*, 1984; Koopman and Kroese, 1986; Shrivastava and Grant, 1985). The natural counterpart in the structural typology of Mintzberg is the professional bureaucracy; in the culture typology of Harrison we should think of the 'person culture'.

Decision making in the *open-end model* is characterized by a limited view of the goals or of the means by which to achieve them. Chance circumstances and unpredictable events cross the path of this approach. Again and again, people must adapt to new demands and possibilities. This forces them to take a step-by-step approach (Quinn, 1980). Another characteristic of the model is that, depending on the problem in question, expertise of various types and locations must be gathered on a temporary basis (project management). The message here is: organize flexibly. Gradually, by way of iterations and recycling, the end product comes into view (Boehm, 1986; Koopman, 1989). Complex innovative decisions (e.g. automation) often take place in this way. Mintzberg's 'adhocracy'

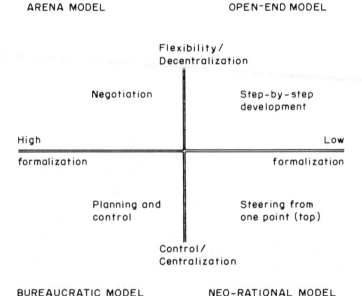

Figure 6.2 Four models of decision making

forms the organizational structure conducive to this type of decision making. The environment is complex and dynamic. Such an organization generally has a 'task culture' (Harrison, 1972).

In the next section the four models will be discussed in greater detail on the basis of research results.

DECISION MAKING MODELS AND EMPIRICAL RESULTS

In this section we will give further empirical basis to the models of decision making, to the context in which they take place and to the subject involved.

The Neo-rational Model

Rational thinking long dominated the decision making literature, and in fact it still does. Students are taught that decisions are the result of conscious choices on the part of management, that they come about on the basis of a clear definition of the problem and a careful consideration of alternatives (Connolly, 1980). However, it is recognized nowadays that all kinds of factors limit this rationality. From this point of view, the rational choice perspective primarily involves cognitive and emotional characteristics of the decision maker.

Research on the effects of cognitive limitations in complex decision making has shown that decision makers work with simplified mental models of reality, and often make do with 'satisficing' rather than maximal results (Simon, 1976; Mason and Mitroff, 1981). To get a grasp on complex reality, managers make use of heuristic techniques, cognitive schemata, strategic assumptions and analogies (Schwenk, 1988). This naturally yields a distorted picture (Hogarth and Makridakis, 1981). For example, managers may overestimate their own impact on the environment, they may only seek information that agrees with their own viewpoints, or they may all too readily assume that previous solutions will work again in a new situation.

Nutt (1984) studied the manner in which solutions to complex problem situations were generated. In an analysis of 73 decision making processes, he distinguished five different phases (formulation, concept development, detailing, evaluation and implementation) and three main activities (search, synthesis and analysis). The combination of phases and activities led to a typology of five different ways in which 'solutions' were found. They were termed as follows:

— Historical process (41%): in this case solutions or ideas of others (e.g. other organizations) are imitated, even if there is no immediate problem. The problem follows the solution. A subcategory is the 'pet idea', hobby-horses of decision makers for which an occasion to put them into practice is sought.

— Off-the-shelf (30%): this approach uses the tender method. Competition arises among various solutions offered from outside, and these offers are then evaluated.

— Appraisal (7%): this is an attempt to find 'objective data' to back up a chosen solution. However, Nutt's remark that this resembles the scientific method is not entirely correct.

— Search (7%): possible solutions are sought to a newly discovered problem. There are no firm ideas about this. The search is passive and takes place through familiar contacts. If a solution is found, it is immediately adopted.

— Nova process (15%): solutions are designed either by outsiders (advisers) or by the decision makers themselves.

In Nutt's typology, solutions do not always follow problems, but sometimes precede them. In some cases it is not so much the solution which must be sought, but the problem! O'Reilly (1983) discussed the role of information in decision making and also recognized these possibilities. Preferences or desired solutions are often present before the search for information starts. Information is then used to support, sell or defend these preferences. Naturally we can no longer speak of an objective or rational choice in such a case.

For that matter, there are important individual differences in cognitive styles, both in the collection of information and in its assessment. In gathering information, some decision makers set to work very systematically, aiming at tracking down all relevant data. Others look more for larger chunks of information, relying on their intuition. An overall vision guides the search process (Middlemist and Hitt, 1988). A similar difference in personal styles plays a role in evaluation and selection. Some people base their opinions on a thorough analysis of objective data, following logical decision rules. Others consciously accept all kinds of subjective elements in the assessment process, relying on their personal opinions (Isenberg, 1984).

In adapting the strategy and structure of the organization to the demands of the environment, the perception of top managers plays a crucial role. Lawrence and Lorsch (1969) saw these perceptions as the best way to define environmental uncertainty. The perceptions of top management determine how strategic issues are formulated. This is a subjective process in which previous experiences play an important role (Lyles, 1981). There are important differences between managers in the extent of early recognition of imminent risks and new chances. Leavitt (1986) distinguished three phases in the management process: pathfinding, problem solving and implementation. Pathfinding, according to Leavitt, is often a neglected phase. Pathfinders are good at taking up questions and, on the basis of all manner of unclear information, they manage to create a meaningful 'Gestalt' (Morgan, 1986). Their own cognitive map of reality is decisive in identifying chances (Neisser, 1967). Using this filter, a manager selects things from 'reality'. A reactive manager will take a different attitude from a proactive manager. The latter is more open to new developments, follows them actively and influences them himself where he can (Vansina, 1986; Weick, 1979).

In addition to cognitions, emotions can play an important role in the decision making process (Kets de Vries and Miller, 1984; Morgan, 1986). In this connection, Janis and Mann (1977) spoke of 'hot cognition'. Managers are not rational decision makers who make entirely disinterested decisions aimed at achieving organizational goals. Their credibility and reputation are at stake. Consciously or intuitively, managers let issues slide if they entail too great risks for their own position and for the organization (Koopman *et al.*, 1988; McCall and Kaplan, 1985). The amount of stress in the decision making depends on the importance of the topic: how much is at stake? Surely when the personal reputation of the decision makers is at stake, tension rises. The amount of stress is also related to the extent to which decision makers feel responsible for current policy. If they are identified with a criticized or even failing policy, loss of face will threaten. Research by Janis and Mann (1977) has shown that decision makers, when confronted with warning signals, first of all tend to choose the road of least resistance. If it proves to be inadequate, a situation of stress ensues. Lacking the prospect of a better solution, 'defensive avoidance' often results: lack of perceptivity, selective attention, twisting facts, rationalizations. When, in addition, time and resources for research and consultation are lacking, decision makers enter into a state of 'hypervigilance': panic, helpless behaviour (such as complaining, blaming others) and decreased constructive thinking.

One of the best known studies of the nature of the work of managers is that of Mintzberg (1973). This study altered the picture of the ruminating, policy-oriented manager who looks almost exclusively to the strategic issues touching the organization. Alongside the familiar typology of roles fulfilled by one manager, this study primarily showed how the nature of the work of a manager is very hectic and fragmentary. There is comparatively brief attention to the matters on which a decision must be made. Mintzberg's characterization of the work of the manager was confirmed by several other studies (Carroll and Gillen, 1987; Kotter, 1982; Sayles, 1979; Stewart, 1982).

In addition to the sheer amount of work, the unpredictability of the questions that come at a manager is another reason for an often fragmentary approach to matters. A manager's schedule is constantly being interrupted by all kinds of unexpected calamities, large and small. These disturbances of his or her schedule make the work very fragmented, yielding a picture of chaos and a rushed, 'stressed' manager. It is therefore not surprising that many decisions are made quickly, without much reflection. In this connection, McCall and Kaplan (1985) used the metaphor of 'shooting from the hip'. But as the complexity of the problem increases, the decision making process generally takes on the characteristics of the bureaucratic model.

The Bureaucratic Model

In this model decisions are not so much seen as the result of a conscious choice, as in the previous model, but as the outcome of a great many organizational processes, systems and structures—planning systems, competencies, evaluation and remuneration systems, etc. (Schwenk, 1988). A certain structure and phasing come about as a result of formalization. In part, the basis for the regulations must sometimes be sought outside of the organization (e.g. in legislation, or in guidelines from the head office). The decision making process is circumscribed by formalization; the number of degrees of freedom of the process decreases (Heller *et al.*, 1988; Mintzberg *et al.*, 1976; Nutt, 1984).

There are large differences between types of organizations in the number of such procedures. Government agencies, for instance, are frequently characterized by detailed regulations and well-delineated tasks and competencies, while business and industry have fewer regulations. In addition, the structure of authority—traditionally more or less hierarchical—is not given, but can itself be the topic of decision making (Bobbitt and Ford, 1980; Child, 1972).

Aside from the existing organizational role division, separate agreements may be made per decision making process about the procedure to be followed. Mintzberg *et al.* (1976) called this 'meta decision making'. This covers agreements about who will do what and when, what criteria will be applied and what the schedule will be (van Aken and Matzinger, 1983). What this in fact amounts to is determining the structure of the decision making process (Kickert, 1979), or decisions about the way in which decisions will be made. Most decisions that must be made will take place within such a network of rules and agreements. In

Table 6.3 Some empirical phase models

Lyles (1981)	Fahey (1981)	Nutt (1984)
Awareness/ incubation	Establishment of overall corporate goals and objectives	Formulation
Triggering	Development of detailed divisional plans	Conceptualization
Information gathering	Development of implementation programs	Detailing
Resolution		Evaluation
		Implementation

the discussion of the open-end model we will see that, in a less formalized context, decision making assumes a more chaotic and less goal-oriented course.

In the literature we encounter many phase models, most of them normative, for decision making (e.g. Brim et al., 1962; Harrison, 1987). But until recently there was little or no empirical evidence about the extent to which decision making actually followed such norms. This started to change in the 1970s. Based on a study of 25 strategic decisions, Mintzberg et al. (1976) developed a sequential cyclic model. This model contained the following phases and activities: (1) identification phase: recognition and diagnosis, (2) development phase: search or design, (3) selection phase: screening, evaluation/choice, authorization. Furthermore, the model described a number of cyclic processes (reversions to earlier phases) and dynamic factors (accelerations, delays). Other studies lent confirmation and support to these results (Schwenk, 1988; see also Table 6.3).

The research by Mintzberg et al. showed that many decision making processes are prematurely broken off or blocked, either for technical or for political reasons. The authors described the following possibilities:

— Simple impasse: as a result of contrasting interests, decision making is blocked in the diagnosis phase.
— Political design: the decision making meets impasses and interruptions in the design phase.
— Basic search: decision making emphasizes a search for existing solutions, and involves uncontested technical decisions.
— Modified search: a technical modification of an existing solution is taking place.
— Basic design: demands much creativity, few interruptions and little political activity.
— Blocked design: like 'basic design', but with additional resistance that is recognized too late.
— Dynamic design: a complicated process with many interruptions, a long duration and repeated feedback loops to earlier phases.

Heller et al. (1988), who studied 217 strategic and tactical decisions in three countries, pointed out the importance of involving the implementation phase in the decision making research, not only because all kinds of decisions must still be made in that phase, but also because it is often the stage when 'negative' power becomes visible: who is obstructing the implementation of the decision?

In a study of reallocations in a multi-national, Koopman et al. (1984) found the following phases (See Figure 6.3):

— Recognition of problems at division and concern level.
— Development of plans at division level.

— Negotiations on plans at division level with national managers (the organization in question is a matrix organization).
— Negotiations on plans at plant level with works council and trade unions.
— Implementation.

In the decision making process studied in this research, formalization and constriction came, on the one hand, from the Dutch Works Council Act and the collective labour agreement, which regulate the rights of the works council and trade unions respectively; on the other hand, it was the result of an internal demarcation of competencies between various management positions. A striking difference with the above-mentioned phase models is that there were in fact two rounds of negotiations, one at the division level and one at the plant level. During the first round, consultation and negotiation were concentrated on the division management and various national organizations, while the second round primarily involved negotiations of plant managers with the works councils and trade unions (Koopman et al., 1984; Koopman and Kroese, 1986). It may be concluded that such complex reorganization decisions exhibit characteristics of both the bureaucratic and the arena model.

Not all studies of decision making have reported such a logically ordered pattern of activities. In part, this depends on the context within which the decision making takes place. But according to Schwenk (1985, 1988), a methodological artefact is also involved. The memory of decision makers is fairly frequently characterized by 'retrospective rationality' (Weick, 1979). This might well imply some degree of distortion, particularly in studies using only interviews. However, Meyer (1984) stated that the rationalization of decision making processes serves a practical purpose, and should not only be termed a 'measurement problem' Symbolic action and rationalizing promote acceptance and consensus formation, and accelerate the healing process of open wounds.

Interesting in this connection is that the study by Witte (1972)—which was based entirely on document analysis—showed that the four primary decision making activities (search for information, development of alternatives, evaluation and selection) occurred simultaneously, with about the same frequency, during the entire decision making process. Witte suggested that decision makers find it difficult to merely collect information without developing and evaluating alternatives at the same time. Isenberg's (1984, 1986) study of the thought processes of managers points in this direction. Furthermore, various studies have shown that goals sometimes only become clear during the process (e.g. Anderson, 1983). We will come back to this in the discussion of the open-end model.

Research results are not unanimous on the effect of formal planning of the quality of the decision making. Some authors emphasize that planning systems promote a thorough, analytical approach (Steiner, 1979). Others state that formal planning obstructs an innovative strategy (Quinn, 1980). Perhaps the

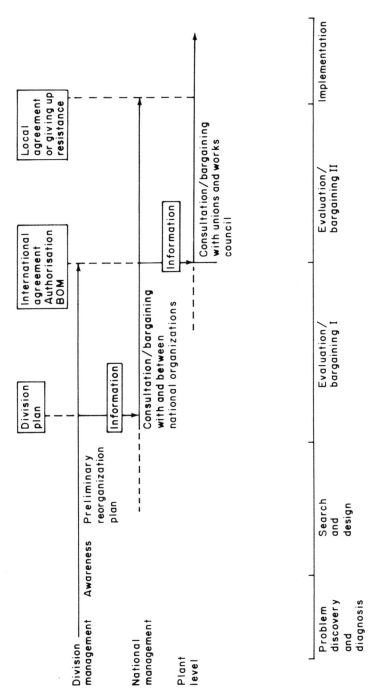

Figure 6.3 Phasing of a large scale reorganization decision (from Koopman, Kroese and Drenth, 1984)

effects vary depending on the branch of industry in which the decisions are being made. Fredrickson (1984) found a negative relationship between the thoroughness of decision making processes and operating results for companies in unstable industries, but a positive relationship for companies in stable industries.

The Arena Model

The political or arena model assumes that various parties involved in organizational decision making often have divergent interests. Hall and Saias (1980) and Pfeffer (1981) stated that differentiation within organizations influences decision making in the sense that the perceptions of the participants are determined by their primary concern for their own departments. In addition to internal groups, external interested parties will try to influence the outcome of the decision making process. Politics in organizations is influenced by both internal and external power relations (Mintzberg, 1983). A divided but active external coalition promotes political behaviour within the organization, certainly when internal power differences are relatively small. In government organizations, decision making is often fragmentized as a result of the necessary approval (initialling) by many people; this makes it incremental or negotiating in nature (Murray, 1978). Utilizing power sources, negotiating, coalition formation and utilization of 'strategies' are the central theme in the arena model.

Following Emerson (1962), Thompson (1967) stated that the extent to which an organization must rely on certain elements of the environment is dependent on the specific needs for the resources and achievements of the group in question, and on how far they can be replaced by other suppliers. Pfeffer and Salancik's (1978) view was that organizations aim at legitimizing themselves to parties on which they are dependent.

The possibility of controlling critical uncertainties also determines the power position within organizations (Crozier, 1964; Kanter, 1977; Pfeffer, 1981). The power of management can be considerably restricted by its dependence on experts or supporting services. Hickson et al. (1971) postulated that the power of individuals or departments is based on the extent to which they can resolve problematic matters for the organization. Jemison (1981) found that departments that are in contact with the environment, and particularly with critical elements of it, have more influence on strategic decision making (cf. boundary spanning, Jemison, 1984). Information is thus an important source of power. Mintzberg's (1983) typology is based on the same line of thought: the organizational form expands in the direction of the group that controls the primary processes and thus maximally influences the success or failure of the organization. If there are several internal coalitions, a political arena results. If this situation lasts for a longer period of time, it can threaten the survival of the organization.

Table 6.4 Phasing of involvement and power

Enderud (1980)	Kanter (1983)	Pettigrew (1986)
Exploring	Information collecting and problem formulation	Arousing interest
Negotiating	Building a coalition	Recognizing a problem
Legitimizing	Mobilization and finalization	Planning and execution
Adjustment		Stabilization

One of the primary sources of power is access to the decision making. Various studies have investigated in what way different groups in the organization are involved in decisions, and in what phase of the decision making process (DIO, 1983; Heller et al., 1988; IDE, 1981). Early involvement is important, because the way in which a problem is defined plays a role in the choice of the approach. Several authors have shown that power processes take place in a relatively early stage of the decision making process (see Table 6.4). Part of the exercise of power remains largely implicit. 'Power maintains its effectiveness not so much through overt action, as through its ability to appear to be natural convention. It is only when this taken-for-grantedness fails . . . that the overt exercise of power is necessary' (Clegg and Dunkerley, 1977, p. 35). Lukes spoke in this connection of the third dimension. In his view, the most grievous form of abuse of power is 'to prevent people . . . from having grievances by shaping their perceptions, cognitions and preferences in such a way that they accept their role in the existing order of things . . . without conflict' (Lukes, 1974, p. 24).

The organizational culture, defined as shared views and values, brings in view the internal power structures of organizations (Pfeffer, 1981). The perceptions of organizational members are influenced by the culture (histories, ideologies, rituals). Pettigrew (1979) stated that leaders create a culture which increases involvement by the organization. Riley (1983) suggested that politics determine the culture, subsequently legitimizing a certain type of political behaviour and defining it as correct.

Kanter (1977) and Mintzberg (1983) discussed ways to acquire power. Narayanan and Fahey (1982) identified the following phases of coalition formation and operation:

— Activation (becoming aware of strategic issues).
— Mobilization (of others in the organization).
— Coalition formation (around a certain 'solution').

— Confrontation (of outsiders with own option).
— Decision (whereby degree of consensus becomes clear).

The authors stated that much power was exerted in the three middle phases. Because much information is exchanged during the mobilization phase, those who control the information have a great deal of power during this phase. An internal political structure can come about during the coalition phase (MacMillan and Jones, 1986).

Open-end Model

Various authors have shown that decision making sometimes follows a capricious, unpredictable, almost accidental course (i.e. Grandori, 1984; Hickson *et al.*, 1986). Decision making processes seldom have clear beginnings and ends. Problems present themselves within a certain context, one that makes the situation even more confusing (McCall and Kaplan, 1985). Burns remarked in this regard: 'Executive decision making is not a series of linear acts like baking a pie. It is a process, a sequence of behavior, that stretches back into a murky past and forward into a murkier future. [It is] a turbulent stream rather than . . . an assembly-line operation . . . a twisted, unshapely halting flow' (Burns, 1978, p. 379).

Best known in this connection are the publications on the garbage can model (Cohen *et al.*, 1972; Cohen and March, 1974; March, 1988; March and Olsen, 1976), which were preceded by studies of the 'Carnegie School' (Cyert, Dill, and March, 1958; Cyert and March, 1963). The garbage can model describes the decision making process as an 'organized anarchy' in which incoherent problems exist alongside potential solutions. It also contains decision makers who try to bide their time as well as possible, and opportunities where solutions can be linked to problems. In this model, decision making is the almost coincidental concurrence of various independent currents within the organization. The elements are more or less arbitrarily mixed in the garbage can. Combinations arise almost unpredictably. There is no *a priori* chronology. Solutions can precede problems, or problems and solutions can wait for a suitable opportunity for a decision. Clearly, the traditionally assumed order of 'identification and definition of the problem, search for solutions, consideration of alternatives and selection' is turned upside-down. 'Although it may be convenient to imagine that choice opportunities lead first to the generation of decision alternatives, then to an examination of their consequences, then to an evaluation of those consequences in terms of objectives, and finally to a decision, this type of model is often a poor description of what actually happens' (Cohen *et al.*, 1972, p. 2).

Concepts such as 'garbage can model' and 'anarchy' can be misleading. The authors certainly do not imply that no systematic decision making can be discovered in such organizations. On the contrary, the central message of these authors is that the seeming anarchy has a structure and an organization which form a reasonable, although not optimal, answer to the great environmental uncertainty in which the participants find themselves.

In order for decision making to progress, it is essential that the organization manages to attract sufficient attention from the participants to solve the problems in question. However, participants generally have more on their minds. Thus it is not unusual that decision making takes place without explicit attention to the problem, or even by simply postponing the problem. The authors, however, see it as the task of management to coordinate and steer the required attention in a direction desired by the organization. Research by Anderson (1983) showed that decision makers sometimes scarcely even consider the available alternatives, and that goals often only gradually become clear. Goals come about through argumentation, and in interaction with demands, often new, made by the situation. The task of management is to give meaning to today and tomorrow ('management of meaning', Bouwen, 1987).

Research by Mayntz and Scharpf (1975) on decision making in the West German government yielded a variant on the garbage can model. The correctness of the assumption that policy initiatives are taken by the administrative top was investigated. Mayntz and Scharpf found that the course taken by these decision making processes was characterized by a dialogue between the decision makers and those who prepare policy. The policy formulation process—certainly in governmental organizations—is often characterized by highly obscure, or even absent, policy objectives, which offers little guidance to those who prepare policy. Initiatives for concrete policy usually come from the employees who are in close contact with specific interest groups. These initiatives find their way up along the hierarchical ladder as draft policy proposals. On their way, they are screened, altered or sent back by senior officials, on the basis of estimates of what is attainable and acceptable higher up in the organization. These estimates often must be based on vague statements or casual remarks on the part of higher officials. Once elaborated, the proposals ultimately land on the right desks. There the reactions to the proposals gradually make policy clearer. Each decision provides information for the policy makers which can be taken into account in following proposals (see also Mayntz, 1976; van der Krogt and Vroom, 1988).

Flexibility is an important requirement in innovative decision making (Koopman and Pool, 1986). Cooperation in temporary teams (adhocracy) is related to this. In particular, complex (Fahey, 1981) and new decisions (Fahey, 1981; Nutt, 1984) demand an open approach. Mintzberg (1988) showed that the strategy pursued may often deviate considerably from the intended strategy. Problems gradually become clearer and goals are formulated along the way, in an interactive process (McCall and Kaplan, 1985).

CONCLUSIONS AND FUTURE RESEARCH

Several matters are important to a good comprehension of the phenomenon of complex decision making in organizations:

1. Good insight into the relevant situational factors—the environment of the organization, the organizational context and personal characteristics of central decision makers—and into the most pertinent characteristics of the subject—complexity and politicality. This context determines how many degrees of freedom remain for management in its approach to the decision making process.
2. Good insight into the available steering mechanisms (strategic choices) with respect to complex decision making: in our view, this mainly involves the extent to which decision making is centralized and formalized, the extent to which it is supported by information and the amount of confrontation.
3. A good understanding of the advantages and disadvantages linked to the various strategic choices (Koopman, Kamerbeek, and Pool, 1986). Here one must not only consider their effects on the current decision making process (for example, it is of short duration), but also the long-term consequences (for example, disrupted relations that will take their toll later).

The four models sketched in this chapter and illustrated by research results may be regarded as metaphors of a reality as it is given shape in decision making processes in organizations. Each metaphor explains a certain aspect, and the extent to which it does so depends on the situation. Perhaps a decision on a large investment by a medium-size company in a dynamic environment can best be described using the neo-rational model, while the decision naturally has political, formalization, and open-end aspects as well. In research presently being conducted (Pool and Koopman, 1989), we attempt to chart different sorts of decision making processes in different types of organizations and contexts in this way, and to relate the course of a decision making process to the context variables.

As stated at the beginning of this chapter, research on decision making in organizations does not yet have a long tradition. Much work must still be done in a number of areas to increase our insight into these basic and central organizational processes. Below is a summary—which is not meant to be exhaustive—of important fields for future research.

1. Most studies of decision making start their analysis at a moment when a problem has been pointed out, and it has been decided that, no matter what, something must change. Several authors (Kanter, 1983; McCall and

Kaplan, 1985) have shown that important steps or events may have preceded this, which can have a substantial influence on decision making. Lyles (1987) and Lyles and Thomas (1988) have done preliminary work on the topic of problem recognition and formulation. Further elaboration in the direction of political aspects in the earlier phases (expanding on the non-decision topic of Bachrach and Baratz (1963)) and the cognitive, personal and political processes of the emergence of decisions (e.g. Narayanan and Fahey, 1982) seems promising.

2. A second field of research is to obtain more insight into the way in which important changes, often referred to as a paradigm shifts, occur in organizations. A crisis, perhaps accompanied by changes in key officials, seems to be one line of explanation (Donaldson and Lorsch, 1983; Miller and Friesen, 1982; Pettigrew, 1986). Further research on the existence of organizational mind sets, belief systems, dominant logics (Bouwen and De Visch, 1989) and other synonyms for what is held to be shared reality in an organization, and especially of the ways in which and circumstances under which they change, is recommended.

3. In our view, further research of the relationship of personality, personal characteristics and skills to decision making is necessary. Although preliminary work has been done in this field (see section on context and subject matter of decision making), better knowledge of these relationships is of crucial importance to a good policy in the selection, training and career support of managers, and to the design of good management training. We must guard against a revival of the 'great men' concept.

4. More research should be performed on the relationship between organizational characteristics and decision making. The basic assumption should be that there is no such thing as unidirectional causality, but reciprocal influence and interaction. The organization influences the way in which decisions are made, but these decisions can—directly or indirectly—influence organizational characteristics. Manipulation of the structural context (Bower, 1970) can even be adopted as a conscious strategy, to facilitate later decisions. Finally, it may be stated that many interpersonal contacts are often intended as strategic, and that networking (Hosking, 1988) is used as an intentional tactic for future decision making. With this in mind, more study of the interaction between the organization and decision making seems particularly fruitful.

5. Much research on decision making in organizations is descriptive in nature, and at best quasi-experimental. There is a dichotomy between field research, which sticks close to reality and often works with case studies, and the more experimental laboratory research to improve decision making methods (e.g. dialectical inquiry and devil's advocacy (Cosier, 1978; Schweiger, Sandberg, and Ragan, 1986)). By converging these two schools, perhaps in the form of experimental field research, real life data

could be obtained: for instance, by training managers in decision making techniques and then evaluating the effects based on an analysis of decisions made before and after training.

6. Although we have not devoted any attention in this chapter to Decision Support Systems (DSS) and Management Information Systems (MIS) (Davis and Olsen, 1984; Koopman *et al.*, 1988), it seems to us of eminent importance to study the effects of the emergence of such systems on the course and the effectiveness of organizational decision making. In an area where bounded rationality is one of the best known explanatory concepts, making the bounds smaller may have great consequences. The rapid increase in the information processing capacity of organizations does not leave decision making unaffected. Although initial results of DSS have not been earth-shaking (Monger, 1987)—and part of the explanation is that better information does not alter the political side of decision making but may even emphasize it—it is important to increase our insight into its operation. In addition, the availability of a multitude of data files and the possibility of transporting and manipulating them (telematics) appears to have a great influence on organizations and their decision making. The influence of such developments should also be studied carefully.

7. Finally, as a possible further development we mention the necessity to arrive at a more methodical research approach. The previously mentioned case study method, one of the most common which has proved to be very fruitful, should be further developed to make the comparison of studies possible. Another step on the road to comparative methods of decision making research is the scenario method developed by Fredrickson (1986b). The advantage of this method lies in the larger scale as compared to case studies. It would even be possible—and extremely interesting—to set up international comparative research in this way.

REFERENCES

Abell, P. (ed.) (1975) *Organizations as Bargaining and Influence Systems.* New York: Halstead.

Aken, J. E. van, and Matzinger, B. (1983) Een neo-rationeel model van besluitvorming. *M&O, Tijdschrift voor Organisatiekunde en Sociaal Beleid,* **37**, 478–493.

Allison, G. T. (1971) *Essence of Decision: Explaining the Cuban Missile Crisis.* Boston: Little Brown.

Anderson, C., and Paine, F. T. (1975) Managerial perceptions and strategic behavior. *Academy of Management Journal,* **18**, 811–823.

Anderson, P. A. (1983) Decision-making by objection and the Cuban missile crisis. *Administrative Science Quarterly,* **28**, 201–222.

Ansoff, H. (1965) *Corporate Strategy.* New York: McGraw-Hill.

Axelsson, R., and Rosenberg, L. (1979) Decision-making and organizational turbulence. *Acta Sociologica*, **22**, 45–62.

Bacharach, S. B., and Lawler, E. J. (1980) *Power and Politics in Organizations.* San Francisco: Jossey Bass.

Bachrach, P., and Baratz, M. S. (1963) Decisions and non-decisions: An analytical framework. *American Political Science Review*, **57**, 641–651.

Beach, L. R., and Mitchell, T. R. (1978) A contingency model for the selection of decision strategies. *Academy of Management Review*, **3**, 439–444.

Beyer, J. M. (1983) Ideologies, values and decision-making in organizations. In P. C. Nystrom & W. H. Starbuck (eds), *Handbook of Organizational Design*, Vol. 2. Oxford: Oxford Univeristy Press, pp. 166–202.

Blankenship, L. V., and Miles, R. E. (1968) Organization structure and management decision behavior. *Administrative Science Quarterly*, **13**, 106–120.

Bobbitt, H. R., and Ford, J. D. (1980) Decision-maker choice as a determinant of organizational structure. *Academy of Management Journal*, **5**, 13–23.

Boehm, B. W. (1986) A spiral model of software development and enhancement. *ACM Sigsoft Software Engineering Notes*, **11**, 22–42.

Bouwen, R. (1987, April) Organizational psychological analysis and understanding of innovation. Paper presented at the 3rd European Congress on the Psychology of Work and Organization, Antwerp, Belgium.

Bouwen, R., and De Visch, J. (1989, April) Innovation projects in organizations: Complementing the dominant logic by organizational learning. Paper presented at the 4th European Congress on the Psychology of Work and Organization, Cambridge, England.

Bower, J. L. (1970) *Managing the Resource Allocation Process: A Study of Corporate Planning and Investment.* Boston: Harvard University School.

Brim, O., Glass, D. C., Larvin, D. E., and Goodman, N. E. (1962) *Personality and Decision Process.* Stanford: Stanford University Press.

Brunsson, N. (1982) The irrationality of action and action rationality: Decisions, ideologies, and organizational actions. *Journal of Management Studies*, **19**, 29–44.

Burgelman, R. (1983) A model of the interaction of strategic behavior, corporate context and the concept of strategy. *Academy of Management Review*, **8**, 61–70.

Burns, J. M. (1978) *Leadership.* New York: Harper & Row.

Butler, R. J., Astley, W. G., Hickson, D. J., Mallory, G., and Wilson, D. C. (1979) Strategic decision-making in organizations: Concepts of content and process. *International Studies of Management and Organization*, **9**, 5–36.

Carroll, S. J., and Gillen, D. J. (1987) Are the classical management functions useful in describing managerial work? *Academy of Management Review*, **12**, 38–51.

Child, J. (1972) Organizational structure, environment and performance: The role of strategic choice. *Sociology*, **6**, 1–22.

Clegg, S., and Dunkerley, D. (1977) *Critical Issues in Organizations.* London: Routledge and Kegan Paul.

Cohen, M. D., March, J. G., and Olsen, J. P. (1972) A garbage can model of organizational choice. *Administrative Science Quarterly*, **17**, 1–25.

Cohen, M. D., and March, J. G. (1974) *Leadership and Ambiguity.* New York: McGraw-Hill.

Connolly, T. (1977) Information processing and decision-making in organizations. In B. M. Staw and G. M. Salancik (eds), *New Directions in Organizational Behavior.* Chicago: St. Clair Press, pp. 205–234.

Connolly, T. (1980) Uncertainty, action and competence: Some alternatives to omniscience in complex problem-solving. In S. Fiddle (ed.), *Uncertainty: Social and Behavioral Dimensions*. New York: Praeger.

Cosier, R. A. (1978) The effects of three potential aids for making strategic decisions on prediction accuracy. *Organizational Behavior and Human Performance*, **22**, 295–306.

Crozier, M. (1964) *The Bureaucratic Phenomenon*. Chicago: University of Chicago Press.

Cyert, R. M., Dill, W. R., and March, J. G. (1958) The role of expectations in business decision-making. *Administrative Science Quarterly*, **3**, 307–340.

Cyert, R. M., and March, J. G. (1963) *A Behavioral Theory of the Firm*. Englewood Cliffs, NJ: Prentice-Hall.

Davis, G. B., and Olson, M. H. (1984) *Management Information Systems*. New York: McGraw-Hill.

Dess, G. G., and Beard, D. W. (1984) Dimensions of organizational task environments. *Administrative Science Quarterly*, **29**, 52–73.

DIO-International Research Team (1983) A contingency model of participative decision-making: An analysis of 56 decisions in three Dutch organizations. *Journal of Occupational Psychology*, **56**, 1–18.

Dirsmith, M., and Covaleski, M. (1983) Strategy, external communication and environmental context. *Strategic Management Journal*, **4**, 137–151.

Donaldson, G., and Lorsch, J. W. (1983) *Decision-making at the Top: The Shaping of Strategic Direction*. New York: Basic Books.

Duncan, R. B. (1972) Characteristics of organizational environments and perceived environmental uncertainty. *Administrative Science Quarterly*, **17**, 313–327.

Duncan, R. B. (1973) Multiple decision-making structures in adapting to environmental uncertainty: The impact on organizational effectiveness. *Human Relations*, **26**, 273–292.

Emerson, R. M. (1962) Power-dependence relations. *American Sociological Review*, **27**, 31–41.

Enderud, H. (1980) Administrative leadership in organized anarchies. *International Journal of Management in Higher Education*, 235–253.

Etzioni, A. (1967) Mixed-scanning: A third approach to decision-making. *Public Administration Review*, **27**, 385–392.

Fahey, L. (1981) On strategic management decision processes. *Strategic Management Journal*, **2**, 43–60.

Fredrickson, J. W. (1984) The comprehensiveness of strategic decision processes. *Academy of Management Journal*, **27**, 445–466.

Fredrickson, J. W. (1986a) The strategic decision process and organizational structure. *Academy of Management Review*, **11**, 280–297.

Fredrickson, J. W. (1986b) An exploratory approach to measuring perceptions of strategic decision process constructs. *Strategic Management Journal*, **7**, 473–483.

Fredrickson, J. W., and Mitchell, T. R. (1984) Strategic decision processes: Comprehensiveness and performance in an industry with an unstable environment. *Academy of Management Journal*, **27**, 399–423.

Grandori, A. (1984) A prescriptive contingency view of organizational decision-making. *Administrative Science Quarterly*, **29**, 192–209.

Greiner, L. E. (1972) Evolution and revolution as organizations grow. *Harvard Business Review*, **50**, 37–46.

Gupta, A., and Govindarajan, V. (1984) Business unit strategy, managerial characteristics and business unit effectiveness. *Academy of Management Journal*, **27**, 25–41.

Hall, D., and Saias, M. A. (1980) Strategy follows structure! *Strategic Management Journal*, **1**, 149–163.

Hambrick, D. C. (1981) Environment, strategy and power within top management teams. *Administrative Science Quarterly*, **26**, 253–276.

Hambrick, D. C., and Mason, P. (1984) Upper echelons: The organization as a reflection of its top managers. *Academy of Management Review*, **9**, 193–206.

Hambrick, D. C., and Snow, C. C. (1977) A contextual model of strategic decision-making in organizations. In R. L. Taylor, M. J. O'Connell, R. A. Zawacki, and D. D. Warrick (eds), *Academy of Management Proceedings* pp. 109–112.

Handy, C. B. (1985) *Understanding Organizations*. New York: Penguin.

Harrison, E. F. (1987) *The Managerial Decision-making Process*, 3rd edn. Boston: Houghton Mifflin.

Harrison, R. (1972) Understanding your organizations character. *Harvard Business Review*, **50**, 119–128.

Hart, P.'t (1988) Verstrikte besluitvormers: 'Entrapment' in beleidsvoering. *Beleid en Maatschappij*, **15**, 277–289.

Hazewinkel, A. (1984) Organization structure and contingency-theory. In P. J. D. Drenth, Hk. Thierry, P. J. Willems, and Ch. J. de Wolff (eds), *Handbook of Work and Organizational Psychology*, chap. 4.3. New York: Wiley.

Hedberg, B. L. T., Nystrom, P., and Starbuck, W. H. (1976) Camping on seesaws: Prescriptions for a self-designing organization. *Administrative Science Quarterly*, **21**, 41–65.

Heller, F. A. (1976) Decision processes: An analysis of power-sharing at senior organizational levels. In R. Dubin (ed.), *Handbook of Work, Organization and Society*. Chicago: Rand McNally, pp. 687–745.

Heller, F. A., Drenth, P. J. D., Koopman, P. L., and Rus, V. (1988) *Decisions in Organizations: A Three Country Comparative Study*. London: Sage.

Hickson, D. J., Hinings, C. R., Lee, A. C., Schneck, R. E., and Pennings, J. M. (1971) A strategic contingency theory of intra-organizational power. *Administrative Science Quarterly*, **16**, 216–229.

Hickson, D. J., Butler, R. J., Cray, D., Mallory, G. R., and Wilson, D. C. (1986) *Top Decisions: Strategic Decision-making in Organizations*. Oxford: Basil Blackwell.

Hogarth, R. M., and Makridakis, S. (1981) Forecasting and planning: An evaluation. *Management Science*, **27**, 115–138.

Horvath, D., and McMillan, C. J. (1979) Strategic choice and the structure of decision processes. *International Studies of Management and Organization*, **9**, 87–112.

Hosking, D. M. (1988) Organization, leadership and skilful process. *Journal of Management Studies*, **25**, 147–166.

Hrebiniak, L. G., and Joyce, W. F. (1985) Organizational adaption: Strategic choice and environmental determinism. *Administrative Science Quarterly*, **30**, 336–349.

IDE-International Research Group. (1981) *Industrial Democracy in Europe*. Oxford: Clarendon Press.

Isenberg, D. J. (1984) How senior-managers think. *Harvard Business Review*, **62**, 81–90.

Isenberg, D. J. (1986) Thinking and managing: A verbal protocal analysis of managerial problem solving. *Academy of Management Journal*, **29**, 775–788.

Janis, I. L. (1972) *Victims of Group Think*. Boston: Houghton Mifflin.

Janis, I. L. (1982) *Groupthink*, 2nd edn. Boston: Houghton Mifflin.

Janis, I. L. (1985) Sources of error in strategic decision-making. In J. M. Pennings (ed.), *Organizational Strategy and Change*. San Francisco: Jossey-Bass, pp. 157–197.

Janis, I. L., and Mann, L. (1977) *Decision-making: A Psychological Analysis of Conflict, Choice and Commitment*. New York: Free Press.

Jemison, D. B. (1981) Organizational versus environmental sources of influence in strategic decision-making. *Strategic Management Journal*, **2**, 77–89.

Jemison, D. B. (1984) The importance of boundary spanning roles in strategic decision-making. *Journal of Management Studies*, **2**, 131–152.

Jick, T. D., and Murray, V. V. (1982) The management of hard times: Budget cutbacks in public sector organizations. *Organization Studies*, **3**, 141–169.

Kanter, R. M. (1977) *Men and Women of the Corporation*. New York: Basic Books.

Kanter, R. M. (1983) *The Change Masters: Innovation for Productivity in the American Corporation*. New York: Simon and Schuster.

Kets de Vries, M. F. R. and Miller, D. (1984) *The Neurotic Organization*. San Francisco: Jossey-Bass.

Kickert, W. J. M. (1979) Rationaliteit en structuur van organisatorische besluitvormings-processen. *Bestuurswetenschappen*, **33**, 21–30.

Klootwijk, J. W., and Wagenaar, R. B. (1983) Veranderingsprocessen in bureaucratische organisaties: Varianten op een traditioneel model. *M&O, Tijdschrift voor Organisatiekunde en Sociaal Beleid*, **37**, 402–415.

Koopman, P. L. (1980) *Besluitvorming in Organisaties*. Assen: Van Gorcum.

Koopman, P. L. (1983) Communicatie en overleg bij afbouw. *M&O, Tijdschrift voor Organisatiekunde en Sociaal Beleid*, **37**, 48–68.

Koopman, P. L. (1989, April) Between control and commitment. Paper presented at the 4th West European Congress on the Psychology of Work and Organizations, Cambridge, England.

Koopman, P. L., Broekhuysen, J. W., and Meijn, O. (1984) Complex decision-making at the organizational level. In P. J. D. Drenth, Hk. Thierry, P. J. Willems, and Ch. J. de Wolff (eds), *Handbook of Work and Organizational Psychology*, chap. 4.10. New York: Wiley.

Koopman, P. L., Broekhuysen, J. W., and Wierdsma, A. F. M. (1988) Complexe besluitvorming in organisaties. In P. J. D. Drenth, Hk. Thierry, and Ch. de Wolff (eds), *Nieuw Handboek Arbeids- en Organisatiepsychologie*, Chap. 4.11. Deventer: Van Loghum Slaterus.

Koopman, P. L., Kamerbeek, E., and Pool, J. (1986, July) Management dilemmas in organizations. Paper presented at the 21st International Congress of Applied Psychology, Jerusalem (Israel).

Koopman, P. L., Kroese, H. A. F. M., and Drenth, P. J. D. (1984) Rationaliteit bij reallocatie. *M&O, Tijdschrift voor Organisatiekunde en Sociaal Beleid*, **38**, 151–170.

Koopman, P. L., and Kroese, H. A. F. M. (1986) Medezeggenschapstructuren: Bureaucratische fictie of preventieve functie? *Namens*, **1**, 36–40.

Koopman, P. L., and Pool, J. (1986) De bestuurbaarheid van besluitvormingsprocessen bij vernieuwing. In A. J. Cozijnsen and W. J. Vrakking (eds), *Handboek voor Strategisch Innoveren*. Deventer: Kluwer/Nive, pp. 178–193.

Koopman, P. L., and Pool, J. (1990) Besluitvorming in organisaties. In J. von Grumbkow and J. van Hoof (eds), *Perspectieven op Organisaties*, Chaps 15–17. Heerlen: Open Universiteit.

Kotter, J. P. (1982) *The General Managers*. New York: Free Press.

Krogt, Th. W. P. M. van der, and Vroom, C. W. (1988) *Organisatie is Beweging*. Culemborg: Lemma.

Larson, L. L., Bussom, R. S., Vicars, W., and Jauch, L. (1986) Proactive versus reactive manager: Is the dichotomy realistic? *Journal of Management Studies*, **23**, 385–400.

Lawrence, P., and Lorsch, J. (1969) *Organization and Environment*. Homewood, IL: Irwin.

Leavitt, H. J. (1986) *Corporate Pathfinders*. Homewood, IL: Dow Jones-Irwin.

Lindblom, C. E. (1959) The science of muddling through. *Public Administration Review*, **19**, 79–88.

Lukes, S. (1974) *Power: A Radical View*. London: Macmillan Press.

Lyles, M. (1981) Formulating strategic problems: Empirical analysis and model development. *Strategic Management Journal*, **2**, 61–75.

Lyles, M. A. (1987) Defining strategic problems: Subjective criteria of executives. *Organization Studies*, **8**, 263–280.

Lyles, M. A., and Thomas, H. (1988) Strategic problem formulation: Biases and assumptions in alternative decision-making models. *Journal of Management Studies*, **25**, 131–145.

MacCrimmon, K. R., and Taylor, R. N. (1976) Decision-making and problem solving. In M. D. Dunnette (ed.), *Handbook of Industrial and Organizational Psychology*. Chicago: Rand McNally, pp. 1397–1453.

MacMillan, I. C., and Jones, P. E. (1986) *Strategy Formulation: Power and Politics*. St. Paul, MI: West.

March, J. G. (ed) (1988) *Decisions and Organizations*. Oxford: Basil Blackwell.

March, J. G. and Olsen, J. P. (1976) *Ambiguity and Choice in Organizations*. Bergen, Norway: Universitetsforlaget.

March, J. G., and Simon, H. A. (1958) *Organizations*. New York: Wiley.

Mason, R. O., and Mitroff, I. I. (1981) *Challenging Strategic Planning Assumptions*. New York: Wiley.

Mayntz, R. (1976) Conceptual models of organizational decision-making and their application to the policy process. In G. H. Hofstede and S. M. Kassem (eds), *European Contributions to Organization Theory*. Assen: Van Gorcum, pp. 114–125.

Mayntz, R., and Scharpf, F. W. (1975) *Policy-making in the German Federal Bureaucracy*. Amsterdam: Elsevier.

Mazzolini, R. (1981) How strategic decisions are made. *Long Range Planning*, **14**, 85–96.

McCall, M. W., and Kaplan, R. E. (1985) *Whatever it Takes: Decision-makers at Work*. Englewood Cliffs, NJ: Prentice-Hall.

McMillan, C. J. (1980) Qualitative models of organizational decision-making. *Journal of General Management*, **5**, 22–39.

Meyer, A. (1984) Mingling decision-making metaphors. *Academy of Management Review*, **9**, 6–17.

Middlemist, R. D., and Hitt, M. A. (1988) *Organizational Behavior*. New York: West.

Miles, R., and Snow, C. (1978) *Organizational Strategy, Structure and Process*. New York: McGraw-Hill.

Miller, D. (1987) Strategy making and structure: Analysis and implications for performance, *Academy of Management Journal*, **30**, 7–32.

Miller, D., Dröge, C., and Toulouse, J. M. (1988) Strategic process and content as mediators between organizational context and structure. *Academy of Management Journal*, **31**, 544–569.

Miller, D., and Friesen, P. (1980) Momentum and revolution in organizational adaptation. *Academy of Management Journal*, **23**, 591–614.

Miller, D., and Friesen, P. (1983) Strategy making and the environment. *Strategic Management Journal*, **4**, 221–235.

Miller, D., Kets de Vries, M. F. R., and Toulouse, J. M. (1982) Top executive locus of control and its relationship to strategy-making, structure and environment. *Academy of Management Journal*, **25**, 237–253.

Miller, D., and Toulouse, J. M. (1986) CEO-personality and its relationship to strategy and structure. *Management Science*, **32**, 1398–1409.

Mintzberg, H. (1973) *The Nature of Managerial Work*. New York: Harper & Row.

Mintzberg, H. (1977) Strategy formulation as a historical process. *International Studies of Management and Organization*, **7**, 28–40.

Mintzberg, H. (1979) *The Structuring of Organizations: A Synthesis of the Research.* Englewood Cliffs, NJ: Prentice-Hall.

Mintzberg, H. (1983) *Power in and around Organizations.* Englewood Cliffs, NJ: Prentice-Hall.

Mintzberg, H. (1988) Opening up the definition of strategy. In J. B. Quinn, H. Mintzberg, and R. M. James (eds), *The Strategy Process: Concepts, Contexts and Cases.* London: Prentice-Hall, pp. 13–20.

Mintzberg, H., Raisinghani, D., and Théorêt, A. (1976) The structure of 'unstructured' decision processes. *Administrative Science Quarterly*, 21, 246–275.

Monger, R. F. (1987) *Managerial Decision Making with Technology.* New York: Pergamon Press.

Montanari, I. R. (1978) Managerial discretions: An expanded model of organizational choice. *Academy of Management Review*, 3, 231–241.

Morgan, G. (1986) *Images of Organization.* London: Sage.

Murray, E. (1978) Strategic choice as a negotiated outcome. *Management Science*, 24, 960–972.

Narayanan, V., and Fahey, L. (1982) The micro-politics of strategy formulation. *Academy of Management Review*, 7, 25–34.

Neisser, U. (1967) *Cognitive Psychology.* New York: Appleton-Century-Crofts.

Nutt, P. C. (1984) Types of organizational decision processes. *Administrative Science Quarterly*, 29, 414–450.

O'Reilly, C. A. (1983) The use of information in organizational decision-making: A model and some propositions. In L. L. Cummings and B. M. Shaw (eds), *Research in Organizational Behavior*, vol. 5. Greenwich, CT: JAI-Press, pp. 103–139.

Payne, J. W. (1976) Task complexity and contingent processing in decision-making: An information search and protocol analysis. *Organizational Behavior and Human Performance*, 16, 366–387.

Perrow, C. (1972) *Complex Organizations: A Critical Essay.* Glenview, IL: Scott, Foresman & Co.

Pettigrew, A. M. (1973) *The Politics of Organizational Decision-making.* London: Tavistock.

Pettigrew, A. M. (1979) On studying organizational culture. *Administrative Science Quarterly*, 24, 570–581.

Pettigrew, A. M. (1986) Some limits of executive power in creating strategic change. In S. Srivastva (ed.), *The Functioning of Executive Power.* London: Jossey-Bass.

Pfeffer, J. (1981) *Power in Organizations.* Boston: Pitman.

Pfeffer, J., and Salancik, G. R. (1978) *The External Control of Organizations.* New York: Harper and Row.

Pickle, H., and Friedlander, F. (1967) Seven societal criteria of organizational success. *Personnel Psychology*, 20, 165–178.

Pinfield, L. T. (1986) A field evaluation of perspectives on organizational decision making. *Administrative Science Quarterly*, 31, 365–388.

Pool, J., and Koopman, P. L. (1987, April) Managing decision-making processes. Paper presented at the 3rd European Congress on the Psychology of Work and Organization, Antwerp, Belgium.

Pool, J., and Koopman, P. L. (1989, April) Strategic decision-making in organizations: A research model and some initial findings. Paper presented at the 4th European Congress on the Psychology of Work and Organization, Cambridge, England.

Pool, J., Koopman, P. L., and Kamerbeek, E. (1986) Veranderingsprocessen bij de rijksoverheid: Cases en keuzemomenten. *M&O, Tijdschrift voor Organisatiekunde en Sociaal Beleid*, 40, 516–531.

Pounds, W. F. (1969) The process of problem finding. *Industrial Management Review*, 1, 1–19.

Quinn, J. B. (1978) Strategic change: Logical incrementalism. *Sloan Management Review*, 20, 7–21.

Quinn, J. B. (1980) *Strategies for Change: Logical Incrementalism*. Homewood: Irwin.

Quinn, J. B. (1988) Managing strategies incrementally. In: J. B. Quinn, H. Mintzberg, and R. M. James (eds), *The Strategy Process: Concepts, Contexts, and Cases*. Englewood Cliffs, NJ: Prentice-Hall, pp. 671–678.

Quinn, R. E. (1988) *Beyond Rational Management*. San Francisco: Jossey-Bass.

Quinn, R. E., and Cameron, K. (1983) Organizational life cycles and shifting criteria of effectiveness: Some preliminary evidence. *Management Science*, 29, 33–51.

Quinn, R. E., and Rohrbaugh, J. (1983) A spatial model of effectiveness criteria: Toward a competing values approach to organizational analysis. *Management Science*, 29, 363–377.

Riley, P. (1983) A structuralist account of political cultures. *Administrative Science Quarterly*, 3, 414–437.

Robbins, S. P. (1987) *Organization Theory: Structure, Design and Applications*. Englewood Cliffs, NJ: Prentice-Hall.

Rotter, J. B. (1966) Generalized expectancies for internal versus external control of reinforcement. *Psychological Monographs: General and Applied*, 80 (Whole no. 609).

Sayles, L. (1979) *Leadership*. New York: McGraw-Hill.

Schweiger, D., Sandberg, W., and Ragan, J. (1986) Group approaches for improving strategic decision-making: A comparative analysis of dialectical inquiry, devil's advocacy and consensus. *Academy of Management Journal*, 29, 51–71.

Schwenk, C. R. (1984) Cognitive simplification processes in strategic decision-making. *Strategic Management Journal*, 5, 111–128.

Schwenk, C. R. (1985) The use of participant recollection in the modelling of organizational decision processes. *Academy of Management Review*, 10, 496–503.

Schwenk, C. R. (1988) *The Essence of Strategic Decision Making*. Massachusetts: D. C. Heath & Co.

Shrivastava, P., and Grant, J. H. (1985) Empirically derived models of strategic decision-making processes. *Strategic Management Journal*, 6, 97–113.

Simon, H. A. (1947) *Administrative Behavior*. New York: Free Press.

Simon, H. A. (1957) *Models of Man*. New York: Wiley.

Simon, H. A. (1976) *Administrative Behavior*, 3rd edn. New York: Free Press.

Staallekker, L. A. (1984) Afbouw van organisaties: Aandacht voor irrationele aspecten. *M&O, Tijdschrift voor Organisatiekunde en Sociaal Beleid*, 38, 187–199.

Stagner, R. (1969) Corporate decision-making: An empirical study. *Journal of Applied Psychology*, 53, 1–13.

Staw, B. M. (1976) Knee deep in the big muddy. *Organizational Behavior and Human Performance*, 16, 27–44.

Stein, J. (1981a) Contextual factors in the selection of strategic decision methods. *Human Relations*, 34, 819–834.

Stein, J. (1981b) Strategic decision methods. *Human Relations*, 34, 917–933.

Steiner, G. A. (1979) *Strategic Planning: What Every Manager Must Know*. New York: Free Press.

Stewart, R. (1982) A model for understanding managerial jobs and behavior. *Academy of Management Review*, 7, 7–13.

Taylor, R. N. (1975) Psychological determinants of bounded rationality: Implications for decision-making. *Decision Sciences*, 6, 409–429.

Thompson, J. D. (1967) *Organizations in Action*. New York: McGraw-Hill.

Thompson, J. D., and Tuden, A. (1959) Strategies, structures and processes of organizational decision. In J. D. Thompson, P. B. Hammond, R. W. Hawkes, B. H. Junker, and A. Tuden (eds), *Comparative Studies in Administration*. Pittsburgh: Pittsburgh University Press.

Tversky, A., and Kahneman, D. (1974) Judgement under uncertainty: Heuristics and biases. *Science*, **185**, 1124–1131.

Ungson, G., Braunstein, D., and Hall, P. (1981) Managerial information processing: A research review. *Administrative Science Quarterly*, **26**, 116–134.

Vansina, L. (1986) Transformatiemanagement. In H. Stufkes (ed.), *Management voor nieuwe tijd: Transformatie in Bedrijf en Organisatie*. Rotterdam: Lemniscaat.

Vroom, V. H., and Yetton, P. W. (1973) *Leadership and Decision-making*. Pittsburgh: University of Pittsburgh Press.

Weick, K. (1979) *The Social Psychology of Organizing*. Reading: Addison-Wesley.

Wilson, D. C., Butler, R. J., Cray, D., Hickson, D. J., and Mallory, G. R. (1986) Breaking the bounds of organization in decision making. *Human Relations*, **39**, 309–332.

Witte, E. (1972) Field research on complex decision-making processes: The phase theorem. *International Studies of Management and Organization*, **2**, 156–182.

Wrapp, H. E. (1988) Good managers don't make policy decisions. In J. B. Quinn, H. Mintzberg and R. M. James (eds), *The Strategy Process: Concepts, Contexts and Cases*. Englewood Cliffs, NJ: Prentice-Hall, pp. 32–37.

Wright, P. (1974) The harassed decision-maker: Time pressures, distractions and the use of evidence. *Journal of Applied Psychology*, **59**, 555–561.

Chapter 7

CAREERS: A REVIEW OF PERSONAL AND ORGANIZATIONAL RESEARCH

Michael J. Driver
University of Southern California
Los Angeles, California
USA

INTRODUCTION

Given the extreme range and volume of career research, only certain aspects will be covered here. I shall begin with a fundamental analysis of the fragmentation problem among theories in the area and suggest the relevance of differences in career definition as a step toward better integration.

Research dealing with the basic issue of career definition will be reviewed next. I shall then examine individual concerns such as personality factors in careers and the process of career choice. Next, I turn to a more organizational focus and review early career issues such as socialization, and later career issues such as career change. The review will conclude with a look at organization–person congruence models, societal trends and career management and the status of career management practice in organizations.

METATHEORETICAL ISSUES

In his critique of the career field, Schein (1986) essentially focuses on four problems: (a) fragmentation, (b) culture bias, (c) lack of integration via theory and confrontation, and (d) 'tool' obsession.

While not wishing to underplay the importance of US bias and tool preoccupation in some career research, it seems to me that the central problem of this field is addressed by Schein's emphasis on extreme fragmentation enhanced by lack of integrating theory.

That the career field is fragmented is hardly surprising given its history. Sonnenfeld and Kotter (1982) have traced the various themes which have dominated career research from the inception of the twentieth century. The first model to gain ascendancy was the social structure view that individual career choices are constrained by socioeconomic class membership. In the 1920s came the emergence of a more psychological view stressing personality traits, such as interests, as determinants of career choice. During the 1950s a more dynamic concept of career stages, dictated by organization focus, took hold. Finally, they see a current interest in internal life cycle stages as a guide in the career process.

In a similar vein, Arthur (1984) isolates five streams of activity in career research:

1. *Vocational guidance*—which assumes people are 'fixed' and organizations can at best select, but not change people.
2. *Human resource management*—assuming people can adapt to organization needs.
3. *Human potential movement*—which focuses on the individual's need to grow and sees organizations as often becoming impediments.
4. *Women's and minority rights*—which sees a white male culture bias distorting the field.
5. *Life/career stage models*—which posit orderly change processes in careers.

Finally, Hall (1986) divides the career field into career planning, concerned with the individual; and career management, concerned with the organization.

In conducting this review the fragmentation due to these varied streams was extremely obvious. Journals such as the *Journal of Vocational Behavior* seemed heavily focused on individual issues with a strong bias toward vocational guidance or trait orientations. *Human Development* was clearly focused on life-cycle models. Organization behavior journals such as *Academy of Management Review* tended toward career management, organizational socialization and career stage models. Theoretical and empirical integration efforts did emerge as will be stressed subsequently. However, they tended to stay 'within streams' rather than cross-streams.

In addition to factors such as diverse training and reference groups, I suggest a major problem here is basic definition. Each career research stream seems to have its own definition of careers. John Davis and I (1987) have tried to capture the underlying dimensions of this issue (as seen in Figure 7.1). We suggest that two basic issues concerning the definition of careers are:

(a) Do career choices change over time or stay constant?
(b) Are career choices externally generated or internal processes?

One can then locate the various streams in a two-dimensional metatheoretical space as seen in Figure 7.1. The one exclusion is the women's and minority view which, along with Schein's US bias factor, should also be factored in. A fourth factor in career definition not seen in Figure 7.1 is the work/non-work dimension: how much should career definition expand to include non-work activity? Describing the basis of the field's fragmentation is possibly helpful, but we wish to go further. Are there any integrating models which can begin to pull it all together? I suggest that there may well be.

The career concept model was developed precisely to deal with the definitional differences in the career realm (Driver, 1979; 1980; 1982). The model suggests four basic concepts held by people (including career researchers) concerning careers:

CAREER CHOICE FREQUENCY

	Constant	Changing
Inner	Vocational guidance Trait theory	Life cycle stages Human potential
SOURCE OF CAREER CHOICE		Luck
External	Sociological determinism	Organizational career stages Human resource planning

Figure 7.1   A metatheory space for career models

1. *Steady-state*—career choice is made once for a life-time commitment to an occupation.
2. *Linear*—career activity continues throughout life as one moves up an occupational ladder.
3. *Spiral*—career choice evolves through a series of occupations (7–10-year durations) where each new choice builds on the past and develops new skills.
4. *Transitory*—career choice is almost continuous—fields, organizations, jobs change over 1–4-year intervals with variety the dominant force.

In our view, each stream tends to favor, consciously or otherwise, a particular career concept. The vocational guidance/trait stream generally focuses on a Steady-State view of careers in which initial choice of field is vitally important. The organizational career stage theories have taken strongly Linear views on the 'need' to advance and avoid plateaus. The life-cycle and human potential views seem heavily Spiral in their emphasis on inner forces winning through over time as identity unfolds. Finally, a stream not much discussed in the literature, stressing luck, seems well tuned to the Transitory model.

In the material reviewed below, these researcher career concepts will be made as clear as possible. The hope is that each career research stream can begin to recognize its own bias and begin to expand awareness to other career concepts. Our research (e.g. Driver and Coombs, 1983) has shown the existence of people working with *all* four concepts. Clearly any theory or stream focused on only one concept will miss a major segment of career phenomena. A truly integrative career research field needs theories encompassing all types of career definition.

Related to the career concept issue is a second fragmentary force—academic discipline. As Hall (1986) has noted, the field falls into individual focus research with a psychological discipline base (and at least four career concept variants), and organizational research with a sociological discipline base. As the contributors to Arthur's book *Working With Careers* (1984) assert, organizations tend toward what I would call Linear career concepts. Thus, much of the organizational career literature in the past has tended to focus on processes aimed at enhancing Linear careers. In the 1980s, organization behavior career researchers such as Bailyn (1984) and Hall (1986) have revised this trend. They are calling for a more Spiral approach in organizations—or even for a pluralistic approach which would permit many career concepts to flourish.

Unfortunately, the individual and organizational focused research streams are not in close communication. A major need in the career area is for the psychological richness (in theory and method) of the individual theorists to connect better with the growing insights of organizational theorists as to how organizations operate and change in shaping careers. An excellent case example of this process is shown by Campbell and Moses' (1986) analysis of how changes in AT & T are changing career definitions of AT & T employees (see below).

FUNDAMENTAL CAREER DEFINITION RESEARCH

Work–Non-Work

There seems to be a growing consensus that careers involve both work and non-work activities. Super (1986) sees a career as involving six roles: child, student, leisurite, citizen, worker, and homemaker. Over time he suggests that the intensity and breadth of involvement in all these roles change in important ways. Hopefully, research can follow his lead in defining the essential roles in a career. It is not clear yet what set of roles is most helpful. For instance, Sundby (1980) defines four roles—worker, mate, parent and self-developer. A main task ahead will be to define which roles are most useful in defining a career.

On a narrower focus, work continues on the work–leisure activity front. Shaffer (1987) has developed a taxonomy of relationships between work and leisure which could be productive. Research and theory continues to support the notion that leisure activity can compensate for meaningless work. Driver and Coombs (1983) found that individuals with Transitory career concepts in a company with very Steady-State values were not totally alienated—they derived meaning from avocational activity. Levinson (1984) describes a case in which a person, bored at work, builds his real career in his avocation. If Spenner (1985) is right that work complexity is not increasing, the highly educated workers of the future may indeed need to turn to avocations to fulfil career needs.

Another theme receiving attention is the family–work arena. Anderson-Kulman and Paludi (1986) have reviewed the problems faced by working mothers. It is clearly seen as a strain (Hardesty and Betz, 1980) in which family cooperation (Gray, 1983) and good day-care (Perry, 1982) help. Despite the strain, working mothers have high self-esteem (Birnbaum, 1971) and equivalent life satisfaction to non-working women (Warr and Perry, 1982).

Anderson-Kulman and Paludi cite Belsky *et al.*'s (1982) conclusions that working mothers have no adverse effect on children, and Hoffman's data (1980) that working mothers have positive effects on female adolescent children. However, more recent work by Belsky (*Time Magazine*, 1987) seems to cast doubt on this. It appears that some day-care may be adverse. The effect of working mothers on middle class family dynamics seems neutral (Wright, 1978) but may be negative for lower-class families (Nye, 1974). Overall, Anderson-Kulman and Paludi concluded that there is a reciprocal relationship between mother's job satisfaction and family harmony.

Career Concepts

Research directly using the Driver Career Concept model has been sparse but confirmatory. Driver and Coombs (1983) found meaningful frequencies in all four career concepts in a large sample of technical and business administration people. In general, those individuals whose career concepts fit the organization culture (Steady-State) reported high productivity, morale and life satisfaction. Those most out of line (i.e. Linear) reported the opposite. Coombs and Driver (1986) have found that there are interesting age differences in career concepts. The Transitory is most prevalent among younger workers, Steady-State and Linear are most frequent among middle aged, and Spiral is dominant among older workers. Tie-ins with life-cycle models are explored. Prince (1984) examined a version of the career concept model and found that work was more central for Linears as opposed to Steady-State or Transitory persons. Linear and Transitory persons had higher energy than Steady-State. Linear and Steady-State individuals show more organizational commitment than Transitory people.

Latack and D'Amico (1985) used actual job moves among youths to measure concepts (as opposed to the career concept questionnaire, Driver and Brousseau, 1981) used in the studies described above. They found that Steady-State youths enter high status occupations with moderate aspirations. Transitories enter lower-status organizations with low aspirations and Linears simply show high aspirations. In their youth sample, 70 per cent were Linear, 15 per cent Steady-State and 4 per cent Transitory. Some caution is needed in interpreting these studies since a distinction must be made between the ideal career concept a person wants (as measured by questionnaire), and the actual careers pursued or expected.

McKinnon (1987) expanded the career concepts model to study engineers. He described three patterns: a managerial Linear, a technical Linear and a technical Steady-State. The latter accounted for 50 per cent of his sample. They were older and less educated (BS only) than Linears and not interested in organizational advancement. They were interested in getting on to new challenging projects with considerable influence over the job. The two Linear types differed in cognitive style—the managerial being less detailed and complex—but they were similar in wanting to go up a ladder.

It may be noted that despite calls for 'Spiral' career approaches by organization behavior analysts, this concept has emerged least clearly in current concept research.

Several studies not overtly using the concept model, have shed light on career concept issues. For instance, Steiner and Farr (1986) find a strong Linear orientation among engineers. Rynes (1987) also finds a majority of an engineer sample hopeful of a Linear career. In fact, Badawy (1981) finds a majority of engineers do go into management. In other occupations the Linear orientation is not so prevalent. For instance, Burke (1985) reports that 40 per cent of a police sample (and only 12 per cent of a teacher sample) exhibit 'careerist' orientation— which is similar to the Linear in Cherniss's model (1980).

The degree of Linear orientation among managers is a matter of considerable controversy. Direct measures of career concepts among MBA's shows a marked increase in the percentage of Linears over the last ten years (Driver, 1985). No large samples using direct measures of concepts have occurred, but by extending the career concept model to include key motives much light on general trends can be shed. Prior research (Driver and Coombs, 1983) has linked career motives and career concepts. In particular, the motivation to get ahead in management and make money is uniquely tied to the Linear concept. In contrast, the Steady-State concept is tied to motives such as security, and the Spiral and Transitory concepts to motives such as novelty.

This linkage allows one to look at studies of career motives as clues to career concept patterns. One of the most interesting data sets has been developed by Astin and Greene (1987). Their work shows a massive shift from Spiral-like concerns with developing a 'philosophy of life' to a very Linear focus on financial well being and administrative responsibility. This shift began in 1975 and shows no signs of leveling off.

In contrast, research by Miner and Smith (1987) seems to suggest that motivation to manage (Linear) has declined from 1960 to 1980. However, Bartol et al. (1980) found the opposite—a rise in this Linear-type motivation using the same instrument. Disputes about scoring methods arose (Miner et al., 1985; Bartol and Schneier, 1983). However, the Bartol and Schneier view that Miner's results suffer from a too narrow baseline—one college in Oregon—seems most relevant. National trends seem to be largely Linear among managers and engineers as seen above.

Some of the confusion on Linear trends may also be due to the fact that in the 1960s and early 1970s there was a decline of Linear-type motives (Driver, 1985). Some of Miner's data may reflect this earlier pattern. The 'turnaround' to increasing Linear orientation occurred around 1975 for college freshman and probably reached MBA's around 1980. This fall from 1960 to 1975, followed by a rise of Linear thinking may explain why studies of 'baby boomers' (Russell, 1982; Hall and Richter, 1985) report values of autonomy, self-development, entrepreneurism and work–family balance. Such non-Linear values did peak for early baby boomers in the early 1970s. But the trend now seems reversed.

Work Values

Given the close tie-in of work values and career concepts, a look at research in this realm seems in order. MacNab and Fitzsimmons (1987) conducted an exemplary integrative study comparing three research approaches: needs, values and preferences. They found high convergent validity and a strong advancement (Linear) orientation showing in all three methods for their sample.

Further afield, Krau (1987) finds an overall Linear value pattern in Israel but notes interesting ethnic and religious differences which suggest some Spiral dominance in certain groups. Berger (1986) also analysed subgroup differences in work values for Mexican-Americans. The study confirmed prior Anglo results that women emphasize social–emotional work qualities (Bentell and Brennan, 1986) while men stress Linear values such as pay and promotion, as well as security and independence (Bush and Bush, 1978). Berger confirmed a male focus on advancement, prestige, security and safety. Also confirmed were white-collar *v.* blue-collar differences. In general, white-collar individuals stressed advancement, prestige, security and safety more than blue-collar.

In general, a Linear value trend seems to be surfacing, even beyond the US.

Career Anchors

Another framework for integrating career research might be Schein's career anchor theory (1971). His five basic anchors are assumed to be differential bases for careers—and hence lead to varied concepts of careers. The five basic anchors are managerial, technical, security-oriented, autonomy-oriented and entrepreneurial. De Long (1985) has factor-analysed these anchors into two dimensions: a management autonomy cluster, and a security technical cluster. These two dimensions could easily tie into a Linear *v.* Steady-State construct. Indeed, Prince (1984) has factor-analysed career concepts into two groups: stayers and movers (i.e. Linear, Spiral and Transitory).

However, purely quantitative analyses of these models can be deceptive since vagaries of samples are notorious. A more promising direction might be to attempt to integrate career concepts and motives into a 'minimum set' of useful dimensions for describing career orientations. By a minimal set I mean a number of categories which does justice to human complexity, yet avoids proliferation of an operationally useless number of categories.

Derr (1986) has attempted to provide 5 orientations which might be a prototype for a minimal set:

> *Getting ahead*—A fusion of the Linear career concept and the managerial anchor;
> *Getting secure*—a fusion of the Steady-State concept and the security anchor;
> *Getting high*—the Spiral concept;
> *Getting free*—a fusion of the Transitory concept and the autonomy anchor;
> *Getting balanced*—a unique focus on work/non-work balance.

The career concept model has also proposed subdividing concepts by motives. There could be two Steady-State patterns—competence and security-oriented; two Linear types—power and achievement-oriented; two Transitory types—identity seeking and novelty-oriented; and several Spiral types—self-development and nurture/mentor oriented (see Driver, 1979). At present a usable minimal set remains an important target for career research.

Organizational Commitment

A final definitional issue concerns the role of organizational identity or commitment in careers. There is a stream of research on organizational commitment which views this aspect of a career as a very positive indicator—both for individuals and organizations (see Mowday et al., 1974). It is seen as a good indication of work satisfaction as well as a predictor of performance. In this view, factors which reduce commitment, such as education, are seen as problematic since commitment is such a strong value (Mottaz, 1986).

However, from a career concept view, this construction of commitment becomes an extreme case of Steady-State thinking—in which organization and occupation are essential in career definition. Prince (1984) and Driver and Coombs (1983) find that organizational commitment is a strong correlate of Steady-State concepts. The problem here is that there are career concepts for which commitment is low, yet self-satisfaction is not low (e.g. Transitory in Driver and Coombs, 1983).

It would therefore seem useful to broaden research on organizational commitment to include a more positive view of those non-Steady-State people for whom low commitment may not be a sign of trouble (see the idea of resilience, below). On the other hand, this stream of research does suggest the importance of including organizational loyalty as a part of at least some career definitions.

PERSONALITY AND CAREERS

Although we have looked at certain personality factors above, there are many interesting streams of research on personality and careers that do not impinge directly on career definitional issues. I shall review first personality development models and then turn to adult personality factors.

Development Theory

Despite the consensus on the 1980s being the era of life-cycle theories, the research literature reviewed here seems to be dominated by one model—the Erikson view. Although it is a life-cycle theory, the Erikson model focuses on the central issue of careers—identity—but once in a lifespan. For Erikson, once the identity problem has been resolved in one's twenties, or early thirties, one should move on to relationships—e.g. intimacy. As a result, research based on Erikson has tended to view career choice as a one time event—a Steady-State view.

One of the most pervasive variants of Erikson's model was developed by Marcia (1966) with the terms diffuse, foreclosed, moratorium and achieved identity. She defined diffuse as having no identity, foreclosed as reaching an easy, externally given identity with no inner choice, moratorium as still searching and achieved as an inner identity based on self-search. Using Marcia's interview method Larkin (1987) found that diffuse and moratorium types had higher fear of success than the focused/foreclosed and achieved identity types. Grotevant and Thorbecke (1982) found the achieved type to correlate well with Holland's measure of identity. Using an objective measure of Marcia's types, Neimeyer and Metzlar

(1981) found the achieved identity types to be more complex in their thinking about careers. The positive side of the Marcia's work is its emphasis on moving from external identities (foreclosed) to real identity as warmly advocated by Shepard (1986).

What this research suggests is that the person with an achieved, self-realized identity is superior to the more fearful, simplistic types. This clearly favors a Steady-State or possibly Linear view of careers and has come under attack as too narrow a view of the identity process. Gilligan (1982), for instance, has noted that Erikson's model is male-oriented. She suggests that for women, relationship issues precede rather than follow identity issues.

In a far more sweeping revision, Logan (1986) suggests a recapitulation model of the basic Erikson concept. Just as Erikson sees early childhood problems such as trust and autonomy recapitulating in the identity crisis, so Logan suggests that identity issues can reoccur at later life stages when a person is apparently focusing on relationships. Identities can be reshaped even after they are 'achieved' in early adulthood. Logan shows how this view of Erikson is compatible with Levinson's and Gould's models of life-cycle change. It can only be hoped that this view of Erikson can receive research analysis and lead to a view of career identity which can admit to change—even from 'achieved' status.

Another line of developmental research stems from the work of Owens (1979) on life history. Using a largely empirical grouping method Owens found 15 male and 17 female groups with similar background factors. Membership in groups tied into subsequent career patterns. The number of Owens' life-history groups possibly exceeds the 'minimum set' for practical research. Many of these groupings are tantalizing in their affinity for some of the simpler theoretical models underlying career choice. For instance, the 'upward mobile' group suggests the Linear concept; the 'analytic adaptive' group seems like the technical anchor of Schein; the 'virile extravert' may relate to the realist of Holland. The potential for integrative research tying these groups to more parsimonious models is clear.

Neiner and Owens (1985) in fact do tie in life-history factors to the Holland interest groups. Using actual job choices they find connections linking life history groups to the Holland categories. For instance, the life-history factors: academic achievement, science interest and social intraversion connect to the investigative interest group. Eberhart and Mushinsky (1982) did similar analyses using proposed work areas for students.

A possible problem in this life-history approach is its fairly Steady-State orientation. Davis (1984) has suggested that there is some change in life-history groups over seven years. From our view this is positive since it permits some people to shift patterns as their life unfolds—supporting Spiral or Transitory concepts of career.

Adult Personality. 1: Interests

Research on interests is dominated by the overarching Holland schema—which will be considered later. But some further developments on the Strong Campbell Vocational Interest Blank have occurred.

Hill and Hansen (1986) studied sex differences in managers and technical managers. In general, managers show no sex differences (Donnell and Hall, 1980). However, Hill and Hansen found that for technical managers, females were higher on Artistic interests, while males were higher on Realistic interests. They also find technical managers were more Investigative and less Enterprising than general managers (which ties in with McKinnon's data, see above).

On a broader front, Fouad et al. (1986) challenge the previous notion (e.g. Hansen and Campbell, 1985) that there are no cross-cultural differences in interests for occupations. On the contrary, they suggest that only if an occupation has universal norms (e.g. science, accounting, etc.) will one see similarity across cultures. As evidence, their data show similar interests for Mexican and American accountants but not for attorneys whose roles in their two countries are quite dissimilar.

Adult Personality. 2: Achievement Motives

Farmer (1985) conducted a major review and extension of understanding in the area of achievement motivation. She breaks the motive into three parts: level of aspiration (LOA), need for competence, and centrality of work/career. The connection of this construct with the Linear concept should be clear.

Her review of LOA research suggests that high aspiration is a function of higher social status, urban location, intelligence, self-esteem, independence and the support of parents and teachers. Her own data for women support these findings (except for independence) and add the factors of race and a supportive attitude on women working.

Past research on competence motivation suggests a positive role of social status, self esteem, being male, intrinsic (v. instrumental) values and parent–teacher support. Fear of success has a negative effect. In her data she confirms only the support variable, but adds location (urban), math ability, independence and competitiveness. Career centrality has been linked to sex, intelligence, self-esteem, intrinsic values, support and competence. Her data confirm the latter two, and add race and independence.

One can conclude that sex differences in LOA antecedents are minimal, but that for competence and career centrality, sex differences are sizeable. In particular, the female factors in competence motivation suggest the pattern needed to break the 'female stereotype' to be discussed below.

While very intriguing research, it would be more synergistic if it had not such a stand alone quality. For instance, it would be interesting to tie LOA to concepts like Linear v. Steady-State (e.g. is it the absolute level aimed for, or the number of steps on the way that make the difference?). Also, connecting career centrality with the broader work/non-work construct would be most interesting.

Adult Personality. 3: Self-efficacy and Locus of Control

It might seem strange to link these two concepts; however, internal locus of control refers to a belief in self-causation which comes very close to self-efficacy.

Differences due to locus of control continue to emerge in research. On a very general level the internal locus person is more satisfied with work, supervisors and promotions. They are more involved in work and see work as important (Stout, Slocum and Cron, 1987). The internals are more career satisfied but nevertheless initiate more job moves (Hamner and Vardi, 1981). Internals do more self-exploration and have more career information (Noe and Steffy, 1987).

The self-efficacious person also emerges with a 'glow'—they use wider ranges of career choice (Rotburg *et al.*, 1987), and are higher in their integration of vocational material (Neville *et al.*, 1986). Lack of a sense of self-efficacy has been blamed as a cause of females not breaking out of traditional jobs. The implication here is that internal, self-efficacious people make 'better' career choices. There are two problems here. One is: what is cause, and what is effect? Andrisani and Nestel (1976), for instance, find that upward mobility correlates with increased internal locus of control. The question is whether internal locus contributes to success (Linear), or the reverse. Perhaps, Hall has the best answer with his notion that success breeds success—i.e. the two are reciprocal.

A more thorny issue concerns what are 'good' career choices. Are we to assume that high information use is better? Or, that Linear success is the only kind? We will revisit these issues a bit further on.

Adult Personality. 4: Intelligence

As seen above, intelligence plays a role in LOA, competency and career centrality. It has also been linked to interest patterns in another exemplary integrative study by Lowman, Williams and Leeman (1985). The six Holland interest categories were rationally linked to abilities: The Realistic interest is connected to mechanical and spatial ability, the Investigative to general and verbal intelligence, the Artistic to music and art ability, the Social to interpersonal skill, the Enterprising to leadership ability and the Conventional to clerical skill.

The results confirmed the Enterprising, Conventional and Social linkages. Artistic interest broke into separate music and art aptitude factors. Investigative interest tied to general, arithmetic and mechanical, but not verbal, ability. Realistic interests related to no abilities.

In general, the data support a link between content of career choice and ability. It also raises some question about the meaningfulness of the Realistic category which may bear further subdivision. It is also possibly worth noting how relatively sparse are intelligence related studies of career choice. Does this betoken a preference for heart over head in career studies (cf. Shepard, 1984)?

Adult Personality. 5: Cognitive Style

In strong contrast to sparse intelligence related studies, there seems to be a major interest in cognitive styles in career research. Perhaps one reason for this flurry of interest in style is the long standing interest in vocational guidance in constructs like vocational maturity which includes quasi-stylistic factors such as career planning, exploration, decision skill and vocational information. The underlying premise of this maturity construct seems to be the assumption that the more rational the career choice the better (Super, 1980). The assumption has been challenged (Phillips et al., 1984), but a preponderance of opinion in this stream of research seems to favor 'rationality'. This debate naturally suggests an investigation of decision-style in career choice.

Harren (1979) proposed a style model contrasting rational with intuitive and dependent styles. Unlike the orderly information-oriented rational style, the intuitive relies on feeling and little data whereas the dependent style gets direction from others with little internal processing.

The normative flavor of this model is revealed in Phillips and Strohmeyer's (1982) conclusion that the dependent style is not 'effective' in career decisions. However, Bud and Daniels (1985) report the intuitive style is 'surprisingly' not unadaptive in career thinking. Blustein (1987) counters with the suggestion that for well-informed students absence of rational style may not matter, whereas for less sophisticated students, style will matter. He supports this with less-informed students where the rational style positively correlated with vocational maturity while the other two styles showed negative correlations.

The problem surfacing here is one that occurred early in the general cognitive style literature. In particular, Witkin's field independence model had a strong normative bias—and ultimately was found to correlate heavily with intelligence.

Much of the other work on style has tried to avoid this normative, intelligence like bias, taking instead the view that all styles are 'good' for certain types of information settings (see Driver, 1975). The point here is whether a rational approach is always best. Shepard (1984) strongly argues for a more intuitive 'path with a heart'. One could find sociologically-minded defenders of the idea that careers should be fitted to the needs of society—which could favor a dependent style.

The ultimate issue again is: what is a good career choice? Is it one that is logical, one that feels good, one that contributes to society, one that maximizes personal growth or power? Unless we can develop a framework for resolving this question it may be wise to avoid premature closure on any one criterion of what makes a good choice.

Nevertheless, the analysis of styles in the choice process seems a very promising direction of research. It can lead to a far better descriptive analysis of the choice process than earlier efforts. This is clearly seen in the line of research building on the Kelly personal construct model (Bodden, 1970). In this approach vocational areas and attributes are grouped into classes yielding scores on differentiation—the number of distinct categories of thought; and integration—the amount of linkage among categories.

The evolution of this research stream paralleled the earlier work on general cognitive complexity in its initial focus on differentiation, which is still seen in more recent studies; e.g. Brown's (1987) result that using one's own vocational constructs yields a more differentiated structure than using experimenter developed attributes.

However, as Winer and Gati (1986) note, some time ago we (Schroder, Driver and Streufert, 1969) emphasized the danger in equating complexity with pure differentiation. One could have many cognitive dimensions to work with yet deal with any one situation very simplistically if the dimensions were not connected and only one dimension was brought to bear at a time. The distinction between these two complexity factors is shown by the negative correlation usually found between them (Neimeyer and Metzler, 1987).

In fact, most studies of this type do stress integration following Cochran's lead (1977). Research has shown that the more integrated the vocational concept system is, the more one finds:

1. Rapid information processing (Cochran, 1977).
2. More information values (Adams-Webber, 1979).
3. More active exploration of identity (i.e. achieved or moratorium types in Marcia's framework) (Neville et al., 1986).
4. More self-efficacy (Neville et al., 1986).

High integration with low differentiation has been associated with better recall of information on vocations (Neville et al., 1986). Whereas, high integration and high differentiation has been linked to the 'achieved identity' of Marcia's typology.

One might be tempted to see a 'master integration' occurring here: the high-complexity person as the nexus of self-efficacy, achieved identity, rational decision process, etc. However, some caution is urged.

First, the Kelly object sorting methodology almost forces a conflict between differentiation and integration. This has caused many of us in the cognitive style area to seek other methods of measuring integration independent of differentiation (see Schroder et al., 1969; Streufert and Streufert, 1979). Also, the tendency to exalt the complex style may be biased. At this stage in career research can we be sure that simpler styles will always make poor or false career choices?

Finally, the focus on complexity in vocational constructs, while highly relevant to careers, is fraught with a problem noted by Winer and Gati (1986). The problem is that complexity across a particular content domain varies within a person. For instance, Winer and Gati found more complexity underlying rejected occupations than selected occupations. One implication of this finding is that 'achieved' or focused identity may be tied to simpler structures, while uncertainty generates more complexity. I shall pursue this issue later.

Another reaction to the Winer and Gati result is to worry about the generality of complexity scores based on one content domain. In our work (e.g. Driver and Streufert, 1969) we have tried to assess the complexity of a presumed central cognitive processing unit which remains relatively stable across content areas and over time. The complexity of this central processor is most accurately measured when a person is dealing with new information and past memory is minimalized. Becoming too domain specific allows the complexity of past experience (i.e. memory traces) to impact and distort the central processor's own structure. We suggest that the most general measure of cognitive structure—i.e. the central processor's structure—might give the most stable measure of career-related complexity since in our work this measure has predicted choice behavior in many varied settings. The general 'decision style' of a person (Driver and Mock, 1975) might give a broader insight into how people cope with all aspects of careers compared to a more domain specific technique.

At present, only a few studies have explored this general decision style model in relation to career issues. The four basic styles in this model are:

(a) *Decisive*—low differentiation, low integration
(b) *Flexible*—high differentiation, low integration
(c) *Hierarchic*—low differentiation, high integration
(d) *Integrative*—high differentiation and integration

Prince (1979) has linked these general styles to career concepts. The Decisive style was correlated with the Linear career concept while the Steady-State concept was negatively correlated with the Integrative style. Olson (1979) reports similar findings. More recently Coombs (1987) has found a consistent style-concept pattern, e.g. Spiral and Transitory correlations with Flexible and Integrative styles.

Schutt (1979) has found interesting connections between Holland interest patterns and style. For instance, the Enterprising orientation correlates with Decisive style while the Investigative correlates with the Integrative style. Finally, Owens (1979) finds general style variables helpful in defining life-history groupings and Strong Campbell Vocational Interest areas. For instance, Integrative style is linked to interests such as psychiatry, personnel, computer programming and law. One other interesting result in Owens work is a connection of Decisiveness and conformity to the female role. Bartunek and Louis (1985) have found that experienced MBAs had higher Flexible and Integrative scores, and lower Decisive scores than inexperienced MBAs. They found differential reactions to socialization at work for each style. They also reported how various factors contributed to style change at work. (This is reviewed in more detail below.)

In sum, after seeing the diversity of these studies of personality and career choice, I strongly endorse Schein's (1986) call for efforts to integrate these varied personality patterns into a minimal set which can propel career research onto a new level.

CAREER CHOICE PROCESSES

Career Indecision

We now wish to shift the focus from studies of factors affecting career processes to research on the process itself. A transitional topic concerns 'career indecision'.

This topic has been a prime focus in traditional vocational guidance literature. Osipow (1976) has developed a scale concerning decidedness which is similar to the maturity measures of Super *et al.* (1981) and Crites (1973). It also resembles Holland's identity scale (Holland *et al.*, 1980) and even Marcia's concept of achieved identity. Integrative studies have linked these measures.

Graef *et al.* (1985) found the Super, Holland and Osipow scales highly intercorrelated. Grotevant and Thorbeck (1982) and Savickas (1985) empirically linked Marcia's achieved identity and Holland's scales. Fuqua and Seaworth (1987) again find high intercorrelation among decidedness scales as well as a strong relation between all of them and anxiety. Even the complexity model gets on board as Niemeyer and Metzler (1987) find high differentiation tied to indecision.

However, the research literature does raise some caveats on any premature closure on the idea that career decidedness is the 'ultimate state' for career happiness. Hartman *et al.* (1983) found that the indecision variable was not very stable over time. They suggest three 'types': decided, developmentally undecided, and chronic undecided. Hartman *et al.* (1985) found the chronic undecided type had more anxiety, less stable self-perception and more external locus of control than the other two types. However, Hartman *et al.* (1986) also found that the unreliability of the decidedness construct increases from decided, to developmentally undecided, to chronic undecided.

The connection of this research to career concept theory is quite intriguing. If we equate decided with Steady-State, and undecided—particularly chronic undecided—with Transitory or Spiral concepts, this line of research can lift itself above a normative plane in which decided equals good. It may allow fascinating possible insights into the affective and personality dynamics of diverse, yet legitimate 'undecided' career orientations.

Another line of effort here as seen in Graef *et al.* (1985) is work on the antecedents of the Super, Holland and Osipow approaches to decidedness. The three measures did not share similar background factors and in some cases they showed rather socially undesirable associations. The Osipow 'decided' type and much of the super 'mature' person pattern showed correlation with low GPA and, in addition, the Super mature type showed poor social adjustment. Westbrook *et al.* (1985) also found no correlation of maturity and academic success although they do see some connection of maturity with students own satisfaction with their career processes. In a more positive vein, Healey *et al.* (1985) report the 'mature' students (in Crites' model) to be older, have a higher GPA and better college jobs.

Several comments are in order. While it seems clear that a major distinction in career states (or concepts, if you prefer) does exist (e.g. decided Steady-State *v.* undecided Transitory), it is by no means clear that one is superior to the other. For instance, undecidedness may be a wholesome, workable state for chronic Transitory people who have found a proper career setting. On the other hand, we hardly deny that for Steady-State (or Linear) people, undecidedness may be indeed a highly traumatic, anxiety-producing and undesirable state. Putting the decidedness variable in a broader context would illuminate career choice research.

Career Planning

The research on career planning has been mainly covered under previous headings with a few scattered exceptions. One such area concerns sex differences in planning. Brenner and Tomkievicz (1979) found males doing more planning; whereas Rynes and Rosen (1983) found no sex differences. A similar concern for sex difference exists concerning the use of career information. Yanico and Hardin (1986) found that women estimated their vocational knowledge in non-traditional work areas as less than did men. In fact, real knowledge showed no sex effect. Whether those sex factors can be subsumed under broader sex differences (e.g. in cognitive style) should form an interesting research target.

Interventions in Career Process

There continues to be considerable research on interventions to improve career choice processes, despite Holland's (1981) concern that these interventions have little effect.

One general trend is for intervention to produce more decidedness and more positive feeling about career processes (e.g. Remer et al., 1984; Neimeyer and Ebben, 1985; Slaney and Lewis, 1986). Neimeyer and Ebben found that interventions such as the Holland search processes, computer interactive systems and providing vocational information *decreased* complexity. Thus, as noted above, decidedness may actually link to cognitive simplicity, not complexity. A further point is that at least one of these interventions (Ramer et al., 1984) also found an increase in a 'rational' style. It may be that intervention to improve decidedness and rationality decrease complexity.

A counter-trend, however, is found in a few studies showing more explorations after intervention—possibly implying greater complexity. For instance, assessment center feedback (Noe and Steffy, 1987) and problem-solving training (Jepson et al., 1982) increase exploration. And the vocational information treatment in the Neimeyer and Ebben study seemed to produce a slight increase in complexity in a follow-up time period.

It appears that very structured interventions may produce a stable but simple 'identity', whereas more open interventions may raise complexity. Along these lines, Robbins and Tucker (1986) found that 'unstable' types (i.e. non-steady-state) worked better in more open interactive career workshops compared to structured techniques. Would not an interesting line of research be to study effects and affinities of different career orientation types for different types of intervention?

But again, we must ask: by what criteria do we judge the goodness of intervention? Until the field examines the issue of how to define 'good' careers, projections of each researcher's definition will continue to be dominant. I would suggest that the use of a descriptive model, such as career concepts or career anchors, could help us take a broader, less uni-focused, normative view of 'goodness in career choice'.

EARLY CAREER ISSUES

Socialization and the Effect of Work

Several theoretical approaches to socialization have recently surfaced. Reichers (1987) has suggested an interactive framework for viewing the process. He suggests that person factors such as field dependence, tolerance of ambiguity, and affiliation needs will increase the rate of socialization. Environmental facilitators would include task interdependence, orientation programs, training, performance evaluation and mentoring.

Hopefully, new research will focus on this model since certain factors (e.g. tolerance of ambiguity) might work opposite to the role suggested by Reichers and certain personality factors (e.g. general decision style) may be a useful addition in his model (see below).

Morrison and Hock (1986) also propose an interactive model seeing work experience as the major factor in shaping careers. They cite an extensive literature showing how work alters personal factors such as locus of control, authoritarianism, well-being and mental health. In particular they cite studies (such as Kohn and Schooler, 1982; Brousseau, 1983) showing deleterious effects of overly simple work. They propose that careers should be shaped by exposing people to incrementally increasing complexity in work—a view shared by Brousseau (1984). They correctly note that this will require extremely effective job analysis and design. However, they do not focus, as Brousseau does, on the need to specifically measure and design complexity on the job. They do, however, stress the importance in selection of measuring changeable, as well as invariant, characteristics. Complexity of style clearly seems to be of the former class (see Bartunek and Louis, 1985) underlining the potential value in the cognitive complexity approach.

Another aspect of the Bartunek and Louis study deserves a summary at this point. They expected that inexperienced MBAs would be more affected by socialization aids (e.g. training) as opposed to work itself; while the opposite would be true for experienced MBAs. The prediction held for inexperienced MBAs and initially for experienced MBAs. However, over time socialization aids were seen retroactively as important by experienced MBAs, as well as work.

As noted above, interesting differences in decision style also emerged. For instance, formal training decreased complexity for all MBAs; whereas relation factors, such as buddy relations and mentoring, increased complexity for experienced MBAs. Curiously many factors that attracted complex styles initially at work (e.g. task variety) actually were associated with declining complexity over time. This study may have uncovered support for the premise in complexity theory that too great a rate of change in environmental complexity can produce a decline in personal complexity (see Driver and Streufert, 1969).

Success Factors in Different Types of Career

(a) Female careers

Gutek et al. (1986) have provided a thorough review of women at work so only a quick look will be given to this topic here. They note that despite a major influx of women into the world's workforce, sex segregation of jobs is still pandemic. For instance, Von Glinow and Kryczkowska (1985) found no increase in the tiny percentage of women on boards or serving as officers in major corporations. Females are also portrayed in company brochures in typically 'female stereotype' jobs.

The problem of unequal pay is also still prevalent. In the face of this, women appear to be developing increasingly less stereotypical views of their potential work roles. For instance, recently Foss and Slaney (1986) found that more liberal women had higher self-efficacy and chose non-traditional jobs for their daughters. Being a working mother, although a great strain due to simultaneous competing role elements, tends to foster this liberal attitude (e.g. Hoffman, 1974).

(b) Entrepreneur careers

Derr (1984) proposes an interesting typology of entrepreneurs and suggests varied orientations in each. He proposes a small business type who is social and focused on one area; a technical entrepreneur who is a craftsman also focused on one area; an administrative type who pursues not income but new projects inside a company; an adventurer who seeks diverse ventures, risk and profit and an artist driven by creativity. In particular, the distinction of a variety oriented, risk seeking type v. a one-venture security-oriented type seems very useful since they are often grouped together and yet differ profoundly in career orientation (e.g. Steady-State v. Transitory).

Bowen and Hesrick (1986) reviewed the entrepreneur literature particularly for women. They note a lack of general trends in predicting entrepreneurial success. For instance, some studies suggest entrepreneurs are not highly educated, others suggest they are; some are risk-takers, some aren't. Bowen and Hesrick suggest that some of this inconsistency may be due to the different types of industry studied, e.g. high-tech v. low-tech. However, attention to distinctions among types of entrepreneurs such as Derr has proposed might yield much clearer results on success factors in this career area.

(c) Managerial careers

Studies on factors in manager success are not particularly frequent. Howard (1984) found that linear motives, tolerance for ambiguity, dominance and independence predicted managerial success. Jaskolke and Beyer (1985) stressed sociological factors such as education, years with a company and job involvement as success factors.

One important distinction which seems needed in this literature is between levels of management. Dalton and Thompson (1986) provide an impressive analysis of the demands of four organizational levels—apprentice, individual contributor, manager and director. They point out that moves from individual contributor to manager require a relinquishment of technical, inside oriented self-absorption and instead a broader focus on others, the outside world and administration. Moves from manager to director require increased skills in providing vision, representing the organization, exercising power and sponsoring new talent. Kotter (1982) provides a similar role analysis for managers.

Given the discrete job demands at different levels, one would expect greater focus and precision in looking for success factors at each level. Top-level factors have received considerable attention. Bennis and Nanus (1986) provide great insight into the traits needed by top leaders. They find that vision, particularly a positive self-regard, a great ability to ask questions and listen, a strong results focus, and a capacity to create clear, compelling goals are essential qualities. Levinson and Rosenthal (1984) agree with most of these findings and would add a willingness to take risks, to take charge and to combine thinking and doing. Dropping down a level, Kotter (1982) finds traits like being sociable (a networker), being stable and optimistic, above average in IQ, moderately analytical as well as having the pervasive Linear motives of power and achievement are vital in successful general managers.

The changes between levels in required traits suggests a great need for deeper analysis of succession planning and management development that has been typical. Sorcher (1985) describes the actual processes used in succession planning but gives only some general ideas on what traits are involved in the failure to make it to the top (e.g. lack of integrity, selfish, too political, rigid, unpleasant). Brady and Helmich (1984) provide great insight into the relative merits of inside vs. outside succession, but only touch on the issue of personality factors in succession.

One of the more intriguing lines of work which concerns executive cognitive style seems to be gaining interest. Streufert (1986) has stressed a unique integrative complexity among successful managers. Weick (1983), on the contrary, stresses a strong action focus. I have proposed that a combination style using integration under moderate stress and a more simplistic Decisive style under high pressure may be the unique 'executive style' (Driver, 1986). However, future research here may reveal that types of industries and even stages of organization life-cycle may relate to optimal management cognitive style.

(d) Expatriate careers

One area of emerging interest concerns careers outside one's own culture (Conway and Von Glinow, 1986). The US expatriate seems to have a more difficult time adjusting than European or Japanese (Dunn, 1980; Tung, 1982). The key problem seems to be family and personal adjustment.

Prior experience seems to help an expatriate as well as traits of empathy, respect, flexibility, tolerance, interest in local cultures, and task skills. It may be expected that more culture-specific adaptation factors (e.g. success factors for Africa v. Japan) may emerge as this research area develops. Mendenhall and Oddou (1985) begin to address the issue of cultural difference as well as proposing a fairly complex model of expatriate success. They suggest three dimensions of success:

(a) *Self-oriented*—capacity to change means of gratification, capacity to reduce stress and competence.
(b) *Other-oriented*—capacity to relate and to communicate.
(c) *Perceptual*—absence of rigidity and ethnocentric judgement.

Each of these factors needs to be adjusted for 'cultural toughness'; i.e. Asian and African sites seem tougher than others (Torbiorn, 1982).

While a promising start, it might prove useful to connect this line of research more to general personality models—e.g. cognitive styles. It might also be useful to describe cultures on dimensions tied to measurable expatriate personality traits—e.g. if cultures vary in their typical information processing complexity, matching cultures to expatriate decision style might be quite helpful (Meshkati and Driver, 1986).

LATER CAREER ISSUES

Plateauing

Although some earlier work (Bray and Howard, 1980) suggests that plateaued managers adjust well, there is growing concern that plateauing may be a very serious problem. Near (1985) reports that plateaued managers were more absent, had poorer relations with superiors, and impaired health. The plateaued manager had poorer education which tallies with prior data on education and management advancement.

Some of the differences in data on plateauing may be due to age. Hall (1986) reviews studies which show that younger plateaued managers are more adversely affected than older. I would also point to the probability that Linear type people would be most hurt by plateauing, while Steady-State would be least bothered.

Career Change

One response to the mid-career problems has been to increasingly advocate career change (Hall, 1986). Hall sees the primary problem in mid-career being a constriction of opportunity. He sees early career stages as being driven by short run performance goals (achievement). Success breeds more success (Howard, 1984). However, at mid-career, chances to perform run out. Hall suggests that some might cope by shifting energy to non-work channels. Others might benefit by shifting jobs laterally (Bailyn and Lynch, 1983), or even downward (Hall and Isabella, 1985).

The central idea here is that as the gap between expectations and reality widens, a new career search can begin (Mihal et al., 1984). This new career search may focus more on finding deeper identity or on adaptability or resilience (London and Stumpf, 1986).

It is clear that Hall is advocating a 'Spiral'-type solution in which new identities are developed over a lifespan, as Logan has suggested. Hall points to the Spiral-type career structure at Digital Equipment (Kidder, 1981) as a prototype. If one is a Spiral or Transitory-type person, these solutions make sense. The problem here is whether truly Linear types can make a meaningful career concept changes. We have found that many apparent Linears are 'closet Spirals or Transitories' waiting for a chance for the organization to approve of lateral moves. For them, the Hall-type solution is excellent. For 'true' Linears, career change may be a hard solution.

For many Steady-State people, Lorsch and Takayi (1986) may have hit a key solution to mid-life problems. They note that successful plateaued managers have had histories of 'mainline' assignments which leave them committed even when no further linear movement is possible. This ties in with Brousseau's (1978) finding that strong task identity and significance impart greater energy. It also ties in with our proposition that for Steady-State persons' 'centrality' (in Schein's [1971] terms—being in the center of the action—is a substitute for advancement.

For the true Linear, perhaps threat of job loss may cause a self-renewal process and shift to another career concept (e.g. Latack and Dozier, 1985). At this stage the factors enhancing concept change, particularly for Linears, remain a prime target for research.

A final line of research on career change concerns factors that facilitate change. Stout, Slocum and Cron (1987) support Louis's (1980) premise that if either a boss or a subordinate have experienced change and the other has not, things go better. Too much change (i.e. both parties) is disruptive (Latack, 1984). Spousal support also seems crucial in career change and is reported to be present for most changers (Anderson-Kulman *et al.*, 1986). Studies show that after the change, husbands are more at home, marriages improve, self-concepts are better, but social activity decreases. Here again one wonders if this picture would be so idyllic for true Linears.

Job Loss

Fryer and Payne (1986) have recently surveyed this area thoroughly, as have Latack and Dozier (1986) and De Frank and Ivancevich (1986). There is considerable consensus that job loss lowers happiness and increases the frequency of depression, mental illness and physical illness. Less clear but possible consequences are higher death rates, suicide, lowered self-esteem and family disorders. Greenhalgh (1985) even notes that survivors of layoffs show increased anxiety and disengagement.

In general, over time, the impact of job loss is maximum at first then wears down. A key coping mechanism is active job search, which is enhanced by expectations of success (Kanfer and Holin, 1985).

Factors facilitating coping include age (younger or older are better), being male, non-caucasian, highly active, 'hardy' (Kobasa and Puceitti, 1984)—that is, *not* committed (i.e. not Steady-State)—being well-off, having sound support, advance warning, good reasons for being let go, and being told by one's immediate boss.

It is suggested that if the stress is moderate and support such as outplacement is given, the experience can even lead to growth. Again, a career concept view here is that for the Steady-State and Linear person, these results make sense, but for Transitories of Spirals ('hardy' or 'resilient' types), job loss is simply a challenge to move on—especially if it is not due to personal incompetence.

Retirement

Only one review of retirement came to light by Beehr (1986). Surprisingly, he cites studies showing retirement as non-stressful (Kasl, 1980) and productive of less illness (Minkler, 1981). However, Ekerdt *et al.* (1983) note that retirees tend to ignore health problems.

Again, individual differences surface. Lower-status workers die faster (Hayes *et al.*, 1978). May this be due to prolonged effects of job simplicity *à la* Kohn and Schooler? Committed (i.e. Steady-State, Linear) types show low satisfaction in retirement (Glamser, 1981). In fact, we might suggest that retirement is little or no stress for change-oriented career types.

ORGANIZATION–PERSON CONGRUENCE MODELS

The Holland Model

Considerable research has been marshalled by Holland and his associates (e.g. Gottfredson, 1977) that individuals who choose occupations which fit their interest pattern will fare better in subsequent careers.

One challenge to this view comes from Schwartz *et al*. (1986). They suggest that in most cases, Holland supporters show that Investigative types do better in Investigative settings than non-Investigative types. The problem, they point out, is that Investigative types are generally higher achievers. The real test of the Holland congruence model then would be to determine if a non-Investigative setting favored non-Investigative types. They raise serious questions by finding that Conventional type accountants (a Conventional area) achieve poorer salaries than non-Conventional types.

This type of result raises questions as to whether the very popular Holland scheme—especially in the Realistic (see IQ data above) and Conventional interest categories—could not benefit by cross-fertilization with some other variables (e.g. complexity of interest fields may better sort out patterns).

A more fundamental challenge to the entire congruence concept is put forth by Pazy and Zin (1987). They suggest that psychological needs for consistency moderate the effects of occupation-interest congruence. In their view, if interests match occupations, all is well. However, if there is a mismatch, only those people with secondary interest patterns which are similar (congruent) to primary interests will be disturbed. Those with incongruent (dissimilar) secondary interest patterns will not be disturbed. Congruence of interest patterns is defined as having secondary interests adjacent to one's primary interests in the Holland hexagram. In sum, incongruence between interests and occupation is only a problem for those with 'inner congruence'.

Their research generally supports the proposed model. However, there are some concerns. One, 'job involvement' comes out as being low for situations where occupation and interest are congruent, which is not expected. In contrast, satisfaction variables are predictably high for congruent cases. Some explanation of this oddity seems needed.

Secondly, several interpretations of this general view are plausible. One which they favor is that low inner consistency in interest areas is symptomatic of high tolerance for ambiguity, which makes occupation-interest incongruence a positive event. This view, incidentally, is consistent with my General Incongruity Adaptation Level model (Driver, 1984), not inconsistent as Pazy and Zin assert.

Another interpretation, however, is that since inner incongruent types have two divergent sets of interests, when they are in an occupation not matching their primary interests, it may still match their secondary areas. Further analysis, or perhaps new studies using a direct measure of inner uncertainty tolerance, might clarify these issues.

Career Culture–Career Concept Congruence

Coombs and Driver (1983) directly tested the career concept models' prediction that if a company constructs a culture (Driver, 1980) which resonates with a person's career concept, optimal performance will occur. Using questionnaire analysis, a company was determined to be seen as largely Steady-State in culture—particularly in its reward system. It was expected that Steady-State-type people would report higher commitment, satisfaction and productivity in this company, which they did. They also report more life satisfaction, a not unexpected 'spillover' of work satisfaction into non-work.

As expected, the Linear types reported strong lack of commitment, low satisfaction and productivity and negative spillover into life satisfaction. The Spirals showed only moderate discomfort and were possibly sustained by intrinsic job interest. The Transitory result was most interesting—unexpectedly low negativity and an apparent compensatory good feeling about avocational activities.

Organization Change and Congruence

An exciting new trend may be emerging in the more dynamic fitting of changing occupations or organizational settings with career interests, concepts, etc. Hall (1986), for instance, suggests matching individual life stages to organizational development stages. An illuminating example of this type of matching is described by Campbell and Moses (1986). They describe shifts in AT & T culture which included lower company identity, less promotion from within, changing standards for measuring high potential and a shift from manager to employee as career manager. However, hierarchic structure, work identity, and performance standards remained intact.

They also note that work values changed to less work primacy, less commitment and less need for structure. They concluded that employees' career orientations must change to more short-term, achievement-oriented, self-managed and, above all else, multiple-career oriented. In career concept language, they echo calls by theorists like Hall for a shift to Spiral career concepts. As noted, only further research will clarify whether changes in career concepts to match changing culture can easily occur.

Societal Trends and Careers

On a broader scale, London and Stumpf (1986) examine social trends which they believe might impact careers. They propose that automation is increasingly leading to a declining management role. They also see trends toward off site work, declining hierarchy, and declining work identification. In these trends, they see an imperative toward less concern with advancement and argue that workers today must develop 'career resiliency' as well as greater self-insight.

I would agree that trends at present are not moving in favor of a Linear career concept (Driver, 1985). To the above, I would add a baby boom bulge about to wipe out most possible movement in upper management, a lengthening of retirement decisions, a not very dynamic economic growth forecast, and the increasing passion to trim management levels. One might argue with some of these factors, but overall, trends do favor anything but the Linear career concept.

The problem, as noted earlier, is that almost all signals seem to say that the Linear type of concept is on the rise. It seems then that a major concern for theory, research and practice is to deal with how to either alter career concepts, or set up alternative Linear structures—perhaps in the leisure world?

Career Management Practice in Organization

Gutteridge (1986) has once again provided a thorough review of the states of the art in career management. I would group these practices into four areas:

Person assessment

By far and away the most common tools found in corporations are self-description work books usually used in workshops. There is some small use of professional counselors, but most often human resource people conduct such efforts. The problem with such methods is mainly self-deception (as London and Stumpf note), or self-ignorance. Sometimes discussion with supervisors can correct misperceptions, but often they too perceive through distorted lenses as the performance appraisal literature has pointed out.

A second tool of growing importance is the computer-based, interactive self-assessment method (Miner, 1986). It ha penetrated schools (Meyers and Cairo, 1983), and is beginning to be used by companies (Harris-Bowlsby, 1983). Despite the electronics, the heart of most of these systems is the same—self-assessment—with the same caveats as workbooks.

A possible corrective might be in greater use of professionally developed psychological tests, professional counselor interviews, and where economically defensible—assessment center methods. As Gutteridge notes, these methods are useful if feedback is given to the person by professionally trained personnel.

Even with these conditions, Gutteridge worries about rigid cutoffs and self-fulfilling prophesies if such methods are used to identify 'high potential'. I would tend to agree. I have found that testing works best when embedded in an integrated career management program which includes counseling, developmental programs, and reward systems not totally tied to Linear advancement (Von Glinow *et al.*, 1985).

There is evidence that psychological testing, hopefully purged of the inadequacies of the pre-EEOC era, is coming back into use. It is clearly a superior assessment tool to self- or other analysis (Reilly and Chao, 1982). A very useful line of research would be to evaluate how a developmentally-oriented testing approach impacts career processes in organizations. One of the problems here is the need for more intensive training among HR practitioners, and organization behavior researchers in test theory and practice. The general lack of such training is one of the fragmentors alluded to by Schein as plaguing this field.

Job analysis

Gutteridge mentions very little about job analysis. Unfortunately, as testing is heavily oriented toward selection, so job analysis tends to be driven by compensation needs. A technique known as job profiling has been described by Brousseau (1984) which builds a picture of the ideal incumbent's personality and abilities based on links to specific tasks in a job. Techniques like this, if in wider use, could provide a much needed advance over vague job descriptions or job analysis focused solely on motives or on aptitudes.

Given job analyses tied to measurable person traits, techniques such as job posting might become more useful. Unfortunately, at present, they are often meaningless blinds covering up predetermined decisions on vacancies—as Gutteridge notes.

Matching processes

Gutteridge and Miner both observe a renaissance of interest in skills inventories. After an abortive start, they seem to be getting more user friendly and specific. However, they seem largely focused on specific task competencies which as Morrison and Hock note, are not very useful in more abstract jobs such as in professions or management. The skill inventory technique, wedded to an integrated system, using common job–person dimensions has considerable promise—if it can avoid fossilization.

Perhaps the most critical area for matching is succession planning. Unfortunately, this area is so far rather barren of research at a deeper psychological level. Gutteridge sees most practice as biased and top down with little openness to career management issues.

Development

Gutteridge takes a dim view of formal career ladder systems which he sees as too focused on the past. While I see ladders as out of touch with trends toward loose, organic, Spiral systems, I suggest that ladders of some type are important to Linear people. A challenge of the future may be to invent new types of ladders.

Kram (1986) suggests that mentoring is a vitally important developmental process at all career stages—even late in one's career (Clawson, 1980). However, she notes that cross-sex mentoring can raise problems (Clawson and Kram, 1984). Formal mentoring programs can be poor if the fit between parties is poor. She suggests that mentoring is best introduced into an organization through general OD techniques.

Perhaps use of testing could produce a maximally useful mentoring program. For instance, a Spiral-type person might be very prone to mentoring, while a Linear would be threatened by the role. Also, developmental life stage might be crucial as Davis (1982) notes. Individuals at complementary life stages rather than competitive stages seem to work best in mentoring relationships.

Finally, we note that little research comes to light on the effect of developmental programs such as enrichment, rotation, or training on participants, other than the almost automatic 'feels good' response. This seems a rich field for future research—especially in relation to the effects of such program on career concepts.

In doing career management, Gutteridge suggests going slow and starting small. I agree, but must caution that all too often career programs end up isolated and vulnerable to the first cost reduction pressure. We have suggested that only when career programs become integrated with standard HR practice—such as performance appraisal, reward systems, selection programs and training will the real promise of the career area be met in organizations (Von Glinow *et al.*, 1983).

CONCLUSION

If there is one trend that most impressed the reviewer, it is the continued fragmentation of this field. Even within streams, there seems to be an unfortunate tendency to reinvent measures of constructs rather than first test or build on prior relevant materials. I see a great need for more research comparing and condensing overlapping measures into a hopefully general minimal set of measures. It is through shared measures that most scientific inquiry progresses.

At a broader level, I see a need for theories which embrace the psychological insights of vocational guidance and the growing organizational and sociological sensitivity of organizational theorists. If we are to truly understand organizational careers, the major themes discussed here must somehow begin to merge.

REFERENCES

Adams-Webber, J. (1979) *Personal Construct Theory*. New York: John Wiley.

Anderson-Kulman, R. and Paludi, M. (1986) Working mothers and the family context: predicting positive coping. *Journal of Vocational Behavior*, **28**, 241–53.

Andrisani, P. and Nestel, G. (1986) Internal–external control as a contributor to an outcome of work experience. *Journal of Applied Psychology*, **61**, 156–65.

Arthur, M. (1984) The career concept: Challenge and opportunity for its further application. In M. Arthur, L. Bailyn, D. Levinson and H. Shepard *Working With Careers*, New York: Columbia University School of Business.

Astin, D. and Greene, K. (1987) *The American Freshman: twenty-year trends*. Los Angeles: Higher Education Research Institute, UCLA.

Badawy, M. (1983) Why managers fail. *Research Management*, 26–31.

Bailyn, L. (1984) Issues of work and family in organizations: Responding to social diversity. In M. Arthur, L. Bailyn, D. Levinson and H. Shepard *Working With Careers*. New York: Columbia University School of Business.

Bailyn, L. and Lynch, J. (1983) Engineering as a life-long career: its meaning, its satisfactions, its difficulties. *Journal of Occupational Behavior*, **4**, 263–83.

Barton, K., Anderson, C. and Schneier, C. (1980) Motivation to manage among college business students: a reassessment. *Journal of Vocational Behavior*, **17**, 22–32.

Bartol, K. and Martin, D. (1987) Managerial motivation among MBA students: a longitudinal assessment. *Journal of Occupational Psychology*, **30**, 1–12.

Bartol, K. and Schneier, C. (1985) Internal and external validity issues with motivation to manage research: a reply. *Journal of Vocational Behavior*, **26**, 299–305.

Bartunek, J. and Louis, M. (1986) Information processing activities associated with organizational newcomers' complex thinking. Paper given at the Academy of Management, Chicago.

Beehr, T. (1986) The process of retirement. *Personnel Psychology*, **39**, 31–55.

Belsky, J., Steinberg, L. and Walker, A. (1982) The ecology of day care. In M. Lamb (ed.) *Nontraditional Families*. Hillside, N.J.: Lawrence Erlbaum.

Bennis, W. and Nanus, B. (1986) *Leaders*. New York: Harper and Row.

Bentell, N. and Brenner, O. (1986) Sex differences in work values. *Journal of Vocational Behavior*, **28**, 29–41.

Berger, P. (1986) Differences in importance and satisfaction from job characteristics by sex and occupational type among Mexican–American employees. *Journal of Vocational Behavior*, **28**, 203–213.

Birnbaum, J. (1971) Life patterns, personality and self-esteem in gifted family oriented and career oriented women. PhD Dissertation, University of Michigan.

Blustein, D. (1987) Decision-making styles and vocational maturity—an alternative perspective. *Journal of Vocational Behavior*, **30**, 61–71.

Bodden, J. (1970) Cognitive complexity as a factor in appropriate vocational choice. *Journal of Counseling Psychology*, **17**, 364–68.

Bowen, D. and Hesrich, R. (1986) The female entrepreneur—a career development perspective. *Academy of Management Review*, **11**, 393–407.

Bray, D. and Howard, A. (1980) Career success and life statisfaction of middle-aged managers. In L. Bond and J. Rosen (eds) *Competence and Coping During Adulthood.* Hanover, N.H.: University Press of New England.

Brady, G. and Helmich, D. (1984) *Executive Succession.* Englewood Cliffs, N.J.: Prentice-Hall.

Brenner, O. and Tomkiewicz, J. (1979) Job orientations of males and females: are sex differences declining? *Personnel Psychology*, 32, 741–50.

Brousseau, K. (1978) Personality and job experience. *Organizational Behavior and Human Performance*, 22, 235–52.

Brousseau, K. (1983) Toward a dynamic model of job–person relationships. *Academy of Management Review*, 8, 33–45.

Brousseau, K. (1984) Job–person dynamics and career development. In K. Rowland and G. Ferris (eds) *Research in Personnel and Human Resources*, Vol. 2. Greenwich, CT: JAI Press.

Brown, M. (1987) A comparison of two approaches to the cognitive differentiation grid. *Journal of Vocational Behavior*, 30, 155–66.

Bud, J. and Daniels, M. (1985) *Assessment of Career Decision Making: Manual.* Los Angeles: Western Psychology Press.

Burke, R. (1985) Career orientations, work experience and health. Paper given at the Academy of Management, San Diego.

Bush, P. and Bush, R. (1978) Women contrasted to men in the industrial sales force. *Journal of Marketing Research*, 15, 43888.

Campbell, R. and Moses, J. (1986) Careers from an organizational perspective. In D. Hall and Associates (eds) *Career Development in Organizations.* San Francisco, Jossey-Bass.

Cherniss, C. (1980) *Professional Burnout in Human Service Organizations.* New York: Praeger.

Clawson, J. (1980) Mentoring in managerial careers. In C. B. Derr (ed.) *Work, Family, and the Career.* New York: Praeger.

Clawson, J. and Kram, K. (1984) Managing cross-gender mentoring. *Business Horizons*, May–June, 22–32.

Cochran, L. (1977) Differences between supplied and elicited constructs. *Social Behavior and Personality*, 5, 241–47.

Conway, B. and Von Glinow, M. (1986) The successful expatriate: A comparative study of U.S., European, and Japanese expatriates in ASEAN. Unpublished manuscript, Department of Management and Organization, University of Southern California, Los Angeles.

Coombs, M. (1987) Measuring career concepts: an examination of the concepts, constructs, and validity of the career concept questionnaire. PhD Dissertation, University of Southern California, Los Angeles.

Coombs, M. and Driver, M. (1986) Who are you satisfied employees: A comparison of work attitudes and values with individual development. Paper given at the Academy of Management, Chicago.

Crites, J. (1973) *Theory and Research Handbook for the Career Maturity Scale.* Monterey, CA: CTB, McGraw-Hill.

Dalton, G. and Thompson, P. (1986) *Novations.* New York: Scott, Foresman.

Dannell, S. and Hall, J. (1980) Men and women managers. *Organizational Dynamics*, 8, 60–77.

Davis, J. (1982) The influence of life stage on father–son work relationships. Doctoral dissertation, Harvard Business School.

Davis, K. (1984) A longitudinal analysis of biographical sub-groups using Owens' Developmental Integration Model. *Personnel Psychology*, 37, 1–14.

De Frank, R. and Ivancevich, J. (1986) Job loss: an individual-level review and model. *Journal of Vocational Behavior*, **28**, 1–20.

De Long, T. (1985) Comparing rural and urban educators using the variable of career orientation. Unpublished manuscript, Harvard Business School, Boston, Mass.

Derr, C. B. (1984) Entrepreneurs—a career perspective. Paper given at the Academy of Management, Boston.

Derr, C. B. (1986) *Managing the New Careerists*. San Francisco: Jossey-Bass.

Driver, M. (1979) Career concepts and career management in organizations. In C. Cooper (ed.) *Behavioral Problems in Organizations*. Englewood Cliffs, N.J.: Prentice-Hall.

Driver, M. (1980) Career concepts and organizational change. In C. B. Derr (ed.) *Work, Family and the Career*. New York: Praeger.

Driver, M. (1982) Career concepts: a new approach to career research. In R. Katz (ed.) *Career Issues in Human Resource Management*. Englewood Cliffs, N.J.: Prentice-Hall.

Driver, M. (1984) *The Purdue Rutgers Prior Experience Inventory, III (GIAL-SD): Technical Manual*. Santa Monica, CA: Decision Dynamics Corp.

Driver, M. (1985) Demographic and societal factors affecting the linear career crisis. *Canadian Journal of Administrative Science*, December.

Driver, M. (1986) The executive style. Paper given at the Academy of Management, Chicago.

Driver, M. and Brousseau, K. (1981) *The Career Concept Questionnaire*. Los Angeles: Decision Dynamics Corp.

Driver, M. and Coombs, M. (1983) Fit between career concepts, corporate culture, and engineering productivity and morale. *Proceedings, IEEE Careers Conference*, New York: IEEE.

Driver, M. and Davis, J. (1987) Change and consistency in career choice: a career concept integration. Unpublished manuscript, Department of Management and Organization, University of Southern California, Los Angeles.

Driver, M. and Mock, T. (1975) Information processing: decision style theory and accounting information systems. *Accounting Review*, **50**, 490–508.

Driver, M. and Streufert, S. (1969) Integrative complexity. *Administrative Science Quarterly*, **14**, 272–285.

Dunn, F. (1980) *The Successful International Executive*. New York: Transnational Information, Inc.

Eberhardt, B. and Mushinsky, P. (1982) Biodata determinants of vocational typology. *Journal of Applied Psychology*, **69**, 714–727.

Ekerdt, D., Bosse, R. and La Castro, J. (1983) Claims that retirement improves health. *Journal of Gerontology*, **38**, 231–36.

Farmer, H. (1985) A model of career and achievement motivation for women and men. *Journal of Counseling Psychology*, **32**, 363–90.

Foss, C. and Slaney, R. (1986) Increasing nontraditional career choices in women: relations of attitude toward women and responses to a career intervention. *Journal of Vocational Behavior*, **28**, 191–202.

Fouad, N., Hansen, J. and Arias-Garcia, F. (1986) Multiple discriminant analysis of cross-cultural similarity of vocational interests of lawyers and engineers. *Journal of Vocational Behavior*, **28**, 85–96.

Fryer, D. and Payne, R. (1986) Being unemployed. *International Review of Industrial and Organizational Psychology*, **1**, 235–271.

Fugua, D. and Seaworth, T. (1987) The relationship of career indecision and anxiety. *Journal of Vocational Behavior*, **30**, 175–186.

Gilligan, C. (1982) *In a Different Voice: Psychological Theory and Women's Development*. Cambridge, Mass.: Harvard University Press.

Glamser, F. (1981) Predictions of retirement attitudes. *Aging and Work*, **4**, 23–27.

Gottfredson, G. (1977) Career Stability and Redirection in Adulthood. *Journal of Applied Psychology*, **62**, 436–44.

Graef, M., Wells, D., Hyland, A. and Muchinsky, P. (1985) Life history antecedents of vocational indecision. *Journal of Vocational Behavior*, **27**, 276–99.

Gray, J. (1983) The married professional woman. *Psychology of Women Quarterly*, **7**, 235–43.

Greenhalgh, L. (1985) Job insecurity and disinvolvement: Field research on the survivors of layoffs. Paper given at the Academy of Management, San Diego.

Grotevant, H. and Thorbecke, W. (1982) Sex differences in styles of occupational identity formation in late adolescence. *Developmental Psychology*, **18**, 396–405.

Gutek, B., Larwood, L. and Stromberg, A. (1986) Women at work. *International Review of Industrial and Organizational Psychology*, **1**, 217–229.

Gutteridge, J. (1986) Organizational career development systems: The state of the practice. In D. Hall and Associates (eds) *Career Development in Organizations*. San Francisco, Jossey-Bass.

Hall, D. (1986) Breaking career routines: mid-career choice and identity development. In D. Hall and Associates (eds) *Career Development in Organizations*. San Francisco, Jossey-Bass.

Hall, D. and Isabella, L. (1985) Downward moves and career development. *Organizational Dynamics*, **14**, 5–23.

Hall, D. and Richter J. (1985) The baby boom and management: Is there room at the middle? Unpublished manuscript, Boston University, School of Management.

Hamner, J. and Vardi, P. (1981) Locus of control and career self-management among non-supervisory employees in industrial settings. *Journal of Vocational Behavior*, **18**, 13–29.

Hansen, J. and Campbell, D. (1985) *Manual for SVIB-SCII*. Stanford, CA: Stanford University Press.

Hardesty, S. and Betz, N. (1980) The relationship of career salience, attitudes toward women and demographic and family characteristics to marital adjustment in dual career couples. *Journal of Vocational Behavior*, **17**, 242–50.

Harren, V. (1979) A model of career decision making for college students. *Journal of Vocational Behavior*, **14**, 119–33.

Harris-Bowlsby, J. (1985) *Discover for Organizations: Human Resource Development Manual*. Hunt Valley, MD: American College Testing Program.

Hartman, B., Fuqua, D. and Blum, C. (1985) A path analytic model of career indecision. *Vocational Guidance Quarterly*, 231–40.

Hartman, B. Fuqua, D. and Hartman, P. (1983) The predictive potential of the career decision scale in identifying chronic career indecision. *Vocational Guidance Quarterly*, **32**, 103–8.

Hartman, B., Fuqua, D. and Jenkins, S. (1986) The reliability/generalizability of the construct of career indecision. *Journal of Vocational Behavior*, **28**, 142–8.

Haynes, S., Mc Michael, A. and Tyroler, H. (1981) Survival after early and normal retirement. *Journal of Gerontology*. **4**, 23–27.

Healey, C., O'Shea, D. and Crook, R. (1985) The relation of career attitudes to age and career progress during college. *Journal of Counseling Psychology*, **32**, 239–44.

Hill, R. and Hansen, J. (1986) An analysis of vocational interests for female research and development managers. *Journal of Vocational Behavior*, **28**, 70–83.

Hoffman, L. (1974) The effects of maternal employment on the child. *Developmental Psychology*, **10**, 204–28.

Hoffman, L. (1980) The effects of maternal employment on the academic attitudes and performance of school-aged children. *School Psychology Review*, **9**, 319–35.

Holland, J., Daiger, D. and Power, P. (1980) *My Vocational Situation*. Palo Alto, CA: Consulting Psychology Press.

Holland, J., Magoun, T. and Spokane, A. (1981) Counseling psychology: Career interventions research and theory. In M. Rosenzweig and L. Porter (eds) *Annual Review of Psychology*. Palo Alto, CA: Annual Reviews.

Howard, A. (1984) Cool at the top. Paper given at American Psychology Association, Toronto.

Jaskolka, G. and Beyer, J. (1985) Measuring and predicting managerial success. *Journal of Vocational Behavior*, **29**, 189–205.

Jepson, D., Dustin, R. and Miars, R. (1982) The effects of problem-solving training on adolescents' career exploration and career decision-making. *Personnel and Guidance Journal*, November, 149–53.

Kanfer, R. and Hahn, C. (1985) Individual differences in successful job searches following lay off. *Personnel Psychology*, **38**, 835–847.

Kasl, S. (1980) The impact of retirement. In C. Cooper and R. Payne (eds) *Current Concerns in Occupational Stress*. Chichester: John Wiley.

Kealey, D. and Ruben, B. (1983) Cross-cultural personnel selection—criteria, issues, and methods. In D. Landis and R. Brislin (eds) *Handbook of International Training*. Vol. I, *Issues in Theory and Design*. New York: Pergamon.

Kidder, T. (1981) *The Soul of a New Machine*. Boston, Mass.: Little, Brown.

Kobasa, S. and Pucetti, M. (1983) Personality and social resources in stress resistance. *Journal of Personality and Social Psychology*, **40**, 839–50.

Kohn, M. and Schooler, C. (1982) Job conditions and personality. *American Journal of Sociology*, **87**, 1257–86.

Kotter, J. (1982) *The General Managers*. New York: Free Press.

Kram, K. (1986) Mentoring in the workplace. In D. Hall and Associates (eds) *Career Development in Organizations*. San Francisco, Jossey-Bass.

Krau, E. (1987) The crystallization of work values in adolescence—sociocultural approach. *Journal of Vocational Behavior*, **30**, 103–23.

Larkin, L. (1987) Identity and fear of success. *Journal of Counseling Psychology*, **34**, 38–45.

Latack, J. (1984) Career transitions within organizations: an exploratory study of work, non-work, and coping strategies. *Organizational Behavior and Human Performance*, **34**, 296–322.

Latack, J. and D'Amico, R. (1985) Career mobility among young men. In S. Hills, R. D'Amico, D. Ball, J. Golon, J. Jackson, J. Latack, L. Lynch, S. Mangum and D. Shapiro *The Changing Market*. Columbus, OH: Center for Human Resources Research, the Ohio State University.

Latack, J. and Dozier, J. (1986) After the axe falls: job loss as a career transition. *Academy of Management Review*, **11**, 375–392.

Levinson, D. (1984) The career is in the life structure; the life structure is in the career: an adult development perspective. In M. Arthur, L. Bailyn, D. Levinson and H. Shepard (eds) *Working With Careers*. New York: Columbia University School of Business.

Logan, R. (1986) A Reconceptualization of Erikson's theory: the recapitulation of existential and instrumental themes. *Human Development*, **29**, 125–36.

London, M. and Stumpf, S. (1986) Individual and organizational career development in changing times. In D. Hall and Associates (eds) *Career Development in Organizations*. San Francisco, Jossey-Bass.

Lorsch, J. and Takayi, H. (1986) Keeping managers off the shelf. *Harvard Business Review*, July–August, 60–64.

Louis, M. (1980) Career transitions: varieties and communalities. *Academy of Management Review*, **5**, 325–40.

Lowman, R., Williams, R. and Leeman, G. (1985) The structure and relationship of college women's primary abilities and vocational interests. *Journal of Vocational Behavior*, **27**, 298–315.

MacNab, D. and Fitzsimmons, G. (1987) A multi-trait multi-method study of work-related needs, values, and preferences. *Journal of Vocational Behavior*, **30**, 1–15.

Marcia, J. (1966) Development and validation of ego identity status. *Journal of Personality and Social Psychology*, **3**, 551–68.

McKinnon, P. (1987) Steady state people: a third career orientation. *Research Management*, January–February, 26–32.

Mendenhall, M. and Oddou, G. (1985) The dimensions of expatriate acculturation: a review, *Academy of Management Review*, **10**, 39–47.

Meshkati, N. and Driver, M. (1986) A systematic method to analyze the effects of the non-technological infrastructure factors of the industrially developing countries on managerial effectiveness and success. *Proceedings: 30th Meeting of the Human Factors Society*.

Mihal, W., Sorce, P. and Comte, T. (1984) A process model of individual career decision-making. *Academy of Management Review*, **9**, 95–103.

Minkler, M. (1981) Research on the health effects of retirement. *Journal of Health and Social Behavior*, **22**, 117–30.

Miner, J. and Smith, N. (1982) Decline and stabilization of managerial motivation over a 20-year period. *Journal of Applied Psychology*, **67**, 297–05.

Miner, J., Smith, N. and Ebrahimi, B. (1985) Further considerations in the decline and stabilization of managerial motivation. *Journal of Vocational Behavior*, **26**, 290–98.

Minor, F. (1986) Computer applications in career development planning. In D. Hall and Associates (eds) *Career Development in Organizations*. San Francisco, Jossey-Bass.

Morrison, R. and Hock, R. (1986) Career building: learning from cumulative work experience. In D. Hall and Associates (eds) *Career Development in Organizations*. San Francisco, Jossey-Bass.

Mottaz, C. (1986) An analysis of the relationship between education and organizational commitment in a variety of occupational groups. *Journal of Vocational Behavior*, **28**, 214–28.

Mowday, R., Porter, L. and Dubin, R. (1974) Unit performance, situational factors, and employee attitudes in spatially separated work units. *Organizational Behavior and Human Performance*, **12**, 231–48.

Myers, R. A. and Cairo, P. (eds) (1983) Computer-assisted counseling. *The Counseling Psychologist*, **11**, 7–63.

Near, J. (1985) A discriminant analysis of plateaued vs. nonplateaued managers. *Journal of Vocational Behavior*, **26**, 177–88.

Neimeyer, G., and Ebben, R. (1985) The effects of vocational intervention on the complexity and positivity of occupational judgments. *Journal of Vocational Behavior*, **27**, 87–97.

Neimeyer, G. and Metzlar, A. (1987) The development of vocational structures. *Journal of Vocational Behavior*, **30**, 1–17.

Neiner, A. and Owens, W. (1985) Using biodata to predict job choices among college graduates. *Journal of Applied Psychology*, **70**, 127–36.

Nevill, D., Neimeyer, G., Probert, B. and Fukuyama, M. (1986) Cognitive structures in vocational information processing and decision making. *Journal of Vocational Behavior*, **28**, 110–22.

Noe, R. and Steffy, B. (1987) The influence of individual characteristics and assessment center evaluation on career exploration behavior and job involvement. *Journal of Vocational Behavior*, **30**, 187–202.

Nye, F. (1974) Sociocultural factors. In L. Hoffman and F. Nye (eds) *Working Mothers*. San Francisco, Jossey-Bass.

Olson, T. (1979) Career concepts and decision styles. Paper given at the Academy of Management, Atlanta.

Osipow, S. and Reed, R. (1985) Decision-making style and career indecision in college students. *Journal of Vocational Behavior*, **27**, 368–73.

Osipow, S., Carver, C., Winer, J., Yanico, B. and Koschier, M. (1976) *The Career Decision Scale*. Columbus, OH: Marathon Consulting and Press.

Owens, W. and Schoenfeldt, L. (1979) Towards a classification of persons. *Journal of Applied Psychology*, **64**, 569–607.

Pazy, A. and Zin, R. (1987) A contingency approach to consistency: A challenge to prevalent views. *Journal of Vocational Behavior*, **30**, 84–101.

Perry, S. (1978) Survey and analysis of employee sponsored day care in the U.S. PhD Dissertation, University of Wisconsin-Milwaukee.

Phillips, S. and Strohman, D. (1982) Decision-making style and vocational maturity. *Journal of Vocational Behavior*, **20**, 215–22.

Phillips, S., Pazienza, N. and Walsh, D. (1984) Decision Making Styles and Progress in Occupational Decision Making. *Journal of Vocational Behavior*, **25**, 96–105.

Prince, B. (1979) An investigation of career concepts and career anchors. Paper given at the Western Academy of Management, Portland, OR.

Prince, B. (1984) Allocative and opportunity structures and their interaction with career orientation. PhD dissertation, University of Southern California.

Reichers, A. (1987) An interactionist perspective on newcomer socialization rates. *Academy of Management Review*, **13**, 278–87.

Reilly, R. and Chao, G. (1982) Validity and fairness of some alternative employee selection procedures. *Personnel Psychology*, **35**, 1–62.

Remer, P., O'Neill, C. and Gohs, D. (1984) Multiple outcome evaluation of a life-career development course. *Journal of Counseling Psychology*, **31**, 532–40.

Robbins, S. and Tucker, K. (1986) Relation of goal instability to self-directed and interactional career counseling workshops. *Journal of Counseling Psychology*, **33**, 418–24.

Rotberg, H., Brown, D. and Ware, W. (1987) Career self-efficacy expectations and perceived career options in community college students. *Journal of Counseling Psychology*, **34**, 164–70.

Russell, L. (1982) *The Baby Boom Generation and the Economy*. Washington, D.C.: Brookings Institute.

Rynes, S. (1987) Career transitions from engineering to management: are they predictable among students? *Journal of Vocational Behavior*, **30**, 138–54.

Rynes, S. and Rosen, B. (1983) A comparison of males and females reactions to career advancement opportunities. *Journal of Vocational Behavior*, **22**, 105–16.

Savickas, M. (1985) Identity in vocational development. *Journal of Vocational Behavior*, **27**, 329–37.

Schein, E. (1971) The individual, the organization and the career: A conceptual scheme. *Journal of Applied Behavioral Science*, **7**, 401–26.

Schein, E. (1986) A critical look at current career development theory and research. In D. Hall and Associates (eds) *Career Development in Organizations*. San Francisco, Jossey-Bass.

Schroder, H., Driver, M. and Streufert, S. (1967) *Human Information Processing*. New York: Holt, Rinehart, Winston.

Schwartz, R., Andiappan, P. and Nelson, M. (1986) Reconsidering the support for Holland's congruence achievement hypothesis. *Journal of Counseling Psychology*, **33**, 425–8.

Shaffer, G. (1987) Patterns of work and non-work satisfaction. *Journal of Applied Psychology*, **72**, 115–24.

Shepard, H. (1984) On the realization of human potential: A path with a heart. In M. Arthur, L. Bailyn, D. Levinson and H. Shepard *Working With Careers*. New York: Columbia University School of Business.

Slaney, R. and Lewis, E. (1986) Effects of career exploration on career undecided re-entry women: an intervention and follow-up study. *Journal of Vocational Behavior*, **28**, 97–109.

Sonnenfeld, J. and Kotter, J. (1982) The maturation of career theory. *Human Relations*, **35**, 19–46.

Sorcher, M. (1985) *Predicting Executive Success*. New York: John Wiley.

Spenner, K. (1985) The upgrading and downgrading of occupations: issues, evidence, and implications for education. *Review of Educational Research*, **55**, 125–54.

Steiner, D. and Farr, J. (1986) Career goals, organizational reward systems, and technical updating in engineers. *Journal of Occupational Psychology*, **59**, 13–24.

Stout, S., Slocum, J. and Cron, W. (1987) Career transitions of supervisors and subordinates. *Journal of Vocational Behavior*, **30**, 124–37.

Streufert, S. and Streufert, S. (1978) *Behavior in the Complex Environment*. Washington, D.C.: Winston.

Streufert, S. and Swezey, R. (1986) *Complexity, Managers, and Organizations*. Orlando, FL: Academic Press.

Sundby, D. (1980) The career quad: a psychological look at some divergent dual career families. In C. B. Derr (ed.) *Work, Family, and the Career*. New York: Praeger.

Super, D. (1980) A life span life space approach to career development. *Journal of Vocational Behavior*, **16**, 282–98.

Super, D. (1986) Life career roles: self-realization in work and leisure. In D. Hall and Associates (eds) *Career Development in Organizations*. San Francisco, Jossey-Bass.

Super, D., Thompson, A., Lindeman, R., Jordaan, J. and Myers, R. (1981) *Career Development Inventory*. Palo Alto, CA: Consulting Psychology Press.

Time Magazine, 22 June, 1983, p. 63.

Torbiorn, I. (1982) *Living Abroad: Personal Adjustment and Personnel Policy in the Overseas Setting*. New York: John Wiley.

Tung, R. (1982) Selection and training procedures of U.S., European, and Japanese multinationals. *California Management Review*, **25**, 57–71.

Von Glinow, M., Driver, M., Brousseau, K. and Prince, B. (1983) The design of a career-oriented human resource system. *Academy of Management Review*, **89**, 23–32.

Von Glinow, M. and Kryczkowska, A. (1985) The Fortune 500: a caste of thousands. Unpublished manuscript, Department of Management and Organization, University of Southern California.

Warr, P. and Parry, G. (1982) Paid employment and women's psychological well-being. *Psychological Bulletin*, **91**, 498–516.

Weick, K. (1983) Managerial thought in the context of action. In S. Srivastava *The Executive Mind*. San Francisco: Jossey-Bass.

Westbrooke, B., Sanford, E., O'Neill, P., Horne, D., Fleenor, J. and Garren, R. (1985) Predictive and construct validity of six experimental measures of career maturity. *Journal of Vocational Behavior*, **27**, 338–55.

Winer, D. and Gati, I. (1986) Cognitive complexity and interest crystallization. *Journal of Vocational Behavior*, **28**, 48–59.

Wright, J. (1978) Are working women really more satisfied? *Journal of Marriage and the Family*, **40**, 301–13.

Yanico, B. and Haudin, S. (1986) College students self-estimated and actual knowledge of gender traditional and non-traditional occupations. *Journal of Vocational Behavior*, **28**, 229–40.

Chapter 8

MANAGEMENT DEVELOPMENT: A REVIEW AND COMMENTARY

Timothy T. Baldwin
Indiana University, USA
and
Margaret Y. Padgett
Butler University, USA

Management development—the complex process by which individuals learn to perform effectively in managerial roles—has attracted increasing organisational and research interest. The growth in organisational interest is due in large part to an increasing recognition of the efficacy of management development as a strategy to improve firm performance (Hall & Foulkes, 1991; Ulrich, 1989; Fulmer, 1990). Indeed, management development is now a multi-billion dollar undertaking for organisations worldwide and recent survey evidence suggests that over 90% of firms engage in some form of development activities for managers (Loo, 1991; Constable, 1988; Saari, Johnson, McLaughlin, & Zimmerle, 1988). Increasing academic interest in management development is reflected in a burgeoning body of research articles and the emergence of several recent books on the subject (e.g. Bigelow, 1991; McCall, Lombardo & Morrison, 1988; Morgan, 1988; Whetten & Cameron, 1991).

This review focuses primarily on the scholarly literature on management development to appear in the last five years. Earlier reviews of the literature were reported by Wexley and Baldwin (1986) and Keys and Wolfe (1988). To uncover relevant literature, all scholarly journals known to include management development-related manuscripts were searched. In addition, a call for papers was included in newsletters of the Academy of Management (USA) and several outlets in the UK and Australia. We also directly solicited papers from over 100 authors in English-speaking countries who had previously published work in the area of management development.

As with earlier reviews, this one was intended to be comprehensive though certainly not exhaustive of the literature. We did not attempt to make a systematic review of the voluminous literature in practitioner-oriented publications nor of related, but distinct topical areas such as organisation development (Woodman & Passmore, 1987) or personnel training (Tannenbaum & Yukl, 1992; Noe & Ford, 1992). In addition, we did not include review of some methods of content delivery (e.g. management simulations, case studies, computer-based training) which have been subject to recent review elsewhere (Keys, 1989; Keys & Wolfe, 1990).

Based on the literature collected, the chapter is organised into three parts. Part one reviews recent work which has focused on the understanding and assessment of effective management. An underlying theme of much of this recent work is that the managerial role is changing and, therefore, new models of effective management and valid assessment technologies are required to adequately understand and develop successful managerial behaviour in the future. The literature suggests that many initiatives are underway to identify key competencies for specific organisations and managerial populations.

Part two reviews the current literature related to what we have called 'contexts' of managerial learning. Specifically, we have organised this literature into three such contexts: job assignments, relationships and formal training events. Although previous reviews have lamented the lack of attention devoted to on-the-job development (Kelleher, Finestone & Lowy, 1986; Wexley & Baldwin, 1986), our receipt of manuscripts suggests a significant increase in conceptual and empirical work related to managerial development which occurs in the course of job assignments, mentoring and coaching. The current literature on formal managerial training events indicates a greater emphasis on leadership, action learning and experiential approaches such as outdoor challenges.

In Part three we review and comment on three emerging issues in management development: (i) management development as a competitive advantage; (ii) self-directed management development; and (iii) management education in degree-granting institutions. Throughout the chapter we attempt to identify research gaps and highlight issues that need more attention. We conclude with some final comments on the state of management development research.

UNDERSTANDING AND ASSESSING EFFECTIVE MANAGEMENT

A considerable portion of recent work on management development continues to focus on issues related to the understanding and assessment of effective management. The research is reviewed under four categories: (i) general skill taxonomies; (ii) assessment instruments and strategies; (iii) the changing managerial environment; and (iv) specific managerial populations.

General Skill Taxonomies

Models of effective management have long been espoused in popular literature and taxonomies of important managerial skills are ubiquitous (cf. Campbell, Dunnette, Lawler & Weick, 1970; Margerison & Kakabadse, 1984; Katz, 1974; Mintzberg, 1973; Kotter, 1982; Wilson, 1978). Nonetheless, new studies of effective managers and new taxonomies of managerial competencies continue to attract both conceptual and empirical attention (Luthans, Hodgetts & Rosencrantz, 1988; McCall, Lombardo & Morrison, 1988; Powers, 1987; Whetten & Cameron, 1991; Yukl, 1989).

Perhaps the most widely publicised recent effort to systematically identify a taxonomy of managerial competencies is described by Powers (1987) who reports on a study commissioned by the American Management Association. The sample consisted of 2000 working managers in 41 different types of jobs in twelve different organisations. Using the Job Competence Assessment methodology pioneered by Boyatzis (1982), the research identified a group of managerial behaviours which were then grouped into 18 competencies and five larger clusters. The five clusters were: (i) goal and action management; (ii) directing subordinates; (ii) human resources management; (iv) leadership; and (v) focus on others. Specialised knowledge was also an important element in the model.

Another model of managerial effectiveness is presented in a popular text by Whetten and Cameron (1991). The authors identified and interviewed 402 highly effective managers in a variety of different firms and industries and extracted ten most frequently mentioned management skills. They ultimately condensed the list and linked management success to three *personal* skills: developing self-awareness, managing stress, and solving problems creatively, and four *interpersonal* skills: communicating supportively, gaining power and influence, motivating others, and managing conflict. They point out that the skill areas overlap such that managers must rely on parts of all skill areas in order to perform effectively in a managerial role.

A four-year observational study by Luthans, Hodgetts and Rosencrantz (1988) looked at how successful and effective managers differ from unsuccessful and less effective ones. Success was defined as speed of promotion within an organisation. Detailed observation of 44 managers from a variety of organisations indicated twelve behavioural categories associated with managerial success. The authors subsequently organised the behavioural categories into four managerial activities: communication; traditional management; networking; and human resource management. Data were then collected from 248 additional managers and the amount of recorded activity in each area was used to distinguish successful from unsuccessful managers. The largest differences occurred on networking activities such as external communications, socialising, and politicking.

After over a decade of research on many management groups, Yukl (1989) has created an integrated taxonomy that consists of eleven categories of behaviour (e.g. monitoring, networking, motivating, teambuilding). The main method used in his research was a questionnaire but it was also supplemented with diaries, interviews and integration of behaviour categories found in other work on managerial effectiveness. The behaviour categories in the taxonomy have been shown to be related to independent measures of managerial effectiveness (Yukl, Wall & Lepsinger, 1990; Yukl & Lepsinger, 1991).

Finally, a project initiated by the Center for Creative Leadership (McCall, Lombardo & Morrison, 1988) included in-depth interviews with 86 successful (success was defined as still in the running for the top job) executives in three corporations, and open-ended questionnaires from 100 high-performing managers in several additional corporations. Content analysis of this qualitative data resulted in 33 categories of managerial competence which have subsequently been condensed to 16 managerial skill categories (e.g. resourcefulness, being a quick study, acting with flexibility). In addition, a group (19) of top executives at three organisations provided descriptions of two people they knew well—an executive who succeeded and one who had recently derailed. Ten reasons for derailment were derived from these interviews.

In reviewing the recent taxonomic work, several observations can be made. First, though there are some notable differences, there continues to be considerable overlap in models of core managerial competencies. For example, most competency models include a dimension of dealing with subordinates which involves motivating, rewarding, delegating and developing. Each also encompasses familiar interpersonal skills such as managing conflict and building a team. Most models also emphasise the problem-solving aspect of managerial jobs.

Second, one of the criticisms which is commonly levelled at taxonomic work on managerial effectiveness is the failure to identify specific behaviours. Indeed, there is still a tendency for some work to fall prey to the type of imprecise trait labels and global behavioural descriptions which organisational scholars have long lamented (Campbell et al., 1970). However, despite some overlap and cases of hazy description, a significant contribution of recent taxonomic work has been the considerably more precise behavioural specification of managerial competencies.

For example, in the AMA model (Powers, 1987) the key issue is not possession of a competency but its use. An individual manager's command of the competency therefore involves three dimensions—its existence as an underlying characteristic, its expression, and the experience of others of its use in the managerial environment (Powers, 1987). Similarly, the model developed by researchers at the Center for Creative Leadership not only describes a behavioural dimension, but illustrates the dimension with even more specific sample items.

Third, far too much of prior taxonomic work has rested solely on opinion, anecdote and speculation. In contrast, several of the recent models (e.g. Yukl,

1989; McCall, Lombardo & Morrison, 1988) have been supported by some preliminary empirical evidence and refinement based on that evidence is ongoing. Nonetheless, much more needs to be learned and rigorous investigation by researchers *not* connected with model developers would be of particular value.

One recent example of an independent empirical test of core competencies was reported by Penley, Alexander, Jernigan and Henwood (1991). In that study, the authors explored the hypothesis that specific communication competencies are essential to effectiveness as a manager. The authors identified and assessed several specific communication competencies that have been conceptually associated with managerial performance (e.g. Luthans, Hodgetts & Rosencrantz, 1988) and gathered data from both male and female upper-level bank managers. Results indicated that though female managers provided lower self-reports of communication skills than male managers, there was a significant correlation between communications skills and managerial performance for both genders.

Although more empirical tests of the link between demonstrated competencies and indices of managerial effectiveness are sorely needed, one caution is that many of the competency models continue to focus primarily on *frequency* of managerial behaviour with less regard to the level of expertise or *mastery* with which the behaviour is performed. In this regard, Shipper (1991) presented a study which suggested that an increase in frequency of managerial behaviour, with no increase in mastery, had little or no positive impact on performance. Rather, he found that managers of subunits high on morale and performance exhibited significantly higher levels of mastery of managerial behaviours. Higher frequency of some managerial behaviours was found to be associated with *low* performing subunits. Martinko and Gardner (1990) also found little support for the proposition that effective managers simply devote more time to specific managerial behaviours.

Clearly, the thrust of management development must be directed toward improving the mastery of skills and not just the frequency. Future research work that includes both the frequency of specific skills and the mastery or quality of the same skills is needed to further our understanding of this important distinction.

Finally, it should be noted that not all organisational scholars are convinced that the pursuit of competency models is even appropriate. For example, Vaill (1989) has seriously questioned whether a skills-list definition of competency can ever accurately reflect how effective managers function. Similarly, Stewart (1989a) suggests that improving the categorisation of behaviours and relating these to measures of effectiveness is less important than attempts to try and improve our understanding of the actions and thoughts of different managers over time. Taking a qualitative research perspective, she outlined eight specific suggestions for what she feels would be a more fruitful exploration of managerial jobs and behaviours.

Assessment Instruments and Strategies

Parallel to the development of models of effective management has been work on the assessment of managerial behaviour and skills. One emerging theme in the creation of assessment tools is an increased use of upward evaluations (input from subordinates and peers) and several thoughtful treatments of the process and validity of such upward feedback have appeared (Wohlers & London, 1989; London, Wohlers & Gallagher, 1990). One recent study even found that ratings by subordinates were better predictors of uncontaminated performance criteria in the short term than were full assessment centre rankings (McEvoy & Beatty, 1989). Consistent with such evidence, several recent assessment instruments embody upward evaluation along with self and superior assessment in what is known as a multiple perspective or '360-degree' feedback strategy (Van Velsor & Leslie, 1991).

For example, Yukl has used his taxonomic work to develop an assessment instrument known as Compass (aka, The Managerial Practices Survey). Compass is a set of three types of questionnaires used to provide managers with information about their managerial behaviour and developmental needs related to this behaviour (Yukl, Wall & Lepsinger, 1990; Yukl & Lepsinger, 1991). Subordinates and peers describe how much a manager uses each of several managerial practices, and they recommend whether the manager should do more, the same amount or less of each behaviour. Managers compare this feedback to their own self-assessment of behaviour and to norms for similar managers. Ratings of the importance of each type of behaviour for the manager's job provide additional information for selecting relevant training.

Another example of a needs assessment instrument stemming from competency identification work discussed above is Benchmarks (McCauley, Lombardo & Usher, 1989). Benchmarks is a rating form developed to measure relevant skills and traits identified in research on managerial experiences and managerial derailment. Self-ratings and ratings made by subordinates, peers and superiors are used to assess a manager's strengths and weaknesses and identify developmental needs.

Van Velsor and Leslie (1991) present an impressive compilation in which they use established criteria to compare 16 of the most frequently used multiple-perspective management assessment instruments (including Compass and Benchmarks). Each of the 16 measures is reviewed with respect to existing evidence on psychometric properties and utility for management development practice. The comparative information is useful for evaluating instruments as well as suggesting avenues for future research. Another useful collection of information regarding different assessment instruments is presented in a book edited by Clark and Clark, (1990).

With respect to other assessment approaches, Miner (1991) reports on a psychological assessment methodology he argues is particularly appropriate for diagnosing performance *problems*. The focus of the assessment is on the creation of test batteries for assessing ability and personality factors. Though Miner argues against a static or standard battery for assessment of all managerial problems, a central diagnostic is the author's 'Motivation to Manage' sentence completion instrument. Test batteries also typically include multiple measures of intelligence, risk taking, achievement motivation and locus of control.

It is now well documented that assessment centres are likely to be valid predictors of managerial performance in a variety of different organisations (Gaugler, Rosenthal, Thornton & Bentson, 1987; Munchus & McArthur, 1991). Furthermore, since the publication of Howard and Bray's (1988) long-term follow-up of the AT&T assessment centre project, there has been increased attention to the *developmental* applications of assessment centres (Hollenbeck, 1990).

Rayner and Goodge (1988) suggest that changing company attitudes and a growing body of research are progressively influencing the nature of assessment centres. More specifically, they discuss changes in traditional centre evaluation and feedback processes and describe how several of those changes have been incorporated by London Regional transport in their use of assessment centres. Goodge (1991) discusses guidelines and pitfalls of 'development centres', which he defines as an off-site process resulting in effective development actions that go beyond the feedback and assessment of a traditional assessment centre.

With respect to empirical research on centres, Noe and Steffy (1987) found that assessment centre ratings predicted career exploration behaviours. More precisely, participants who had received higher ratings were more accepting of those ratings and more likely to seek information about target jobs. Jones and Whitmore (1992) used data from a follow-up evaluation of a developmental assessment centre to address questions concerning the antecedents and consequences of feedback acceptance from the centre. Results indicated that participants' self-efficacy and perceived support of developmental activities had a significant impact on feedback acceptance. However, acceptance of feedback was not significantly related to managerial level attainment.

In an interesting longitudinal study, Fletcher (1990) explored individuals' reaction to assessment centres. He found that the experience of going through an assessment centre does have an impact on candidates, particularly with respect to variables such as self-esteem and need for achievement, though some of the effects tended to diminish over time.

Finally, Streufert, Pogash and Piasecki (1988) described research on assessment of managerial skills with two *compuer-based* simulations. The simulations were designed for a single individual (like an in-basket) rather than a group in order to regulate the information available to each participant. The authors contend that one significant advantage of this simulation methodology is that managerial behaviour and skills for handling crises can be assessed under standardised conditions.

Clearly, accurate assessment and feedback are keys to managerial effectiveness. Unfortunately, assessment prior to management development interventions continues to be an all too rare and haphazard activity (Saari et al., 1988). Part of the neglect may be attributed to the fact that traditional assessment instruments and methods have often been unreliable and not linked to any recognised theory of effective management. Recent work on assessment, however, includes several examples of empirically tested tools and certainly gives cause for optimism. Continued development and refinement of theoretically based and empirically validated measurement strategies is needed to stimulate more organisational attention to the assessment phase of the management development process.

Changing Managerial Environments

Traditional studies of core management competencies have generally focused on existing managerial positions and those who have already experienced success. Yet a pervasive theme in current organisational literature is that the world of the manager is rapidly changing. Unprecedented competitive pressures, increased technological complexity, globalisation of economies, changing social and cultural values, and a more diverse workforce are all frequently mentioned as relevant considerations for management development (Schein, 1989). With such changes in mind, a number of recent authors have suggested that while traditional core competencies may still be necessary for managerial success, they will not be sufficient in an increasingly turbulent world (Ames & Heide, 1991; Hunt, 1990; Morgan, 1988; Kleiner, 1991).

Predominant among the macro-competencies discussed as crucial for managing in the future are several variants of 'learning how to learn' (Argyris, 1991; Dechant, 1990). For example, Argyris (1991) contends that managerial jobs are increasingly taking on the contours of 'knowledge work' and, as such, a crucial managerial competency is what he has termed 'double loop learning'. In essence, this means that managers must learn how the way they go about defining and solving problems can be a source of problems in its own right. Effective managers in the future will be those who can reflect critically on their own behaviour, identify the ways they often inadvertently contribute to the organisation's problems, and then change how they act (Argyris, 1991).

In a similar vein, Streufert, Nogami, Swezey, Pogash and Piasecki (1988) argue that the majority of senior managers are already very well trained and often excel in many of the specific micro-competencies which are integral parts of most management development programmes. Based on that assumption, the authors argue that to enable managers to function well in changing and uncertain task environments, development interventions should focus not only on the specific content of managerial tasks (i.e. what managers should think or do in response to certain task demands) but also on structural components of managerial effectiveness (i.e. how managers think and function). The authors report on an initiative to develop such structural skills via a computer simulation methodology and results indicated that the inclusion of structural components generated considerable improvement in managerial performance.

Schein (1989) makes a compelling argument that the concept of *hierarchy* colours our most basic assumptions and beliefs about managerial work. He further contends that the advent of technological complexity will force the need to develop a new picture of what an effective manager should be. He suggests that hierarchical authority will probably play a much smaller role in that picture while *coordination skills* will play a much larger role. Morgan (1988) similarly contends that skills such as reading the environment and managing ambiguity and paradox will be essential for the effective manager of the future.

Kolb, Lublin, Spoth and Baker (1985) point out that much more is required of managers in a context of increased environmental complexity. They note that the days of classical organisation structures with limited spans of control, non-overlapping job definitions, single chains of command and formal authority matched to responsibility are already gone. As a result, the authors contend that greater competence is needed in four areas: *behavioural competence* in taking initiative under conditions of risk and uncertainty; *perceptual competence* in gathering and organising information and considering other perspectives; *affective competence* in empathising with others and resolving conflict; and *symbolic competence* to conceptualise the organisation as a system.

Keys and Case (1990) suggest that increasing team interdependence and widening spans of control are diminishing the effectiveness of formal authority and, therefore, authority must be replaced with influence. Using a critical incident approach and building on the work of Kotter (1982) and others, the authors conclude that influence in four directions—superiors, peers, outsiders and subordinates—will be among the most crucial future managerial competencies.

We interpret the literature on the changing management environment as suggesting that traditional core competencies are not wrong or invalid, but only incomplete. That is, because the managerial environment is changing so rapidly, the needed set of knowledge, skills and abilities is a moving target. Though we are beginning to learn how to do future-oriented job analysis to help focus some of our development initiatives (Schneider & Konz, 1989), it is clear that managers of the future will have to be strong self-learners not only to learn autonomously, but to have the capacity to learn about themselves. However, while the importance of skills such as sefl-awareness and knowing how to learn seems clear, there is a definite need to extend the range of human qualities which can be subjected to valid assessment (Raven, 1988). More research work aimed at conceptualising and operationalising the type of macro-competencies discussed in this section would be well directed.

Specific Managerial Populations

Nearly twenty years ago, Katz (1974) suggested that the degree to which managers need different skills is dependent on administrative level. According to Katz, technical skills are most needed at the lower level; conceptual skills are most needed at the executive level; and human skills are needed to about the same degree at all managerial levels. Yet, as the taxonomic work discussed earlier suggests, traditional research on managerial work has generally focused on the common denominators of management jobs. Moreover, a recent descriptive study of 155 organisations found that management development programmes do not significantly differentiate between managerial skill requirements according to hierarchical level (Blakely, Martinec & Lane, 1992).

Results of a study of the importance of managerial activities conducted by Kraut, Pedigo, McKenna and Dunnette (1989) were largely consistent with Katz's theory. A factor they labelled 'instructing subordinates', which contained several items about activities closely related to technical skills, was rated less important by senior managers than by middle- and lower-level managers. A factor they labelled 'monitoring the outside' which contained several items about activities closely related to conceptual skills, was rated more important by senior managers than by middle- and lower-level managers.

Other authors have focused strictly on the skill requirements of upper-level strategic managers (Cox & Cooper, 1989; Jonas, Fry & Srivasta, 1989; Stumpf, 1989): For example, Cox and Cooper (1989) studied 45 chief executives of successful British firms with over 1000 employees. Interviews were semi-structured and explored such aspects of the executives' lives as family background and childhood, education, career pattern, motivation and personality. Self-reported skill assessments indicated that the CEOs felt that decision-making, interpersonal skills and leadership skills, in that order, were most critical to their success. Other skills mentioned were moderate risk taking, ability to learn from failure, and a high work rate.

In an unconventional study of executive language, Jonas, Fry and Srivasta (1989) conducted in-depth interviews with 24 CEOs to determine the dimensions of executive experience. The authors concluded that there are two basic dimensions of executive experience: (i) the degree of their identification with the organisation; and (ii) their general degree of scepticism or optimism. Combining the two dimensions produces four types of executive experience (strategist, analyst, steward, artist) and each approach is expressed primarily through the particular language usage of the chief executive.

More generally, Stumpf (1989) summarised survey work on strategic thinking conducted at New York University which included the observation of several thousand managers. Based on that work he identified four factors that were associated with strategic manager effectiveness: (i) consistently applying a small number of key concepts, (ii) developing skills at thinking and acting strategically, (iii) knowing one's personal style and its impact on others; and

(iv) understanding the strategic management process. He further outlined a set of six crucial strategic thinking skills (e.g. manage subunit rivalry, find and overcome threats).

In an effort to facilitate the targeting of management development interventions for particular contexts, several recent authors have focused on identifying competencies within specific managerial populations. Included among these are secondary school principals (McCauley, 1990); utility and health care executives (Thareau, 1991; Johnson, 1991); team leaders (Komacki, Desselles & Bowman, 1989); global managers (Finney & Von Glinow, 1988; Sanders, 1988); engineers (Cobb & Gibbs, 1990); public sector management (Johnston & Dryssen, 1991); research and development managers (Pearson & McCauley, 1991); and women (Cotter, James, Lucas & Vinnicombe, 1991).

In addition, there has been a proliferation of recent study of important managerial competencies for managers in nearly every region of the world. Examples include the UK (Constable, 1988), Japan (Suzuki, 1989), Asia (Temporal, 1990), the Third World (Blunt & Jones, 1991), Singapore (Williams, 1991), Russia (McCarthy, 1991), Eastern Europe (Fogel, 1990), and Hong Kong (Yau & Sculli, 1990).

Finally, leaders of some progressive firms are stressing the importance of identifying managerial competencies crucial in their own organisations and are concerned with how abstract and general models might manifest themselves in particular firm settings (Kerr, 1990). Among reports of company initiatives to better understand managerial effectiveness within the context of the firm are General Electric (Hayes, 1988); British Airways (O'Neill, 1990); and Bell Canada, (Wilson, 1990).

Summary

In summary, a great deal of recent work has attempted to enhance our understanding of effective management by exploring personal qualities, environmental changes and a variety of different organisational and contextual variables. It should be abundantly clear from the diversity of research that it is incomplete to talk only about personal abilities leading to managerial success or only about the behaviours of good managers or only about the environments conducive to management success. Rather, managerial effectiveness is a function of complex interactions between ability, motivation and environmental variables and the nature of feedback, incentive and reward systems developed by organisational policies and practices. Managerial tasks and problems are highly interdependent, relatively unstandardised, highly susceptible to change, and often specific to situations rather than problems (Whitley, 1989).

Fortunately, recent research seems to be moving in a way that acknowledges this reality. The development of more precisely specified and empirically supported taxonomies facilies the mapping of characteristics of management jobs in different settings and the operationalisation of appropriate development objectives and strategies. Nonetheless, for research in specific contexts to have cumulative value and contribute to our understanding of effective management, rigorous work must continue to define, describe and measure the dimensions of jobs, cultures and organisations relevant to managerial success.

CONTEXTS OF MANAGERIAL DEVELOPMENT

In 1986, McCauley completed a review of the empirical literature examining experiences on the job that contribute to the development of managers. At that time, she noted that there was no systematic body of research which focused on what experiences or events might be significant in managerial careers. Indeed, the majority of traditional research examining management development has focused primarily on learning that takes place in structured training programmes. Yet, when managers are asked to describe their most significant learning experiences, they invariably describe on-the-job experiences as having contributed the most to their development (e.g. McCall, Lombardo & Morrison, 1988; Mumford, 1988; Davies & Easterby-Smith, 1984).

Recent literature suggests a rather dramatic increase in interest in on-the-job experiences and other learning contexts. Our review is organised around three contexts: job assignments, relationships, and formal training. Due to the relatively little attention that the first two contexts have received in the past, we focus our review there. However, several trends in the area of formal training that have received increased attention (e.g. outdoor challenge training and action learning) are reviewed as well.

Job Assignments

Job assignments have been frequently mentioned as an important context for the development of managers (e.g. McCall, Lombardo & Morrison, 1988; Lindsey, Homes & McCall, 1987; Lombardo, 1989). Research in this area has developed around two different but related ways of thinking about how job assignments contribute to development. Some research has focused on how job challenge enhances development. The intent has been to determine what essential or basic job elements contribute to the experience of job challenge (e.g. McCall, 1988; McCauley, Ohlott & Ruderman, 1989). The other approach focuses on identifying specific types of job assignments that contribute to development. The assumption is that these specific assignments provide managers with the opportunity to experience one or more of these challenging job elements (e.g. Lindsey, Homes & McCall, 1987; McCall, Lombardo & Morrison, 1988; Lombardo, 1989; Marsick; 1990; Mumford, 1991; Stumpf, 1989).

A third issue to be examined is the contribution that hardship experiences make to development. While hardship experiences are not a specific type of job assignment, these experiences typically occur within the context of a particular job and hence will be discussed with job assignments.

Sources of job challenge

Among the earliest research examining how job assignments contribute to management development were two studies (Berlew & Hall, 1966; Bray, Campbell & Grant, 1974) which suggested that early job challenge significantly enhances a manager's development. Subsequent research has added to our understanding of how challenging job experiences contribute to managerial learning. The experience of job challenge results from a gap between the skills and abilities of the individual and those required by the situation, which leads to the feeling of being 'stretched' by the job. Experiencing this gap motivates the manager to learn what is necessary to carry out the responsibilities of the job (McCauley, Ohlott & Ruderman, 1989; McCauley, Ruderman, Ohlott & Morrow, 1992). Akin (1987) describes this 'gap' as a 'sense of role' and considers it to be an important precondition for learning.

Until recently, our understanding of what exactly constituted a challenging job experience was limited. In the original studies at AT&T, job challenge involved four components: job stimulation and challenge, supervisory responsibility, degree of structure of assignments and degree to which the boss was an achievement model (Bray, Campbell & Grant, 1974; Bray & Howard, 1983). More recent research by McCall and his associates (e.g. McCall, 1988; McCall, Lombardo & Morrison, 1988) described eight key elements of job challenge that were derived from descriptions by executives of key developmental events. These fundamental challenges are: dealing with bosses; incompetence and resistance from subordinates; having to develop relationships with those whom he/she has never had to deal with before; playing for high stakes; business adversity; coping with scope and scale; missing trumps (i.e. entering a business situation at a disadvantage in some way); and starkness of transitions (i.e. degree of difference from what the manager has done before).

In a recent model of how job challenge contributes to on-the-job development, McCauley, Ohlott and Ruderman (1989) described two major categories of job challenges: job transitions and job demands. Job transitions included such things as changes in organisation level, a move to a new organisational unit or geographical location, and key first experiences, such as the first supervisory position. Four broad job demands were proposed in the model: creating change; performing in high stakes situations, dealing with uncertainty and experiencing supervisory pressure. According to their model, the experience of job challenge could lead to a variety of responses, such as seeking information, trying out new behaviours or building new relationships. These activities are expected to lead to learning, with learning being maximised under conditions where the manager receives feedback on his/her success and where the new behaviours are reinforced and supported. The model also proposes that individual differences, such as self-esteem, past experience and learning orientation, will influence how individuals react to the challenge and how much is learned from it. A preliminary test of the model revealed support for several of the hypothesised linkages.

Subsequent research has further refined our understanding of these fundamental job challenges. Researchers at the Center for Creative Leadership (USA) (McCauley, Ohlott & Ruderman, 1989; Ruderman, Ohlott & McCauley, 1990) have developed an instrument called the Job Challenge Profile (JCP) which is designed to measure the developmental aspects of managerial jobs. The content of the instrument was derived from the McCall, Lombardo and Morrison (1988) studies on executive learning and growth. Job incumbents rate the extent to which each item is seen as descriptive of their job.

In a comprehensive study examining the reliability and validity of the JCP (McCauley, Ruderman, Ohlott & Morrow, 1992), fourteen subscales were identified through factor analysis and grouped into five more general demand scales. The five demand scales were: dealing with scope and scale (including the high stakes, managing business diversity and job overload subscales); job transitions; creating change; coping with situations outside the chain of command (handling external pressure); and working without advice and support.

In addition to research examining challenges across jobs in general, there are a few studies which have focused on the challenges present in special types of jobs or organisations. For example, McCauley and Hughes (1991) examined the developmental opportunities present in the non-profit sector. Pearson and McCauley (1991) studied the challenges in research and development (R&D) jobs and found that, compared to other managers, R&D managers faced more job challenge from lack of top management support and more problemmatic relationships with their bosses and subordinates. However, they also reported learning less from their jobs.

Finally, Eichinger and Lombardo (1990) discussed the developmental potential of staff positions. In comparing line and staff positions on the key sources of developmental challenge described above, staff positions were lacking on all but two (influencing others without authority and involving significant intellectual, strategic or problem-solving challange with little or no guidance). They argued that over time, line managers will accumulate more developmental experiences than will staff managers. This is interesting since McCall, Lombardo and Morrison (1988) found that managers reported spending time in a staff position as a significant developmental experience. Perhaps spending a few years in a staff position is developmental although having a career in staff positions may not be. Eichinger and Lombardo (1990) suggest a variety of ways for maximising the developmental potential of staff positions.

The Job Challenge Profile, as it becomes more widely utilised, should contribute significantly not only to our understanding of how job challenge enhances growth and learning but also to our ability to use this knowledge to better develop managerial talent. One practical application for the instrument is to enable managers to obtain feedback on the developmental opportunities available to them in their current job. This feedback should facilitate career planning among managers. Further, the instrument could be used by organisations engaged in succession planning to periodically audit positions for their developmental potential. This could aid staffing decisions by enabling organisations to place individuals in positions where they would experience new job demands that would have value-added in terms of their growth and learning. This would be particularly valuable for those working in staff positions which, as described above, have fewer developmental opportunities within them (Eichinger & Lombardo, 1990). Being able to connect these challenging experiences with the specific skills, abilities or knowledges acquired would significantly add to our understanding of how job challenge contributes to managerial development.

Specific job assignments

Research examining specific job assignments is, for the most part, very sparse. Much anecdotal evidence exists for the value of serving on a project or task force, or for taking a staff position, but there is little evidence of an empirical nature. One notable exception is a study conducted by McCall, Lombardo and Morrison (1988) at the Center for Creative Leadership. They were interested in understanding what key events managers felt contributed to their development and what, specifically, they believed they had learned from these events. Based upon extensive interviews with 79 executives and survey information from 112 executives, they identified five specific types of job assignments that managers believed facilitated their development. These were: (i) project or task force assignments; (ii) fix-it assignments; (iii) assignments that involved starting something from scratch; (iv) line to staff switches; and (v) managing an operation of significant scope (see Lindsey, Homes & McCall, 1987; for more information concerning these assignments).

McCall, Lombardo and Morrison (1988) examined these five types of job assignments to determine what specific lessons managers learned from them that contributed to their development. A total of 34 lessons were identified by managers with the lessons being grouped into five categories: setting and implementing agendas, handling relationships, executive temperament, basic values and personal awareness.

It is clear that different lessons are learned from different job assignments. Generally speaking, however, job assignments are most likely to teach the lessons in the first three categories, with self-confidence being the lesson most likely to be learned. For example, project or task force assignments are most likely to teach self-confidence, external negotiation and management values. Fix-it assignments are most useful for learning about the directing and motivating of subordinates, lateral cooperation, how the business works and self-confidence. Starting something from scratch is most likely to teach lessons dealing with directing and motivating subordinates, standing alone and acting, and self-confidence. Line to staff switches teach technical knowledge, how business works, comfort with ambiguity and stress, how to work with executives, the organisation as a system and what executives are like. Finally, handling large-scope operations teaches directing and motivating subordinates, technical knowledge and self-confidence.

Bentz (1987) argues that being in jobs possessing scope and scale is an important determinant of the effectiveness of high-level executives. He defines scope in terms of breadth of management—the number of horizontal units included within a position. Scale refers to the internal complexity, diversity and ambiguity of functions within and across units managed, within and across varieties of personal relationships, and across decisions made. He discusses both specific job elements that contribute to the scope and scale of high-level positions and what kinds of experiences prepare managers to handle positions having significant scope and scale (i.e. high-level positions).

Temporal and Burnett (1990) and others (e.g. Beck, 1988) have argued for the use of strategic project assignments in an international setting to help develop international managers. One important example of such an assignment would be responsibility for developing and implementing market entry in a new country or region. An assignment such as this, which takes place in another country, can help to give high potential managers a solid general experience across financial, marketing, production, cultural and personal disciplines. The experience of working overseas, they note, is an essential component in the development of global managers.

Job rotation, while not a specific type of job assignment, has also been linked to managerial development (Wexley & Latham, 1991). Job rotation is believed to provide managers with a diversity of experiences which should, presumably, give them a broader perspective on the organisation. According to McCall and Lombardo (1983) having a wide range of different work experiences is one factor that differentiates between successful and derailed executives. Moreover, job rotation potentially exposes employees to new functional areas, helps them develop an appreciation for the inter-relationships between various parts of the company and assists them in developing a large network of contacts across the organisation.

Despite the widespread belief in the usefulness of job rotation for management development, few empirical studies exist. One exception is a study by London (1989) which evaluated the effectiveness of a job rotation programme for early career scientists and engineers. Results of the study indicated that those participating in the job rotation programme had a greater understanding of the importance of collaboration, the value of eliciting and comparing different problem solutions, and a stronger belief that work unit performance was rewarded and that mutual respect of other functions was important.

More recently, Campion, Cheraskin and Stevens (1991) examined the rewards and costs of job rotation for individuals and organisations. A survey study of 387 employees across a wide variety of occupations and organisational levels indicated that job rotation rates and promotion rates were positively correlated. Further, four categories of rewards were found (in order of importance): stimulating work, organisational integration (understanding of strategy, developing networks), awareness of self and of management styles and career (satisfaction and involvement in career and opportunities for promotion). Three categories of costs to job rotation were found (in order of importance): increased costs associated with the learning curve, increases in workload and decreases in productivity for the individual and his/her coworkers, and decreased satisfaction and motivation of coworkers.

Research by Gabarro (1987) also has some interesting implications for the practice of job rotation as a developmental strategy. Gabarro focused on how people adjust to new job assignments and the learning involved in making the adjustment. Based upon extensive study of 17 successions, he identified five stages in the process of taking charge: (i) taking hold; (ii) immersion; (iii) reshaping; (iv) consolidation; and (v) refinement. He argues that it is not until after the completion of the reshaping stage, where the manager typically makes significant changes based upon the learning acquired during the previous stage, that the manager has had the opportunity to learn enough to make the experience developmental. After the consolidation stage, little new learning occurs. Thus, from a developmental perspective, it appears that most of the value from experiencing job transitions may occur in the first three years (at which time the manager has reached the consolidation stage) and that little is to be gained by remaining in the assignment longer.

On the other hand, Gabarro cautions against moving managers too soon, before they have had time to fully understand the situation and to act upon their new understanding rather than upon their past experience. Others have suggested that the 'fast-track' developmental strategy employed by many organisations may not be beneficial to either the individual or the organisation (e.g. Thompson, Kirkham & Dixon, 1985; Kovach, 1986).

Several authors have suggested that there may be individual differences in the ability of people to learn from experiences, such as job assignments (McCall, 1988; McCauley, Ohlott & Ruderman, 1989; Morrison & Brantner, 1991). Individual differences such as the manager's career history (McCall, Lombardo & Morrison, 1988), learning orientation (Dechant, 1990; Kelleher, Finestone & Lowy, 1986) and self-esteem (Brett, 1984) have been proposed.

Most of the recent research dealing with individual differences has focused on gender (e.g. Van Velsor & Hughes, 1990; Ohlott, Ruderman & McCauley, 1990; 1992). Ohlott, Ruderman and McCauley (1992) found evidence that women experience different demands from managerial jobs than do men in similar types of jobs at comparable levels. For example, women managers reported experiencing higher levels of job demands related to influencing without authority and lacking personal support. Furthermore, male managers were more likely to experience those demands generally believed to have important developmental opportunities (e.g. high stakes assignments) while women faced more problems involving the development of supportive relationships. Also of interest is the finding that, even when the effects of age, tenure and difference of current job from previous job are removed, women seem to learn more from the demands that they face. The authors suggest a variety of possible reasons for this, such as greater openness to learning by women in comparison to men. An earlier study by these authors (Ohlott, Ruderman & McCauley, 1990) supports some of these findings and further suggests that not only are female managers experiencing job demands to a greater extent than are males, but that they are also learning from a greater variety of sources than men.

Of course, job assignment-based development is not without its constraints and barriers. Hall and Foulkes (1991) argue that the barriers to cross-functional movement are greater now than in the past since line managers, faced with tighter headcount restrictions, may be reluctant to give up good people in a trade for an unknown individual. They also note that the trend in companies toward downsizing means that many of the 'key' high-visibility developmental jobs have been eliminated, while the movement toward delayering means that there are fewer promotional opportunities. Corporations may need to explore other forms of organisational movement, such as downward movement (Hall & Isabella, 1985), for their developmental opportunities.

There may also be resistance by bosses to the explicit use of job assignments for development since this necessarily results in placing individuals into positions where they do not currently have all the skills and abilities necessary to be successful. While this is necessary to stretch the individual so that learning occurs, resistance on the part of bosses might occur due to their reluctance to tolerate what they believe could be a longer learning and adjustment period by the individual. Staffing for development thus conflicts with the traditional selection approach which involves trying to achieve a good match between the person and the job, so that the individual hired is the individual whose present skills best match those required by the job (Ruderman, Ohlott & McCauley, 1990; McCauley et al., 1992).

Hardships

Until recently, the literature examining developmental experiences had little to say concerning the developmental potential of hardship experiences. Although some (e.g. Jennings, 1971; Gaylord & Simon, 1984) have suggested that these experiences provided the opportunity for growth and learning, most research has focused on the negative consequences rather than the potential positive outcomes. Recent research dealing with hardships focuses on three themes: identification of hardship experiences, the causes and consequences of experiencing hardships, and issues related to helping managers learn from these experiences.

The research of McCall, Lombardo and Morrison (1988) on key developmental events identified five types of hardship experiences that managers found to be significant in terms of their development as managers. These were: business mistakes and failures (which usually resulted from mistakes in dealing with key people, either superiors, subordinates or peers); demotions/missed promotions/lousy jobs; breaking a rut (i.e. changing careers); subordinate performance problems; and personal trauma (e.g. injury, illness, divorce).

Managers learned a variety of lessons from these experiences, but the most frequent lessons dealt with personal awareness. For example, from business mistakes and failures managers learned to recognise their personal limits, how to deal with people and about organisational politics. From demotions and lousy jobs managers learned to cope with situations outside their control and organisational politics, and they learned to recognise their personal limits.

Lombardo and McCauley (1988) have followed up on previous research examining executive *derailment* (e.g. McCall & Lombardo, 1983; Morrison, White & Van Velsor, 1987). Derailment occurs when a manager who has been judged to have the ability to go higher fails to live up to his/her full potential and is fired, demoted or plateaued below expected levels of achievement. Using supervisor ratings of over 300 middle- to upper-level managers in eight companies, six basic flaws that contribute to derailment were identified: (i) difficulty moulding a staff; (ii) difficulty making strategic transitions; (iii) lack of follow-through; (iv) problems with interpersonal relationships; (v) overdependence; and (vi) strategic differences with management. Additional reasons for derailment that occurred in a study examining derailment among female managers were poor image and narrow business experience (Morrison, White & Van Velsor, 1987).

The research by Lombardo and McCauley (1988) also indicated that managers who were rated by their bosses as having more flaws also had fewer strengths. Moreover, although the first three flaws have the strongest relationship to derailment, the flaws which contribute most to derailment seemed to vary somewhat across companies and across jobs. They concluded that some flaws which do not hinder performance in lower-level jobs become critical as the manager is moved into more challenging, higher-level jobs and this is consistent with previous research (e.g. McCall & Lombardo, 1983; Kovach, 1986). Finally, and perhaps most significantly, they concluded that derailment can be predicted in advance.

Kovach (1989) examined derailment from a somewhat different perspective. Rather than focusing on what causes derailment, she examined what happens to managers *after* they have been derailed. While derailment is possible for everyone, she suggests that it is likely to be particularly prevalent among those managers who are on the 'fast-track'. For example, being on the 'fast track' may produce an imbalance between the manager's work and personal life (Kofodimos, 1990). Fast-track managers may become so involved in their work (in an effort to continue the movement upward that is seen as a sign of success) that they neglect their personal life and eventually become ineffective at work.

Based upon her interviews with 17 managers who had been identified as fast-trackers, Kovach (1989) concluded that a career slowdown leads managers to a period of reflection about themselves and their relationship to others and that their reaction to the derailment and the learning which occurs while derailed can be significant factors in determining if they become mobile again. Derailment gives managers the opportunity to learn about themselves, about others, and about their organisation. From this reflection can develop a new understanding of their priorities and values.

Being able to learn from derailment and other hardship experiences requires a willingness on the part of the manager to examine him/herself and an ability to learn from their mistakes. Yet Argyris (1991) and others (e.g. Hall, 1986; Kaplan, Drath & Kofodimos, 1987) argue that this is very difficult for managers to do, primarily because they have been so successful all their lives. Having never experienced failure, they have an extremely difficult time learning from it. Managers tend to become defensive and find it difficult to admit that they may have inadvertently contributed to their mistakes.

Interestingly, the ability to accept responsibility for mistakes is one of the very characteristics that has been found to distinguish between successful and derailed executives (e.g. McCall & Lombardo, 1983; Kaplan, Drath & Kofodimos, 1987; Hall, 1986). Argyris (1991) describes a process used to help managers break out of what he calls the 'doom loop' of defensive reasoning. It requires getting managers to recognise the conflict between the theory of behaviour which they espouse and the theory which they actually use. Feedback from others can be a valuable source of information to help managers recognise their limitations.

Unfortunately, it appears that the higher managers advance, the more difficult it becomes for them to receive this feedback (Kaplan, Drath & Kofodimos 1987; Bartolome, 1989). A variety of factors, relating to the nature of the executive role, and his/her job and personal characteristics, combine to keep managers from obtaining this critical feedback both from other people and, through introspection, from themselves. For example, the executive's isolation and exaggerated perceptions of his/her impact may keep others from sharing this information with him/her. The many demands, pressures and requirements for action inherent in the job contribute to the problem by inhibiting managers from taking the time to reflect and examine themselves. Finally, the need to be competent may keep managers from being able to accept criticism from others.

Nonetheless, it has been argued that none of the identified barriers to learning are necessarily insurmountable. As noted by Kaplan, Drath and Kofodimos (1987), executives who really want to learn can do so and there are steps that organisations can take to make this process easier. For example, being more tolerant of mistakes and providing an environment where learning (and not just results) is valued can increase the willingness of managers to accept criticism (Kaplan, Drath & Kofodimos, 1987; Lombardo & McCauley, 1988). In addition, organisations can create developmental job assignments that follow a logical progression and build upon each other rather than the haphazard pattern often observed. Finally, organisations need to help managers make 'mental transitions' (p. 18) so they understand that the behaviours or qualities that were rewarded earlier in their careers may need to be modified to fit new situational demands (Lombardo & McCauley, 1988).

In examining the research on job assignments, several observations can be made. The first and most readily apparent is how little empirical research of an evaluative nature there is. We have very little conclusive evidence that these types of job assignments really are developmental. We concur with Noe and Ford's (1992) recommendations for the evaluation of job rotation programmes and argue that they need to be extended to other developmental job assignments as well. Specifically, a rigorous assessment of the value of these job assignments is necessary to determine if those who have them are actually more successful (using a variety of individual and organisational outcome measures) than those who do not. Thus far, almost all that we know concerning the value of different types of job assignments has been based on the opinions of executives/managers. While this is a valuable start, we now need to move beyond reaction and self-reported learning measures to more objective learning, behavioural change and results measures (e.g. London, 1989).

In addition to research evaluating the effectiveness of various job assignments, it would be valuable to learn more about how the specific assignments should be utilised to best enhance managerial development. For example, in order to maximise learning, should managers experience all of the different types of assignments or some subset? In what order should managers experience these assignments? Which should occur earlier in one's career and which later? Should managers experience some of these assignments more than once? McCall, Lombardo and Morrison (1988) have suggested that little additional learning comes from experiencing one type of assignment more than once but there is little empirical support for this contention.

Implicit in the research on specific types of job assignments is an assumption that the reason these assignments are developmental is because they provide an opportunity for the manager to be challenged. Thus, job challenge is assumed to mediate between specific assignments and learning outcomes. Surprisingly, though, research integrating these two streams of research is virtually non-existent. To further our understanding of how job assignments, job challenges and learning outcomes are related, it would be useful to know if certain types of assignments are most likely to provide certain basic elements of job challenge and also, which learning outcomes derive from these challenges.

Another direction for future research would be to determine what specific work experiences are most valuable for teaching which managerial competencies. While McCall, Lombardo and Morrison (1988) do identify the lessons learned from job assignments, most of the lessons do not relate to specific managerial competencies. An example of research which does this is Stumpf (1989) which identified specific work experiences that help to develop a manager's capacity for strategic thinking. Additional research of this nature would be extremely valuable.

Finally, research examining how to help managers actually learn from these informal learning experiences and what can be done to facilitate this process would be useful. As McCall, Lombardo and Morrison (1988) note, there is no guarantee that just because a manager experiences a developmental assignment he/she will learn from it. A variation on action learning, a developmental approach that is gaining popularity, has the potential to be very useful in terms of helping managers learn from their experiences (Marsick, 1990).

Relationships with Others

A growing body of recent literature supports the long-held belief that relationships play an important role in the development of managers, both as professionals and as individuals (McCall, Lombard & Morrison, 1988; Kram, 1985; Gabarro, 1987; Kovach, 1989; London & Mone, 1987). In this section we will review recent research examining how three different relationships (mentor, boss, peer) may contribute to managerial development.

Mentoring relationships

Perhaps the most frequently examined relationship in the context of management development is that of mentoring. The term 'mentor' is generally used to describe 'a relationship between a young adult and an older, more experienced adult that helps the younger individual to navigate in the adult world and the world of work' (Kram, 1985: p. 2). Recent research on mentoring has focused on three issues: the benefits of mentoring (for the protégé, the mentor and the organisation), dynamics within mentoring relationships, including issues related to the gender of the mentor and protégé, and structured mentoring programmes.

Prior research on mentoring relationships has identified two important functions which these relationships serve for the protégé: career and psycho-social (Kram, 1985). Career functions are those that enhance career advancement (e.g. exposure, visibility, coaching) while psycho-social functions enhance the protégé's sense of competence, identity and effectiveness in a professional role (e.g. role modelling, counselling and friendship).

Recently, some additional benefits of mentoring have also been reported. For example, Kram and Hall (1989) have found that mentor-protégé relationships may be a way to alleviate the stress that occurs during times of organisational change (e.g. corporate restructuring or downsizing). During these times, individuals reported a greater desire to serve as a mentor to others and were more likely to indicate both that mentoring was important and was not of sufficient quality in the organisation. Ostroff and Kozlowski (1992) reported that mentoring may influence the socialisation experiences of newcomers. Those newcomers with mentors were able to learn more about organisational issues and practices than newcomers without mentors. Interestingly, these two groups also differed in their information acquisition strategies. Newcomers with mentors relied on their mentor while newcomers without mentors relied more on their coworkers.

An important question is whether mentoring has any significant impact on the career outcomes of protégés. Yet beyond a study conducted a number of years ago (Roche, 1979) which found that executives who had sponsors earned more money at an earlier age, little research has emerged. One recent study, however, reported that individuals who had extensive experience in mentoring relationships (as the protégé) received more promotions, had higher incomes and were more satisfied with their pay and benefits than individuals who had experienced less extensive mentoring relationships (Dreher & Ash, 1990).

Recent work in this area has also begun to take into account benefits of relationships for the mentor and the organisation. For example, Smith (1990) argues that mentoring relationships foster the growth of mentors, give them satisfaction and increased motivation and help to develop their leadership skills.

Organisations are believed to benefit since younger employees have the opportunity to be guided by those with more experience, which should lead to more effective utilisation of human resources (Wright & Werther, 1991). The potential for mentoring relationships to aid in training and development is another important benefit to organisations (Zey, 1988), as is the ability to foster teamwork, shared values and improved communication (Smith, 1990).

In describing the nature of mentor/protégé relationships, Bushardt, Fretwell and Holdnak (1991) argue that mentors, regardless of their gender, utilise predominantly masculine sex-role behaviour. On the other hand, protégés, regardless of their gender, utilise predominantly feminine sex-role behaviour. Taking a socio-biological perspective, they draw parallels between the mentoring process and the mating process in terms of selection criteria, acquisition strategies and demographic characteristics of the relationship.

Several researchers have examined factors influencing the formation of mentor-protégé relationships and the reactions of the protégé and the mentor to those relationships. Olian, Carroll, Giannantonio and Feren (1988) studied the impact of both mentor characteristics and behaviours (gender, age, interpersonal competence, and integration into the organisation's decision-making network) and protégé characteristics (gender, age and previous work experience) on attraction to a mentoring relationship. Results of three laboratory studies involving a total of 675 participants found that the interpersonal competence of the mentor significantly increased protégé attraction to the mentoring relationship, that mentor integration into decision-making networks only increased protégé attraction to the relationship when mentor interpersonal competence was weak, and that protégé work experience and mentor age had no effect on protégé attraction. There was no consistent evidence that protégés are more attracted to same sex mentor-protégé relationships.

More recently, Olian, Carroll and Giannantonio (1992) examined several protégé factors (e.g. protégé performance, mentor-protégé gender similarity and protégé marital status) thought to influence mentor reactions to the mentoring relationship. Results revealed that protégé performance was positively related to mentor intentions to engage in mentoring behaviours and anticipated rewards from the relationship. Protégé marital status interacted with protégé sex such that mentors anticipated greater inclination to engage in career-enhancing behaviours and greater rewards to themselves when male protégés were married and when female protégés were single. Finally, mentors perceived somewhat greater drawbacks to mentoring single protégés.

Gender may be an important factor influencing the nature and formation of mentoring relationships. For example, it has been suggested that not only may mentoring relationships be more important to females seeking advancement but that they may be harder for women to obtain (Noe, 1988b; Ragins, 1989). Ragins (1989) describes some potential barriers for women in obtaining mentoring relationships. First, women may fail to recognise the importance of gaining sponsorship and may be less likely than men to seek mentors. Or, if they do realise the importance of having a mentor, they may not have the knowledge, skills or strategies necessary to obtain a mentor. A contributing factor is that mentors may be less willing to select female protégés.

Ragins and Cotton (1991a) examined some of these barriers empirically to determine if there actually are gender differences in barriers to gaining a mentor. The survey results obtained from 510 men and women indicated that women perceived more barriers than did men in gaining a mentor, even after controlling for experience as a protégé, age, rank and tenure. As noted by Ragins and Cotton (1991a), although this study is suggestive of greater barriers for women in mentoring, it focused entirely on *perceptions* of mentoring barriers which may or may not correspond to actual barriers. In fact, in a survey of 440 business school graduates, Dreher and Ash (1990) found little evidence that females were less likely than males to have mentors. Furthermore, there was no evidence that gender moderated the relationship between mentoring and career outcomes as was expected. It is conceivable that the perception of greater barriers by women may actually be a defense mechanism employed to rationalise their personal limitations, inability to obtain a mentor, or lack of advancement. Future research needs to examine more objective indices of mentoring barriers to resolve this issue.

Examining gender differences from the perspective of the mentor, Ragins and Cotton (1991b) found that although there was no difference between men and women in their willingness to serve as a mentor, women perceived more drawbacks and obstacles to becoming a mentor. Women were more likely than men to report that they did not feel qualified to be a mentor, that they did not want the risk of being made to look bad by their protégé's failure and that they lacked the time to be a mentor.

Another variation on the research examining gender differences in mentoring concerns cross-gender mentoring relationships. Cross-gender mentoring refers to a mentor-protégé relationship involving a male and female (Bushardt, Fretwell & Holdnak, 1991). There are special problems involved in these mentoring relationships due to latent and/or manifest sexual themes and these vary depending on whether the male or female is the mentor (Bushardt, Fretwell & Holdnak, 1991). Ragins and McFarlin (1990) compared protégé perceptions of mentor roles in both cross-gender and same-gender mentoring relationships. They found few differences between these types of relationships. However, cross-gender protégés reported that they were less likely than same-gender protégés to spend time in after-work social activities with their mentors. It is possible that sexual concerns may result in cross-gender relationships not being as close as same-gender relationships. Also of interest was the finding that female protégés with female mentors were more likely to report that their mentor served as a role model to them.

As described above, there are a number of benefits both to individuals and organisations from having mentoring relationships develop within the organisation. Yet it is clear that not everyone is able to establish such relationships. This has led some to suggest that organisations should establish formal mentoring programmes rather than relying on those relationships that develop naturally (e.g. Zey, 1988; Bernstein & Kaye, 1986). Indeed, a number of companies, (e.g. Johnson & Johnson, Motorolla, Honeywell) have already established such programmes.

It has been argued that formal mentoring programmes are somewhat risky because there is some question about whether appointed mentors will develop the 'favorable chemistry' (Wright & Werther, 1991: p. 27) with the protégé needed to make the relationship a success. There is a number of other possible problems with assigned mentors. There may be personality conflicts between the parties and a lack of true commitment to the relationship since it was not formed of their own volition (Kram, 1985; Kram & Bragar, in press). Furthermore, formal programmes might create expectations in those mentors of rapid career progress, which might lead to frustration or even turnover if those expectations are not met (Wright & Werther, 1991).

Thus far, most of the concerns raised about mentoring programmes are speculative in nature and there has been little empirical research examining actual mentoring programmes. One exception is a study by Noe (1988a) that examined determinants of successful assigned mentoring relationships. Results of this study suggest that organisations should not expect the same benefits to protégés from assigned mentoring relationships as those which arise naturally. More specifically, protégés in assigned relationships reported receiving valuable psychosocial outcomes from the mentoring relationships but limited career functions. Interaction between the mentor and the protégé appeared to be limited, which suggests the possible need to increase the accessibility of the mentor to the protégé, perhaps by requiring weekly meetings.

There appear to be a number of core components necessary to make planned mentoring programmes successful (Kram & Bragar, in press; Zey, 1988, 1989; Alleman, 1989). These include such things as specific objectives for the programme, a careful selection process that incorporates voluntary participation and an attempt to match mentors and protégés so that both will find value in the relationship, a monitoring and evaluation process, and a programme coordinator.

Smith (1990) describes an interesting variation on typical mentoring programmes that attempts to combine two developmental methods, mentoring and project work, to capitalise on the strengths of both. The programme, called 'mutual mentoring on projects', involves having managers identify real organisational problems that need to be solved but which they cannot solve on their own with their current skills and knowledge. A group of people who can contribute to solving the problem are identified and each member develops a learning contract that identifies what he/she intends to learn from the process as well as what he/she is responsible for teaching others. This process appears to have much in common with action learning programmes, which are reviewed later.

Other important relationships

In examining the research on relationships, it is clear that much more attention has been paid to mentoring than to other important relationships on the job. We know comparatively little about how bosses, peers and subordinates may help to contribute to the development of managers.

Given the large number of researchers and writers who have argued that bosses can play an important role in the development of managers (e.g. Kovach, 1989; London & Mone, 1987; Gabarro, 1987; McCall, Lombardo & Morrison, 1988), surprisingly little research of an empirical nature has been conducted. The importance of the relationship with one's boss can be seen in Gabarro's (1987) research examining the taking charge process. All of the failed successions examined were characterised by poor working relationships with their supervisor.

Clearly, ineffective relationships with bosses can negatively impact development. The research conducted by McCall and his colleagues (McCall, Lombardo & Morrison, 1988; Lindsey, Homes & McCall, 1987) examining key events in the development of managers identified two key events, both involving bosses, in which other people were the central feature. One type of key event was when the boss served as a role model. This event usually occurred over an extended period of time (from six months to three years). In contrast, the other event involving bosses (called 'values playing out') was typically a brief episode in which superiors (or sometimes the managers themselves) demonstrated their values by doing something either extremely bad or extremely good. The lessons learned from these two events were usually similar and they dealt mostly with values, either human, managerial or political. From observing the behaviour and seeing its impact on others, managers learned a great deal about not only their own values but also the values of the organisation.

Bosses can also aid in development by serving as a source of feedback to the manager about his/her strengths and weaknesses and as a source of advice and counselling (e.g. Hillman, Schwandt & Bartz, 1990). London and Mone (1987) described the various ways bosses can affect the career motivation (career resilience, insight and identity) of their employees. Career motivation is important because it has implications for how managers view their careers, how hard they work at them and how long they stay in them, all of which are important for management development. For example, career resilience should be strengthened by treating subordinates with respect, giving them challenging job assignments, allowing them to make their own mistakes, and encouraging them to use others as resources.

Since the pioneering work of Kram and Isabella (1985) examining peer relationships, the role of peers in the development of managers has been almost entirely ignored. Part of this inattention may be due to the belief that peer relationships will have less impact on development because peers do not typically have the knowledge and history of success that make true mentors such valuable career assets (Wright & Werther, 1991). This is a serious omission, given research by Gabarro (1987) which found that three out of four failed successions involved managers who had poor working relationships with two or more peers. Furthermore, peer relationships represent an alternative to mentoring, which, as noted earlier, may be less available to minorities and women (Ilgen & Youtz, 1986; Ragins, 1989; Noe, 1988b). These relationships may not only be more readily available but may also be more effective because the non-hierarchical nature of the relationship might make it easier to achieve communication, mutual support and collaboration.

One function that can be provided by peers that makes them an important developmental source is their ability to give the manager feedback of both a job-related and a personal nature (e.g. London & Mone, 1987). As noted earlier, feedback about his/her strengths and weaknesses is critical if the manager is to grow and develop and several studies have examined the use of feedback from both peers and subordinates to facilitate development (London & Wohlers, 1991; London, Wohlers & Gallagher, 1990). The 'mutual mentoring on projects' programme (Smith, 1990) described above represents another innovation in management development that relies heavily on lateral relationships and how peers learn from one another.

Research examining how significant relationships contribute to development is in its infancy. We have made some progress in our understanding of mentoring relationships but much more needs to be done. For example, Noe (1988) suggested the need to study the types of functions provided by mentors at different career stages and specifically to determine if the functions desired differed by gender or other minority status. Empirical research examining the value of mentoring relationships to the mentors would also be beneficial. Finally, more research on the dynamics of mentoring relationships is needed since it is these dynamics which will most influence the success or failure of the relationship.

Our understanding of the role that bosses play in the development of managers would be enhanced by identifying the characteristics of bosses that make them effective coaches since it is unlikely that all bosses are equally effective at this. Clawson (1980), for example, found that bosses who were consistent in their behaviour, informal in their interactions, and willing to share information had more effective developmental relationships. Personality correlates of effectiveness in developing managers might include high self-esteem and high self-monitoring.

Research is also needed to determine how individual differences contribute to preferences for peer relationships versus mentoring relationships. It is possible that some people would learn more from the non-hierarchical peer relationships than from mentoring relationships (Kram & Isabella, 1985) . For example, highly authoritarian people might respond better to mentoring due to its hierarchical nature. Finally, we need a better understanding of the utility of lateral and upward feedback for management development. Valuable areas for future research include how managers interpret and apply the feedback data (regardless of whether it is upward or lateral feedback), how they interpret differences in ratings across people, and variables that influence their acceptance or denial of the results (London & Wohlers, 1991). The literature on feedback as a communication process (e.g. Ilgen, Fisher & Taylor, 1979) would be helpful in doing this.

Formal Training

Formal training programmes represent the third important context for management development. Formal programmes have always been an integral part of management development and have been the backbone of the management development efforts of most organisations (Mumford, 1991).

Traditionally, these formal development programmes have utilised lectures, discussions and case analyses to facilitate the development of managerial talent.

However, the growing recognition that managers (and adults in general) learn best by actually doing things that are of practical relevance to them, has led to changes in the content and process of formalised management development programmes (e.g. Braddick, 1988; Prideaux & Ford, 1988a; Knowles, 1984). In this section, we focus on three topics—outdoor challenge training, action learning and leadership training—that reflect this changing perspective and have received significant attention in the literature.

Outdoor challenge training

Outdoor challenge training is a rapidly growing innovation in formal training programmes. In a typical outdoor challenge programme, participants work as groups to complete a variety of outdoor activities that encompass an increasing level of challenge and risk, and that require greater trust in and dependence on group members. The focus of these programmes can be individual growth and change (e.g. Galagan, 1987) or leadership development and team building (e.g. Long, 1987). Two important components of outdoor challenge programmes are the development of action plans for transferring the learning of participants back to the workplace and follow-up on the success of these efforts by programme providers (Gall, 1987).

Descriptions of typical (e.g. Gall, 1987; Galagan, 1987; Long, 1987) and atypical (e.g. Blashford-Snell, 1991) outdoor learning programmes can be found in a variety of practioner-oriented journals. Unfortunately, despite the growing popularity of outdoor learning and its extensive use in many progressive organisations, little is known about how effective these programmes are at facilitating learning and bringing about changes in behaviour and attitudes. Some authors have argued that the extremely favourable anecdotal reports must be at least partially discounted given that participants almost uniformly experience a type of 'post-group euphoria' at the conclusion of novel outdoor experiential exercises (e.g. Baldwin, Wagner & Roland, 1991; Gall, 1987; Galagan, 1987; Long, 1987).

There is, however, some evidence that outdoor challenge programmes can produce changes in the attitudes and behaviour of participants (Galagan, 1987; Long, 1987; Marsh, Richards & Barnes, 1986, 1987; Baldwin, Wagner & Roland, 1991). For example, Marsh, Richards and Barnes (1986, 1987) found that participation in an adventure learning programme resulted in improvements in self-concept while Ewert (1988) found that trait anxiety declined for participants in the programme.

In one recent study of outdoor challenge training Baldwin, Wagner and Roland (1991) found some additional evidence for its effectiveness. They collected data from 343 programme participants, 115 non-participants and 13 team supervisors on a variety of individual and group measures. Results suggested that outdoor challenge training had a modest effect on some perceptions of group awareness and effectiveness as well as individual problem-solving measured three months after the training. However, no significant changes in trust or self-concept were observed. Group level analyses suggested that both the facilitator and the participation of intact work groups may be related to positive training outcomes.

Finally, in a study conducted at Federal Express, Inc. (USA), it was found that turnover dropped 10 percentage points in a group that had participated in an outdoor challenge learning programme and stayed the same in a group that had not (Gall, 1987).

Action learning

The growth of management development programmes based upon action learning principles represents a second important innovation in the area of management development (cf. Mumford, 1987). Action learning is most accurately thought of as a theory of adult learning rather than a training technique *per se* (Jones, 1990). It is based upon the idea that people learn best from their personal experience of doing something. It further assumes that managers can: (i) learn from experience; (ii) share that experience with others; (iii) have their colleagues criticise and advise them on possible actions; (iv) implement the advice; and (v) review the action taken and the lessons that are learned with those colleagues (Margerison, 1988).

All management development programmes utilising an action learning framework are project driven, meaning that participants work on solving real problems being faced by real organisations (often their own). In this way, the learning is practical and immediately relevant. While actual programme characteristics differ, other typical features include an emphasis on developing management competencies (rather than acquisition of knowledge), self-managed learning and learning from peers (Prideaux & Ford, 1988a,b).

Using the typology of management development formulated by Mumford (1991), action learning represents a 'middle ground' (Type 2) between the informal, unplanned, accidental (Type 1) learning processes described by the researchers at the Center for Creative Leadership (e.g. McCall, Lombardo & Morrison, 1988) and the formal, planned, deliberate (Type 3) management development practices that have been so heavily utilised by organisations in the past. These Type 2, 'opportunistic' learning processes share some characteristics with each type of learning process. Like Type 1 processes, they occur within the context of managerial activities and have task performance as an explicit goal. However, unlike Type 1 processes, development is also an explicit goal. In contrast, Type 3 learning processes occur outside the context of managerial activities and have development as the only explicit goal.

Essentially, action learning attempts to capitalise on the benefits of both the planned and unplanned learning processes that typically occur during the development of managers. Unfortunately, writings about action learning are not always clear about what, exactly, managers are expected to learn as a result of participating in these programmes. Very few descriptions of programmes have articulated much of a specific nature about programme outcomes. One exception is a study by Prideaux and Ford (1988b) which described seven major learnings reported by participants in their action learning programme: self-awareness and self-management, proactivity and vision, learning skills such as learning how to learn, staying power and emotional resilience, interactive skills, team skills, and analytical skills. Note the similarity of their list of learnings with the lists of management competencies described earlier.

Thus far, action learning programmes have been utilised most extensively in the UK and outside the United States. The literature provides examples of formal action learning programmes (both within companies, by external management development centres and within MBA programmes) as well as informal application of action learning principles in the UK (e.g. Mumford, 1991), Australia (e.g. Hubbard, 1990; Kable, 1989; Margerison, 1988; Prideaux & Ford, 1988a,b), Sweden (e.g. Marsick, 1990) and Africa (e.g. Safavi & Tweddell, 1990).

Though Marsick (1990) discusses some reasons why action learning has not been as popular in the United States, a few examples of applications exist (e.g. Lawrie, 1989; Noel & Charan, 1988). For example, Noel and Charan (1988) describe how General Electric changed their Business Management Course (part of their executive programme) at the Crotonville Management Development Institute to incorporate action learning principles.

Leadership development

Research on the development of leadership skills continues to receive a significant amount of attention in the management development literature and extensive reviews of leadership training programmes (Latham, 1988; Bass, 1990a,b) and leadership models (Yukl, 1989) have recently appeared. Our brief review of recent leadership literature is intended solely to give the reader a sense of the current research direction in this area.

Two research streams in the leadership area have been receiving a great deal of attention: (i) transformational leadership and the related concepts of charismatic leadership and inspirational leadership (e.g. Bass, 1990a,b; Bass & Avolio, 1991; Bennis & Nanus, 1985; Conger & Kanungo, 1988); and (ii) self-leadership (e.g. Manz, 1986; Neck & Manz, 1992; Gilbert-Smith, 1991). Current research in each of these areas will be briefly described.

According to Bass and his colleagues, an understanding of transformational leadership is necessary to account for the extraordinary efforts often exerted by followers. Transformational leaders, in contrast to transactional leaders, try to elevate follower needs to higher levels, try to develop followers into leaders and to bring about changes in the culture and strategies of the organisation. Recent research in this area has focused on gaining an understanding of how transformational leaders develop. Avolio and Gibson (1988) utilised a life-span approach to describe some of the factors that are believed to account for the development of transformational leaders and explored such variables as family factors, birth order, conflict and disappointments, previous leadership experience and mentors. From a somewhat different perspective, Bass and Avolio (1991) describe a workshop to develop transformational leadership and preliminary results of studies evaluating the effectiveness are promising.

Another major development in the leadership area is the emergence of self-leadership (e.g. Manz, 1986). Self-leadership is defined as 'the process of influencing oneself to establish the self-direction and self-motivation needed to perform' (Neck & Manz, 1992: p. 5). Neck and Manz (1992) discuss one aspect of self-leadership which involves controlling one's thoughts through the application of such cognitive strategies as self-dialogue and mental imagery.

The authors argue that self-leadership will lead to enhanced individual and organisational performance and suggest a number of propositions to guide future research in this area. The development of self-leadership skills is the first step toward becoming a superleader (Manz & Sims, 1991). Manz and Sims (1991) argue that leaders become superleaders by helping followers to develop their own leadership and self-leadership skills. Manz (1990) argued for the need to integrate the literature on self-managing teams with that on self-leadership, so that we can move beyond self-managing teams toward self-leading teams. Manz, Keating and Donnellon (1990) describe issues involved in preparing managers for their new role as facilitators of a self-managed work team.

Finally, research examining the application of established leadership models to the development of managers is ongoing. For example, research continues to be undertaken on path-goal (e.g. Neider & Schreisheim, 1988), the Vroom–Yetton model of participation in decision-making (e.g. Vroom & Jago, 1988; Maczynski, 1992), cognitive resources theory (e.g. Fiedler, in press), and an extension of the leader-member exchange model called leadership-making (e.g. Graen & Uhl-Bien, 1991a,b; Uhl-Bien & Graen, in press a). Other interesting developments in the area of leadership include a cross-cultural study examining how Japanese leadership techniques are utilised in US transplants (Graen & Wakabayashi, in press) and an attempt to enhance organisational effectiveness by linking leader requirements to the stage of the organisational life cycle (Hunt, Baiga & Peterson, 1988).

Recent developments in formal management programmes are exciting and have a great deal of intuitive appeal. Action learning programmes, in particular, seem uniquely suited for developing managers. It is difficult to argue with the logic of using actual work experiences as the basis for learning. It appears to be a strategy well suited to overcoming the difficulties of transferring learning back to the job when the learning was acquired in a very different context

(Baldwin & Ford, 1988). As noted by Kable (1989), the transfer problem occurs not only because the system often fails to reinforce the new behaviours, but because there is frequently direct pressure applied to individuals to keep their behaviour the same once they return to the job. This is much less likely to be a problem with action learning programmes because the projects that form the basis for the programme are of real concern to the organisation. In addition, action learning principles may help maximise the learning potential of the informal, unplanned experiences that occur naturally on the job.

Nevertheless, in our enthusiasm for new approaches to formal training we cannot overlook the need to carefully evaluate programmes to see how effective they truly are. As with all management development initiatives, we continue to lack evidence concerning the impact of these programmes on management behaviour and organisational effectiveness. To date, there have been few reported studies looking at the outcomes from either action learning or outdoor challenge programmes. In both cases, there are many positive testimonials but we know little about other outcomes.

Indeed, with respect to action learning, very little has even been said about *expected* outcomes. Future research similar to that of Prideaux and Ford (1988b) is necessary to determine what specific competencies managers acquire from participating in action learning programmes. One general concern is that, given the project-driven nature of these programmes, learning may be highly situation-specific and, therefore, not generalisable. On the other hand, given that the success of projects assigned to managers can be ascertained, action learning may lend itself to evaluation on objective outcome measures even more so than other development strategies.

Both action learning and adventure learning rely heavily on the use of teams for learning. For both types of programmes, it would also be valuable to know more about the characteristics that influence dynamics within the teams and how both team characteristics and team dynamics influence the success of programmes. Marsick (1990) has suggested that the action learning process is more effective when participants have different backgrounds (e.g. education, age, gender, ethnicity, experience and functional specialities), but research is needed which specifically examines this issue. Similarly, Marsick argues that participants should be from several different companies or organisations rather than just one (so that they will be working on a project outside their 'home environment' and presumably feel more free to ask questions), but there is also a pressing need for empirical evidence to support this contention.

Several team characteristics might be relevant to understanding the effectiveness of adventure learning. Baldwin, Wagner and Roland (1991) found preliminary evidence which suggests that more positive outcomes might be obtained when intact work teams are used rather than groups of strangers who come together only for purposes of participating in the training. Along similar lines, it is possible that newly formed teams in the earlier stages of development might be able to gain more than those who are further advanced because they have less 'history' to overcome. Other relevant team characteristics might include the size of the team and the extent of interdependence among team members on the job.

Summary

As this review of developmental contexts has shown, managers learn in a variety of ways from a variety of different experiences. As we attempt to make better use of the developmental opportunities present in day-to-day job experiences it would be valuable to have a better understanding of which individuals will benefit most from which experiences. Akin's (1987) learning themes might be useful in helping to differentiate between those who learn best from job assignments versus relationships with others versus formal developmental opportunities. Since legal constraints suggest that it may be difficult to differentially offer developmental experiences based upon learning style preferences, an understanding of these differences would enable human resource professionals to help managers maximise their own learning from each of the experiences they face.

EMERGING ISSUES IN MANAGEMENT DEVELOPMENT

Management Development as a Competitive Advantage

To gain competitive advantage, businesses have traditionally focused on technological, economic and strategic capabilities (Porter, 1985). However, a growing body of evidence supports the role of effective management on organisation and subunit performance (*Harvard Business Review*, 1987; Shipper, 1991; Day & Lord, 1988). Indeed Kotter (1988) argues that one thing that seems to distinguish excellent companies from the also rans is the amount of time and energy spent in the planning, designing and carrying out of development activities.

Such findings have prompted consideration of how organisations may treat development of managerial talent as a 'strategic weapon' (Ulrich, 1989; Hall & Foulkes, 1991; Fulmer, 1990). The traditional philosophy of development has often been that it should be aimed at benefiting the individual and, in some indirect way, would ultimately benefit the company. However, firms are now demanding development that is results oriented and aimed at implementing business strategy and corporate objectives (Bolt, 1987). More than ever before, organisations are stressing the importance of translating education into greater managerial effectiveness and responsiveness to a quickly changing business environment.

Ulrich reports on several case studies (e.g. Whirlpool, Borg-Warner) and presents eight transitions required to make executive development a competitive weapon. He presents a summary checklist of 24 key questions which he contends will focus development as a means of gaining competitiveness.

Hall and Foulkes (1991) make a similar case for the potential role of development as a competitive weapon. They debunk seven myths of existing executive development, present several corporate examples and emphasise the importance of organisation design, reward systems and CEO commitment for successful strategy-driven development to occur.

Rosow and Zager (1988) suggest that the evolution in training underway in organisations today is actually a movement towards a continuous learning philosophy. Pedler, Boydell and Burgoyne (1989) define the continuous learning organisation as one where learning is considered an everyday activity for all employees and the organisation continuously transforms itself. They argue that conditions for a learning organisation include extending the development to other significant shareholders and making the development strategy central to the business strategy so that learning becomes a major business activity. They further outline a set of nine guidelines for a firm to become a learning organisation.

In a widely acclaimed book, Senge (1990) identifies a number of specific organisational learning 'disabilities' and suggests that such disabilities cripple competitiveness. He argues that learning disabilities are eventually fatal in organisations and, because of them, few corporations live even half as long as a person. Senge identifies five disciplines (systems thinking, personal mastery, mental models, building shared visions, team learning) which he contends are key to the building of a learning organisation.

Of course, a shift to more strategic development is a complex process and several authors have discussed obstacles to the evolution of a continuous learning environment. For example, Culley (1989) discusses the factors that can cause resistance to development efforts and some key elements in overcoming such resistance. More specifically, he identified three factors that often conspire to work against a continuous learning environment: (i) executives are action-oriented and very sensitive to demands on time; (ii) bias against training and development activities and (iii) executives are preoccupied with what they left behind and what will be waiting upon return. To deal with this, Culley suggests that organisations need to be particularly sensitive to the organisation calendar, reinforce key learning, and use locations which symbolise the organisation's commitment to development efforts. Baldwin and Magjuka (1991) also make a case for the importance of management actions in signalling organisational commitment to development activities.

It seems clear that one key to long-term competitiveness in the years ahead is the ability of an organisation to continuously change and evolve in order to maintain leadership positions in quality, profitability and performance. Further, if management development is going to be a strategic weapon for achieving competitive advantage then firms must become increasingly self-renewing. The emerging, continuous learning paradigm of management development is a key driving force for building and sustaining this essential capacity. However, we still need a much better understanding of how organisations can stimulate continuous learning behaviours from their managers. Noe and Ford (1992) suggest that human resource strategies such as skill-based pay, reward for innovation and using learning as an evaluation dimension may be useful in this regard. In any case, more research devoted to the individual and organisational factors associated with continuous learning activities is clearly warranted.

Self-directed Management Development

Traditional research and writing on management development has generally reflected an implicit assumption that management development was something that was done *to* managers by some external force. However, the recent interest in continuous learning and experience-based development has prompted something of a revolution in thinking about management development.

The 'revolution' has involved a change in the assumed locus of control for learning. Responsibility for learning is shifting away from the trainer and toward the learner. The move toward becoming more learner centred is indicated by a growing literature on self-directed management development (e.g. Stewart, 1989b; Kaplan, Drath & Kofodimos, 1985; Manz & Manz, 1991; Knowles, 1984).

Manz and Manz (1991) outline a model of 'self-directed learning capacity' and propose four strategies that can be used to increase such a capacity. The authors assert that increases in the capacity for self-directed learning are a function of increases in an individual's self-efficacy and increases in self-leadership skills.

Spitzer (1991) attempts to more fully specify an operational definition of self-directed learning by describing it as a continuum in which the key defining attribute is choice (topic, timing, etc.). He further explores how principles of instructional design can help establish the conditions under which self-directed learning can be operationalised in a business setting.

Not surprisingly, the growth in interest in self-development has raised questions regarding the feasibility and utility of it for nurturing managerial talent. For example, several authors (e.g. Stewart, 1989b; Kinzie, 1990) express some reservations regarding the capability of learners to manage their own learning in an effective way (e.g. will they make good choices? will they be motivated to learn?). Kinzie (1990) reviewed the limited research relevant to this question and identified areas where more research is needed.

Stewart (1989b) argues that for self-development to be an effective strategy in organisational environments there must be an acceptance of the need to learn, a view of development as a continuous process, and the perspective that learning is something for which individual managers take a personal responsibility. Stewart questions whether these conditions typically exist in organisations and argues that the culture of a company will discourage or encourage the practice of individual development.

Finally, Kaplan, Drath and Kofodimos (1985) have suggested that high-level executives have trouble charting a self-development course because they are often isolated from criticism by their positional power, structurally detached by their executive suites and pressed by the staggering demands on their time.

Despite some significant challenges, the increased interest in self-development is consistent with the belief that the most significant managerial development occurs on the job (McCall, Lombardo & Morrison, 1988). Few would argue with the contention that self-development, in conjunction with constructive input from others (e.g. bosses, educators), is critical in a turbulent world. Moreover, learner self-control over training is becoming increasingly feasible with the advent of interactive training methods that allow individualised instruction and greater flexibility. Perhaps most importantly, the rapid globalisation of business is creating managerial tasks and roles that are so different from anything that we can imagine today that we cannot possibly develop stable development programmes which allow for all such contingencies (Schein, 1991). Thus, the role of self-directed learning will be even more crucial in the future and research aimed at making the linkage from theory to practice is sorely needed in this area.

Management Development in Degree-granting Institutions

A large body of recent literature continues to be devoted to management education in degree-granting institutions—most predominantly schools of management and business. Criticisms levelled at traditional business school education are pervasive in the literature and include claims that graduates are too analytical, lack interpersonal and communication skills, have unrealistic expectations about their first jobs after graduation, and do not work well in groups (Porter & McKibbin, 1988; Louis, 1990). In response to these criticisms, considerable effort has been centred around the design of business school curriculums in the United States (Bigelow, 1991), Europe (Porter, Muller & Rehder, 1991), Japan (Kimura & Yoshimori, 1989), and Australia (Hubbard, 1990). Much of this effort has focused on the development of skills or competency-based courses.

Perhaps the most visible effort in this regard is the outcome measurement project sponsored by the American Association of Collegiate Schools of Business (AACSB, 1987). Originally begun in 1976, the outcome measurement project sampled business school deans, consultants, corporate advisors and more than 2000 college students to identify clusters of skills and personal characteristics thought to comprise an effective business graduate. Skills and personal characteristics tests were created using assessment centre techniques (AACSB, 1987; Porter & McKibbon, 1989).

Boyatzis and colleagues (Boyatzis, Cowen and Kolb, 1991) report on a project undertaken at the Weatherhead School of Management at Case Western Reserve University. The objective of the project was to dramatically change the MBA programme to become distinctive as an outcome-oriented, competency-based, and value-added programme. In a study of 72 students participating in that programme, Boyatzis and Renio (1989) found significant improvement on six of the nineteen management skill variables assessed. The programme appeared to have a significant positive effect on students' abilities in areas of information collection and analysis, quantitative analysis, the management of technology, entrepreneurial and action skills. Unfortunately, the programme did not appear to have an impact on abilities that involve interaction with people.

McConnell and Seyboldt (1991) also argued for the usefulness of assessment centre technology in curriculum design and Mullin, Shaffer and Grelle (1991) present results of a study using that technology for teaching basic management skills. As predicted, students who participated in experimental assessment centre method classes demonstrated higher levels of competence on a target set of basic management skills with no loss of content knowledge. However, the difference between experimental assessment centre and traditional (lecture-intensive approaches) was of relatively small magnitude which the authors attributed to the limits of one course and lack of congruency with other courses in the business curriculum.

Other literature in the area of management education has focused on the changes in university-based executive programmes (Vicere, 1991). Until recently, it was possible to draw a distinct line between management training and education leading to academic qualifications (Wexley & Baldwin, 1986). However, this line is blurring with the growth of executive education and MBA schemes that are designed for a particular company or for a group of companies. Organisations are stressing more customised programmes, emphasising pragmatism in the programmes, and working more closely with universities (Bolt, 1987; Verlander, 1989). Moreover, organisations continue to increase their capacity to be their own educational provider as evidenced by the growth of corporate universities and campuses (Green & Lazarus, 1988).

Of particular note is the development of the International Management Centre from Buckingham (UK) which has adopted a decidedly client-based orientation. In designing curriculum, the Centre relies less on traditional content and more on the needs of the organisation footing the bill. As a result, the Centre is one of the fastest growing business schools in the UK and a leader in the provision of in-company action learning programmes (Lethbridge, 1989).

Of course, not all organisational scholars are enamoured with the growth of university-based executive education and some feel that it is nothing more than commercial activity with little academic credibility. However, Vicere (1988) argues that universities can add research capabilities, methodological expertise, and objectivity to the executive education process. Furthermore, a growing body of literature indicates that company-specific programmes may provide greater benefits to the organisation and are therefore more appropriate investments than traditional university programmes (Bolt, 1987; Armenakis, Flowers, Burdge, Kuerten, McCord & Arnold, 1989). For example, Armenakis et al. (1989) conclude that, while the instruction and research missions of universities will affect organisational competitiveness in the long run, tailored business extension programmes have greater potential for short-term impact.

Summary

As Keys and Wolfe (1988) point out, the competency movement and growing popularity of tailored executive education has prompted a soul searching on the part of organisations and academicians alike. With respect to the competency movement, we continue to need a better understanding of ways to integrate competency-based teaching within existing business school curricula and of how to motivate faculty to teach competencies (Wexley & Baldwin, 1986). With respect to executive education programming, research is needed which explores ways to identify the appropriate content and process for specific executive audiences and means to link those with institutional and organisational objectives.

CONCLUDING COMMENTS

Prior reviewers have often lamented the faddish and non-empirical nature of much management development literature and it is still prone to those tendencies (Wexley & Baldwin, 1986). However, we were pleasantly surprised by the volume and quality of the work that has appeared in the last five years and think it gives much cause for optimism.

For example, there has been a dramatic improvement in the behavioural specificity of models of effective management and a move toward more empirical work with generalisable samples. Although the efficacy of the billions of dollars spent on management development still remains largely an article of faith, and much more research is needed, at least some work documenting effects of development on criteria of organisational effectiveness is emerging. In addition, researchers have seemingly become far more cognisant of the distinction between management positions and the various contexts of managerial learning. That is, authors are now far less likely to treat 'management as management' or 'development as development', wherever they find it (Schein, 1989).

Research on the developmental value of job assignments and relationships such as mentoring and coaching is providing information with which to improve on-the-job learning of relevant skills and allow better integration of developmental experiences and formal training. Researchers at the Center for Creative Leadership have been at the forefront in examining how job assignments contribute to development.

In addition, conceptions of formal training have expanded to include consideration of both relevant content and issues related to the process of instruction which is appropriate for adult executive learners. Attention to exciting new approaches such as action learning and outdoor challenges reflect this expanded perspective. Finally, more than ever before, organisations are beginning to view management development as an integral component of competitive advantage and an activity that requires a great deal of self-directed effort and lifelong learning.

While the recent advances are encouraging, some concerns with the research and practice of management development persist. For example, there is still a paucity of research which illustrates attempts to systematically identify development objectives, choose an appropriate development strategy, and evaluate the outcomes to determine whether the objectives were met. Historically, most firms have not 'closed the loop' by evaluating their management development efforts and therefore have made subsequent decisions based on reactions, hunches or inertia (Tannenbaum & Woods, 1992).

In this regard, we would contend that it is time to move beyond research designed to show that a particular type of management development 'works'. Rather, we need to proceed to the more specific questions of why, when, and for whom a particular development strategy is effective. Furthermore, both practitioners and researchers need to do a better job of describing the nature and purpose of development initiatives. We need to be clear not only about the development strategy employed, but also about the basic content and purpose of the development. Making these distinctions should greatly enhance the ability to compare studies in future reviews of this type (Tannenbaum & Yukl, 1992).

The interest in continuous learning organisations has also prompted a need for renewed interest in learner motivation. As Campbell (1989) notes, everyone intuitively appreciates that motivational effects can completely swamp the potential benefits of a well-designed development initiative. We should therefore pay more attention to issues related to managers' goals and their correspondence with development goals, the reinforcement and punishment contingencies associated with development in organisations, and the socialisation and group processes that will influence managers' 'motivation for development'.

Finally, we need more published work on what progressive and successful companies are doing with respect to management development. An unfortunate paradox is that the more organisations truly believe that management development is a source of competitive advantage, the less inclined they are to share their secrets with the world. We hope that organisational scholars and corporate practitioners can be creative in finding mutually beneficial ways to share important concepts and data without violating proprietary concerns of progressive firms.

REFERENCES

AACSB (1987) *Outcome Measurement Project: Phase III report.* St. Louis: American Assembly of Collegiate Schools of Business.

Akin, G. (1987) Varieties of managerial learning. *Organizational Dynamics,* **16**, 36–48.

Alleman, E. (1989) Two planned mentoring programs that worked. *Mentoring International,* **3**, 6–12.

Ames, M. & Heide, D. (1991) The keys to successful management development in the 1990s. *Journal of Management Development,* **10**(2), 20–30.

Argyris, C. (1991) Teaching smart people how to learn. *Harvard Business Review,* **69**(3), 99–109.

Armenakis, A. A., Flowers, J. D., Burdge, H. B., Kuerten, K. M., McCord, S. O., & Arnold, H. D. (1989) The business schools' impact on US competitiveness. *Journal of Management Development,* **8**(1), 49–54.

Avolio, R. J. & Gibson, T. G. (1988) Developing transformational leaders: A lifespan approach. In J. Conger, R. Kanungo & Associates (eds), *Charismatic Leadership: The Elusive Factor in Organizational Effectiveness.* San Francisco, CA: Jossey-Bass.

Baldwin, T. T. & Ford, J. K. (1988) Transfer of training: A review and directions for future research. *Personnel Psychology,* **41**, 63–105.

Baldwin, T. T. & Magjuka, R. J. (1991) Organizational training and signals of importance: Linking pre-training perceptions to intentions to transfer. *Human Resource Development Quarterly,* **2**, 25–36.

Baldwin, T. T., Wagner, R. J., & Roland, C. C. (1991) Effects of outdoor challenge training on group and individual outcomes. Paper presented at the Annual Meeting of the Society for Industrial & Organizational Psychology (USA), St. Louis, MO.

Bartolome, F. (1989) Nobody trusts the boss completely—Now what? *Harvard Business Review,* **67**, 135–142.

Bass, B. M. (1988) The inspirational processes of leadership. *Journal of Management Development,* **7**, 21–31.

Bass, B. M. (1990a) *Handbook of Leadership: Theory, Research and Managerial Implications* (3rd edn.). New York: Free Press.

Bass, B. M. (1990b) From transactional to transformational leadership: Learning to share the vision. *Organizational Dynamics,* **18**, 19–36.

Bass, B. M. & Avolio, B. J. (1990) The implications of transactional and transformational leadership for individual, team and organizational development. In W. Pasmore & R. W. Woodman (eds), *Research on Organizational Change and Development,* **4**, 231–272. Greenwich, CT: JAI Press.

Bass, B. M. & Avolio, B. J. (1991) Developing transformational leadership: 1992 and beyond. *Journal of European Industrial Training,* **14**, 21–27.

Beck, J. E. (1988) Expatriate management development: Realizing the learning potential of overseas assignment. *Proceedings of the National Academy of Management (USA),* pp. 112–116.

Bennis, W. & Nanus, B. (1985) *Leaders: The Strategies for Taking Charge.* New York: Harper & Row.

Bentz, V. J. (1987) Explorations of scope and scale: The critical determinant of high-level executive effectiveness. (Report No. 31.) Greensboro, NC: Center for Creative Leadership.

Berlew, D. E. & Hall, D. T. (1966) Teacher, tutor, colleague, coach. *Personnel Journal*, 65(11), 44–51.

Bigelow, J. D. (1991) *Managerial Skills: Explorations in Practical Knowledge*. Newbury Park, CA: Sage.

Blakely, G. L., Martinec, C. L. & Lane, M. S. (1992) Management development programmes: The effects of management level and corporate strategy. Unpublished manuscript, Morgantown, WV: West Virginia University.

Blashford-Snell, J. (1991) Executive explorers. *Executive Development*, 4, 15–17.

Blunt, P. & Jones, M. L. (1991) Management development in the third world. *Journal of Management Development* [Special Issue], 10(6).

Bolt, J. F. (1987) Trends in management training and executive education: The revolution continues. *Journal of Management Development*, 6(5), 5–15.

Boyatzis, R. E. (1982) *The Competent Manager: A Model for Effective Performance*. New York: Wiley.

Boyatzis, R. E. (1991) Developing the whole student: An MBA required course called managerial assessment and development. Paper presented at the National Academy of Management (USA), Miami, August.

Boyatzis, R. E., Cowen, S. S., & Kolb, D. A. (1991) Curricular innovation in higher education: The new Weatherhead MBA program. *Selections*, 8(1), 27–37.

Boyatzis, R. E. & Renio, A. (1989) The impact of an MBA program on managerial abilities. *Journal of Management Development*, 8(5), 66–77.

Braddick, W. (1988) How top managers really learn. *Journal of Management Development*, 7, 55–62.

Bray, D. W., Campbell, R. J., & Grant, D. L. (1974) *Formative Years in Business*. New York: Wiley.

Bray, D. W. & Howard, A. (1983) The AT&T longitudinal studies of managers. In K. W. Shaie (ed.), *Longitudinal Studies of Adult Psychological Development* (pp. 266–312). New York: Guilford Press.

Brett, Jeanne M. (1984) Job transitions and personal and role development. In K. M. Rowland and G. R. Ferris (eds), *Research in Personnel and Human Resources Management*. Greenwich, CT: JAI Press.

Bushhardt, S. C., Fretwell, C. & Holdnak, B. J. (1991) The mentor/protégé relationship: A biological perspective. *Human Relations*, 44, 619–635.

Campbell, J. P., Dunnette, M., Lawler, E. E., & Weick, K. E. Jr (1970) *Managerial Behavior, Performance and Effectiveness*. New York: McGraw-Hill.

Campbell, R. J. (1989) Human resource development strategies. In K. N. Wexley (ed.), *Developing Human Resources* (pp. 5/1–34), Washington, DC: Bureau of National Affairs.

Campion, M. A., Cheraskin, L., & Stevens, M. J. (1991) The rewards and costs of job rotation as a means of preparing for promotion. Paper presented at the Society for Industrial-Organizational Psychology, St. Louis, Missouri, April.

Clark, K. E. & Clark, M. B. (1990) *Measures of Leadership*. West Orange, NJ: Leadership Library of America.

Clawson, J. G. (1980) Mentoring in managerial careers. In C. B. Derr (ed.), *Work, Family and Career* (pp. 144–165). New York: Praeger.

Cobb, J. & Gibbs, J. (1990) A new competency-based, on-the-job programme for developing professional excellence in engineering. *Journal of Management Development*, 9(3), 60–72.

Conger, J. A. & Kanungo, R. N. (1988) *Charismatic Leadership: The Elusive Factor in Organizational Effectiveness*. San Francisco: Jossey-Bass.

Constable, J. (1988) Developing the competent manager in a UK context. Report for the Manpower Services Commission, United Kingdom.

Cotter, S., James, K., Lucas, D. & Vinnicombe, S. (1991) Developing women managers at British Telecom. *Executive Development*, 4(2), 3–11.

Cox, C. J. & Cooper, C. L. (1989) The making of the British CEO: Childhood, work experience, personality and management style. *Academy of Management Executive*, 3, 241–245.

Culley, H. C. (1989) Overcoming resistance to management development. *Journal of Management Development*, 8(5), 4–10.

Davies, J. & Easterby-Smith, M. (1984) Learning and developing from managerial work experiences. *Journal of Management Studies*, 21(2), 169–183.

Day, D. V. & Lord, R. G. (1988) Executive leadership and organisational performance: Suggestions for a new theory and methodology. *Journal of Management*, 14, 453–464.

Dechant, K. (1990) Knowing how to learn: The 'neglected' management ability. *Journal of Management Development*, 9(4), 40–49.

Dreher, G. F. & Ash, R. A. (1990) A comparative study of mentoring among men and women in managerial, professional and technical positions. *Journal of Applied Psychology*, 75, 539–546.

Eichinger, R. W. & Lombardo, M. M. (1990) Twenty-two ways to develop leadership in staff managers. (Report No. 144.) Greensboro, NC: Center For Creative Leadership.

Ewert, A. (1988) Reduction of trait anxiety through participation in outward bound. *Leisure Sciences*, 10, 107–117.

Fiedler, F. E. (in press) The role and meaning of leadership experience. In K. E. Clark, M. B. Clark & D. Campbell (eds), *The Impact of Leadership*. Greensboro, NC: Center for Creative Leadership.

Finney, M. & Von Glinow, M. A. (1988) Integrating academic and organisational approaches to developing the international manager. *Journal of Management Development*, 7(2), 16–27.

Fletcher, C. (1990) Candidates' reactions to assessment centres and their outcomes: A longitudinal study. *Journal of Occupational Psychology*, 63, 117–127.

Fogel, D. S. (1990) Management education in central and eastern Europe and the Soviet Union. *Journal of Management Development*, 9(3), 14–19.

Fulmer, R. (1988) Corporate management development and education: The state of the art. *Journal of Management Development*, 7(2), 57–68.

Fulmer (1990) Executive learning as a strategic weapon. *Executive Development*, 3(3), 26–28.

Gabarro, J. J. (1987) *The Dynamics of Taking Charge*. Boston, MA: Harvard Business School Press.

Galagan, P. (1987) Between two trapezes. *Training and Development Journal*, 41(3), 40–53.

Gall, A. L. (1987) You can take the manager out of the woods, but . . . *Training and Development Journal*, 41(3), 54–61.

Gaugler, B. B., Rosenthal, D. B., Thornton, G. C. III, & Bentson, C. (1987) Meta-analysis of assessment center validity. *Journal of Applied Psychology*, 72, 493–511.

Gaylord, M. C. & Simon, E. B. (1984) Coping with job loss and job change. *Personnel*, 61(5), 70–75.

Gilbert-Smith, D. (1991) Training for leadership. *Executive Development*, 4, 25–27.

Goodge, P. (1991) Development centres: Guidelines for decision makers. *Journal of Management Development*, 10(3), 4–12.

Graen, G. B. & Uhl-Bien, M. (1991a) The transformation of professionals into self-managing and partially self-designing contributors: Toward a theory of leadership-making. *Journal of Management Systems*, 3, 33–48.

Graen, G. B. & Uhl-Bien, M. (1991b) Leadership-making applies equally well to sronsors, competence networks and teammates. *Journal of Management Systems*, **3**, 49–54.

Graen, G. B. & Wakabayashi, M. (in press) Adapting Japanese leadership techniques to their transplants in the United States: Focusing on manufacturing. *Research in International Business and International Relations*.

Green, W. A. & Lazarus, H. (1988) Corporate campuses: A growing phenomenon. *Journal of Management Development*, **7**(3), 56–67.

Hall, D. T. (1986) Dilemmas in linking succession planning to individual executive learning. *Human Resource Management*, **25**, 235–265.

Hall, D. T. (1989) How top management and the organization itself can block effective executive succession. *Human Resource Management*, **28**(1), 5–24.

Hall, D. T. & Foulkes, F. K. (1991) Senior executive development as a competitive advantage. *Advances in Applied Business Strategy*, **2**, 183–203. Greenwich, CT: JAI Press.

Hall, D. T. & Isabella, L. A. (1985) Downward movement and career development. *Organizational Dynamics*, **14**, 5–23.

Harvard Business Review (1987) Competitiveness survey; *Harvard Business Review* readers respond, **65**(5), 8–12.

Hayes, H. M. (1988) Internationalising the executive education curriculum at General Electric. *Journal of Management Development*, **7**(3), 5–12.

Hillman, L. W., Schwandt, D. R. & Bartz, D. E. (1990) Enhancing staff members' performance thru feedback and coaching. *Journal of Management Development*, **9**, 20–27.

Hollenbeck, G. P. (1990) The past, present, and future of assessment centers. *The Industrial-Organizational Psychologist*, **28**, 13–17.

Howard, A. & Bray, D. W. (1988) *Managerial Lives in Transition: Advancing Age and Changing Times*. New York: Guilford Publishing.

Hubbard, G. (1990) Changing trends in MBA education in Australia. *Journal of Management Development*, **9**(6), 41–49.

Hunt, J. G., Baiga, B. R. & Peterson, M. F. (1988) Strategic apex leader scripts and an organisational life cycle approach to leadership and excellence. *Journal of Management Development*, **7**, 61–83.

Hunt, J. W. (1990) Management development for the year 2000. *Journal of Management Development*, **9**(3), 4–13.

Ilgen, D. R., Fisher, C. D. & Taylor, M. S. (1979) Consequences of individual feedback on behavior in organizations. *Journal of Applied Psychology*, **64**, 349–371.

Ilgen, D. R. & Youtz, M. A. (1986) Factors influencing the evaluation and development of minorities. In K. Rowland & G. Ferris (eds), *Research in Personnel and Human Resource Management*, **4**, 307–337. Greenwich, CT: JAI Press.

Jennings, E. (1971) *Routes to the Executive Suite*. New York: McGraw-Hill.

Jonas, H. S. III, Fry, R. E. & Srivasta, S. (1989) The office of the CEO: Understanding the executive experience. *Academy of Management Executive*, **4**, 36–47.

Jones, M. L. (1990) Action learning as a new idea. *Journal of Management Development*, **9**, 29–34.

Jones, R. G. & Whitmore, M. D. (1992) When will developmental feedback from an assessment center make a difference in people's careers? Paper presented at the Annual Meeting of the Society for Industrial and Organizational Psychology (SIOP), Montreal.

Johnson, J. (1991) Health care management development. *Journal of Management Development* [Special Issue], **10**(4).

Johnston, A. & Dryssen, H. (1991) Co-operation in the development of public sector management skills: The SIDA experience. *Journal of Management Development*, **10**(6), 52–59.

Kable, J. (1989) Management development through action learning. *Journal of Management Development*, **8**, 77–80.

Kaplan, R. E., Drath, W. H. & Kofodimos, J. R. (1985) High hurdles: The challenge of executive self-development. (Technical Report No. 25). Greensboro, NC: Center for Creative Leadership.

Kaplan, R. E., Kofodimos, J. R. & Drath, W. H. (1987) Development at the top: A review and a prospect. In W. Pasmore & R. W. Woodman (eds), *Research on Organizational Change and Development*. Greenwich, CT: JAI Press.

Katz, R. L. (1974) Skills of an effective administrator. *Harvard Business Review*, **52**(1), 90–102.

Kelleher, D., Finestone, P. & Lowy, A. (1986) Managerial learning: First notes from an unstudied frontier. *Group and Organization Studies*, **11**, 169–202.

Kerr, S. (1990) British Telecom: On the right lines. *Executive Development*, **3**(2), 3–10.

Keys, B. (1989) Management development review. *Journal of Management Development* [Special Issue], **8**(2).

Keys, B. & Case, T. (1990) How to become an influential manager. *Academy of Management Executive*, **4**(4), 38–49.

Keys, B. & Wolfe, J. (1988) Management education and development: Current issues and emerging trends. *Journal of Management*, **14**, 205–229.

Keys, B. & Wolfe, J. (1990) The role of management games and simulations in education and research. *Journal of Management*, **16**, 307–336.

Kimura, Y. & Yoshimori, M. (1989) Japan imports American management methods through an MBA programme. *Journal of Management Development*, **8**(4), 22–31.

Kinzie, M. B. (1990) Requirements and benefits of effective interactive instruction: Learner control, self-regulation and continuing motivation. *Educational Technology Research & Development*, **38**, 1–21.

Kleiner, B. H. (1991) Developing managers for the 1990s. *Journal of Management Development*, **10**(2), 5–7.

Knowles, M. (1984) *The Adult Learner: A Neglected Species*. Houston: Gulf.

Kofodimos, J. (1990) Why executives lose their balance. *Organizational Dynamics*, **19**, 58–73.

Kolb, D., Lublin, S., Spoth, J. & Baker, R. (1985) Strategic management development: Using experiential learning theory to assess and develop managerial competencies. *Journal of Management Development*, **5**(3), 13–24.

Komacki, J. L., Desselles, M. L. & Bowman, E. D. (1989) Definitely not a breeze: Extending an operant model of effective supervision to teams. *Journal of Applied Psychology*, **74**, 522–529.

Kotter, J. P. (1982) *The General Managers*. New York: Free Press.

Kotter, J. P. (1988) *The Leadership Factor*. New York: Free Press.

Kovach, B. E. (1986) The derailment of fast-track managers. *Organizational Dynamics*, **15**, 41–48.

Kovach, B. E. (1989) Successful derailment: What fast-trackers can learn while they're off the track. *Organizational Dynamics*, **18**, 33–47.

Kram, K. E. (1985) *Mentoring at Work: Developmental Relationships in Organizational Life*. Glenview, IL: Scott, Foresman.

Kram, K. E. & Bragar, M. C. (in press) Development through mentoring: A strategic approach for the 1990s. In D. Montrose & C. Shinkman (eds), *Career Development in the '90s*.

Kram, K. E. & Hall, D. T. (1989) Mentoring as an antidote to stress during corporate trauma. *Human Resource Management*, **28**, 493–510.

Kram, K. E. & Isabella, L. A. (1985) Mentoring alternatives: The role of peer relationships in career development. *Academy of Management Journal*, **28**, 110–132.

Kraut, A. I., Pedigo, P. R., McKenna, D. D. & Dunnette, M. D. (1989) The role of the manager: What's really important in different managerial jobs. *Academy of Management Executive*, **3**, 286–93.

Latham, G. P. (1988) Human resource training and development. *Annual Review of Psychology*, **39**, 545–582.

Lawrie, J. (1989) Taking action to change performance. *Personnel Journal*, **68**, 59–69.

Lethbridge, D. (1989) University degrees for sale—the Buckingham experience. *Journal of Management Development*, **8**(3), 38–49.

Lindsey, E., Homes, V. & McCall, M. W., Jr (1987) Key events in executive lives. (Tech. Report No. 32.) Greensboro, NC: Center for Creative Leadership.

Lombardo, M. M. (1989) The road to the top is paved with good assignments. *Executive Development*, **2**, 4–7.

Lombardo, M. M. & McCauley, C. D. (1988) The dynamics of management derailment. (Tech. Report No. 134.) Greensboro, NC: Center for Creative Leadership.

London, M. (1989) *Managing the Training Enterprise*. San Francisco, CA: Jossey-Bass.

London, M. & Mone, E. M. (1987) *Career Management and Survival in the Workplace*. San Francisco, CA: Jossey-Bass.

London, M. & Wohlers, A. J. (1991) Agreement between subordinate and self-ratings in upward feedback. *Personnel Psychology*, **44**, 375–390.

London, M., Wohlers, A. J. & Gallagher, P. (1990) A feedback approach to management development. *Journal of Management Development*, **9**(6), 17–31.

Long, J. W. (1987) The wilderness lab comes of age. *Training and Development Journal*, **41**(3), 30–39.

Loo, R. (1991) Management training in Canadian organisations. *Journal of Management Development*, **10**(5), 60–72.

Louis, M. R. (1990) The gap in management education. *Selections*, **6**(3), 1–12.

Luthans, F., Hodgetts, R. M. & Rosencrantz, S. A. (1988) *Real Managers*. Cambridge, MA: Ballinger.

Maczynski, J. (1992) A cross-cultural comparison of decision-making based on the Vroom–Yetton model of leadership. (Tech. Report No. 23.) Wroclaw: Institute of Management.

Manz, C. C. (1986) Self leadership: Toward an expanded theory of self influence processes in organizations. *Academy of Management Review*, **11**, 585–600.

Manz, C. C. (1990) Beyond self-managing work teams: Toward self-leading teams in the workplace. In W. Pasmore & R. W. Woodman (eds), *Research on Organizational Change and Development*, **4**, 273–299. Greenwich, CT: JAI Press.

Manz, C. C., Keating, D. E. & Donnellon, A. (1990) Preparing for an organizational change to employee self-management: The managerial transition. *Organizational Dynamics*, **19**, 15–26.

Manz, C. C. & Manz, K. P. (1991) Strategies for facilitating self-directed learning: A process for enhancing human resource development. *Human Resource Development Quarterly*, **2**, 3–12.

Manz, C. C. & Neck, C. P. (1991) Inner leadership: Creating productive thought patterns. *Executive*, **5**, 87–95.

Manz, C. C. & Sims, H. P. (1991) SuperLeadership: Beyond the myth of heroic leadership. *Organizational Dynamics*, **20**, 18–35.

Margerison, C. J. (1988) Action learning and excellence in management development. *Journal of Management Development*, **7**, 43–54.

Margerison, C. J. & Kakabadse, A. (1984) *How American Chief Executives Succeed: Implications for Developing High Potential Employees*. New York: American Management Association.

Marsh, H. W., Richards, G. E. & Barnes, J. (1986) Multidimensional self-concepts: The effectors of participation in an Outward Bound program. *Journal of Personality and Social Psychology*, **50**, 195–204.

Marsh, H. W., Richards, G. E. & Barnes, J. (1987) A long-term follow-up of the effects of participation in an Outward Bound Program. *Personality and Social Psychology Bulletin*, **12**, 475–492.

Marsick, V. (1990) Experience-based learning: Executive learning outside the classroom. *Journal of Management Development*, **9**, 50–60.

Martinko, M. J. & Gardner, W. L. (1990) Structured observation of managerial work: A replication and synthesis. *Journal of Management Studies*, **27**, 329–357.

McCall, M. W. (1988) Developing executives through work experience. (Tech. Report No. 33.) Greensboro, NC: Center for Creative Leadership.

McCall, M. W. Jr & Lombardo, M. M. (1983) Off the track: Why and how successful executives get derailed. (Tech. Report No. 21.) Greensboro, NC: Center for Creative Leadership.

McCall, M. W., Lombardo, M. M. & Morrison, A. M. (1988) *The Lessons of Experience: How Successful Executives Develop on the Job*. Lexington, MA: Lexington Books.

McCarthy, D. J. (1991) Developing a programme for Soviet managers. *Journal of Management Development*, **10**(5), 26–31.

McCauley, C. D. (1986) Developmental experiences in managerial work: A literature review. (Tech. Report No. 26.) Greensboro, NC: Center for Creative Leadership.

McCauley, C. D. (1990) Effective school principals: Competencies for meeting the demands of educational reform. (Tech. Report No. 146.) Greensboro, NC: Center for Creative Leadership.

McCauley, C. D. & Hughes, M. W. (1991) Leadership challenges for human service administrators. *Nonprofit Management and Leadership*, **1**, 267–281.

McCauley, C. D., Lombardo, M. M. & Usher, C. J. (1989) Diagnosing management development needs: An instrument based on how managers develop. *Journal of Management*, **15**, 389–403.

McCauley, C. D., Ohlott, P. J. & Ruderman, M. N. (1989) On-the-job development: A conceptual model and preliminary investigation. *Journal of Managerial Issues*, **1**(2), 142–158.

McCauley, C. D., Ruderman, M. R., Ohlott, P. J. & Morrow, J. E. (1992) Assessing the developmental potential of managerial jobs. Unpublished manuscript: Center for Creative Leadership.

McConnell, R. V. & Seyboldt, J. W. (1991) Assessment center technology: One approach for integrating and assessing management skills in the business school curriculum. In J. Bigelow (ed.), *Managerial Skills: Explorations in Practical Knowledge* (pp. 105–115). Newbury Park, CA: Sage.

McEvoy, G. M. & Beatty, R. W. (1989) Assessment centers and subordinate appraisals of managers: A seven year examination of predictive validity. *Personnel Psychology*, **42**, 37–52.

Miner, J. B. (1991) Psychological assessment in a developmental context. In C. P. Hansen & K. A. Conrad (eds), *A Handbook of Psychological Assessment in Business* (pp. 226–237). New York: Quorum Books.

Mintzberg, H. (1973) *The Nature of Managerial Work*. New York: Harper-Row.

Morgan, G. (1988) *Riding the Waves of Change: Developing Managerial Competencies for a Turbulent World*. San Francisco, CA: Jossey Bass.

Morrison, A. M., White, R. P. & Van Velsor, E. (1987) *Breaking the Glass Ceiling: Can Women Reach the Top of America's Largest Corporations?* Reading, MA: Addison-Wesley.

Morrison, R. F. & Brantner, T. M. (1991) What affects how quickly a new job is learned? *Proceedings of the National Academy of Management*, 52–56.

Mullin, R. F., Shaffer, P. L. & Grelle, M. J. (1991) A study of the assessment center method of teaching basic management skills. In J. Bigelow (ed.), *Managerial Skills: Explorations in Practical Knowledge* (pp. 116–139). Newbury Park, CA: Sage.

Mumford, A. (1987) Action learning. *Journal of Management Development* [Special Issue], **6**(2), 1–70.

Mumford, A. (1988) *Developing Top Managers*. Aldershot: Gower.

Mumford, A. (1991) Developing the top team to meet organisational objectives. *Journal of Management Development*, **10**, 5–14.

Munchus, G. III & McArthur, B. (1991) Revisiting the historical use of the assessment center in management selection and development. *Journal of Management Development*, **10**(1), 5–13.

Neck, C. P. & Manz, C. C. (1992) Thought self-leadership: The influence of self-talk and mental imagery on performance. Unpublished manuscript: Arizona State University (USA).

Neider, L. L. & Schreisheim, C. A. (1988) Making leadership effective: A three-stage model. *Journal of Management Development*, **7**, 10–20.

Noe, R. A. (1988a) An investigation of the determinants of successful assigned mentoring relationships. *Personnel Psychology*, **41**, 457–79.

Noe, R. A. (1988b) Women and mentoring: A review and research agenda. *Academy of Management Review*, **13**, 65–78.

Noe, R. & Ford, J. K. (1992) Emerging issues and new directions for training research. In K. Rowland & G. Ferris (eds), *Research in Personnel and Human Resource Management*. Greenwich, CT: JAI Press.

Noe, R. A. & Steffy, B. D. (1987) The influence of individual characteristics and assessment center evaluation of career exploration behavior and job involvement. *Journal of Vocational Behavior*, **30**, 187–302.

Noel, J. L. & Charan, R. (1988) Leadership development at GE's Crotonville. *Human Resource Management*, **27**, 433–447.

Northcraft, G. B., Griffith, T. L. & Shalley, C. E. (1992) Building top management muscle in a slow growth environment: How different is better at Greyhound Financial Corporation. *Academy of Management Executive*, **6**(1), 32–41.

Ohlott, P. J., Ruderman, M. N. & McCauley, C. D. (1990) Women and men: Equal opportunity for development. Paper presented at the National Academy of Management (USA). San Francisco, CA: August.

Ohlott, P. J., Ruderman, M. N. & McCauley, C. D. (1992) Gender differences in managerial job demands and learning from experience. Unpublished manuscript: Center for Creative Leadership.

Olian, J. D., Carroll, S. J. & Giannantonio, C. M. (1992) Mentor reactions to protégés: An experiment with managers. Unpublished manuscript: University of Maryland (USA).

Olian, J. D., Carroll, S. J., Giannantonio, C. M. & Feren, D. B. (1988) What do protégés look for in a mentor? Results of three experimental studies. *Journal of Vocational Behavior*, **33**, 15–37.

O'Neill, B. (1990) The top-flight initiative at British Airways. *Executive Development*, **3**(2), 11–15.

Ostroff, C. & Kozlowski, S. (1992) The role of mentoring in the information gathering processes of newcomers during early organizational socialization. Unpublished manuscript: University of Minnesota (USA).

Pate, L. E. (1988) Developing leadership excellence. *Journal of Management Development* [Special Issue], **7**(5).

Pearson, A. W. & McCauley, C. D. (1991) Job demands and managerial learning in the research and development function. *Human Resource Development Quarterly*, **2**, 263–275.

Pedler, M., Boydell, T. & Burgoyne, J. (1989) Towards the learning company. *Management Education and Development*, **20**(1), 1–8.

Penley, L. E., Alexander, E. R., Jernigan, I. E. & Henwood, C. I. (1991) Communication abilities of managers: The relationship to performance. *Journal of Management*, **17**, 57–76.

Porter, J. L., Muller, H. J. & Rehder, R. R. (1991) Graduate management education in Europe. *Executive Development*, 4(2), 23–24.

Porter, L. W. & McKibbon, L. E. (1988) *Management Education and Development: Drift or Thrust into the 21st Century*. New York: McGraw-Hill.

Porter, M. (1985) *Competitive Advantage*. New York: Free Press.

Powers, E. A. (1987) Enhancing managerial competence: The American Management Association competency programme. *Journal of Management Development*, 6(4), 7–18.

Prideaux, G. & Ford, J. E. (1988a) Management development: Competencies, contracts, teams and work-based learning. *Journl of Management Development*, 7, 56–68.

Prideaux, G. & Ford, J. E. (1988b) Management development: Competencies, teams, learning contracts, and work experience based learning. *Journal of Management Development*, 7, 13–21.

Ragins, B. R. (1989) Barriers to mentoring: The female manager's dilemma. *Human Relations*, 42, 1–22.

Ragins, B. R. & Cotton, J. L. (1991a) Easier said than done: Gender differences in perceived barriers to gaining a mentor. *Academy of Management Journal*, 34, 939–951.

Ragins, B. R. & Cotton, J. L. (1991b) Gender differences in willingness to mentor. *Proceedings of the National Academy of Management* (USA), 57–61.

Ragins, B. R. & McFarlin, D. B. (1990) Perceptions of mentor roles in cross-gender mentoring relationships. *Journal of Vocational Behavior*, 37, 321–339.

Raven, J. (1988) Toward measures of high-level competencies: A re-examination of McClelland's distinction between needs and values. *Human Relations*, 41, 281–294.

Rayner, T. & Goodge, P. (1988) New techniques in assessment centres: LRT's experience. *Journal of Management Development*, 7(4), 21–30.

Revans, R. (1982) *The Origin and Growth of Action Learning*. Hunt, England: Chatwell Bratt, Bickley.

Roche, G. R. (1979) Much ado about mentors. *Harvard Business Review*, 57(1), 14–28.

Rosow, J. M. & Zager, R. (1988) *Training—The Competitive Edge*. San Francisco, CA: Jossey-Bass.

Ruderman, M. N., Ohlott, P. J. & McCauley, C. D. (1990) Assessing opportunities for leadership development. In K. E. Clark & M. B. Clark (eds), *Measures of Leadership* (pp. 547–562). West Orange, NJ: Leadership Library of America.

Saari, L. M., Johnson, T. R., McLaughlin, S. D. & Zimmerle, D. M. (1988) A survey of management training and education practices in US companies. *Personnel Psychology*, 41, 731–743.

Safavi, F. & Tweddell, C. E. (1990) Attributes of success in African management development programmes: Concepts and applications. *Journal of Management Development*, 9, 50–63.

Sanders, P. (1988) Global managers for global corporations. *Journal of Management Development*, 7(1), 33–44.

Schein, E. H. (1989) Reassessing the 'divine right' of managers. *Sloan Management Review*, 30(2), 63–68.

Schein, E. H. (1990) Career stress in changing times: Some final observations. In J. C. Quick, R. E. Hess, J. Hermalin & J. D. Quick (eds), *Career Stress in Changing Times: Prevention in Human Services*, 8(1), 251–261.

Schein, E. H. (1991) What are the pressing career issues of the 90s? Paper presented to the Annual Conference of Drake Beam Morin, Inc. San Francisco, CA.

Schneider, B. & Konz, A. M. (1989) Strategic job analysis. *Human Resource Management*, 28, 51–64.

Senge, P. M. (1990) *The Fifth Dimension: The Art and Practice of the Learning Organization*. New York: Doubleday.

Shipper, F. (1991) Mastery and frequency of managerial behaviours relative to subunit effectiveness. *Human Relations*, 44(4), 371–388.

Smith, B. (1990) Mutual mentoring on projects: A proposal to combine the advantages of several established management development methods. *Journal of Management Development*, **9**, 51–57.

Spitzer, D. R. (1991) Response to Manz and Manz's article on self-directed learning: An instructional design perspective. *Human Resource Development Quarterly*, **2**, 175–179.

Stewart, R. (1989a) Studies of managerial jobs and behaviour: The ways forward. *Journal of Management Studies*, **26**(1), 1–10.

Stewart, R. (1989b) Self-development. *Executive Development*, **2**(3), 15–16.

Streufert, S., Nogami, G. Y., Swezey, R. W., Pogash, R. M. & Piasecki, M. T. (1988) Computer assisted training of complex managerial performance. *Computers in Human Behavior*, **4**, 77–88.

Streufert, S., Pogash, R. & Piasecki, M. (1988) Simulation-based assessment of managerial competence: Reliability and validity. *Personnel Psychology*, **41**, 537–557.

Stumpf, S. A. (1989) Work experiences that stretch managers' capacities for strategic thinking. *Journal of Management Development*, **8**(5), 31–39.

Suzuki, N. (1989) Management development in Japan. *Journal of Management Development* [Special Issue], **8**(4).

Tanaka, T. (1989) Developing managers in the Hitachi Institute of management development. *Journal of Management Development*, **8**(4), 12–21.

Tannenbaum, S. I. & Woods, S. (in press) Determining a strategy for evaluating training: Operating within organizational constraints. *Human Resource Planning Journal*.

Tannenbaum, S. I. & Yukl, G. (1992) Human resource training and development. *Annual Review of Psychology*, **43**, 399–441.

Temporal, P. (1990) Management development in Asia. *Journal of Management Development* [Special Issue], **9**(5).

Temporal, P. & Burnett, K. (1990) Strategic corporate assignments and international management development. *Journal of Management Development*, **9** 58–64.

Thareau, P. (1991) Managers' training needs and preferred training strategies. *Journal of Management Development*, **10**(5), 46–59.

Thompson, P. H., Kirkham, K. L. & Dixon, J. (1985) Warning: The fast track may be hazardous to organizational health. *Organizational Dynamics*, **13**, 21–33.

Uhl-Bien, M. & Graen, G. B. (in press a) An empirical test of the leadership-making model in professional project teams. In K. E. Clark, M. B. Clark & D. Campbell (eds), *The Impact of Leadership*. Greensboro, NC: Center for Creative Leadership.

Uhl-Bien, M. & Graen, G. B. (in press b) Self-management and team-making in cross-functional work teams: Discovering the keys to becoming an integrated team. *Journal of High Technology Management*.

Ulrich, D. (1989) Executive development as a competitive weapon. *Journal of Management Development*, **8**(5), 11–22.

Vaill, P. (1989) *Managing as a Performing Art: New Ideas for a World of Chaotic Change.* San Francisco, CA: Jossey Bass.

Van Velsor, E. & Hughes, M. W. (1990) Gender differences in the development of managers: How women managers learn from experience. (Tech. Report No. 145.) Greensboro, NC: Center for Creative Leadership.

Van Velsor, E. & Leslie, J. B. (1991) *Feedback to Managers/Volume II: A Review and Comparison of Sixteen Multi-rater Feedback Instruments.* (Tech. Report No. 150.) Greensboro, NC: Center for Creative Leadership.

Vedder, J. (1992) How much can we learn from success? *Academy of Management Executive*, **6**(1), 56–66.

Verlander, E. G. (1989) Improving university executive programmes. *Journal of Management Development*, **8**(1), 5–19.

Vicere, A. A. (1988) University-based executive education: Impacts and implications. *Journal of Management Development*, 7(4), 5–13.

Vicere, A. A. (1991) The changing paradigm for executive development. *Journal of Management Development*, 10(3), 44–47.

Vroom, V. & Jago, A. G. (1988) Managing participation: A critical dimension of leadership. *Journal of Management Development*, 7, 32–42.

Wexley, K. N. & Baldwin, T. T. (1986) Management development. *Journal of Management*, 12, 277–294.

Wexley, K. N. & Latham, G. P. (1991) *Developing and Training Human Resources in Organizations*. New York: HarperCollins.

Whetten, D. A. & Cameron, K. S. (1991) *Developing Management Skills* (2nd edition). New York: HarperCollins.

Whitley, R. (1989) On the nature of managerial tasks and skills: Their distinguishing characteristics and organisation. *Journal of Management Studies*, 26(3), 209–224.

Williams, E. C. (1991) Management development programmes for the Asia Pacific Region maritime industry: The Singapore port institute. *Journal of Management Development*, 10(7), 66–69.

Wilson, C. L. (1978) The Wilson multi-level management surveys: Refinement and replication of the scales. JSAS: Catalog of selected documents in Psychology 8 (Ms. no 1707) American Psychological Association, Washington, DC.

Wilson, W. B. (1990) The changing bell(e) of the north. *Journal of Management Development*, 9(3), 35–41.

Wohlers, A. J. & London, M. (1989) Ratings of managerial characteristics: Evaluation difficulty, co-worker agreement and self-objectivity. *Personnel Psychology*, 42, 235–261.

Woodman, R. & Passmore, W. A. (1987) *Research in Organizational Change and Development*. Greenwich, CT: JAI Press.

Wright, R. G. & Werther, W. B. (1991) Mentors at work. *Journal of Management Development*, 10, 25–32.

Yau, W. S. L. & Sculli, D. (1990) Managerial traits and skills. *Journal of Management Development*, 9(6), 32–40.

Yukl, G. A. (1989) *Leadership in Organizations* (2nd edition). Englewood Cliffs, NJ: Prentice-Hall.

Yukl, G. & Lepsinger, R. (1991) An integrative taxonomy of managerial behavior: Implications for improving managerial effectiveness. In J. W. Jones, B. D. Steffy & D. W. Bray (eds), *Applying Psychology in Business* (pp. 563–572). Lexington, MA: Lexington Books.

Yukl, G., Wall, S. & Lepsinger, R. (1990) Preliminary report on validation of the managerial practices survey. In K. E. Clark & M. B. Clark (eds), *Measures of Leadership* (pp. 223–237). West Orange, NJ: Leadership Library of America.

Zey, M. G. (1988) A mentor for all reasons. *Personnel Journal*, 67, 46–51.

Zey, M. G. (1989) Building a successful mentor program. *Mentoring International*, 3, 48–51.

Chapter 9

ORGANIZATION THEORY: CURRENT CONTROVERSIES, ISSUES, AND DIRECTIONS

Arthur G. Bedeian
Department of Management
Louisiana State University
USA

INTRODUCTION

The field of organization theory is alive and apparently thriving. A sense of excitement and vitality has transcended national boundaries as researchers throughout the world have turned their attention to examining organizations as distinct units in a larger system of relations. An interdisciplinary field, organization theory is defined by its focus upon the *organization as the unit of analysis* (Cummings, 1978). It has roots in sociology, political science, anthropology, and economics, and deals with questions of organization structure, processes, and outcomes within social/economic contexts.

Organization theory thus focuses on the actions of organizations viewed as total entities. This stands in contrast to the field of organizational behavior that examines the behavior of individuals and groups within the context of organizations. The distinction here is not only one of unit of analysis, but of nature of dependent variables. Within the field of organizational behavior, the relevant dependent variables are measures of individual or subunit (e.g. work clusters, departments, authority ranks) affective or behavioral reactions. By comparison, organization theory takes as its primary concerns dependent variables such as effectiveness, efficiency, and environmental relations. As a consequence, while organizations furnish a common locus of research for investigators from both fields, their questions of interest and the corresponding conceptual schemes which guide their inquiries vary (Schneider, 1985). The present review will concentrate solely on the organization theory field. Those readers interested in reviews of the organizational behavior field are referred to representative sources such as Mitchell (1979), Cummings (1982), Staw (1984), and Schneider (1985).

Focus and Format of the Review

The literature associated with organization theory since its emergence as a field four or so decades ago is enormous. In a review such as this it is impossible to cover all areas or to do justice to areas that have received considerable attention in the literature. In general, as the number of contributions to a research domain increases, the pressures for review and integration grow. The mass of available information becomes too large for assimilation. This pressure has produced a number of earlier reviews of the organization theory field (Cyert and MacCrimmon, 1968; Donaldson, 1985; March, 1965; Miner, 1982; Pfeffer, 1986; Scott, 1964; Scott, 1975; Nystrom and Starbuck, 1981).

My intent is not to cover the same ground again. Rather, this review will focus on current controversies and issues associated with four topics on which substantial scholarship has been conducted recently. These topics are: (1) organizational effectiveness, (2) organization-environment relations, (3) organizational learning, and (4) organizational decline. For each topic, a summary will be provided of the prevailing theoretical approaches and research trends. Theoretical issues will be discussed more fully than any particular study, and ideas are emphasized over methods. The historical works of the field will be used as a framework for interpretation. A section at the end of the review comments on the field's present state of health.

ORGANIZATIONAL EFFECTIVENESS

In a recent commentary on the state of contemporary organization theory, it was observed that research themes seem to have changed not so much because issues are resolved and phenomena understood, but rather because investigators run out of steam and interest turns to 'newer, more exciting' topics (Bedeian, 1986b). Perhaps no topic better exemplifies this observation than that of organizational effectiveness.

Although it was identified by Cummings (1982) as a reemerging area of research likely to continue to accelerate as a focus of scholarship, the last few years have seen a virtual abandonment of organizational effectiveness studies, as investigators have turned to 'hotter' topics. The latest heyday of organizational effectiveness research began building up steam in the late 1970s (Cameron, 1978; Campbell, 1976; Goodman et al., 1977; Steers, 1975, 1976, 1977).

Effectiveness Models

The goal model

Initial interest in organizational effectiveness can be traced to early economic, accounting, and general management theories. Viewed historically, theorists have traditionally defined effectiveness as the meeting or surpassing of organizational goals (see, for example, Barnard, 1938). This perspective has become known as the goal model approach to the study of organizational effectiveness, since it views organizations as principally concerned with the attainment of certain end products or goals. The goal model thus rests on the implicit assumption that an organization's goals can be clearly established and that necessary human and material resources can be manipulated for goal attainment.

Various shortcomings in the goal model have been noted repeatedly. For instance, it has been observed that most contemporary organizations are multifunctional, pursuing numerous goals at the same time (Cameron, 1981a). Consequently, effectiveness in attaining one goal may be inversely related to effectiveness in attaining other goals. This suggests the likelihood that an organization will find it impossible to be effective in all areas simultaneously if it has multiple goals.

A second common criticism leveled at the goal model concerns the establishment of unambiguous criteria for measuring effectiveness. An ability to assess effectiveness on the basis of goal attainment depends upon the extent to which goals are measurable. Business firms, for example, have identifiable 'bottom line' objectives. No comparable yardstick exists for public organizations such as social welfare agencies and voluntary associations (Keating and Keating, 1981; Meyer, 1985). The determination of what constitutes goal attainment in these and similar situations can be quite unclear.

Despite these and other such criticisms, the goal model remains the dominant approach for studying organizational effectiveness (Clinebell, 1984). 'Its dominance,' as suggested by Hall (1980, p. 538), 'is linked to the fact that organizations do in fact utilize goals, as witnessed by annual reports and planning documents.' Hall further notes that 'while these can be labeled as rationalizations for past actions, goals remain a central component of most theories of organizations and of organizational effectiveness'.

The system resource model

Perhaps the most widely accepted alternative to the goal model is known as the system resource model of organizational effectiveness. Incorporating an open-systems viewpoint, this approach defines effectiveness as the degree to which an organization is successful in acquiring scarce and valued resources. The system resource model focuses on the interaction between an organization and its environment. In contrast to the goal model, inputs replace outputs as the primary consideration (Shipper and White, 1983). Organizations are viewed as involved in a continuous bargaining relationship with their environment, importing scarce resources to be returned as valued outputs. An organization's survival through time clearly depends upon its ability to establish and maintain a favorable input–output ratio. That is, to establish and maintain a greater resource intake than is required to produce its output.

Like the goal model, the system resource model has also received its share of criticism. Principal among these is that it is difficult to operationalize. While the system resource model holds that an organization is most effective when it optimizes its resource intake, it provides little guidance as to what constitutes optimum procurement. Moreover, it does not elaborate on *which* scarce and valued resources are relevant for assessing an organization's effectiveness and how, once obtained, they should be internally allocated.

More recent models for studying organizational effectiveness have been largely integrative. Two of these models, the 'multiple constituency approach' and the 'competing values approach', have generated sufficient interest to be considered separately. Each will be examined in turn.

Multiple constituency model

Individuals become involved with different organizations for various reasons. As would be anticipated, these reasons are reflected in differential preferences for performance. The multiple constituency approach (Connally, Conlon, and Deutsch, 1980) to organizational effectiveness defines effectiveness as the extent to which an organization satisfies the goals of its strategic constituents (or stakeholders). Thus, it represents an expansion of the goal model in the sense that it incorporates in the assessment process the goals of constituencies other than managers. As generally portrayed, a typical organization's constituencies (stakeholders) include society in general, customers, governments (local, state and federal), owners, employees, suppliers and competitors (Bedeian, 1986a). The multiple constituency model, thus, avoids problems of specifying and assessing organizational goals inherent in the goal model, as well as problems of identifying and assessing optimal resource acquisition as required by the system resource model.

As with its predecessors, however, critics have been quick to note several shortcomings associated with the multiple constituency model. Most notably, it incorporates several underlying value-based issues. Major among these is that selecting specific constituents to participate in assessing an organization's effectiveness involves a value judgement (Mark and Shotland, 1985). Except in instances where there is a limited constituent set or an unlikely consensus among constituents about what is important, practical constraints will prohibit an organization from satisfying *all* concerns that might interest its various constituents.

This dilemma has obvious implications for the actual measurement of organizational effectiveness. Admittedly, perceptions of an organization's effectiveness depend largely upon its constituents' frames of reference (Zammuto, 1984). As Bedeian (1986b) has observed, this presents three rather complicated measurement issues:

1. Any and all effectiveness criteria that are proposed will doubtlessly be viewed in terms of self-interest by each of the constituents involved.
2. Despite claims to the contrary, no criteria will be viewed impartially. Assessments of effectiveness do not take place in a neutral vacuum. Each criterion will likely benefit some constituents more than others.
3. Given the above considerations, in a situation in which resources are scarce, we would have every reason to expect a wide divergence and commensurate conflict in the criteria different constituents propose for assessing effectiveness.

Competing values model

The most recent approach to studying organizational effectiveness is that developed by Quinn and Rohrbaugh (1981, 1983; Rohrbaugh, 1981, 1983; Faerman and Quinn, in press). Known as the 'competing values' approach, it provides a means for integrating different models of organizational effectiveness with respect to three underlying value dimensions: (1) an internal focus versus an external focus, (2) a concern for flexibility versus a concern for control, (3) a concern for ends versus a concern for means.

Casting these underlying value dimensions on a Cartesian plane, Quinn and Rohrbaugh found a parallel with four alternative models of organizational effectiveness (see Figure 9.1). The 'human relations' model emphasizes an internal focus together with flexibility. It stresses effectiveness criteria such as cohesion and morale (as means) and human resource development (as an end). The 'open-systems' model emphasizes an external focus along with flexibility. It stresses effectiveness criteria such as innovation and readiness (as means) and organizational growth (as an end). The 'rational goal' model emphasizes an external focus, as well as control. It stresses effectiveness criteria such as planning and goal setting (as means) and productivity (as an end). Finally, the 'internal process' model emphasizes an internal focus together with control. It stresses effectiveness criteria such as the role of information management and communication (as means) and stability and predictability (as ends).

Each of the four organizational effectiveness models identified by Quinn and Rohrbaugh (1981) is embedded in a set of competing values. Indeed, while each does have a polar opposite with a directly competing emphasis, it also shares parallel

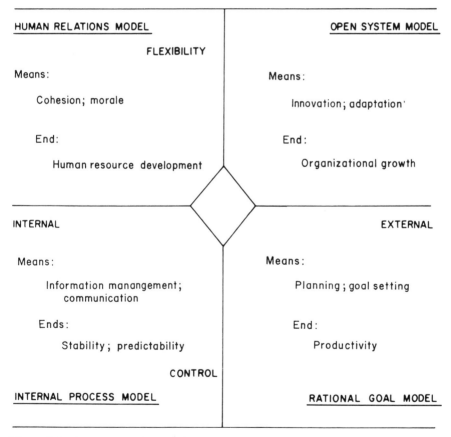

Figure 9.1 A summary of competing value dimensions and four effectiveness models Based on Quinn and Rohrbaugh (1981, 1983; Rohrbaugh, 1981, 1983)

emphases with the two models it adjoins on common axes. The critical point to note, however, is that while certain pairs of effectiveness criteria reflect competing values, in practice they are not mutually exclusive. To be effective may require that an organization be both cohesive *and* productive, or stable *and* innovative.

The competing values approach clearly recognizes that multiple criteria and potentially conflicting constituent interests underlie any effort at assessing an organization's effectiveness. Moreover, given an understanding of the values different constituencies hold, it provides a basis for predicting the effectiveness criteria a constituency will likely employ in judging an organization's performance. Such knowledge should be of great value to an oganization attempting to satisfy a maximum number of stakeholders.

Measurement Concerns

As the preceding discussion suggests, irrespective of approach, assessing effectiveness is difficult and potentially controversial. Much frustration, as well as numerous methodological problems, surround the measurement of organizational effectiveness (Cameron, 1986). Several authors have even called for a moratorium on studies of organizational effectiveness and, in the extreme, have suggested that efforts to develop a theory of effectiveness be abandoned (Bluedorn, 1980; Goodman, Atkin, and Schoorman, 1982). The work of Quinn and Rohrbaugh (1981) is especially notable in integrating what has largely been a fragmentary and scattered area. The development of an accepted methodology for assessing an organization's overall effectiveness has been hampered by acknowledged measurement problems (Bedeian, 1986b).

Of particular concern in measuring effectiveness is the assessment of organizational performance across time (Cameron and Whetten, 1984). Three issues are particularly noteworthy. First, since organizations do not perform in standard units that are uniformly distributed over time, effectiveness is cyclical (Warner, 1967). Thus, the specific period or era and the actual time—short-run versus long-run—used in assessing an organization's performance may influence the resulting evaluation. Second, organizations are necessarily at different stages in their life cycles. Thus, effectiveness criteria appropriate at one stage may be unsuitable at another as organizational goals at each stage generally have a different focus (Cameron, 1981b; Cameron and Whetten, 1981; Quinn and Cameron, 1983). Third, taking a multiple constituency perspective, it is likely that an organization's constituents will change over time (Zammuto, 1982a, 1984). Moreover, the preferences of any continuing constituents are unlikely to remain stable. Measurement techniques for incorporating such changes and, in turn, determining how an organization's attempts to satisfy constituent preferences at one point in time will likely change constituent expectations for an organization's future performance simply do not exist.

A further measurement problem hampering the development of an accepted methodology for assessing effectiveness concerns the translation of criteria across levels of analysis (Mossholder and Bedeian, 1983a, 1983b). Effectiveness can be and has been conceptualized at the individual, group, and supra-system levels. It should not be assumed, however, that assessing an organization's overall effectiveness is a substitute for assessing its components or vice versa. Moreover, as Schneider (1985, p. 597) notes, it is becoming increasingly recognized that studies which include 'data derived from a focus on only one unit of analysis will likely yield relatively weak relationships because phenomena exist at multiple levels'. In the context of the present discussion, our ability to measure organizational effectiveness would be significantly enhanced by the identification of processes that operate across levels.

A final, but certainly not last, measurement problem hindering the development of an accepted methodology for assessing effectiveness concerns the appropriateness of criteria across organizations (Lewin and Minton, 1986). Research supports the view that since different types of organizations (e.g. profit versus not-for-profit) have different goals and constituencies, different criteria are appropriate for judging their performance (see, for example, Bozeman, 1982). Thus, while certain criteria (e.g. market share) may be relevant for certain types of organizations (e.g. business firms), they may have little relevance for others (e.g. public service agencies). A valid means for establishing appropriate effectiveness criteria that accurately reflect such contrasting orientations awaits development.

ORGANIZATION–ENVIRONMENT RELATIONS

Environmental relations have probably attracted more research than any other dependent variable in the organization theory field. The issue of organization–environment relations has drawn the attention of investigators for the greater part of the last two decades. Recent research, maintaining a longstanding tradition, has continued to examine environmental management strategies. Likewise, it has extended its focus in the allied areas of organization–environment 'fit' and strategic choice and environmental determinism. Of additional current interest, population ecologists have emerged in force as a vocal group attempting to explain the dynamics of organization–environment relations. The following discussion will review recent work in the areas of (1) organization–environment fit, (2) strategic choice and environmental determinism, (3) population ecology, and (4) environmental management strategies, including environmental scanning.

Organization–Environment 'Fit'

Structural contingency theory models have long dominated the study of organization design and performance (Venkatraman and Camillus, 1984). The basic proposition of these models is that performance is contingent on a fit between two or more factors, e.g. the fit between environmental demands, strategy, structure, and technology. Recently, however, structural contingency theory has drawn increasing criticism for a seeming inability to address its basic theoretical and empirical problems (e.g. Schoonhoven, 1981; Schreyogg, 1980; Takahashi, 1983).

In specific response to this mounting criticism, Van de Ven and Drazin (1985; Drazin and Van de Ven, 1985; Van de Ven, 1979) have argued that much of this criticism arises from the inadequate specification of the 'fit' concept. Van de Ven

(1979), for instance, has noted that there are at least four different conceptual meanings of fit, each with its own unique theoretical implications. Contending that little scientific progress will be made until more detailed specifications of fit are established, Van de Ven and Drazin (1985) have made a significant contribution to the organization theory literature by addressing the current confusion surrounding contingency theory models.

Focusing on three approaches to fit—selection, interaction, and systems—Van de Ven and Drazin (1985) have not only suggested alternate means for testing the fit concept, but have empirically tested their own recommendations (Drazin and Van de Ven, 1985). Their evidence provides support for the selection and systems approaches, but not the interaction approach. Commenting on the generalizability of this finding, Drazin and Van de Ven urge the design of further contingency studies to permit additional comparative evaluation of alternative approaches to fit. In doing so, they stress that the resulting complementary information can result in more comprehensive explanations of context–structure–performance relationships than any single approach to fit alone.

Strategic Choice and Environmental Determinism

Although research suggests that some form of fit between an organization's structure and its environment affects its performance, the role of managerial perceptions and strategic choice in this adaptive process is still unclear (Bourgeois, 1985). As Hrebiniak and Joyce (1985, p. 336) note, 'The prevailing assumption in recent literature is that strategic choice and environmental determinism represent mutually exclusive, competing explanations of organizational adaptation'. On the one hand, environmental determinists, focusing on objective environments as determinants of structures, have disregarded the influence of managerial perceptions on organizational adaptations. On the other hand, strategic choice advocates, emphasizing the role of managerial perceptions, have ignored the influences of objective environments. Despite the general recognition that organizations and their environments are parts of a complex interactive system both groups have assumed one-way causality. Yasai-Ardekani's (1986, p. 9) conclusion that 'objective and perceptual approaches to the study of environment-structural fit have yielded equally suspect results' should thus not be surprising.

Environmental determinists essentially view organizations as passive recipients being acted upon by their environment. By contrast, strategic choice advocates view organizations as perceptually modeling their world and taking actions accordingly. A recognition of the relevance of both the environment and top managers' choices in determining organizational performance is beginning to emerge (Astley and Van de Ven, 1983; Dess and Beard, 1984). Hrebiniak and Joyce (1985), for instance, have argued that classifying organizational adaptations as either managerially or environmentally derived is misleading. They suggest instead that strategic choice and environmental determinism are independent variables that in interaction yield four types of organizational adaptation: (1) natural selection: low strategic choice and high environmental determinism, (2) differentiation: high strategic choice and high environmental determinism, (3) strategic choice: high strategic choice and low environmental determinism, and (4) undifferentiated choice: low strategic choice and low environmental determinism. The key point emerging from Hrebiniak and Joyce's analysis is that organizational adaptation is a dynamic process in which strategic choice and environmental determinism exist simultaneously.

Hrebiniak and Joyce thus view strategic choice and environmental determinism as variables whose effects can only be understood in relation to one another. Their model of organizational adaptation suggests that strategic choice and environmental determinism never operate in isolation. In an extension of Hrebiniak and Joyce's logic, Bedeian (1986b) contends that strategic choice and environmental determinism stand in a relationship of continuous reciprocal influence in which organizations respond to their environments as well as change them. His argument is that environmental attributes and strategic choice continuously influence each other in a multidirectional interaction process that Pervin and Lewis (1978) term 'reciprocal action–transaction'. What makes the reciprocal action–transaction model even more different from traditional models is that it requires consideration of a time orientation. In traditional models, strategic choice and environmental determinism are viewed interdependently. By contrast, from a reciprocal action–transaction perspective, strategic choice and environmental determinism exist in continual interaction over time. Thus, reciprocal action–transaction derives from two factors: (1) organizations not only react to their individual environments, they also create or enact them, and (2) the resulting new environments in turn influence future organization actions, which alternately change the environments again. The continuous reciprocal influence underlying the cognitive interpretation and reinterpretation of environments by organizations hence emphasizes the need to attend to both subjective and objective phenomena as they interact across time. As two examples, recently published case studies of the historical development of the Du Pont Company (McNamee, 1983) and how the cigarette industry has protected its environmentally threatened cigarette operations (Dunbar and Wasilewski, 1985) clearly underscore the continuous reciprocal interplay of organization and environment.

Population Ecology

Following a deterministic slant, the population ecology perspective has quickly become one of the most influential approaches for explaining the dynamics of organization–environment relations. Proponents of this perspective focus on the appearance, development, and disappearance of organizations. They contend that extreme environmental demands in effect 'select out' stronger, more dominant organizational forms as 'weaker' organizations cease to exist, or survive only as markedly different forms of organization. Thus, organizational forms which are successful spread through growth and imitation, while unsuccessful forms disappear or are absorbed into other organizations. A complete development of population ecology as it applies to organizations is given by Aldrich, McKelvey, and Ulrich (1984), Aldrich and McKelvey (1983), Bidwell and Kasarda (1985), Kasarda and Bidwell (1984), McKelvey and Aldrich (1983), Ulrich (1984), and Ulrich and Barney

(1984). Astley (1985a) has recently gone beyond population ecology to develop a more encompassing community ecology perspective.

A fundamental aspect of population ecology lies in the identification of environmental niches — 'distinct combinations of resources and other constraints that are sufficient to support an organizational form' (Aldrich, 1979, p. 28). Of particular interest has been the question of niche width. That is, a population of organizations' 'tolerance for changing levels of resources, its ability to resist competitors, and its response to other factors that inhibit growth' (Carroll, 1985, p. 1266). Populations with a broad niche (generalists) have a wide tolerance, being able to reproduce in diverse circumstances. Those with a narrow niche (specialists) have more limited ranges of tolerance, being able to survive only in specific environmental conditions. To date, studies investigating the notion of niche width (Carroll, 1985; Freeman and Hannan, 1983; McPherson, 1983) have been more distinguished by their statistical manipulations than their clarity of results. Likewise, analyses of the general population ecology model have largely reported inconsistent results (Korsching, 1983; Marple, 1982, 1983; Rundall and McClain, 1982; Staber, 1985).

Criticism of the population ecology perspective has been far-reaching (Betton and Dess, 1985). Critics have claimed that the selection process incorporated in population ecology is much more complicated than presented. As Weick (1979, p 125) explains, 'their objection is that "selection" can occur in so many ways that the concept does not explain very much of what happens. It is easy to attribute everything that occurs to some kind of selection, and for this reason the explanation loses its power'. Others (McPherson, 1983; Van de Ven, Hudson and Schroeder, 1984) have noted that unless the population ecology logic is tested with longitudinal experimental evidence, it contains an inherent tautology: organizations are successful because they have survived, and they have survived because they were successful. Equally vocal are those (Astley and Fombrun, 1983; Astley and Van de Ven, 1983) who argue that environments may not really consist of open niches waiting to be filled, but rather of potential space that needs to be carved out. Additionally, there are critics (Büschges, 1985; Foo, Aliga and Puxty, 1981) who object to population ecology's virtually ignoring the role played by managerial decision makers. The population ecology perspective views organizations as adopting a passive, reactive posture in relation to environmental events. It depicts the process of selection among organizational forms continuing almost regardless of managerial decision makers. Finally, it has also been noted (Astley, 1984; Strauss, 1982) that population ecologists have focused almost exclusively on the dynamics of competition and ignored the cooperative social and political features regulating the vital intersections between organizations.

Environmental Management Strategies

Environmental scanning

Theorists rejecting the notion of a deterministic relationship between environment and structure generally argue that strategic choice plays an important role in influencing an organization's responses to its environment. In this respect, a close relationship has been repeatedly shown between performance and gathering of environmental data. On the upscale side, most research shows a positive correlation between superior performance and the extent to which organizations scan their environment (e.g. Miller and Friesen, 1980). On the downscale side, organizational decline has been repeatedly associated with a failure to adequately identify and assess environmental trends (e.g. Schendel, Patton and Riggs, 1976).

As generally conceptualized, scanning involves monitoring and evaluating events and trends in an organization's environment. Recognizing the importance of adequately identifying and assessing environmental trends, organization theorists have continued their study of formal environmental scanning activities. A two-dimensional matrix for guiding scanning activities has been developed by Camillus and Venkatraman (1984). Diffenbach (1983) and Higgins (1986) have surveyed the extent of environmental analysis in *Fortune 500* and British firms, respectively. Klein and Linneman (1984) have similarly surveyed the nature of environmental scanning in a worldwide sample of international corporations. Other more or less comprehensive studies have also been recently reported (e.g. Fahey, Narayanan, 1981; Jain, 1984; Stubbart, 1982).

Studies investigating specific hypotheses relating to environmental scanning behavior have been performed by Nishi, Schoderbek, and Schoderbek (1982; Nishi, 1979) and Culnan (1983). In a test of eight propositions, Nishi *et al.* (1982) found, among other things, that executives' scanning behaviors (surveillance and search) were related to different environmental states (dynamic versus stable), as well as to different hierarchical levels of management (upper versus lower). Culnan's (1983) findings also confirm that scanning is influenced by an organization's environment, but that the information-gathering requirements (e.g. complexity) associated with a manager's environment are related to the use of different information sources (e.g. periodicals, consultants, databases). In a methodological advance, Farh, Hoffman, and Hegarty (1984) have adapted Hambrick's (1981) environmental scanning scale for use at the subunit level. Finally, Lenz and Engledow (1986) have explored the administrative problems associated with structuring, sustaining, and using environmental scanning units in ten 'leading-edge' corporations.

Assuming a benefit from environmental scanning, the specific strategies organizations employ hopefully to manage their environment vary extensively. What have been generally classified as *direct* strategies include coopting, interlocking directorates, illegal activities, mergers, and joint ventures. More *indirect* strategies include involvement of third parties such as trade associations (e.g. National Association of Furniture Manufacturers), professional organizations (e.g. American Medical Association), and, in the US, political action committees. The extent of research on each of these strategies varies. Mergers, joint ventures, and similar coalescing activities have been extensively reviewed in the general management literature (e.g. Bedeian, 1986a) and will, thus, not be covered here. Comments, however, will be offered on a majority of the remaining identified strategies.

Coopting

A *direct* strategy for dealing with environmental uncertainty, coopting is the process of absorbing external elements into an organization's decision-making or policy-determining structure as a means of averting threats to its stability or existence.

The naming of International Union–United Auto Workers President (Emeritus) Douglas A. Fraser to the Chrysler Corporation board is a typically cited example of cooptation (Zeithaml and Zeithaml, 1984). Cooptation is selected as a strategy to manage environmental relations on the assumption that if threatening elements from the environment are absorbed or coopted into an organization, the effects of uncertainty can be partially neutralized. The classic case is the non-financial corporation that is seriously indebted to a particular bank and coopts a representative of the bank onto its board (Pennings, 1980). The notion of cooptation, however, has been more broadly defined. Hirsch (1975) has shown how the pharmaceutical industry coopted the American Medical Association. More recently, Burt (1983a, 1983b) has suggested that corporate philanthropy can be employed as a means of coopting the consumer sector of a nation's economy.

Interlocking directorates

Interlocking directorates is a second *direct* strategy for attempting to manage environmental uncertainty. The literature dealing with interlocking boards of directors is voluminous (e.g. recently, Burt, 1982, 1983a; Fennema, 1982; Mintz and Schwartz, 1985; Mizruchi, 1982; Pennings, 1980; Scott and Griff, 1984). The goal of director interlocks is to help manage external dependencies, and thus make an organization's environment more manageable. Research suggests that this is primarily accomplished in four ways: (1) establishment of horizontal coordination, whereby two or more competitors are linked, can communicate, and can jointly benefit; (2) establishment of vertical coordination, whereby an organization can reduce uncertainty concerning either its input or its outputs; (3) appointment of outside directors who can contribute information and skills from which an organization can benefit; and (4) appointment of prestigious people as directors to provide confirmation for the larger environment as to the wealth and responsibility of an organization (Bazerman and Schoorman, 1983; Mintz and Schwartz, 1981; Ornstein, 1984; Palmer, 1983; Roy, 1983; Schoorman, Bazerman, and Atkin, 1981).

Illegal activities

Interest in organizational illegality, a third *direct* strategy for managing organization-environment relations, has grown steadily (e.g. Sonnenfeld, 1981). The exact extent of such deviant behavior is, of course, unknown. Available evidence, however, suggests that it is quite extensive (Clinard, 1983a, 1983b; Ermann and Lundman, 1982; Wagel, Ermann, and Horowitz, 1981). As identified by Szwajkowski (1985), three explanatory variables appear to form the building blocks of organizational crime theory. They are: environment (press, need or distress); structure (corporate, industrial or legal); and inner-directed choice processes (pathology, intent or proactive exploitation). Szwajkowski contends that these variables may occur in isolation or combination and may be manifested in numerous ways. Moreover, he notes that their explanatory power may vary considerably across violation type and setting, with their effect differing depending upon whether relevant laws are new and uncertain or well-established and tested.

Political action committees

Of the various *indirect* strategies employed by organizations hopefully to manage their environment, political action committees (PACs) have perhaps generated the most interest. While corporations in Britain are permitted to donate money to political parties and candidates they favor, US corporations by law cannot (Useem, 1984). The US ban on direct corporate financing of political campaigns has prompted a substantial number of organizations of all types (corporate, labor, trade) to establish PACs to collect funds from employees and channel them to friendly political parties and candidates. The growth in PAC activity has spawned a good deal of concern in both the academic (e.g. Handler and Mulkern, 1982) and popular press (Grover, 1986). This concern is far too wide to chronicle here. Some researchers have concluded that PACs do have a major effect on legislative behavior (Kau and Rubin, 1981; Kau, Keenan, and Rubin, 1982). Others, however, contend that the influence of PACs is overstated (Banthin and Stelzer, 1986; Chappell, 1982; Keim, Zeithaml, and Baysinger, 1984; Malbin, 1979). Of the studies in this area, the works of Masters and his colleagues (e.g. Masters and Keim, 1985) are of particular interest. More specifically, Masters and Baysinger (1985) have developed a theoretical framework to explain variation in corporate PAC fundraising. Findings based on hypotheses derived from the model suggest that the federal government, through its actions as a purchaser and regulator, seems to have a significant impact on how corporations act in the political arena. For instance, it is not surprising to find that corporations highly affected by government attempt to influence policy making through electoral campaign financing. Similarly, Masters and Delaney (1985) have developed and tested an exploratory model to explain differences in union PAC contributions. Their findings suggest that political activity among union PACs is at least partly a function of being situated in a highly regulated economic sector. In any case, evidence is mounting to suggest that organizations, especially US corporations, are becoming increasingly involved in political activity (Baysinger, 1984; Baysinger and Woodman, 1982; Dickie, 1984; Keim, 1985; Yoffie and Bergenstein, 1985).

ORGANIZATIONAL LEARNING

Interest in oganizational learning can be traced to the early work of Cyert and March (1959, 1963; March, 1962). This interest, however, did not reach its full stride until the publication of March and Olsen's (1975, 1976) research on ambiguity and choice. A conceptually appealing notion, organizational learning has recently emerged as a key concept in the popular management press. Writing in their *Leaders: The Strategies for Taking Charge*, Bennis and Nanus (1985) see 'innovative' learning as essential for an organization's survival. Similarly, O'Toole (1985) sees 'continuous' learning as a general characteristic of organizations practicing the 'New Management', or what he terms 'Vanguard Management'.

Generally defined, organizational learning is the process by which an organization obtains knowledge about the associations between past actions, the effectiveness of those actions, and future actions (cf. Fiol and Lyles, 1985). As presented by March and Olsen (1975), organizational learning rests on two fundamental foundations: (1) rational calculation and (2) experiential learning. The notion of rational calculation incorporates the idea that organizations use expectations about future outcomes as a basis for selecting among current alternatives. Experiential learning assumes that organizations adjust their activities based on past experiences in an effort to increase their competence.

Just as in the case of 'organizational goals', the concept of organizational learning raises the issue of reification. That is, it grants to the concept of organization anthropomorphic (human) characteristics that it does not possess. Acknowledging that organizations exhibit adaptive behavior over time, it seems naïve to assume that organizations learn in the same manner as human beings. Bennis and Nanus (1985) sidestep this issue by simply declaring that organizational learning occurs at all levels in an organization—among individuals and groups as well as systemwide. Friedlander (1983) avoids this issue by coining the term 'learning organism' to include both individual and organizational learning. Perhaps most satisfactorily, Argyris (1985) states that organizational learning is produced through the actions of individuals acting as an 'agent' for an organization. Exactly how individual and organizational learning relate remains unclear. Organizational learning is, however, certainly real. In adapting over time, organizations obviously employ individual members as behavioral instruments. However, the learning process involved seems independent of individuals and to proceed uninterrupted through repeated turnover of personnel, as well as despite some variation in the actual behaviors people contribute. This would suggest that the organizational learning process is influenced not only by the specific individuals involved, but by a broad set of exogenous (i.e. social, political and structural) variables.

Organizational learning has reached its current prominence on the basis of its importance for bringing about successful change. As Friedlander (1983, p. 194) remarks, 'Learning is the process that underlies and gives birth to change. Change is the child of learning'. This reasoning, of course, reflects a basic logic that has long been a part of the literature on innovation. For instance, Shepard (1967), writing on innovation-resisting and innovation-producing organizations, considered an organization to have innovated when it had learned to do something it did not know how to do before. The conceptual overlap in the organizational learning and innovation literatures suggests that the latter might be an important knowledge base for understanding (1) how learning (innovation) is induced, (2) how to design organizations which are productive of innovations (learning), and (3) how to change an innovation (or learning) resistant organization into an innovation (or learning) producing organization. Recognizing a close relationship between strategic action and innovativeness, this conceptual overlap further suggests that the development of a strategic management capability is closely related to an organization's ability to learn and be creative. Indeed, Normann (1985) contends that a high organizational learning capability is an underlying variable explaining performance in strategic action. This contention squares completely with Shrivastava and Grant's (1985; Shrivastava, 1985) research into strategic decision-making processes and organizational learning. While their work reveals that there is no perfect organizational learning system, it underscores the necessity of developing organizational learning systems that support an organization's strategic decision-making processes.

Theories of Action

Building on their learning, organizations develop what Argyris and Schön (1978; Argyris, 1985) have termed theories of action. These theories represent beliefs that organizations hold about the environmental consequences (outcomes) of their actions. Shrivastava and Schneider (1984) contend that such theories allow employees to share organizational frames of reference and institutionalize them as consensual knowledge. Hedberg (1981), however, warns that difficulties commonly occur in relating organizational actions to specific environmental responses. He introduces the concept of myth to denote invalid theories of action which guide organizational learning. Myths are undermined as they fail to produce desired results or as exogenous events raise doubts about their validity. As this occurs, new theories of action will emerge. The theory of action generating the most convincing strategy will rule until it is no longer valid (becomes a myth). An understanding of the emergence of theories of action would be of considerable importance in comprehending the dynamics of organizational learning (Brunsson, 1985; Ford and Hegarty, 1984). To the extent that theories of action permit the sharing of oganizational frames of reference and their institutionalization as consensual knowledge, a clear implication thus emerges: what organizations learn does not depend on their environment in general, but on those elements in the environment from which they form their theories of action (Dery, 1982, 1983).

Organizational Memory

A point yet unmentioned is that experiential learning, the second fundamental foundation upon which organizational learning rests, presupposes a capacity to recall. Therefore, organizations must accumulate and maintain an adequate organizational memory (Etheredge, 1981). As described by Covington (1985), memory contributes to two organizational attributes: (1) a learning capability that informs and conditions decisions with knowledge of the past, and (2) an independent and self-sustaining identity—a continuing characteristic sense of mission. In an interesting analysis, Covington (1985) studied the organizational memory of the staff components attached to the National Security Council, the Office of Management and Budget, and the Council on Environmental Quality. Six features were identified as determinates of organizational memory: (1) staff turnover, (2) record-keeping regulations, (3) veteran-newcomer cooperation, (4) goal compatibility over time, (5) job routine, and (6) recruitment control. A study by Green, Bean, and Snavely (1983) of idea flows in an R&D lab extends our knowledge in this area further. Their results suggest that the critical key in idea management for organizational learning may be moving ideas from an organization's short-term memory into a long-term memory.

Organizational learning occurs along several simultaneous dimensions. Learning from direct experience (experiential learning) is supplemented by other forms of learning. Organizations also learn from (1) imitation, (2) novel interpretations of prosaic facts, (3) errors, and (4) superstition.

Imitative Learning

Learning through imitation results from the diffusion of experience. Imitation, or simply copying others, is a common method for increasing the amount of experience from which an organization can draw (March, 1982). Indeed, March and Sevón (1982) observe that organizations copying each other can be seen as reflecting contagion, and that such learning can be seen spreading through a population of actors like measles through a population of children. Imitation allows new organizations to start further along the learning curve and possibly out-compete older organizations (Aldrich, 1986). This copying often takes the form of 'reverse engineering' (Eells and Nehemkis, 1984), where an organization examines in detail its competitors' products as they appear in the marketplace. Imitation is thus one way for an organization to neutralize an advantage enjoyed by its competition. Citing research by Ijiri and Simon (1967), Dutton and Freedman (1985) suggest that the inability of *Fortune* 500 firms to maintain or replicate past successes may result from competitors imitating their successful techniques. This is one example of what DiMaggio and Powell (1983) have called 'mimetic processes' whereby organizations mimic each other as a means for nullifying the perceived advantages of their competitors. Commenting on such situations, Herriott, Levinthal, and March (1985), however, argue that while 'fast learners' often do better than 'slow learners', there are many plausible situations in which slow learners do better than fast learners. In a related finding, Sahal (1981) presents evidence to suggest a lack of interindustry transmission of technical know-how. Knowledge largely seems to be product and industry specific. The process of learning associated with the development of technology appears context dependent, typically isolated in the industry of its origin. Sahal (1981, p. 57) has labeled this phenomenon the 'principle of technological insularity'.

Novel Learning

A second form of organizational learning involves the novel interpretation of prosaic facts. As Smirich and Stubbart (1985) observe, successful organizations have often considered the same facts available to their competitors, but done so in a way as to invent startling insights. They cite as one example Ray Kroc and McDonald's fast-food hamburger restaurant chain. Smirich and Stubbart further note that such novel interpretations frequently occur when organizations enter an environment in which they have no experience. Not burdened by prior theories of action (myths?), they introduce novel strategies that run counter to conventional assumptions. As an example they cite Philip Morris in the beer industry. The introduction of Lite Beer through the firm's Miller Brewing unit flew in the face of traditional knowledge that a diet beer could not be sold. Such erroneous industrywide theories of action (myths) stress the fragile nature of so-called industry wisdom (Cooper and Schendel, 1983). The dynamics underlying industrywide learning have only recently been studied (Stokey, 1986). Such occurrences draw attention to the fragile nature of theories in use.

Learning from Errors

Organizations also learn through their errors. While little cumulative research is available on this form of organizational learning, its importance should not be underestimated. Dery (1982, p. 217) contends that 'the learning organization is, by definition, an erring organization'. Notably, Dery argues that error recognition is a function of interpretation rather than simply observation of events. This argument stresses the significance of converting data into information. The story is told at Proctor & Gamble (P & G) of how a crutcher (a device to mix ingredients) was left on too long and inadvertently put air bubbles into an early product, thus accidently producing a buoyant soap, Ivory. P & G was aware of the error (data), but it carried no meaning (information) until shoppers started asking for more of 'the soap that floats'. To restate Dery's position, error recognition (i.e. interpretation of events) rather than simple error detection is a basic prerequisite to organizational learning.

Superstitious Learning

Finally, organizational learning can be superstitious. This is likely to be the case in situations where organizational outcomes are affected by both random and systematic environmental effects, and where the rate of environmental change exceeds an organization's ability to adapt (Levinthal and March, 1981). In general, superstitious learning develops because cognitive limitations distort managerial perceptions of action-outcome relations in such a way that environmental responses to organizational initiatives are erroneously interpreted. Notwithstanding, organizational actions are assumed to produce intended environmental responses and subsequent actions are modified in what is judged to be an appropriate manner. Despite the fact that the real situation is substantially different from what is believed, 'learning' continues. Implications are drawn from environmental events and succeeding altered organizational actions (Rice, 1985). As an example of superstitious learning, one only need consider the marketing efforts of most major corporations. While advertising and other marketing efforts doubtlessly have an impact on consumer expenditures, the full extent and nature of their effectiveness remains unknown. Indeed, it could be easily argued that the marketplace is actually indifferent to much advertising, and that advertising expenditures are based as much on superstition as on fact.

In sum, most forms of organizational learning are adaptively rational (Comfort, 1985). As viewed by March (1982), they allow organizations to identify good alternatives for most of the choice situations they will encounter. However, March further observes that the organizational learning process can produce some surprises:

> If goals adapt rapidly to experience, learning what is likely may inhibit discovery of what is possible. If strategies are learned quickly relative to the development by competence, a decision maker will learn to use strategies that are intelligent given the existing level of competence, but may fail to invest in enough experience with a suboptimal strategy to discover that it would become a dominant choice with additional competence. (March, 1982, p. 35)

While such derivations are unlikely to occur frequently, they do provide a link between the organizational learning process and surprising results.

ORGANIZATIONAL DECLINE

Over the past decade, organizational decline has emerged as a major research topic in organization theory. Building from a small base (Whetton, 1980a), research interest in this area has grown tremendously (for a bibliography see Zammuto, 1983). Traditionally, most general theories of organization have reflected inherent biases in favor of growth. These biases have proven quite dysfunctional for managers who must deal with declining organizations. Mounting research clearly indicates that the effects of growth and decline on organizations and their members are asymmetrical (Zammuto, 1982b).

Current interest in decline can be largely traced to Hedberg, Nystrom, and Starbuck's (1976) early work on the behaviors of declining organizations in their transition from growth to non-growth. Building on this base, present research has primarily focused on both the sources and dynamics of decline (Kaufman, 1985). The following review will center on these two subjects.

Sources of Decline

In general, the types of crises that, if responded to improperly, precipitate organizational decline can be classified as either internally or externally generated. That is to say, crises may be classified as originating from either deficiencies within an organization itself or from sudden and unpredictable events or changes in an organization's environment. Whetten (1980b), building on Levine (1978), has developed a particularly useful typology for examining both internally and externally generated sources of decline. The four sources of decline which he has identified are (1) organizational atrophy, (2) vulnerability, (3) loss of legitimacy, and (4) environmental entropy. Research into these sources has been uneven.

Organizational atrophy

Unless appropriate counteractions are taken organizational atrophy is a phenomenon to be expected in any organization (Levine, 1978). It results from the breakdown of an organization's internal operating systems, leading to declining performance and weakening productive capacity. Attempts to understand why organizations are vulnerable to internal atrophy and its consequences are being made. Most impressive in this regard is the continuing work of Nystrom and Starbuck (1984a, 1984b; Starbuck 1983, 1985). Their findings suggest that many organizations fall victim to atrophy as a consequence of their accumulated past successes. Bolstered by recollections of former triumphs, they create action generators (automatic behavior programs that are similar to routinized or scripted behavior of individuals) that go unchallenged long after their usefulness has expired (Starbuck, 1983). As a consequence of clinging to inappropriate beliefs and perceptions, atrophic organizations act non-adaptively most of the time. Nystrom and Starbuck (1984a, 1984b) contend that organizations must unlearn these cognitive structures if they are to survive.

Vulnerability

Vulnerability, the second source of organizational decline identified by Whetton (1980b), is an internal property indicating a high level of fragility that limits an organization's capacity to resist environmental demands. Factors contributing to vulnerability include small size (Dalton and Kesner, 1985a), internal conflict (Gilmore and Hirschhorn, 1984; Krantz, 1985), and changes in leadership (Gilmore and Hirschhorn, 1983). Evidence suggests, however, that an organization's age may be the strongest predictor of its vulnerability. Young organizations are more likely to be vulnerable than their older counterparts because they lack initial legitimacy to claim resources, have yet to develop a wide range of adaptive skills, possess a limited capacity for learning, and wield only limited environmental influence (Storey, 1985; Wiewel and Hunter, 1985). The research in this regard is lengthy and virtually unequivocal (see, most recently, Aldrich and Auster, 1986; Altman, 1983; Carroll, 1983; Carroll and Delacroix, 1982; Delacroix and Carroll, 1983; Freeman, 1982; Freeman, Carroll, and Hannan, 1983; Hannan and Freeman, 1984). This is not to say, however, that a wide range of factors (e.g. elite sponsorship, government support in the form of subsidies or favorable tax laws, etc.) cannot mitigate selection pressures associated with youth (DiMaggio and Powell, 1983).

Loss of legitimacy

Loss of legitimacy represents a third source of decline. Organizations seek to maintain a congruence between the social values associated with their activities and the standards of acceptable behavior in the society of which they are a part (Dowling and Pfeffer, 1975). When a disparity exists between the two, there will exist a threat to organizational legitimacy. This threat may take the form of legal, economic and other social sanctions. Loss of legitimacy can thus have direct consequences for an organization's continued existence. Perhaps most significantly, failure to establish and maintain legitimacy will immeasurably inhibit an organization's ability to deflect criticism and obtain resources and other support from its surrounding environment (Berger, 1981). The exact process by which society views an organization as proper and worthy of support — that is, as legitimate — remains unexplored. It is a topic greatly in need of empirical research.

Environmental entropy

The fourth source of decline, environmental entropy, occurs when the capacity of an environment to support an organization at an existing level of activity is no longer adequate. This kind of decline typically results from market and technological shifts that render ineffective an organization's established processes of self-maintenance. The decline in demand for domestic textiles and steel provides two examples of market shifts that have prompted increased entropy in a number of economic sectors. The greatly diminished demand for mechanically based products and systems as a consequence of advancements in electronics and software would exemplify a technological shift that has given rise to similar entropy.

Based on a review of the relevant literature, Zammuto and Cameron (Zammuto, Whetten, and Cameron, 1983; Zammuto and Cameron, 1985; Cameron and Zammuto, 1983) have proposed an integrative model depicting four different types of environmental decline resulting from entrophy (see Figure 9.2). The four types vary by (1) type of change in ecological niche configuration (size versus shape) and (2) the continuity of change (continuous versus discontinuous). Organizations that encounter continuous decline in the size of their ecological niche experience 'erosion'. Those that encounter a discontinuous decline in their niche's size experience 'contraction'. 'Dissolution' is experienced when a continuous change in the shape of a niche occurs. Finally, 'collapse' refers to a rapid, unanticipated shift in an organization's existing niche and the emergence of a new niche. Zammuto and Cameron's (1985) model is important because it suggests that different types of environmental entrophy result in diffenent types of organizational decline. Moreover, it underscores that to survive and prosper, organizations must select domain strategies that address the challenges presented by different environmental conditions.

Dynamics of Decline

A declining organization encounters many difficult challenges. Most notably, decline induces changes in virtually all relationships within an organization and between an organization and its environment. Research on the various organizational processes affected by decline has been uneven. It has ranged from theoretical models of organizational responses to scarcity (Nottenburg and Fedor, 1983) to analyses of stress caused by budget cuts (Jick, 1983) to suggestions for managing organizational retrenchment and death (Harris and Sutton, 1986; Robinson, 1985). The following review will survey findings on the two organizational attributes which have received the most attention in the decline literature. These are top management leadership and workforce composition.

Top management leadership

One nearly universal generalization emerges from the literature on organizational decline. Research supports the view that a declining organization's successful turnaround is dependent on the replacement of its current leadership (top management). Both recent case (Kothari and Near, 1982) and policy (O'Neill, 1986)

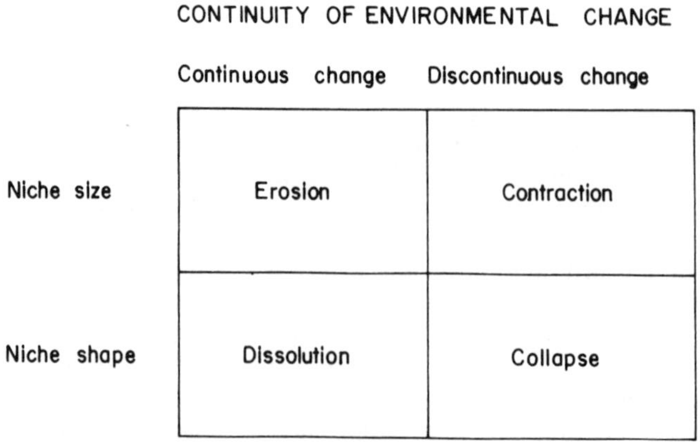

CONTINUITY OF ENVIRONMENTAL CHANGE

	Continuous change	Discontinuous change
Niche size	Erosion	Contraction
Niche shape	Dissolution	Collapse

Figure 9.2 A model of environmental decline
Based on Cameron and Zammuto (1983), Zammuto, Whetten, and Cameron (1985), and Zammuto and Cameron (1985)

studies offer similar results. These results are consistent with research extending back at least a decade (Hofer, 1980; Khandwalla, 1981, 1983–1984; Schendel, Patton, and Riggs, 1976; Starbuck, Greve, and Hedberg, 1978). It is generally held that outside recruitment of top management is associated with the introduction of novel viewpoints and practices (Dalton and Kesner, 1983, 1985b). New top-level managers are not shackled to existing administrative patterns and resource allocations. By voicing their opinions and questioning old knowledge, new managers can trigger organizational learning. The exact manner in which new top-level managers prompt organization recoveries deserves further research (cf. Hambrick, 1985; Tushman, Virany, and Romanelli, 1985). Especially intriguing would be a more complete understanding of what the popular press has labeled 'masters of the corporate turnaround' (Cole, 1983; Eklund, 1986).

Workforce composition

One of the most disturbing effects of decline is that while voluntary turnover of all employees typically increases, it is usually the most qualified (hence mobile) employees who leave first (Greenhalgh, 1983a, 1983b). The net consequence is a 'regression to the mean' in labor pool qualifications (Whetten, 1981). Between the human resource management and business policy literatures, this dilemma has been dealt with extensively. While general economic conditions will affect the extent to which more valuable workers exit (Levine and Wolohojian, 1983; Levine, 1984), it is generally reasoned that those most qualified do not want their record marred by failure and are drawn away by attractive job alternatives in more prosperous organizations. Thus, those employees with the greatest potential for turning around a declining organization see little incentive for making the effort. Case evidence suggests, however, that there are at least two exceptions to this pattern: (1) high-quality employees who are extremely loyal, and (2) better employees retained by promises of equal or better positions in a parent organization (Sutton, 1983). The more prescriptive business policy literature echoes the importance of enacting this second exception (Harrigan, 1984).

Perhaps the most extensive outline of a role for human resource management in a declining organization has been provided by Ferris, Schellenberg, and Zammuto (1984). Taking the Cameron and Zammuto (1983) model of environmental decline, they have developed a model identifying different roles and responsibilities within the human resource function under different conditions of environmental decline. Although the model must still be tested, it clearly suggests that organizations must take into account the capacity of their human resource managers in implementing strategic responses to decline.

Clearly, gaps yet remain in our understanding of how to manage human resources more effectively in a declining organization. Improvements in our understanding of ways to prevent the exit of key employees are especially needed. Drawing on case analyses of the declines experienced by companies such as Continental Illinois Bank and Itel Corporation, Perry (1984) suggests that in addition to increasing career opportunities in order to reduce ill-timed employee exit, organizations should strive to reduce organizational uncertainty by creating the impression that survival is guaranteed or turnaround is imminent. He indicates that this can be accomplished in numerous ways. Perhaps the most powerful means involves creating a new organizational image. In one example, he cites Lee Iacocca as spokesperson for the advertising campaign that introduced 'The New Chrysler Corporation'. Regardless of the means chosen for countering key employee loss, it is generally acknowledged that how an organization treats its employees during stressful periods is of critical importance to its long-term health (Smith, 1982).

Although the preceding review has focused on the two organizational attributes which have received the most attention in the decline literature, others should not be ignored. As identified by Greenhalgh (1983a), other major organizational attributes affected by decline include various structural properties, e.g. formalization, centralization, differentiation (Cullen, Anderson, and Baker, 1986), and administrative intensity (Goh and Evans, 1985); slack, meaning a surplus of resources over what is required to maintain equilibrium in an ecological niche; adaptive innovation (McKinley, 1984); and relationships with employees, unions, competitors, and regulatory agencies. A more complete understanding of the complex interrelated processes that occur during decline would enable a more complete response to be made to questions such as (Wilson, 1985), 'Which organizations will die?' 'Which survive?' 'What can be done to revive a wounded organization?' and 'Why did this organization decline or, in transmigrating, become a different creature?'.

CONCLUSION

A review of the literature in four topic areas in which substantial scholarship has been conducted recently suggests that the organization theory field is alive. Important work is being conducted not only in such traditional strongholds as Great Britain and the United States, but throughout Europe, Canada, Australia, Israel, and Japan. However, if the field is alive, does this (as our opening sentence suggests) mean that it is also well? In the eyes of some, the answer to this question is less certain. Organization theorists, they concede, are undoubtedly investigating important issues, but they yet wonder whether the field is progressing as a result of such investigations. As in so many other instances associated with organization theory, different opinions have emerged (Donaldson, 1985). Based on the preceding four-part literature review, the position advanced here is that progress is being made; perhaps not as quickly as some might wish, but nevertheless advances have been real. Indeed, over the past four decades, organization theory has emerged as a purposeful, coherent area of study with its own criteria and traditions.

This emergence and its accompanying progress are manifest in several ways. First, organization theorists are interested in an ever-increasing number of phenomena and are exploring these phenomena in a greater variety of ways. There are strong incentives for researchers to 'create intellectual novelty and pursue distinctive paradigms' (Astley, 1985b, p. 504). Given its multidisciplinary roots, the organization theory field has resisted advancing a given world view or a single preferred analytical perspective. This has contributed greatly to the dynamic and pluralistic growth of organization research. Moreover, it has served as a substantial safeguard against academic isolationism and conceptual stagnation.

A second manifestation of progress is the many efforts to relate organization theory to developments in other areas, especially business policy/strategic management and industrial economics. The resulting cross-fertilization of ideas has led to a wide range of issues being studied and to the development of differing methods of research. Boundaries which were once clearly labeled organizational sociology, industrial economics, business policy/strategy management, public administration, and so on, are now quite vague.

A final manifestation of progress is the growing international exchange of knowledge concerning organizations. The international editorial board of the relatively new journal *Organization Studies*, published by the European Group for Organizational Studies (EGOS), is one sign of an excitement and vitality that transcends national boundaries. In the United States, an increasing internationalization of the Academy of Management's Organization and Management Theory Division is another. Both efforts have been supported by an international emphasis long evident in traditional research outlets such as the *Administrative Science Quarterly*, and their newer counterparts such as the *Journal of Management*.

Attention to such progress is not meant to suggest that there are no reasons for concern. As suggested in the instance of organizational effectiveness studies, too often it seems that the popularity of research themes has either grown or declined in direct proportion to their marketability rather than the degree to which basic issues have been resolved and critical phenomena understood.

One consequence of this tendency to focus on 'hot' topics is what some see as an extreme iconoclasm resulting in an unhealthy fragmentation of the field (Astley, 1985b). Instead of that being a tendency to build on previous findings, a vogue seems to exist in some quarters that encourages a preoccupation with 'fad and fashion'. As Staw (1985, p. 97) has observed, this would seem to explain why a measure of organization theory research tends to be 'literature driven' rather than problem driven. One predictable consequence is that much organization research is non-cumulative and non-communicable across quarters. Needless to say, such difficulties have led to substantial and frequent disagreements. Confusion and controversy, however, are traditionally characteristic of a new and growing field of study. In this regard, organization theory has been no exception.

ACKNOWLEDGMENTS

The critical comments of Edward R. Kemery (University of Baltimore), Robert T. Lenz (Indiana University—Indianapolis), Robert E. Quinn (State University of New York at Albany), James D. Werbel (Louisiana State University), and Raymond R. Zammuto (University of Colorado at Denver) on an earlier draft manuscript are gratefully acknowledged.

REFERENCES

Aldrich, H. (1979). *Organizations and Environments*. Engelwood Cliffs, NJ: Prentice-Hall.
Aldrich, H. (1986). *Population Perspectives on Organizations*. Uppsala: Acta Universitatis Upsaliensis.
Aldrich, H., and Auster, E. R. (1986). Even dwarfs started small: Liabilities of age and size and their strategic implications. *Research in Organizational Behavior*, **8**.
Aldrich, H., and McKelvey, B. (1983). The population perspective and the organization form concept. *Economia Aziendale*, **2** (1), 63–86.

Aldrich, H., McKelvey, B., and Ulrich, D. (1984). Design strategy from the population perspective. *Journal of Management*, **10**, 67-86.

Altman, E. I. (1983). Why businesses fail. *Journal of Business Strategy*, **3** (4), 15-21.

Argyris, C. (1982). The executive mind and double-loop learning. *Organizational Dynamics*, **11** (5), 5-22.

Argyris, C. (1985). Developing with threat and defensiveness. In *Organizational Strategy and Change*, ed. J. M. Pennings *et al.*, pp. 412-430. San Francisco: Jossey-Bass.

Argyris, C., and Schön, D. A. (1978). *Organizational Learning: A Theory of Action Perspective*, Reading, MA: Addison-Wesley.

Astley, W. G. (1984). Toward an appreciation of collective strategy. *Academy of Management Review*, **9**, 526-535.

Astley, W. G. (1985a). The two ecologies: Population and community perspectives on organizational evolution. *Administrative Science Quarterly*, **30**, 224-241.

Astley, W. G. (1985b). Administrative science as socially constructed truth. *Administrative Science Quarterly*, **30**, 497-513.

Astley, W. G., and Fombrun, C. J. (1983). Collective strategy: The social ecology of organizational environments. *Academy of Management Review*, **8**, 576-587.

Astley, W. G., and Van de Ven, A. (1983). Central perspectives and debates in organization theory. *Administrative Science Quarterly*, **28**, 245-273.

Banthin, J., and Stelzer, L. (1986). Political action committees: Facts, fancy, and morality. *Journal of Business Ethics*, **5**, 13-19.

Barnard, C. I. (1938). *The Functions of the Executive*. Cambridge: Harvard University Press.

Baysinger, B. D. (1984). Domain maintenance as an objective of business political activity: An expanded typology. *Academy of Management Review*, **9**, 248-258.

Baysinger, B. D., and Woodman, R. W. (1982). Dimensions of the public affairs/government relations function in American corporations. *Strategic Management Journal*, **3**, 27-41.

Bazerman, M. H., and Schoorman, F. D. (1983). A limited rationality model of interlocking directorates. *Academy of Management Review*, **8**, 206-217.

Bedeian, A. G. (1986a). *Management*. Hinsdale, IL: Dryden Press.

Bedeian, A. G. (1986b). Contemporary challenges in the study of organizations. Yearly Review, *Journal of Management*, **12**, 185-201.

Bennis, W., and Nanus, B. (1985). *Leaders: The Strategies for Taking Charge*. New York: Harper & Row.

Berger, P. L. (1981). New attack on the legitimacy of business. *Harvard Business Review*, **59** (11), 82-89.

Betton, J., and Dess, G. G. (1985). The applications of population ecology models to the study of organizations. *Academy of Management Review*, **10**, 750-757.

Bidwell, C. E., and Kasarda, J. D. (1985). *The Organization and its Ecosystem; A Theory of Structuring in Organizations*. Greenwich, CN: JAI Press

Bluedorn, A. C. (1980). Cutting the Gordian knot: A critique of the effectiveness traditional in organizational research. *Sociology and Social Research*, **64**, 477-497.

Bourgeois, L. J. (1985). Strategic goals, perceived uncertainty, and economic performance in volatile environments. *Academy of Management Review*, **28**, 548-573.

Bozeman, B. (1982). Organization structure and the effectiveness of public agencies: An assessment and agenda. *International Journal of Public Administration*, **4**, 235-296.

Brunsson, N. (1985). *The Irrational Organization: Irrationality as a Basis for Organizational Action and Change*. Chichester, UK: Wiley

Burt, R. S. (1982). *Toward a Structural Theory of Action*. New York: Academic Press.

Burt, R. S. (1983a). *Corporate Profits and Cooptation: Networks of Market Constraints and Directorate Ties in the American Economy*. New York: Academic Press.

Burt, R. S. (1983b). Corporate philanthropy as a cooptive relation. *Social Forces*, **62**, 419-449.

Büschges, G. (1985). [Review of *Organizational Systematics*: taxonomy, evolution, classification] . *Organization Studies*, **6**, 191-193.

Cameron, K. S. (1978). Measuring organizational effectiveness in institutions of higher education. *Administrative Science Quarterly*, **23**, 604-632.

Cameron, K. S. (1981a). Domains of organizational effectiveness. *Academy of Management Journal*, **24**, 25-47.

Cameron, K. S. (1981b). The enigma of organizational effectiveness. In *New Directions for Program Evaluation: Measuring Effectiveness*, ed. D. Baugher, pp. 1-13 San Francisco: Jossey-Bass.

Cameron, K. (1986). A study of organizational effectiveness and its predictors. *Management Science*, **32**, 87-112.

Cameron, K. S., and Whetten, D. A. (1981). Perceptions of organizational effectiveness across organizational life cycles. *Administrative Science Quarterly*, **26**, 525-544.

Cameron, K. S., and Whetten, D. A. (1984). Models of the organizational life cycle: Applications to higher education. In *College and University Organization: Insights from the Behavioral Sciences*, ed. J. L. Bess, pp. 31-61 New York: New York University Press.

Cameron, K. S., and Zammuto, R. (1983). Matching managerial strategies to conditions of decline. *Human Resource Management*, **22**, 359-375.

Camillus, J. C., and Venkatraman, N. (1984). Dimensions of strategic choice. *Planning Review*, **12** (1), 26-31, 46.

Campbell, J. P. (1976). Contributions research can make in understanding organization effectiveness. *Organization and Administrative Science*, **7** (1), 29-45.

Carroll, G. R. (1983). A stochastic model of organizational mortality: Review and reanalysis. *Social Science Research*, **12**, 303-329.

Carroll, G. R. (1985). Concentration and specialization: Dynamics of niche width in populations of organizations. *American Journal of Sociology*, **90**, 1262-1283.

Carroll, G. R., and Delacroix, J. (1982). Organizational mortality in the newspaper industry of Argentina and Ireland: An ecological approach. *Administrative Science Quarterly*, **27**, 169-198.

Chappell, H. W., Jr (1982). Campaign contributions and congressional voting: A simultaneous probit-tobit model. *Review of Economics and Statistics*, **64**, 77-83.

Clinard, M. B. (1983a). *Corporate Ethics and Crime*. Beverly Hills: Sage

Clinard, M. B. (1983b). *Corporate Crime, Ethics and Middle Management*. Beverly Hills: Sage.

Clinebell, S. (1984). Organizational effectiveness: An examination of recent empirical studies and the development of the contingency view. In *Proceedings 27th Annual Conference Midwest Academy of Management*, ed. W. D. Terpening and K. R. Thompson, pp. 92-102. Notre Dame, IN: Department of Management, University of Notre Dame.

Cole, R. J. (1983). Masters of the corporate turnaround. *New York Times*, 31 July, Section 3, pp. 1, 9-10.

Comfort, L. K. (1985). Action research: A model for organizational learning. *Journal of Policy Analysis and Management*, **5**, 100-118.

Connally, T., Conlon, E. J., and Deutsch, S. J. (1980). Organizational effectiveness: A multiple-constituency approach. *Academy of Management Review*, **5**, 211-217.

Cooper, A. C., and Schendel, D. (1983). Strategic responses to technological threats. In *Business Policy and Strategy; Concepts and Readings*, ed. D. J. McCarthy, pp. 207-219. Homewood, IL: Irwin

Covington, C. R. (1985). Development of organizational memory in presidential agencies. *Administration and Society*, **17**, 171-196.

Cullen, J. B., Anderson, K. S., and Baker, D. D. (1986). Blau's theory of structural differentiation revisited: A theory of structural change or scale? *Academy of Management Journal*, **29**, 203-229.

Culnan, M. J. (1983). Environmental scanning: The effects of task complexity and source accessibility on information gathering behavior. *Decision Sciences*, **14**, 194-206.

Cummings, L. L. (1978). Toward organizational behavior. *Academy of Management Review*, **4**, 90-98.

Cummings, L. L. (1982). Organizational behavior. *Annual Review of Psychology*, **33**, 541-579.

Cyert, R. M., and MacGrimmon, K. R. (1968). Organizations. In *Handbook of Social Psychology*, 2nd edn, ed. G. Lindzey and E. Aronson, vol. 1, pp. 568-611 Reading, MA: Addison-Wesley.

Cyert, R. M., and March, J. G. (1959). A behavioral theory of organizational objectives. In *Modern Organization Theory*, ed. M. Haire, pp. 76-90. New York: Wiley.

Cyert, R. M., and March, J. G. (1963). *A Behavioral Theory of the Firm*. Englewood Cliffs, NJ: Prentice-Hall

Dalton, D. R., and Kesner, I. F. (1983). Inside/outside succession and organizational size: The pragmatics of executive replacement. *Academy of Management Journal*, **26**, 736-742.

Dalton, D. R., and Kesner, I. F. (1985a). Organizational growth: Big is beautiful. *Journal of Business Strategy*, **6**, 38-48.

Dalton, D. R., and Kesner, I. F. (1985b). Organizational performance as an antecedent of inside/outside chief executive succession: An empirical assessment. *Academy of Management Journal*, **28**, 749-762.

Delacroix, J., and Carroll, G. R. (1983). Organizational foundings: An ecological study of the newspaper industries of Argentina and Ireland. *Administrative Science Quarterly*, **28**, 274-291.

Dery, D. (1982). Erring and learning: An organizational analysis. *Accounting, Organizations and Society*, **7**, 217-223.

Dery, D. (1983). Decision-making, problem-solving and organizational learning. *Omega*, **11**, 321-328.

Dess, G. G., and Beard, D. W. (1984). Dimensions of organizational task environments. *Administrative Science Quarterly*, **29**, 52-73.

Dickie, R. B. (1984). Influence of public affairs offices on corporate planning and of corporations on government policy. *Strategic Management Journal*, **5**, 15-34.

Dittenbach, J. (1983). Corporate environmental analysis in large U. S. corporations. *Long Range Planning*, **16** (3), 107-116.

DiMaggio, P. J., and Powell, W. W. (1983). The iron cage revisited: Institutional isomorphism and collective rationality in organizational fields. *American Sociological Review*, **48**, 147-160.

Donaldson, L. (1985). *In Defence of Organization Theory: A Reply to the Critics*. Cambridge: Cambridge University Press.

Dowling, J., and Pfeffer, J. (1975). Organizational legitimacy: Social values and organizational behavior. *Pacific Sociological Review*, **18**, 122-135.

Drazin, R., and Van de Ven, A. H. (1985). Alternative forms of fit in contingency theory. *Administrative Science Quarterly*, **30**, 514-539.

Dunbar, R. L. M., and Wasilewski, N. (1985). Regulating external threats in the cigarette industry. *Administrative Science Quarterly*, **30**, 540-559.

Dutton, J. M., and Freedman, R. D. (1985). External environment and internal strategies: Calculating, experimenting, and imitating in organizations. *Advances in Strategic Management*, **3**, 39-67.

Eells, R., and Nehemkis, P. (1984). *Corporate Intelligence and Espionage*, New York, Macmillan

Eklund, C. S. (1986). Stan Hiller is old-fashioned: He fixes broken companies. *Business Week*, 31 March, pp. 74-75.

Ermann, M. D., and Lundman, R. J. (1982). *Corporate Deviance*. New York: Holt, Rinehart, & Winston.

Etheredge, L. S. (1981). Government learning: An overview. In *Handbook of Political Behavior*, ed. S. L. Long, vol. 2, pp. 73-161. New York: Plenum.

Faerman, S., and Quinn, R. E. (in press). Effectiveness: The perspective from organizational theory. *Higher Education Review*.

Fahey, L., King, W., and Narayanan, V. (1981). Environmental scanning and forecasting in strategic planning—the state-of-the-art. *Long Range Planning*, **14** (1), 32-39.

Farh, J., Hoffman, R. C., and Hegarty, W. H. (1984). Assessing environmental scanning at the subunit level: A multitrait-multimethod analysis. *Decision Sciences*, **15**, 197-220.

Fennema, M. (1982). *International networks of banks and industry*. The Hague: Martinus Hijhoff

Ferris, G. R., Schellenberg, D. A., and Zammuto, R. F. (1984). Human resource management strategies in declining industries. *Human Resource Management*, **23**, 381-394.

Fiol, C. M., and Lyles, M. A. (1985). Organizational learning. *Academy of Management Review*, **10**, 803-811.

Foo, W. F., Oliga, J. C., and Puxty, A. G. (1981). The population ecology model and management action. *Journal of Enterprise Management*, **2**, 317-325.

Ford, J. D., and Hegarty, W. H. (1984). Decision makers' beliefs about the causes and effects of structure: An exploratory study. *Academy of Management Journal*, **27**, 271-291.

Freeman, J. H. (1982). Organizational life cycles and natural selection processes. *Research in Organizational Behavior*, **4**, 1-32.

Freeman, J., Carroll, G. R., and Hannan, M. T. (1983). Age dependence in organizational death rates. *American Sociological Review*, **48**, 692-710.

Freeman, J., and Hannan, M. T. (1983). Niche width and the dynamics of organizational populations. *American Journal of Sociology*, **88**, 1116-1145.

Friedlander, F. (1983). Patterns of individual and organizational learning. In *The Executive Mind*, ed. S. Shrivastava *et al.*, pp. 192-220. San Francisco: Jossey-Bass.

Gilmore, T., and Hirschhorn, L. (1983). The downsizing dilemma: Leadership in the age of discontinuity. *Wharton Annual, 1984*, **8**, 94-104.

Gilmore, T., and Hirschhorn, L. (1984). Management challenges under conditions of retrenchment. *Human Resource Management*, **22**, 341-357.

Goh, S. C., and Evans, M. G. (1985). Organization growth and decline: The impact on direct and administrative components of a university. *Canadian Journal of Sociology*, **10**, 121-138.

Goodman, P. S., Atkin, R. S., and Schoorman, F. D. (1982). On the demise of organizational effectiveness studies. In *Organizational Effectiveness: A Comparison of Multiple Models*, ed. K. S. Cameron and D. A. Whetten, pp. 163-183. New York: Academic Press

Goodman, P. S., Pennings, J. M., *et al.* (eds.) (1977). *New Perspectives on Organizational Effectiveness*. San Francisco: Jossey-Bass.

Green, S. G., Bean, A.S., and Snavely, B. K. (1983). Idea management in R&D as a human information processing analog. *Human Systems Management*, **4**, 98-112.

Greenhalgh, L. (1983a). Organizational decline. *Research in the Sociology of Organizations*, **2**, 231-276.

Greenhalgh, L. (1983b). Managing the job insecurity crisis. *Human Resource Management*, **22**, 431-444.

Grover, R. (1986). Campaign reformers just can't catch up with the PACs. *Business Week*, 20 January, pp. 24-26.

Hall, R. H. (1980). Effectiveness theory and organizational effectiveness. *Journal of Applied Behavioral Science*, **16**, 536-545.

Hambrick, D. C. (1981). Environment, strategy, and power within top management teams. *Administrative Science Quarterly*, **26**, 253-276.

Hambrick, D. C. (1985). Turnaround strategies. In *Handbook of Business Strategy*, ed. W. D. Guth, pp. 10/1-10/32 Boston: Warren, Gorham & Lamont.

Handler, E., and Mulkern, J. R. (1982). *Business in Politics*. Lexington MA: Lexington Books.

Hannan, M. T., and Freeman, J. (1984). Structural inertia and organizational change. *American Sociological Review*, **49**, 149-164.

Harrigan, K. R. (1984). Managing declining businesses. *Journal of Business Strategy*, 4 (3), 74-78.

Harris, S. G., and Sutton, R. I. (1986). Functions of parting ceremonies in dying organizations. *Academy of Management Journal*, **29**, 5-30.

Hedberg, B. L. T. (1981). How organizations learn and unlearn. In *Handbook of Organizational Design*, ed. P. C. Nystrom and W. H. Starbuck, vol. 1, pp. 3-27. New York: Oxford University Press

Hedberg, B. L. T., Nystrom, P. C., and Starbuck, W. H. (1976). Camping on seesaws: Presciptions for a self-designing organization. *Administrative Science Quarterly*, **21**, 41-64.

Herriott, S. R., Levinthal, D., and March, J. G. (1985). Learning from experience in organizations. *American Economic Review* (Papers and Proceedings), **75**, 298-302.

Higgins, J. C. (1986). Progress in monitoring the sociopolitical environment of the firm. *Omega*, **14**, 49-55.

Hirsch, P. (1975). Organizational effectiveness and the institutional environment. *Administrative Science Quarterly*, **20**, 327-344.

Hofer, C. W. (1980). Designing turnaround strategies. *Journal of Business Strategy*, 1 (1), 19-31.

Hrebiniak, L. G., and Joyce, W. F. (1985). Organizational adaptation: Strategic choice and environmental determinism. *Administrative Science Quarterly*, **30**, 336-349.

Ijiri, Y., and Simon, H. A. (1967). A model of business firm growth. *Econometrica*, **35**, 348-355.

Jain, S. (1984). Environmental scanning in U.S. corporations. *Long Range Planning*, **17** (2), 117-128.

Jick, T. D. (1983), The stressful effects of budget cuts in organizations. In *Topics in Managerial Accounting*, ed. A Rosen, pp. 267-280 Toronto: McGraw-Hill

Kasarda, J. D., and Bidwell, C. E. (1984). A human ecological theory of organizational structuring. In *Sociological Human Ecology: Contemporary Issues and Applications*. In *Sociological Human Ecology: Contemporary Issues and Applications*, ed. M. Micklin and H. M. Choldin, pp. 183-236. Boulder, CO: Westview.

Kau, J. B., Keenan, D., Rubin, P. H. (1982). A general equilibrium model of congressional voting. *Quarterly Journal of Economics*, **97**, 271-293.

Kau, J. B., and Rubin, P. H. (1981). The impact of labor unions on the passage of economic legislation. *Journal of Labor Research*, 2, 133-145.

Kaufman, H. (1985). *Time, Chance and Organizations: Natural Selection in a Perilous Environment*. Chatham, NJ: Chatham House.

Keating, B. P., and Keating, M. O. (1981). Goal setting and efficiency in social service agencies. *Long Range Planning*, **14** (1), 39-48.

Keim, G. (1985). Corporate grassroots programs in the 1980's. *California Management Review*, **28**, 110-123.

Keim, G. D., Zeithaml, C. P., and Baysinger, B. D. (1984). New directions for corporate political strategy. *Sloan Management Review*, **25** (3), 53-62.

Khandwalla, P. N. (1981). Strategy for turning around complex sick organizations. *Vikalpa*, **6** (3-4), 143-165.

Khandwalla, P. N. (1983-1984). Turnaround management of mismanaged complex organizations. *International Studies of Management and Organization*, **8** (4), 5-41.

Klein, H. E., and Linneman, R. E. (1984) Environmental assessment: An international study of corporate practice. *Journal of Business Strategy*, **5** (1), 66-75.

Korsching, P. F. (1983). The ecology of an ecological study: Comments on Marple's 'Technology Innovation and Organizational Survival'. *Sociological Quarterly*, **24**, 151-153.

Kothari, R. M., and Near, J. P. (1982). Decline and revival of a sick enterprise: A case discussion. *Indian Management*, **21** (7), 9-15.

Krantz, J. (1985). Group process under conditions of organizational decline. *Journal of Applied Behavioral Science*, **21**, 1-17.

Lenz, R. T., and Engledow, J. L. (1986). Environmental analysis units and strategic decision-making: A field study of selected 'leading-edge' corporations. *Strategic Management Journal*, **7**, 69–89.

Levine, C. H. (1978). Organizational decline and cutback management. *Public Administration Review*, **38**, 316–325.

Levine, C. H. (1984). Retrenchment, human resource erosion, and the role of the personnel manager. *Public Personnel Management Journal*, **13**, 249–263.

Levine, C. H., and Wolohojian, G. G. (1983). Retrenchment and human resources management: Combatting the discount effects of uncertainty. In *Public Personnel Management: Problems and Prospects*, ed. S. W. Hays and R. C. Kearney, pp. 175–188. Englewood Cliffs, NJ: Prentice-Hall

Levinthal, D., and March, J. G. (1981). A model of adaptive organizational search. *Journal of Economic Behavior and Organization*, **2**, 307–333.

Lewin, A. Y., and Minton, J. W. (in press). Determining organizational effectiveness: Another look, and an agenda for research. *Management Science*, **32**, 514–538.

McKelvey, B., and Aldrich, H. (1983). Populations, natural selection, and applied organizational science. *Administrative Science Quarterly*, **28**, 101–128.

McKinley, W. (1984). Organizational decline and innovation in manufacturing. In *Strategic Management of Industrial R&D*, ed. B. Bozeman, M. Crow, and A. Link), pp. 147–159 Lexington, MA: Lexington Books.

McNamee, S. J. (1983). Capital accumulation and the Du Pont Company: An historical analysis. *Organization Studies*, **4**, 201–218. Errata. *Organization Studies* (1984) **5**, 208–209.

McPherson, M. (1983). An ecology of affiliation. *American Sociological Review*, **48**, 519–532.

Malbin, M. J. (1979). Campaign financing and the 'special interests'. *Public Interest*, **56**, 21–42.

March, J. G. (1962). Some recent substantive and methodological developments in the theory of organizational decision-making. In *Essays on the Behavioral Study of Politics*, ed. A. Ranney, pp. 191–208. Urbana: University of Illinois Press.

March, J. G. (ed.) (1965). *Handbook of Organizations*. Chicago: Rand McNally.

March, J. G. (1982). Theories of choice and making decisions. *Society*, **20**, 29–39.

March, J. G., and Olsen, J. P. (1975). The uncertainty of the past: Organizational learning under ambiguity. *European Journal of Political Research*, **3**, 147–171.

March, J. G., and Olsen, J. P. (1976). *Ambiguity and Choice in Organizations* Bergen: Universitetsforlaget.

March, J. G., and Sevón, G. (1982). Gossip, information, and decision making. *Advances in Information in Organizations*, **1**, 95–105.

Mark, M. W., and Shotland, R. L. (1985). Stakeholder-based evaluations and value judgments. *Evaluation Review*, **9**, 605–626.

Marple, D. (1982). Technological innovation and organizational survival: A population ecology study of nineteenth-century American railroads. *Sociological Quarterly*, **23**, 107–116.

Marple, D. (1983). Reply to Korshing's 'The Ecology of an Ecological Study: Comments on Marple's Technological Innovation and Organizational Survival'. *Sociological Quarterly*, **24**, 155–157.

Masters, M. F., and Baysinger, B. D. (1985). The determinants of funds raised by corporate political action committees: An empirical examination. *Academy of Management Journal*, **28**, 654–664.

Masters, M. F., and Delaney, J. T. (1985). Interunion variation in congressional campaign contributions. *Industrial Relations*, **23**, 410–416.

Masters, M. F., and Keim, G. D. (1985). Determinants of PAC participation among large corporations. *Journal of Politics*, **47**, 1158–1173.

Meyer, M. W. (1985). *Limits to Bureaucratic Growth*. Berlin: Gruyter.

Miller, D., and Friesen, P. (1980). Archtypes of organizational transition. *Administrative Science Quarterly*, **25**, 268–269.

Miner, J. B. (1982). *Theories of Organizational Structure and Processes.* Hinsdale, IL: Dryden

Mintz, B., and Schwartz, M. (1981). Interlocking directorates and interest group formation. *American Sociological Review,* **46**, 851–869.

Mintz, B., and Schwartz, M. (1985). *The Power Structure of American Business* Chicago: University of Chicago Press.

Mitchell, T. R. (1979). Organizational behavior. *Annual Review of Psychology,* **30**, 243–281.

Mizruchi, M. S. (1982). *The American Corporate Network: 1904–1974.* Beverly Hills: Sage.

Mossholder, K. W., and Bedeian, A. G. (1983a). Cross-level inference and organizational research: Perspectives on interpretation and application. *Academy of Management Review,* **8**, 547–558.

Mossholder, K. W., and Bedeian, A. G. (1983b). Group interaction processes: Individual and group effects. *Group and Organization Studies,* **8**, 187–202.

Nishi, K. (1979). *Management Scanning Behavior: A Study of Information-Acquisition Behavior.* Tokyo: Saikon.

Nishi, K., Schoderbek, C., Schoderbek, P. P. (1982). Scanning the organizational environment: Some empirical results. *Human Systems Management,* **3**, 233–245.

Normann, R. (1985). Developing capabilities for organizational learning. In *Organizational Strategy and Change,* ed., J. M. Pennings *et al.*, pp. 217–248 San Francisco: Jossey-Bass.

Nottenburg, G., and Fedor, D. B. (1983). Scarcity in the environment: Organizational perceptions, interpretations and responses. *Organization Studies,* **4**, 317–337.

Nystrom, P. C., and Starbuck, W. H. (eds.) (1981). *Handbook of Organizational Design,* vols. 1–2. New York: Oxford University Press.

Nystrom, P. C., and Starbuck, W. H. (1984a). To avoid organizational crises, unlearn. *Organizational Dynamics,* **12** (4), 53–65.

Nystrom, P. C., and Starbuck, W. H. (1984b). Managing beliefs in organizations. *Journal of Applied Behavioral Science,* **20**, 277–287.

O'Neill, H. M. (1986). Turnaround strategy and recovery: What strategy do you need? *Long Range Planningy,* **19** (1), 8–88.

Ornstein, M. (1984). Interlocking directorates in Canada: Intercorporate or class alliance? *Administrative Science Quarterly,* **29**, 210–231.

O'Toole, J. (1985). *Vanguard Management.* Garden City, NY: Doubleday.

Palmer, D. (1983). Broken ties: Interlocking directorates and intercorporate coordination. *Administrative Science Quarterly,* **28**, 40–55.

Pennings, J. M. (1980). *Interlocking Directorates: Origins and Consequences of Connections Among Organizations' Boards of Directors.* San Francisco: Jossey-Bass.

Perry, L. T. (1984). Key human resource strategies in an organization downturn. *Human Resource Management,* **23**, 61–75.

Pervin, L. A., and Lewis, M. (1978). Overview of the internal–external issue. In *Perspectives in Interactional Psychology.* ed. L. A. Pervin and M. Lewis, pp, 1–22 New York: Plenum.

Pfeffer, J. (1986). Organizations and organization theory. In *Handbook of Social Psychology,* 3rd edn, ed. G. Lindzey and E. Aronson, vol. 1, pp. 379–440. New York: Random House.

Quinn, R. E., and Cameron, K. (1983). Organizational life cycles and shifting criteria of effectiveness: Some preliminary evidence. *Management Science,* **29**, 33–51.

Quinn, R. E., and Rohrbaugh, J. (1981). A competing values approach to organizational effectiveness. *Public Productivity Review,* **5**, 122–140.

Quinn, R. E., and Rohrbaugh, J. (1983). A spatial model of effectiveness criteria: Towards a competing values approach to organizational analysis. *Management Science,* **29**, 363–377.

Rice, G. H., Jr (1985). Available information and superstitious decision making. *Journal of General Management,* **11** (2), 35–44.

Robinson, I. (1985). Managing retrenchment in a public service organization. *Canadian Public Administration,* **28**, 513–530.

Rohrbaugh, J. (1981). Operationalizing the competing values approach: Measuring performance in the employment service. *Public Productivity Review*, **5**, 141-159.

Rohrbaugh, J. (1983). The competing values approach: Innovation and effectiveness in the job service. In *Organizational Theory and Public Policy*, ed. R. H. Hall and R. E. Quinn, pp. 265-280. Hollywood: Sage.

Roy, W. G. (1983). The unfolding of the interlocking directorate structure of the United States. *American Sociological Review*, **48**, 248-257.

Rundall, T. G., and McClain, J. O. (1982). Environmental selection and physician supply. *American Journal of Sociology*, **87**, 1090-1112.

Sahal, D. (1981). *Patterns of Technological Innovation*. Reading, MA: Addison-Wesley.

Schendel, D., Patton, G. R., and Riggs, J. (1976). Corporate turnaround strategies: A study of profit decline and recovery. *Journal of General Management*, **3** (3), 3-11.

Schneider, B. (1985). Organizational behavior. *Annual Review of Psychology*, **36**, 573-611.

Schoonhoven, C. B. (1981). Problems with contingency theory: Testing assumptions hidden within the language of contingency 'theory'. *Administrative Science Quarterly*, **26**, 349-377.

Schoorman, F. D., Bazerman, M. H., and Atkin, R. S. (1981). Interlocking directorates: A strategy for reducing environmental uncertainty. *Academy of Management Review*, **6**, 243-251.

Schreyogg, G. (1980). Contingency and choice in organization theory. *Organization Studies*, **1**, 305-326.

Scott, J., and Griff, C. (1984). *Directors of Industry: The British Corporate Network 1904-76*. Cambridge, UK: Polity.

Scott, W. R. (1964). Theory of organizations. In *Handbook of Modern Sociology*, ed. R. E. L. Faris, pp. 485-529 Chicago: Rand McNally.

Scott, W. R. (1975). Organizational structure. *Annual Reivew of Sociology*, **1**, 1-20.

Shepard, H. A. (1967). Innovation-resisting and innovation-producing organizations. *Journal of Business*, **40**, 470-477.

Shipper, F., and White, C. S. (1983). Linking organizational effectiveness and environmental change. *Long Range Planning*, **16** (3), 99-106.

Shrivastava, P. (1985). Knowledge systems for strategic decision making. *Journal of Applied Behavioral Science*, **21**, 95-107.

Shrivastava, P., and Grant, J. H. (1985). Empirically derived models of strategic decision-making processes. *Strategic Management Journal*, **6**, 97-113.

Shrivastava, P., and Schneider, S. (1984). Organizational frames of reference. *Human Relations*, **37**, 795-809.

Smirich, L., and Stubbart, C. (1985). Strategic management in an enacted world. *Academy of Management Review*, **10**, 724-736.

Smith, M. E. (1982). Shrinking organizations: A management strategy for downsizing. *Business Quarterly*, **47** (4), 30-33.

Sonnenfeld, J. (1981). Executive apologies for price fixing: Role biased perceptions of causality. *Academy of Management Journal*, **24**, 192-198.

Staber, U. (1985). A population perspective on collective action as an organizational form: The case of trade associations. *Research in the Sociology of Organization*, **4**, 181-219.

Starbuck, W. H. (1983). Organizations as action generators. *American Sociological Review*, **48**, 91-102.

Starbuck, W. H. (1985). Acting first and thinking later: Theory versus reality in strategic change. In *Organizational Strategy and Change*, ed. J. M. Pennings *et al.* pp. 336-372. San Francisco: Jossey-Bass.

Starbuck, W. H., Greve, A., and Hedberg, B. L. T. (1978). Responding to crises: Theory and the experience of European business. In *Studies in Crisis Management*, ed. C. F. Smart and W. T. Stanbury, pp. 111-137. Toronto: Butterworth.

Staw, B. M. (1984). Organizational behavior: A review and reformation of the field's outcome variables. *Annual Review of Psychology*, **35**, 627-666.

Staw, B. M. (1985). Repairs on the road to relevance and rigor: Some unexplored issues in publishing organizational research. In *Publishing in the Organizational Sciences*, ed. L. L. Cummings and R. J. Frost, pp. 96-107. Homewood, IL: Irwin.

Steers, R. M. (1975). Problems in the measurement of organizational effectiveness. *Administrative Science Quarterly*, **20**, 546-558.

Steers, R. M. (1976). When is an organization effective? A process approach to understanding effectiveness. *Organizational Dynamics*, **5** (2), 50-63.

Steers, R. M. (1977). *Organizational Effectiveness* Santa Monica, CA: Goodyear.

Stokey, N. L. (1986). The dynamics of industry-wide learning. In *Equilibrium Analysis: Essays in Honor of Kenneth J. Arrow*, ed. W. P. Heller, R. M. Starr and D. A. Starrett, vol. 2, pp. 81-104 Cambridge: Cambridge University Press.

Storey, D. J. (1985). The problem facing new firms. *Journal of Management Studies*, **22**, 327-345.

Strauss, A. (1982). Interorganizational negotiation. *Urban Life*, **11**, 350-367.

Stubbart, C. (1982). Are environmental scanning units effective? *Long Range Planning*, **15** (3), 139-145.

Sutton, R. I. (1983). Managing organizational death. *Human Resource Management*, **22**, 391-412.

Szwajkowski, E. (1985). Organizational illegality: Theoretical integration and illustrative application. *Academy of Management Review*, **10**, 558-567.

Takahashi, N. (1983). Efficiency of management systems under uncertainty: Short-run adaptive processes. *Behaviormetrika*, **14**, 59-72.

Tushman, M. L., Virany, B., and Romanelli, E. (1985). Executive succession, strategic reorientations, and organization evolution: The minicomputer industry as a case in point. *Technology in Society*, **7**, 297-313.

Ulrich, D. (1984). Specifying external relations: Definition of and actors in an organization's environment. *Human Relations*, **37**, 245-262.

Ulrich, D., and Barney, J. B. (1984). Perspectives in organizations: Resource dependence, efficiency, and population. *Academy of Management Review*, **9**, 471-481.

Useem, M. (1984). *The Inner Circle: Large Corporations and the Rise of Business Political Activity in the U.S. and U.K.* New York: Oxford University Press.

Van de Ven, A. H, (1979) [Review of *Organizations and Environment*] *Administrative Science Quarterly*, **24**, 320-326.

Van de Ven, A. H., and Drazin, R. (1985). The concept of fit in contingency theory. *Research in Organizational Behavior*, **7**, 333-365.

Van de Ven, A. H., Hudson, R., and Schroeder, D. M. (1984). Designing new business startups: Entrepreneurial, organizational, and ecological considerations. *Journal of Management*, **10**, 87-108.

Venkatraman, N., and Camillus, J. C. (1984). Exploring the concept of 'fit' in strategic management. *Academy of Management Review*, **9**, 513-525.

Wagel, W. B., Ermann, M. D., and Horowitz, A. M. (1981). Organizational responses to imputations of deviance. *Sociological Quarterly*, **22**, 43-55.

Warner, W. K. (1967). Problems in measuring the goal attainment of voluntary organizations. *Adult Education*, **19**, 3-14.

Weick, K. E. (1979). *The Social Psychology of Organizing*, 2nd edn. Reading, MA: Addison-Wesley

Whetten, D. (1980a). Organizational decline: A neglected topic in organizational science. *Academy of Management Review*, **5**, 577-588.

Whetten, D. (1980b). Organizational decline: Causes, responses, and effects. In *The Organizational Life Cycle*, ed. J. Kimberly, R. Miles, *et al.* pp. 354-362 San Francisco: Jossey-Bass.

Whetten, D. A. (1981). Organizational responses to scarcity: Exploring the obstacles to innovative aproaches to retrenchment in education. *Educational Administration Quarterly*, **17** (3), 80-97.

Wiewel, W., and Hunter, A. (1985). The interorganizational network as a resource: A comparative case study on organizational genesis. *Administrative Science Quarterly*, **30**, 482-496.

Wilson, E. K. (1985). What counts in the death or transformation of an organization? *Social Forces*, **64**, 259-280.

Yasai-Ardekani, M. (1986). Structural adaptations to environments. *Academy of Management Review*, **11**, 9-21.

Yoffie, D. B., and Bergenstein, S. (1985). Creating political advantage: The rise of the corporate political entrepreneur. *California Management Review*, **28**, 124-139.

Zammuto, R. F. (1982a). *Assessing organizational effectiveness: Systems change, adaptation, and strategy*. Albany, NY: SUNY Press.

Zammuto, R. F. (1982b). Organizational decline and management education. *Exchange: The Organizational Behavior Teaching Journal*, **7** (3), 5-12.

Zammuto, R. F. (1983). *Bibliography on Decline and Retrenchment* Boulder, CO: National Center for Higher Education Management Systems.

Zammuto, R. F. (1984). A comparison of multiple constituency models of organizational effectiveness. *Academy of Management Review*, **9**, 606-619.

Zammuto, R. F., and Cameron, K. S. (1985). Environmental decline and organizational response. *Research in Organizational Behavior*, **7**, 223-262.

Zammuto, R. F., Whetten, D. A., and Cameron, K. S. (1983). Environmental change, enrollment decline and institutional response: Speculations on retrenchment in colleges and universities. *Peabody Journal of Education*, **60**, 93-107.

Zeithaml, C. P., and Zeithaml, V. A. (1984). Environmental management: Revising the marketing perspective. *Journal of Marketing*, **48**, 46-53.

INDEX

Index compiled by Caroline Sheard